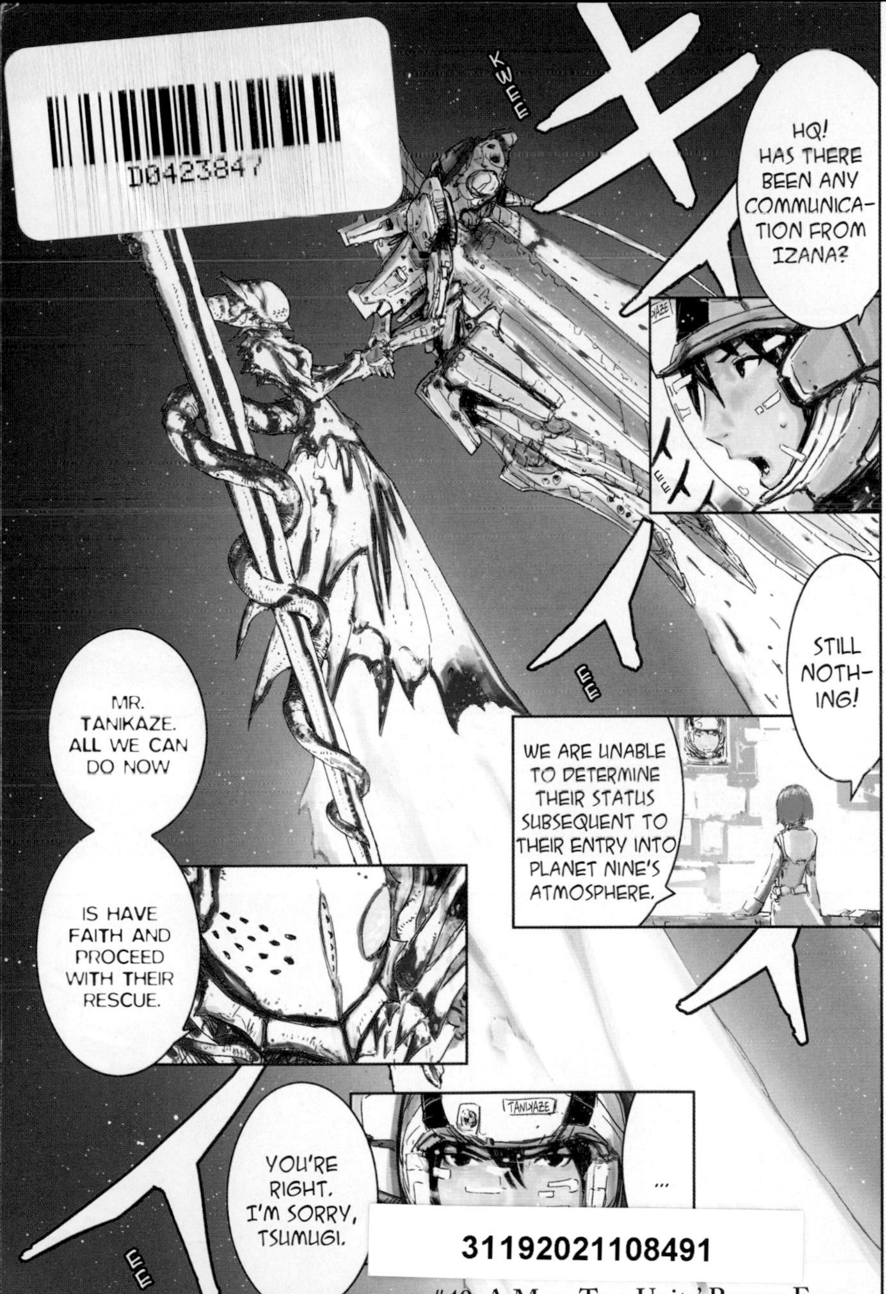
KWEE
HQ! HAS THERE BEEN ANY COMMUNICATION FROM IZANA?
STILL NOTHING!
WE ARE UNABLE TO DETERMINE THEIR STATUS SUBSEQUENT TO THEIR ENTRY INTO PLANET NINE'S ATMOSPHERE.
MR. TANIKAZE. ALL WE CAN DO NOW
IS HAVE FAITH AND PROCEED WITH THEIR RESCUE.
TANIKAZE
...
YOU'RE RIGHT. I'M SORRY, TSUMUGI.

#40 A Mere Two Units' Rescue Force

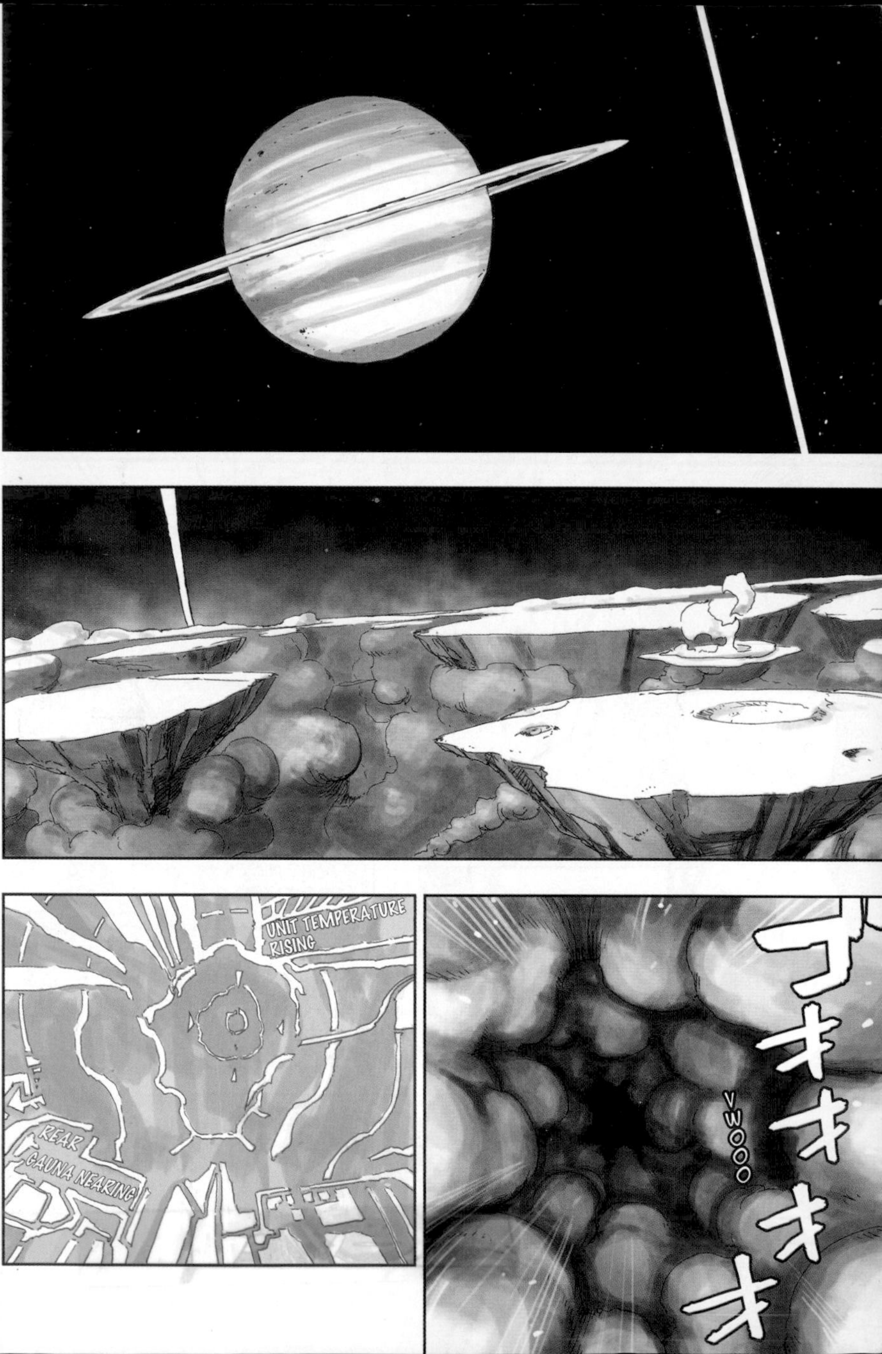
ゴオオオオ
VWOOO
UNIT TEMPERATURE RISING
REAR GAUNA NEARING

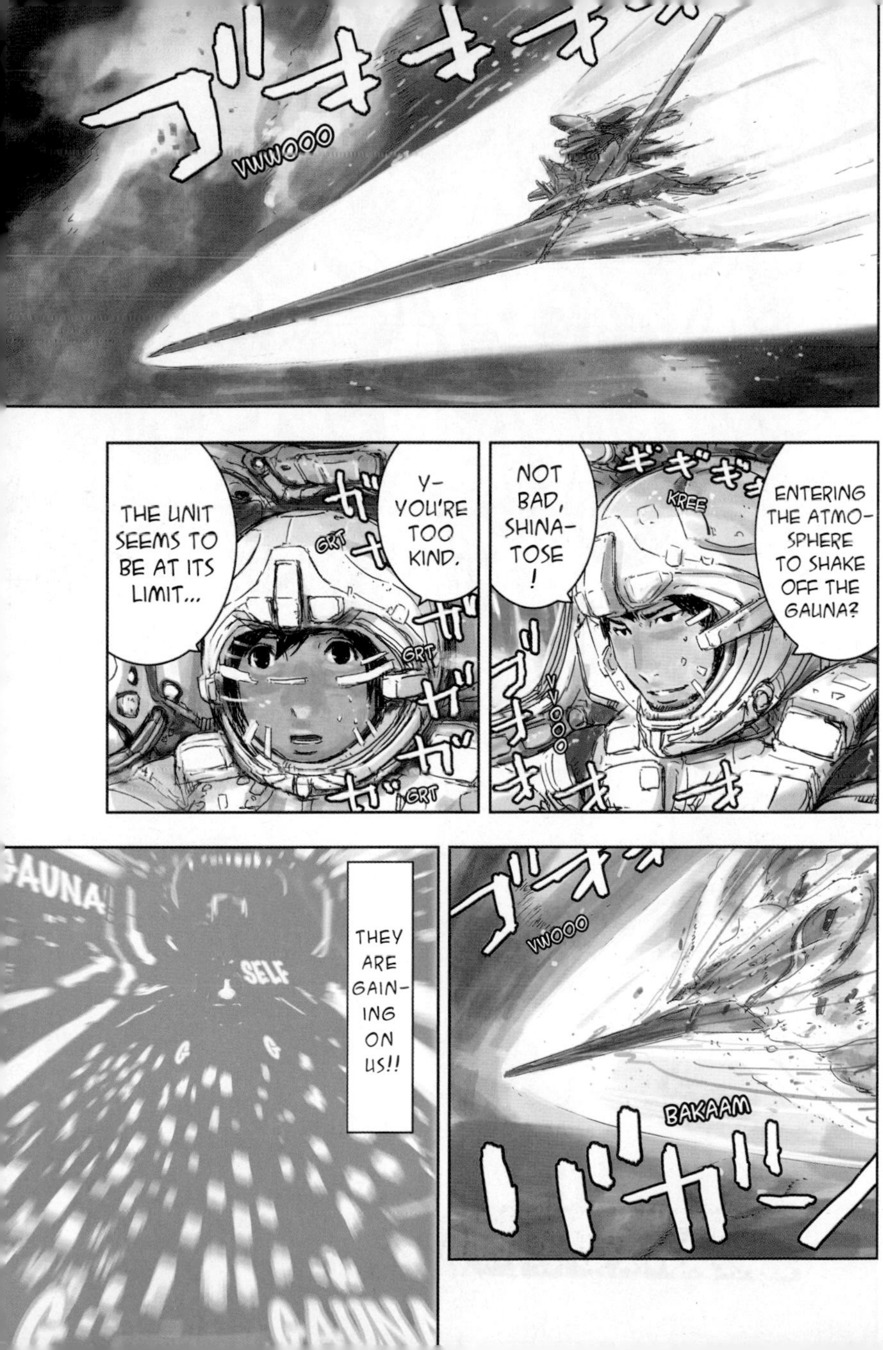
VWWOOO
ENTERING THE ATMOSPHERE TO SHAKE OFF THE GAUNA?
KREE
NOT BAD, SHINATOSE!
Y-YOU'RE TOO KIND.
THE UNIT SEEMS TO BE AT ITS LIMIT...
GRT
GRT
GRT
GRT
VWOOO
BAKAAM
THEY ARE GAINING ON US!!
GAUNA
SELF
GAUNA

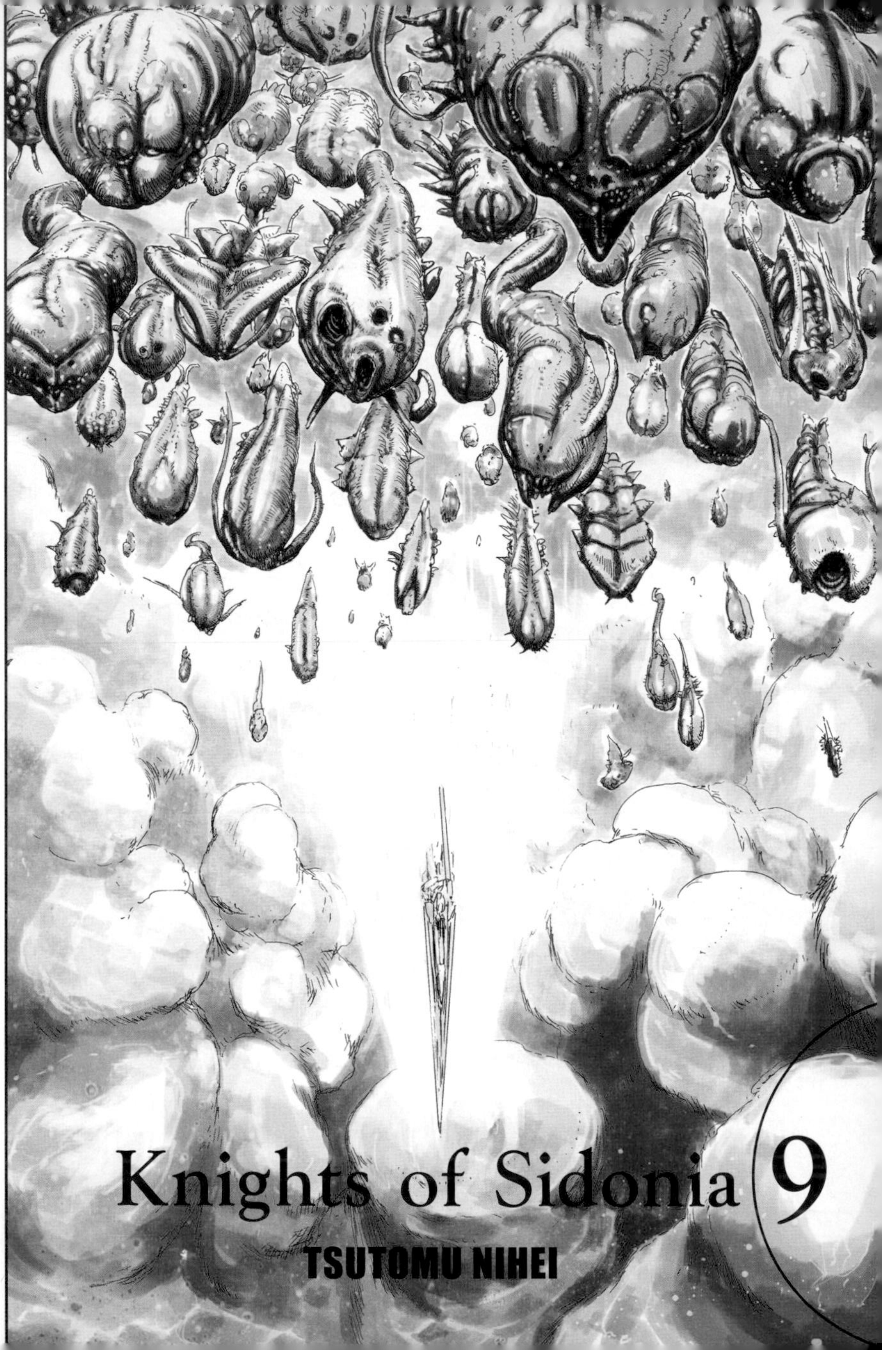

Knights of Sidonia 9

TSUTOMU NIHEI

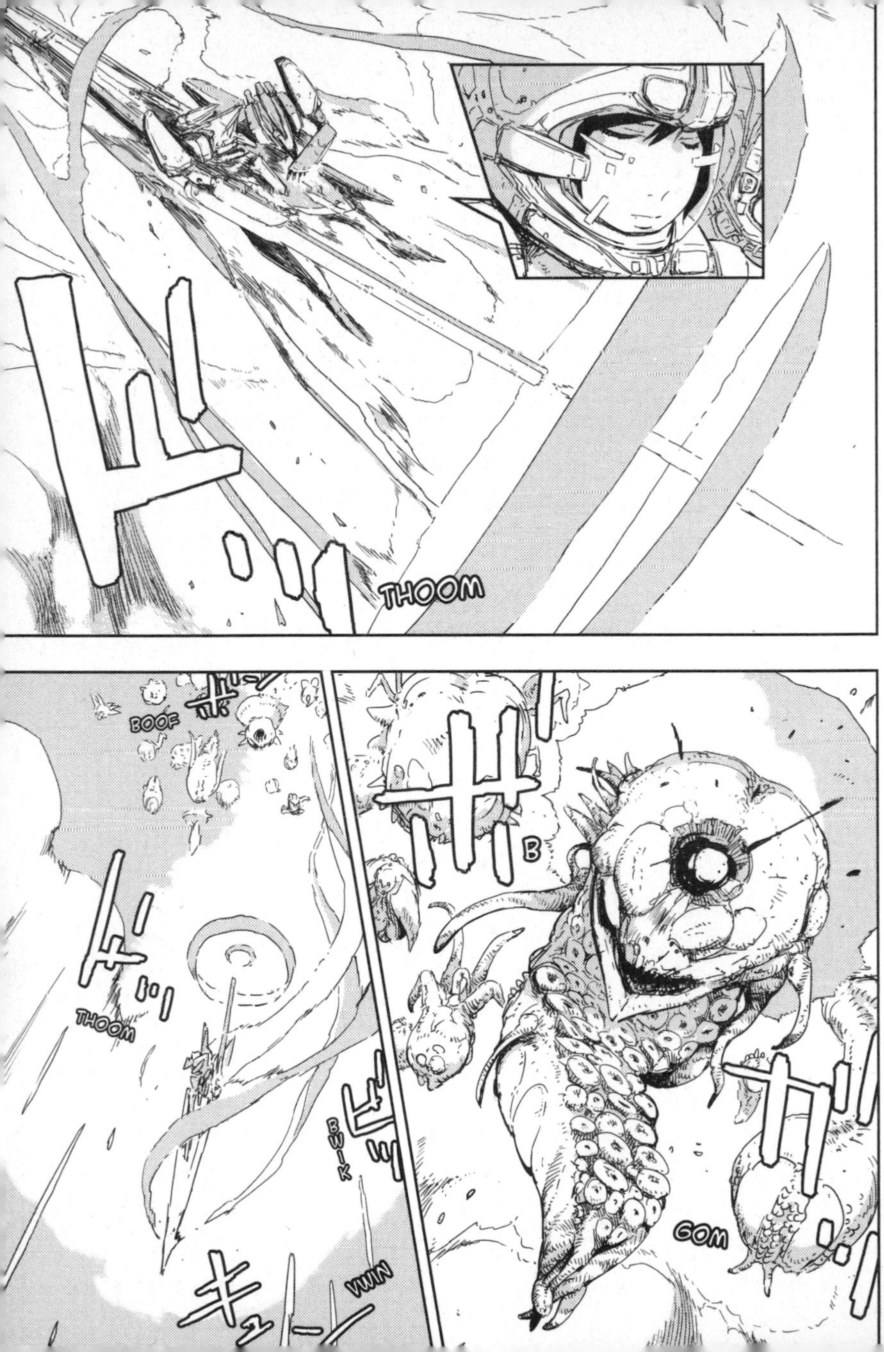
THOOM
B
GOM
BOOF
THOOM
BWIK
VWIN

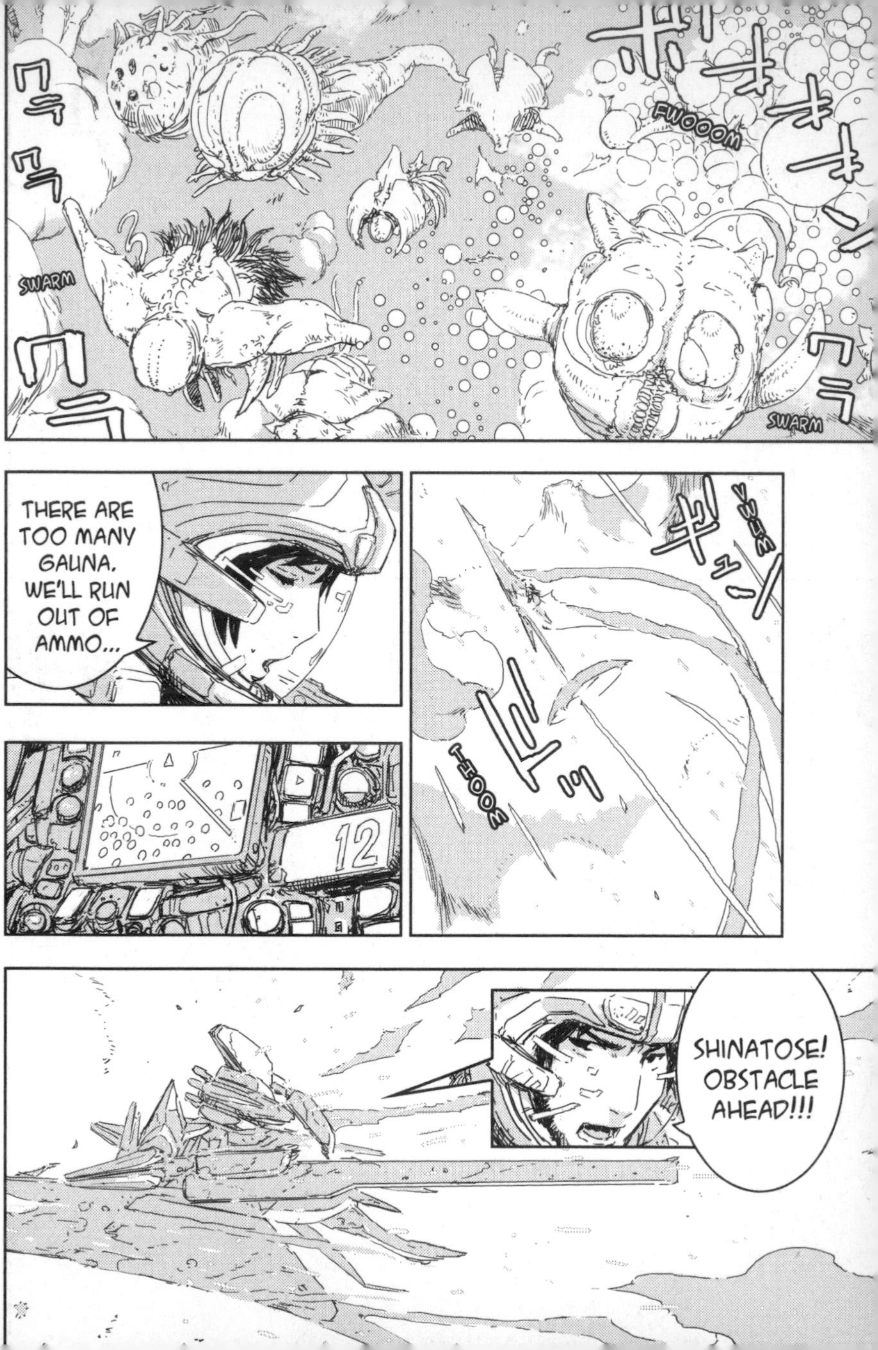
FWOOOM
SWARM
SWARM
WOOF!
THERE ARE TOO MANY GAUNA. WE'LL RUN OUT OF AMMO...
12
SHINATOSE! OBSTACLE AHEAD!!!

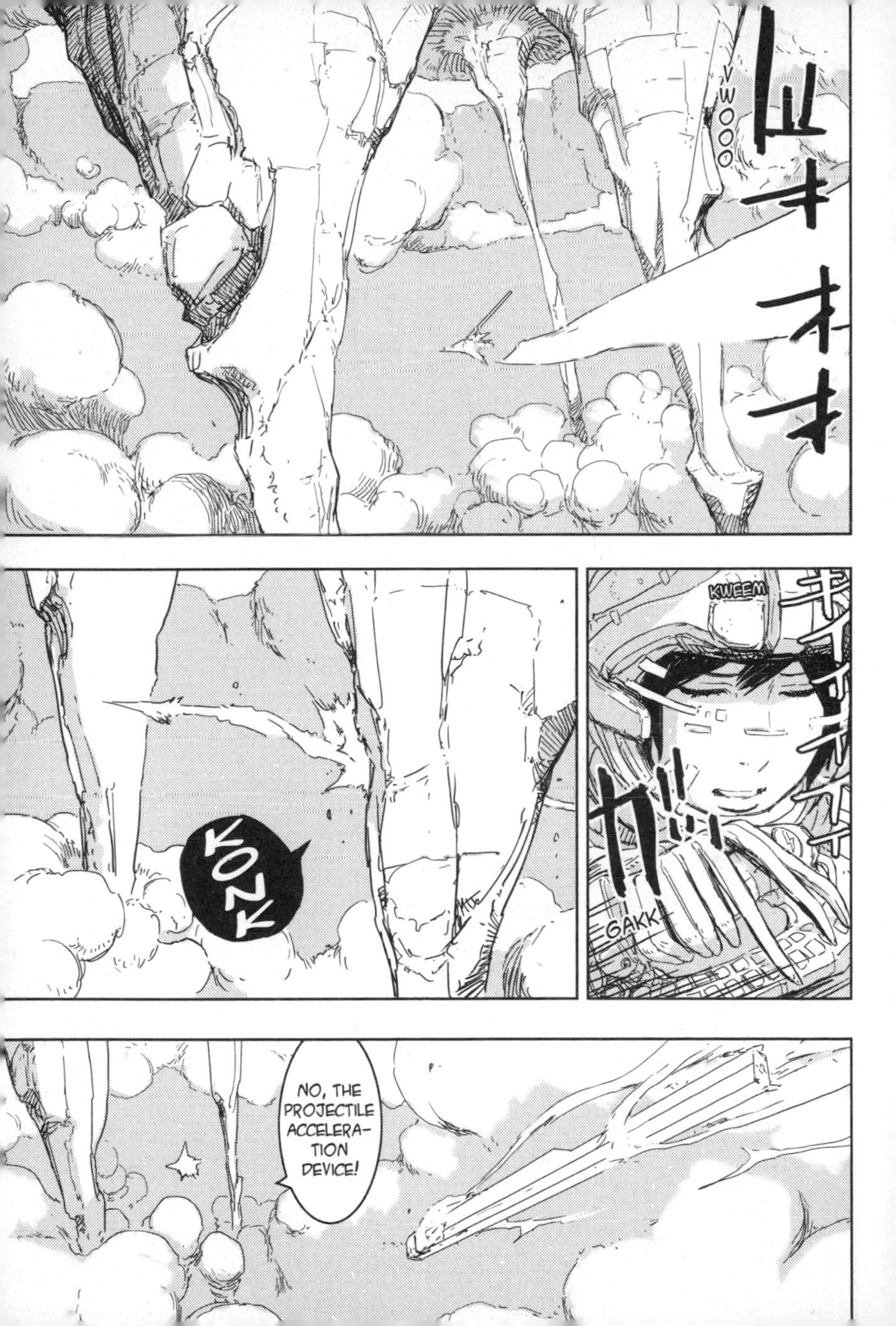
VWOOO
KWEEM
GAKK
KONK
NO, THE PROJECTILE ACCELERATION DEVICE!

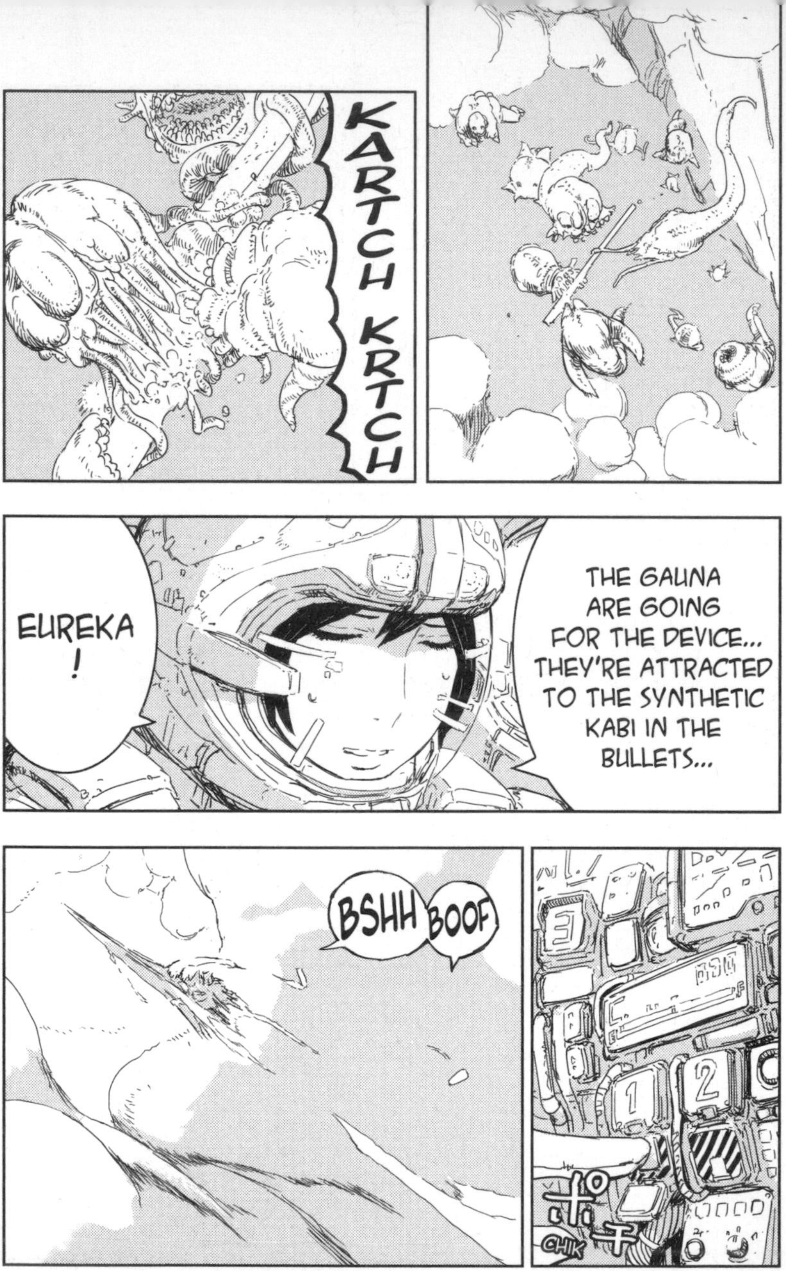
KARTCH KRTCH
THE GAUNA ARE GOING FOR THE DEVICE... THEY'RE ATTRACTED TO THE SYNTHETIC KABI IN THE BULLETS...
EUREKA !
ポチ
CHIK
BSHH
BOOF

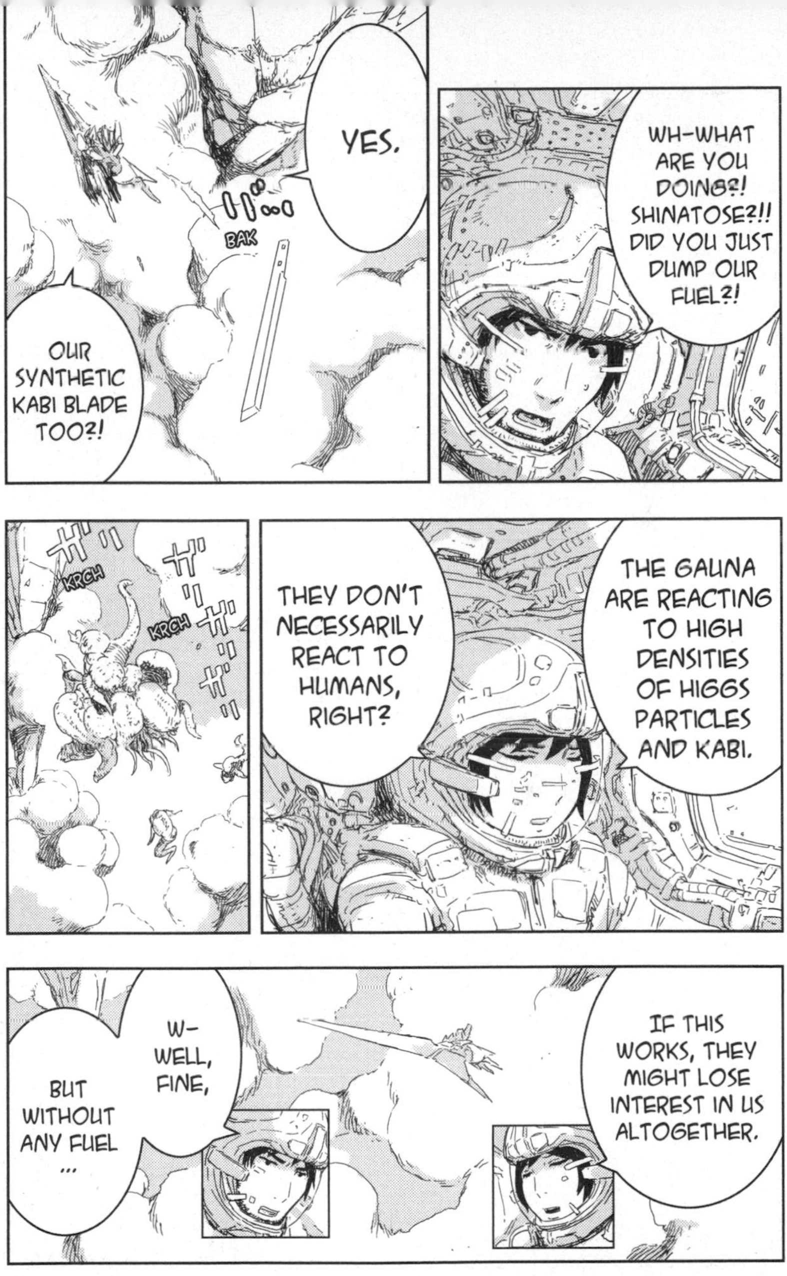
WH-WHAT ARE YOU DOING?! SHINATOSE?!! DID YOU JUST DUMP OUR FUEL?!
YES.
BAK
OUR SYNTHETIC KABI BLADE TOO?!
THE GAUNA ARE REACTING TO HIGH DENSITIES OF HIGGS PARTICLES AND KABI.
THEY DON'T NECESSARILY REACT TO HUMANS, RIGHT?
KRCH
KRCH
IF THIS WORKS, THEY MIGHT LOSE INTEREST IN US ALTOGETHER.
W-WELL, FINE,
BUT WITHOUT ANY FUEL ...

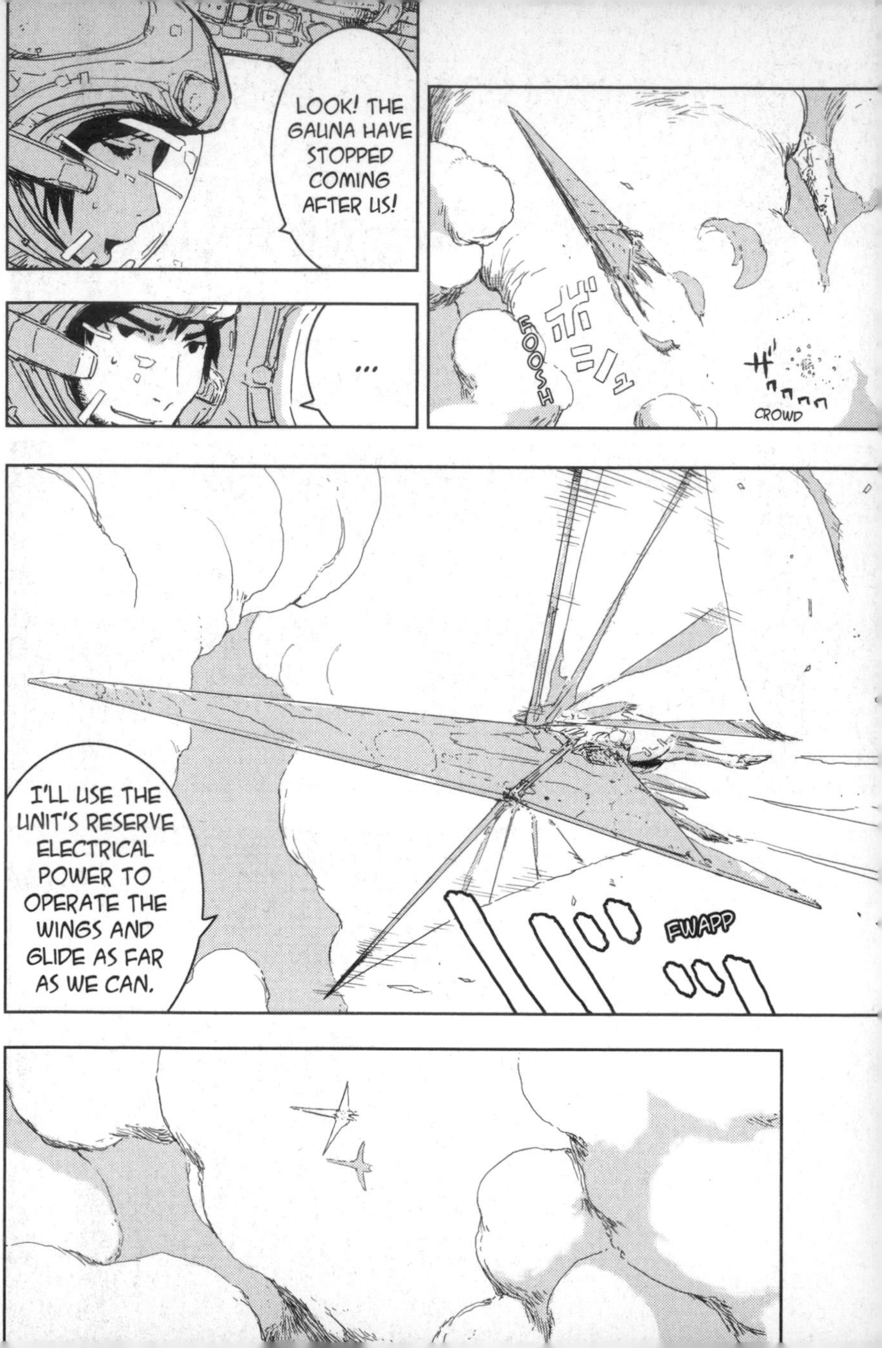
WHOOSH
CROWD
LOOK! THE GAUNA HAVE STOPPED COMING AFTER US!
...
I'LL USE THE UNIT'S RESERVE ELECTRICAL POWER TO OPERATE THE WINGS AND GLIDE AS FAR AS WE CAN.
FWAPP

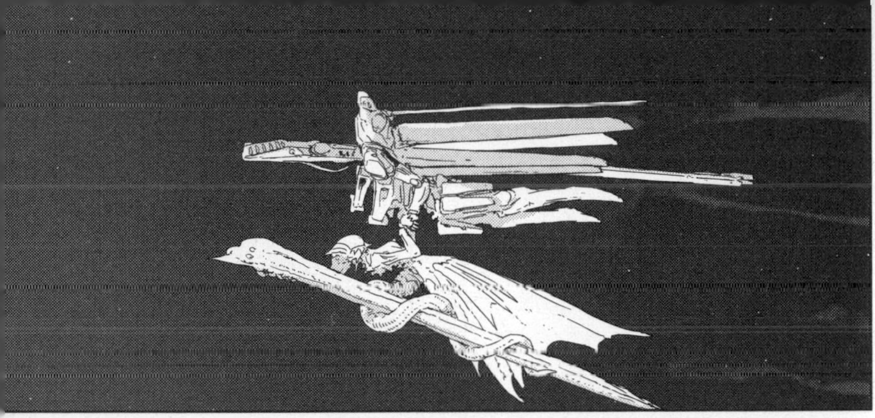
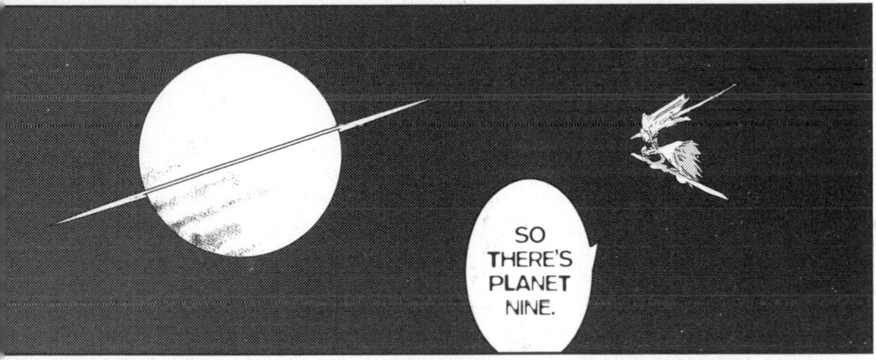
SO THERE'S PLANET NINE.
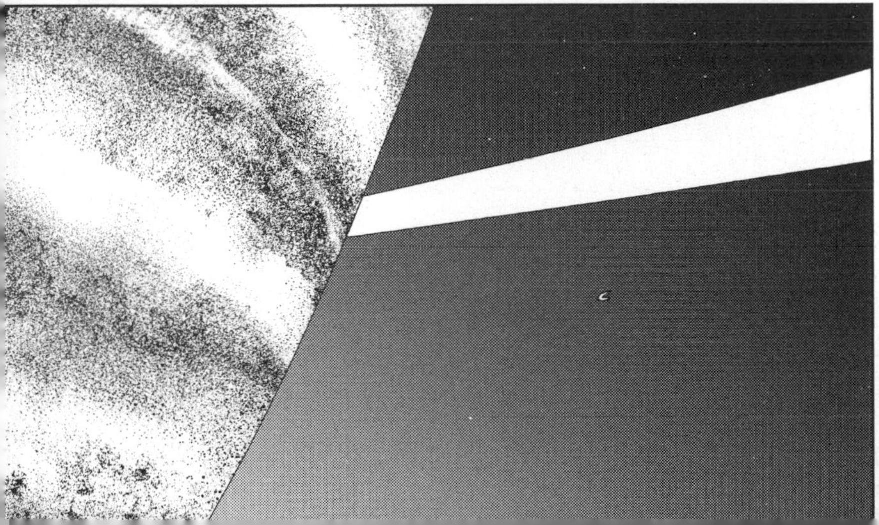

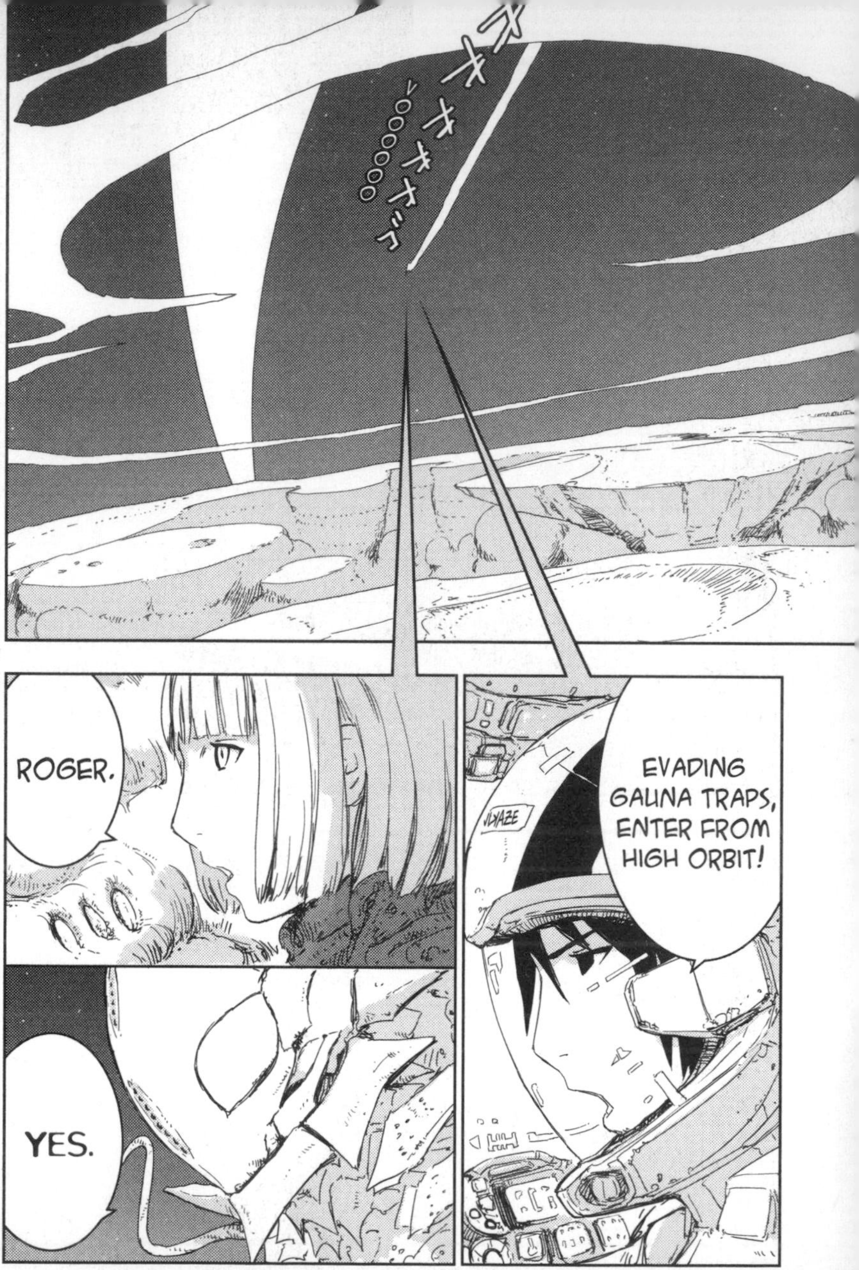
オオオオッ
VOOOOOO
EVADING GAUNA TRAPS, ENTER FROM HIGH ORBIT!
ROGER.
YES.

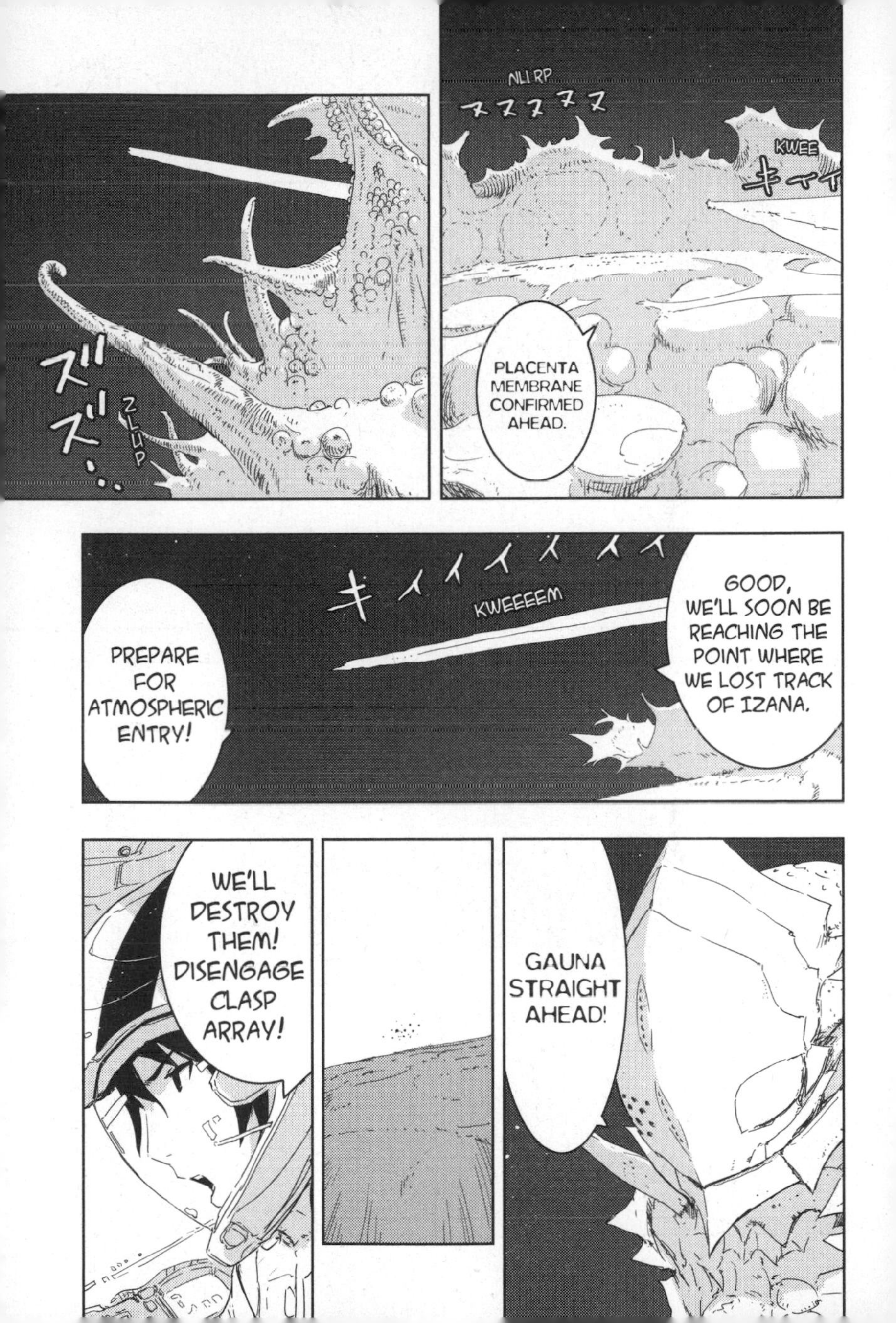
NLIRP
KWEE
PLACENTA MEMBRANE CONFIRMED AHEAD.
ZLUP
GOOD, WE'LL SOON BE REACHING THE POINT WHERE WE LOST TRACK OF IZANA.
KWEEEEM
PREPARE FOR ATMOSPHERIC ENTRY!
GAUNA STRAIGHT AHEAD!
WE'LL DESTROY THEM! DISENGAGE CLASP ARRAY!

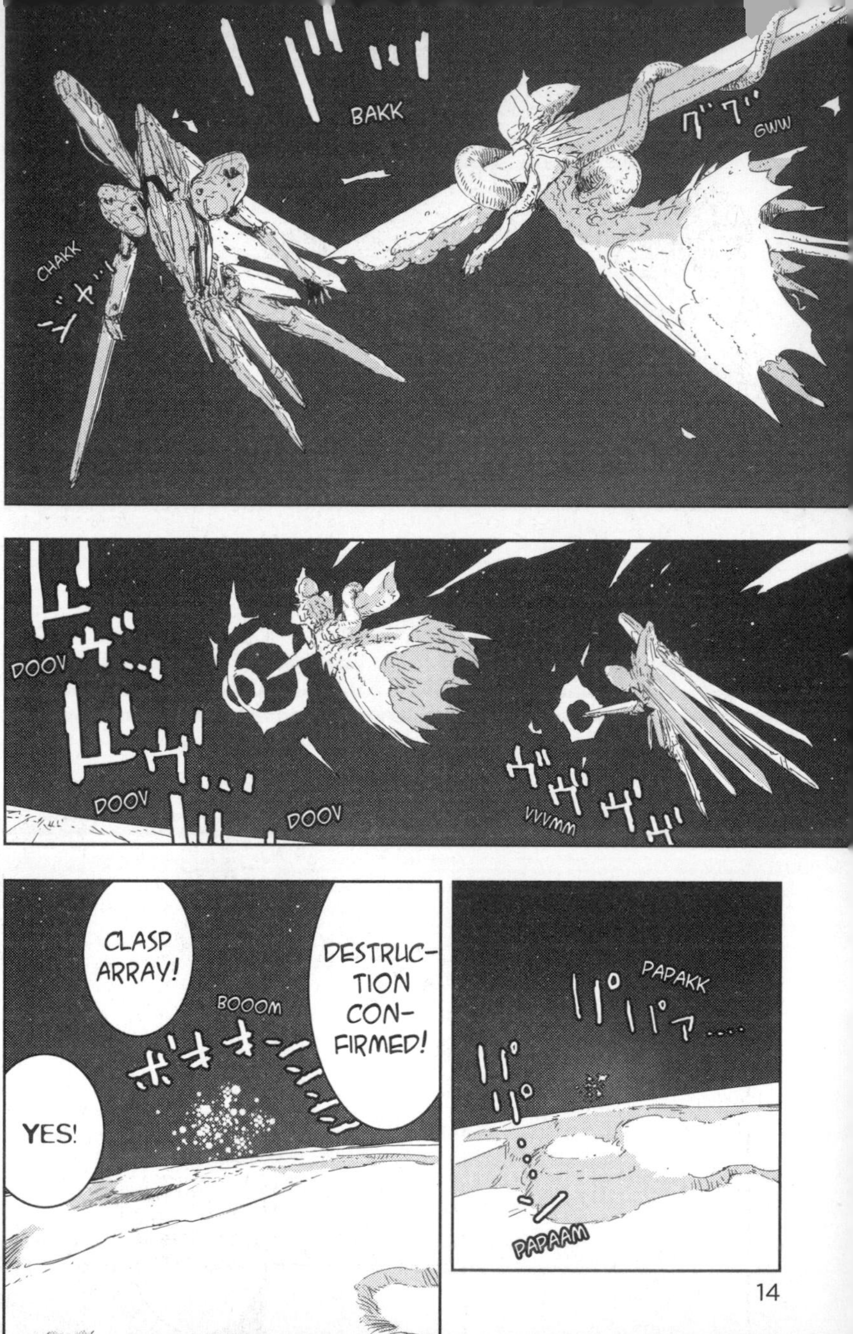
GWW
BAKK
CHAKK
VVVMM
DOOV
DOOV
DOOV
PAPAKK
PAPAAM
DESTRUC-TION CON-FIRMED!
CLASP ARRAY!
BOOOM
YES!

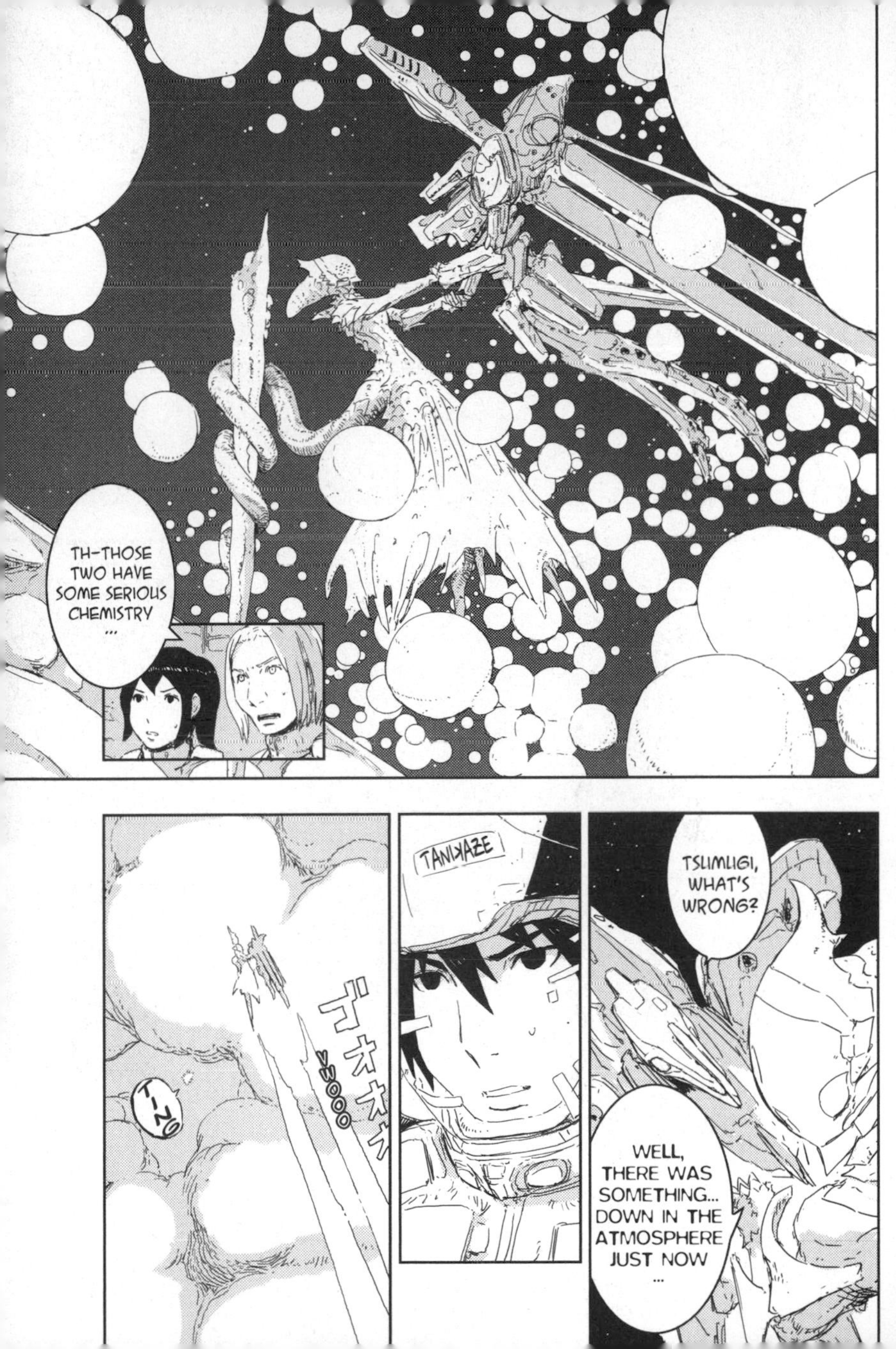
TH-THOSE TWO HAVE SOME SERIOUS CHEMISTRY ...
TSUMUGI, WHAT'S WRONG?
WELL, THERE WAS SOMETHING... DOWN IN THE ATMOSPHERE JUST NOW ...
TANIKAZE
ゴオオオ
VWOOO
T-20

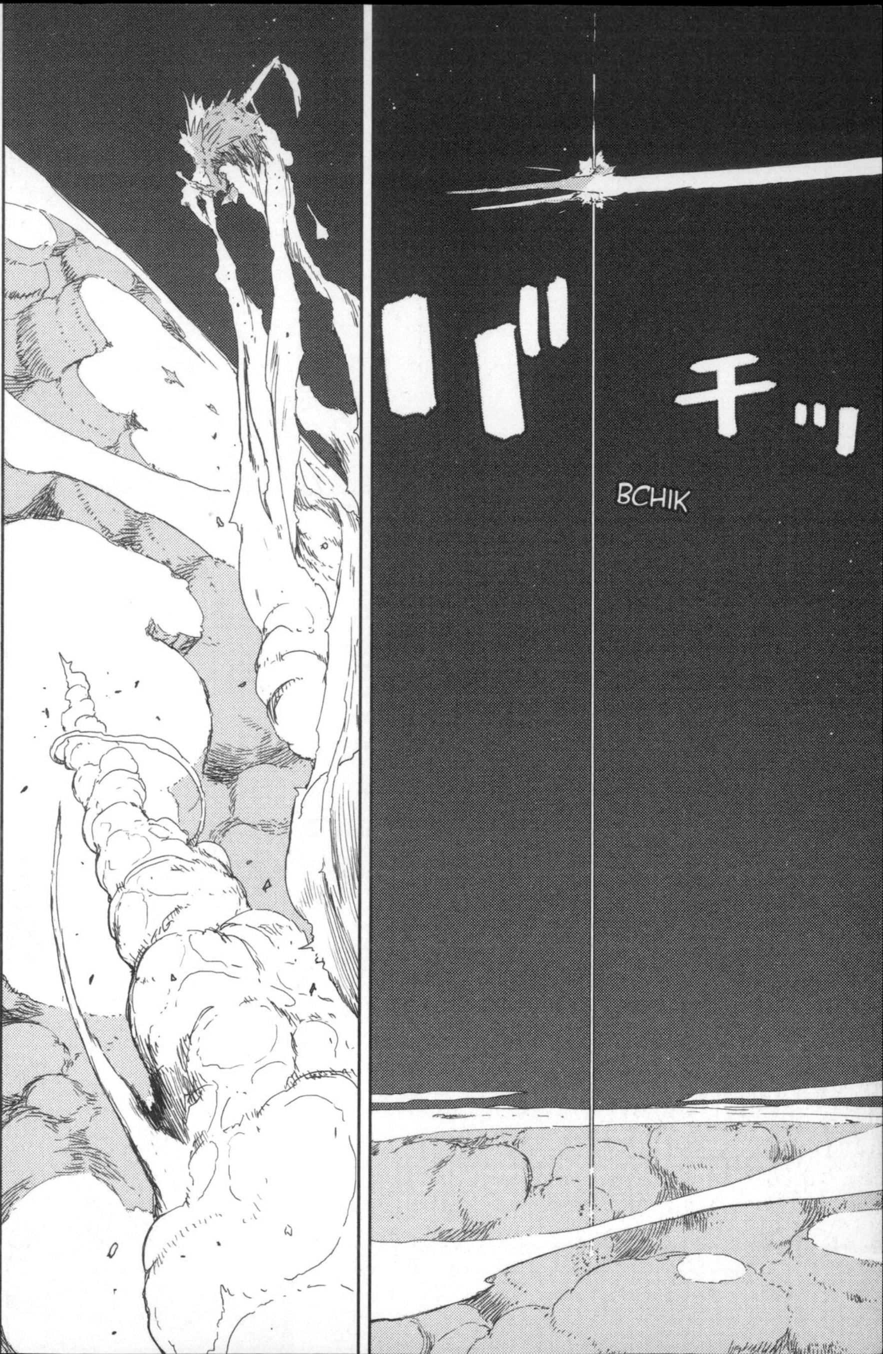
バチッ
BCHIK

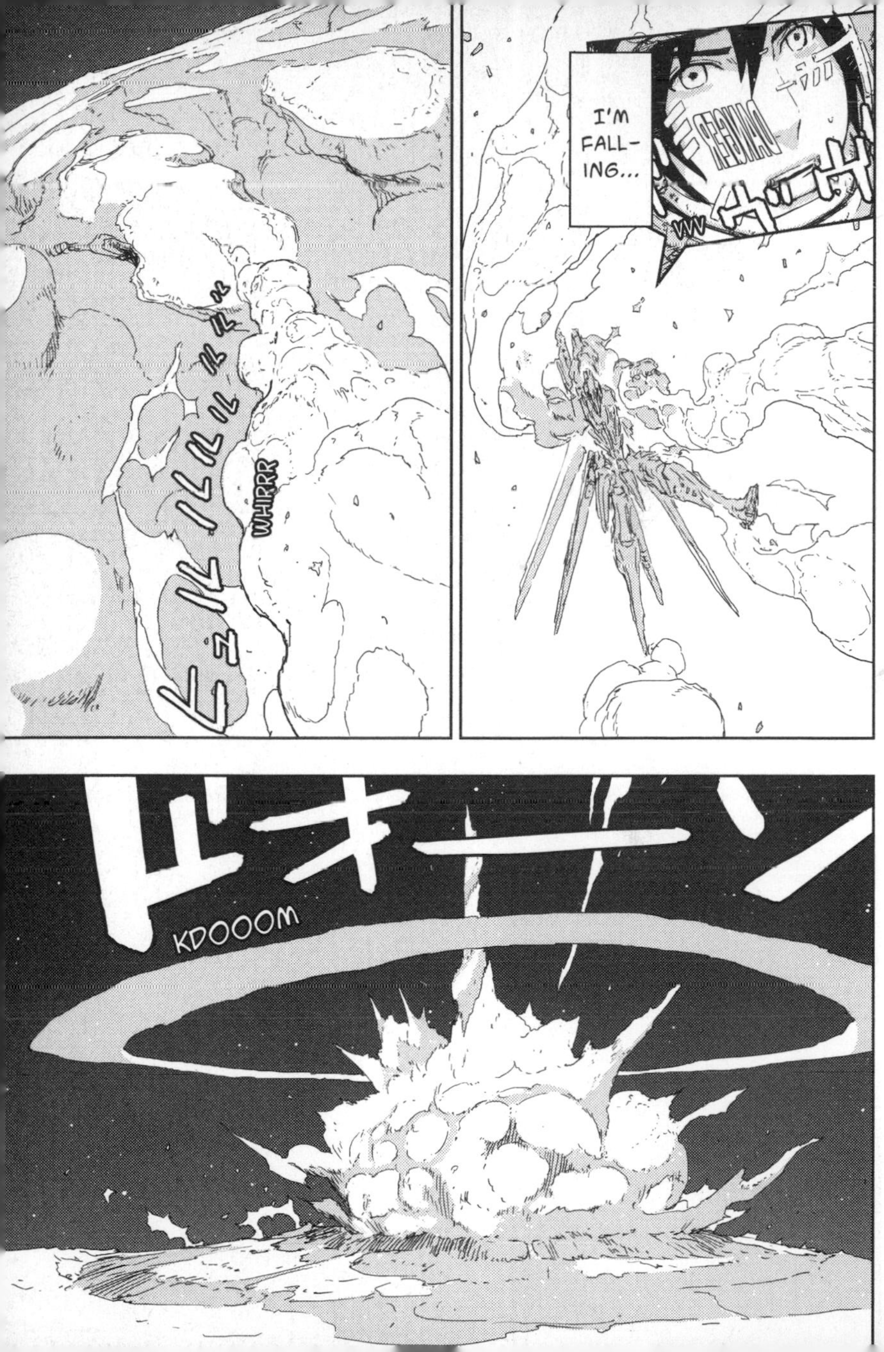
I'M FALLING...
WHIRRR
KDOOOM

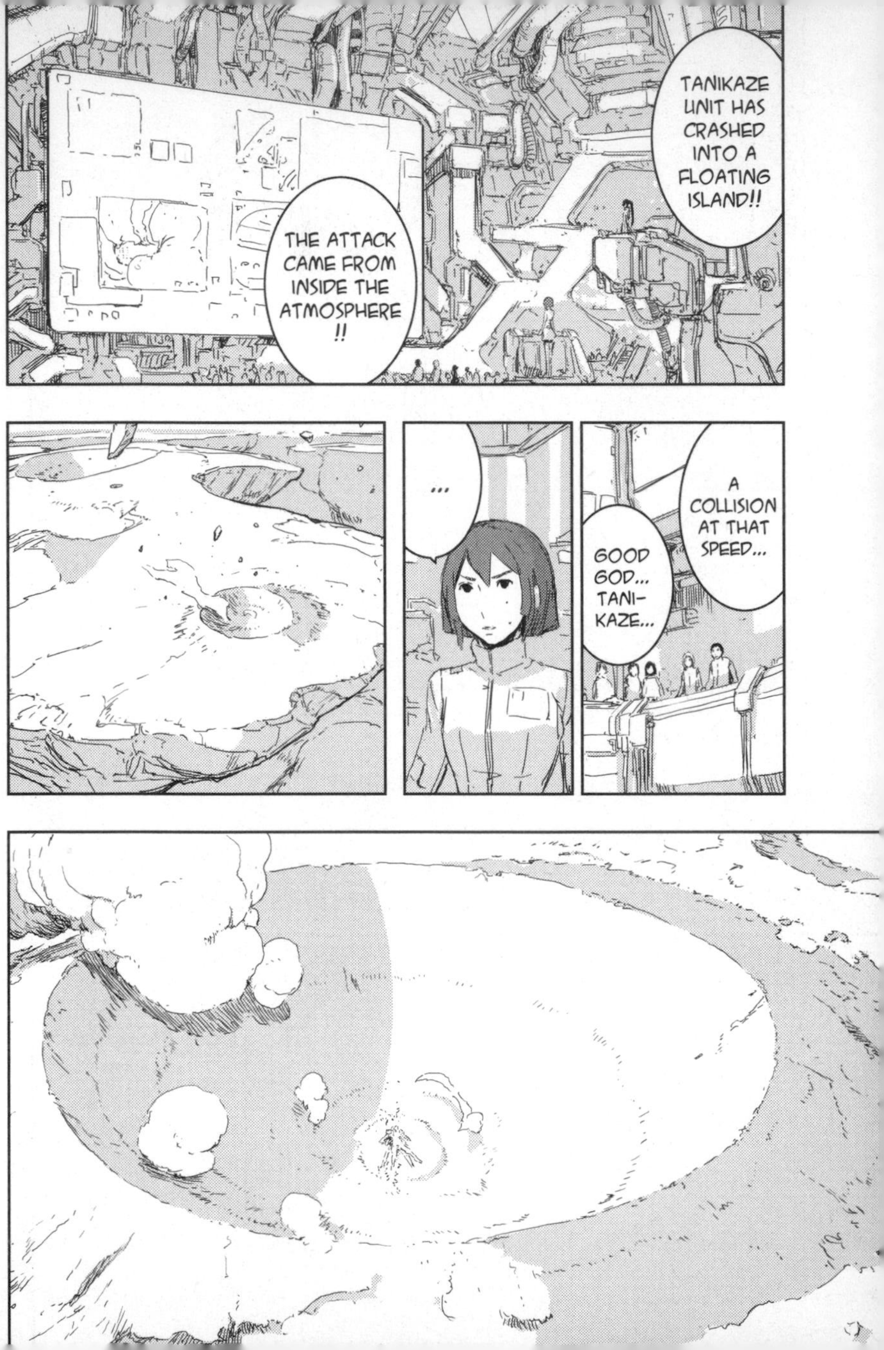
TANIKAZE UNIT HAS CRASHED INTO A FLOATING ISLAND!!
THE ATTACK CAME FROM INSIDE THE ATMOSPHERE!!
A COLLISION AT THAT SPEED...
GOOD GOD... TANI-KAZE...
...

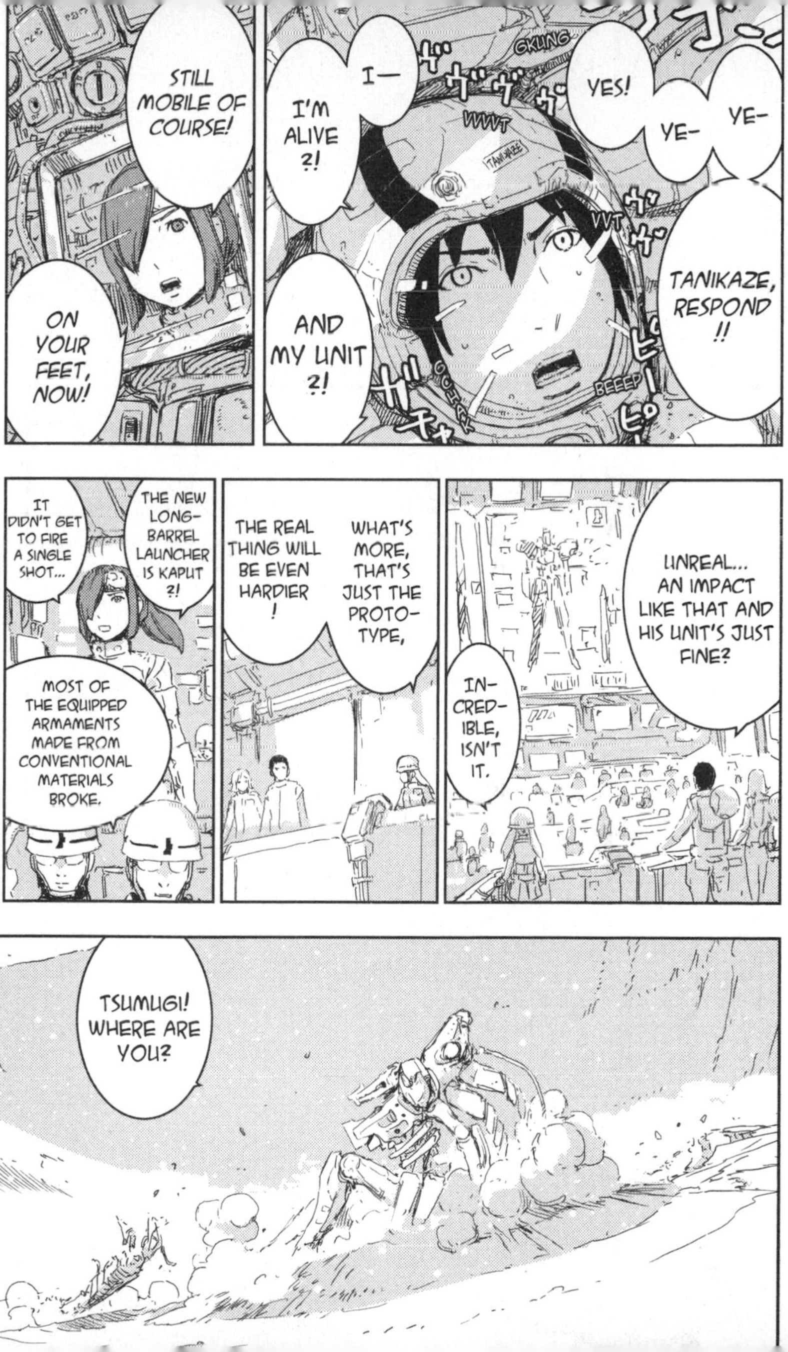
YE-
YE-
YES!
GKUNG
VVVVT
TANIKAZE, RESPOND!!
VVT
BEEEP
I—
I'M ALIVE?!
AND MY UNIT?!
GCHAK
STILL MOBILE OF COURSE!
ON YOUR FEET, NOW!
UNREAL... AN IMPACT LIKE THAT AND HIS UNIT'S JUST FINE?
INCRED-IBLE, ISN'T IT.
WHAT'S MORE, THAT'S JUST THE PROTO-TYPE,
THE REAL THING WILL BE EVEN HARDIER!
THE NEW LONG-BARREL LAUNCHER IS KAPUT?!
IT DIDN'T GET TO FIRE A SINGLE SHOT...
MOST OF THE EQUIPPED ARMAMENTS MADE FROM CONVENTIONAL MATERIALS BROKE.
TSUMUGI! WHERE ARE YOU?

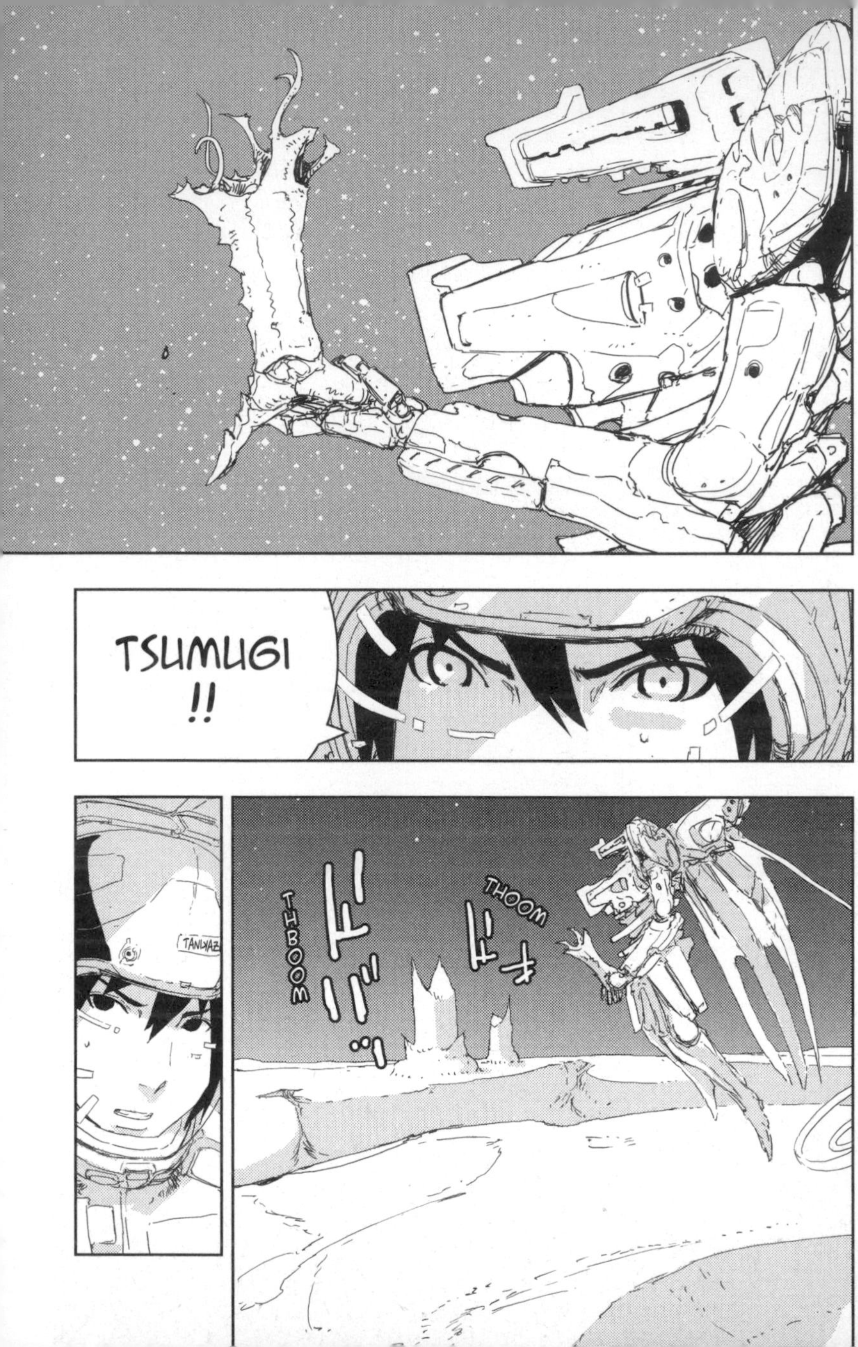
TSUMUGI !!
THOOM
THBOOM

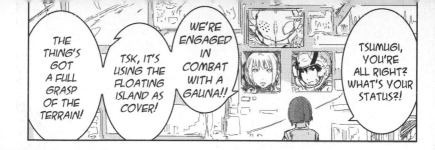

TSUMUGI, YOU'RE ALL RIGHT? WHAT'S YOUR STATUS?!
WE'RE ENGAGED IN COMBAT WITH A GAUNA!!
TSK, IT'S USING THE FLOATING ISLAND AS COVER!
THE THING'S GOT A FULL GRASP OF THE TERRAIN!
THZZT
BABAM
FLASH
BOOF
GWUMM
TSUMUGI, GET OUT OF THE ATMOSPHERE!

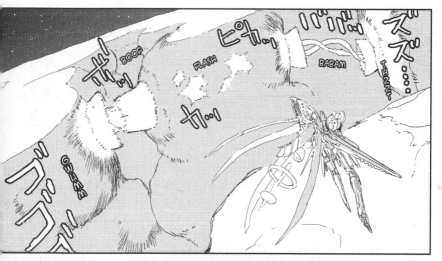

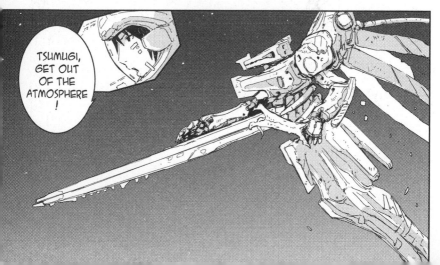

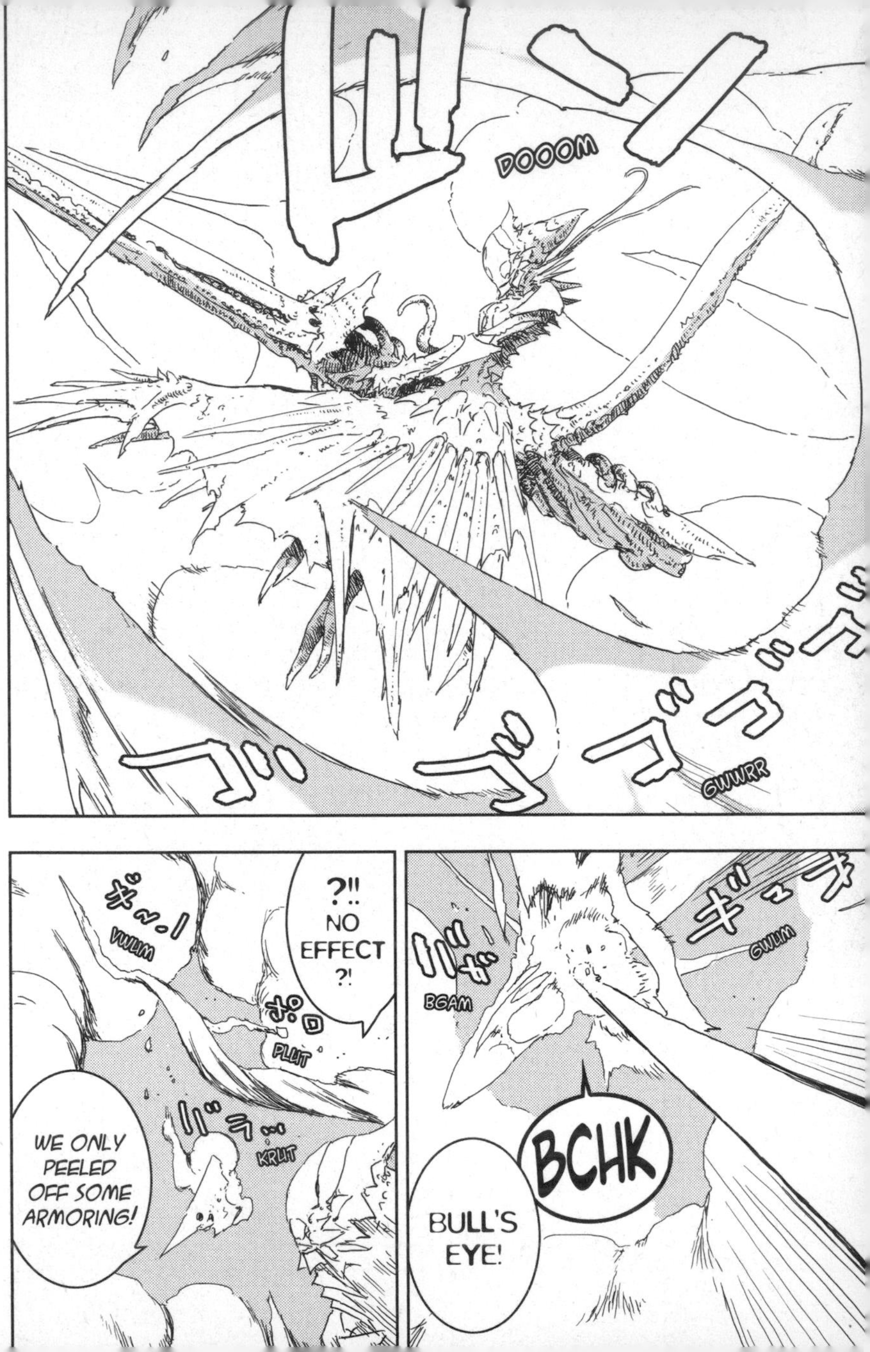
DOOOM
GWURR
GWUM
BGAM
BCHK
BULL'S EYE!
VWUM
?!! NO EFFECT ?!
PLUT
KRUT
WE ONLY PEELED OFF SOME ARMORING!

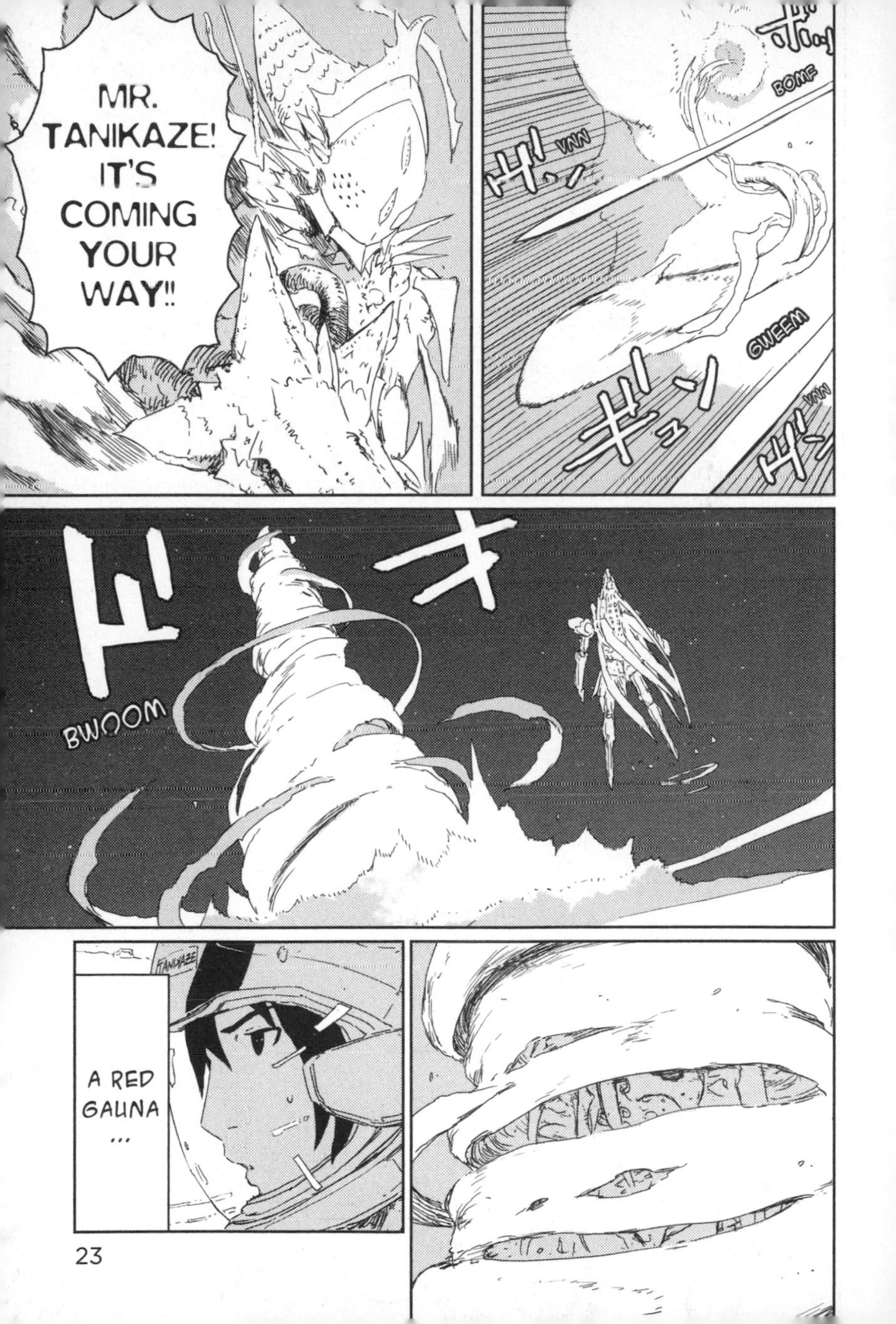
BOMF
VNN
GWEEM
VNN
MR. TANIKAZE! IT'S COMING YOUR WAY!!
BWOOM
TANIKAZE
A RED GAUNA ...

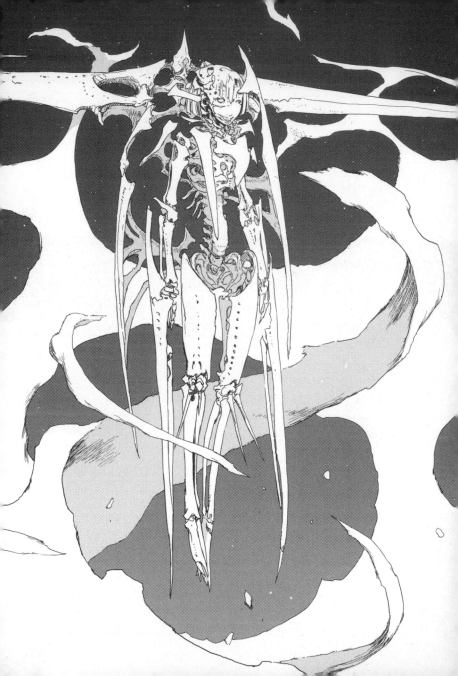

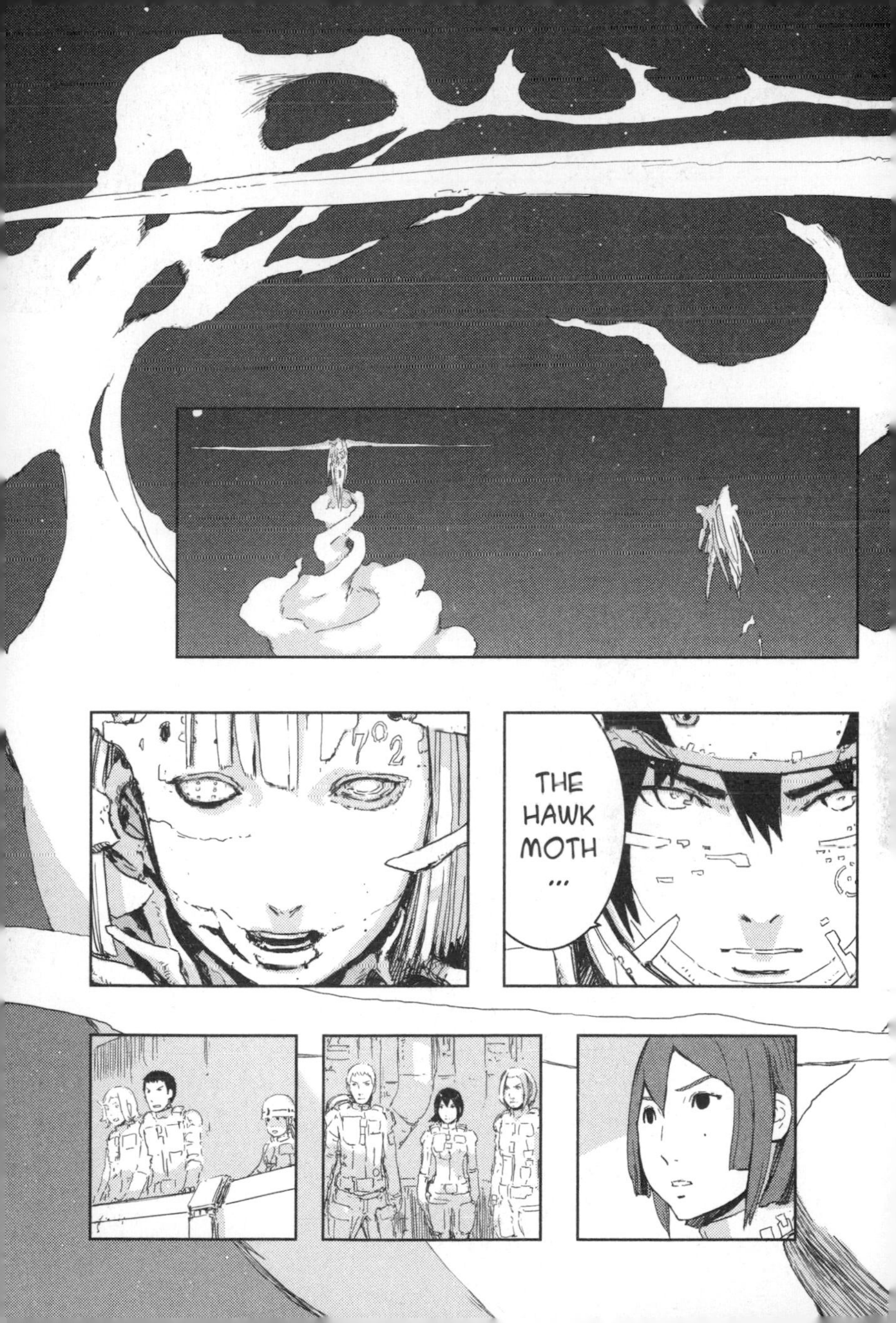
THE HAWK MOTH ...

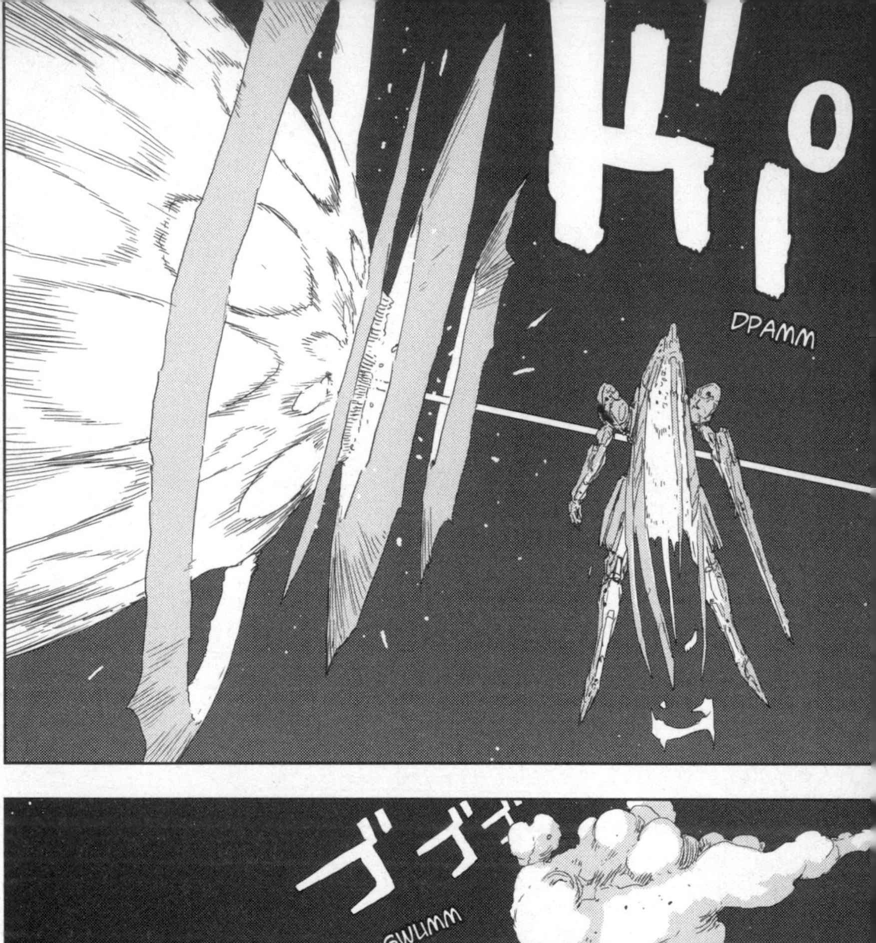
DPAMM
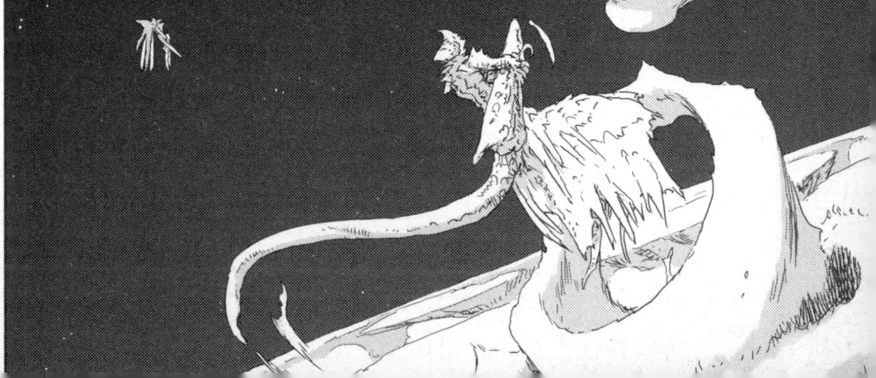
GWUMM

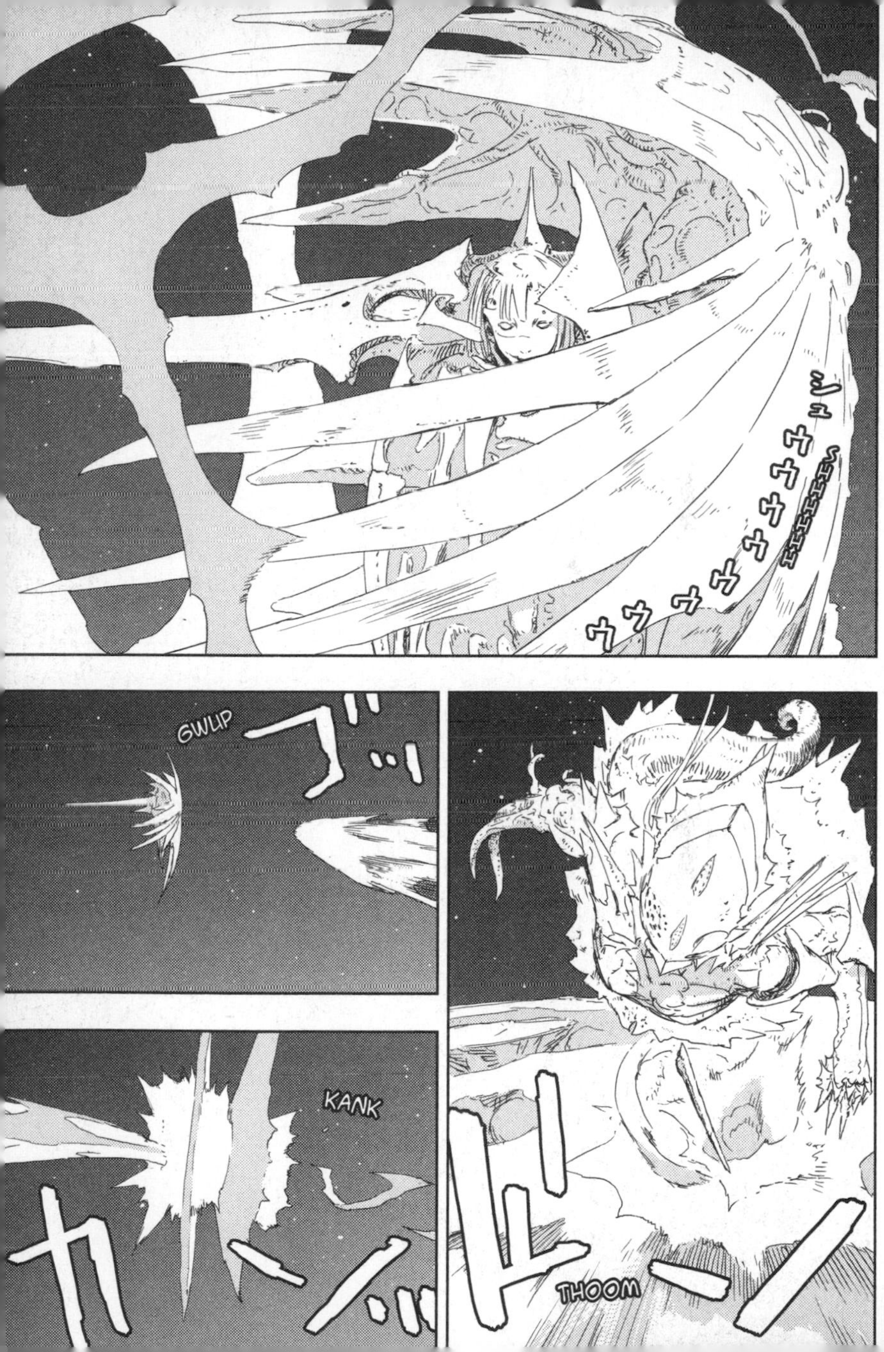

シュウウウウウウウウ
SHHHHHHHH
ドーン
THOOM
ゴッ
GWLUP
カーン
KANK

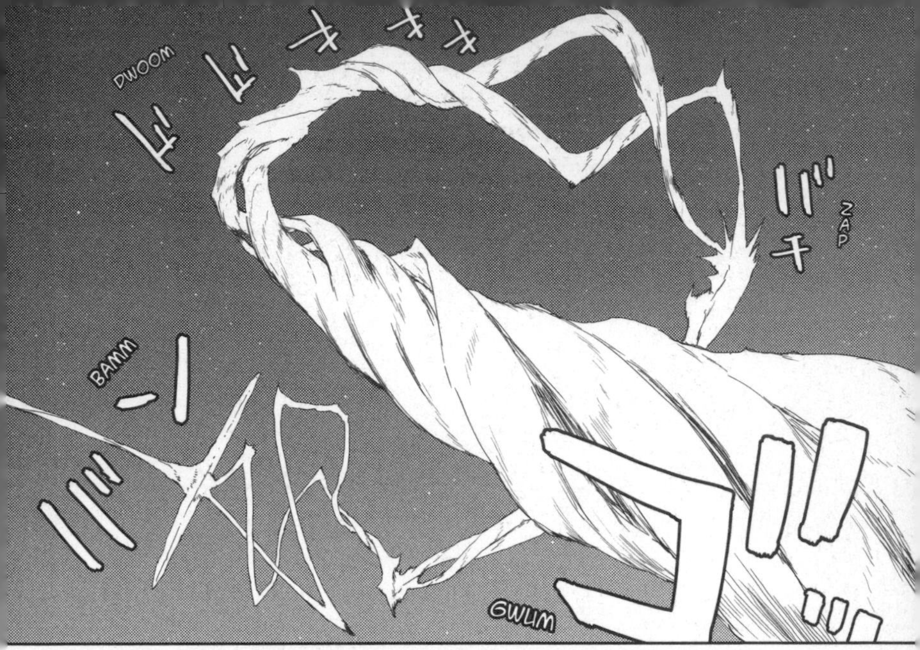
ZAP
DWOOM
GWUM
BAMM
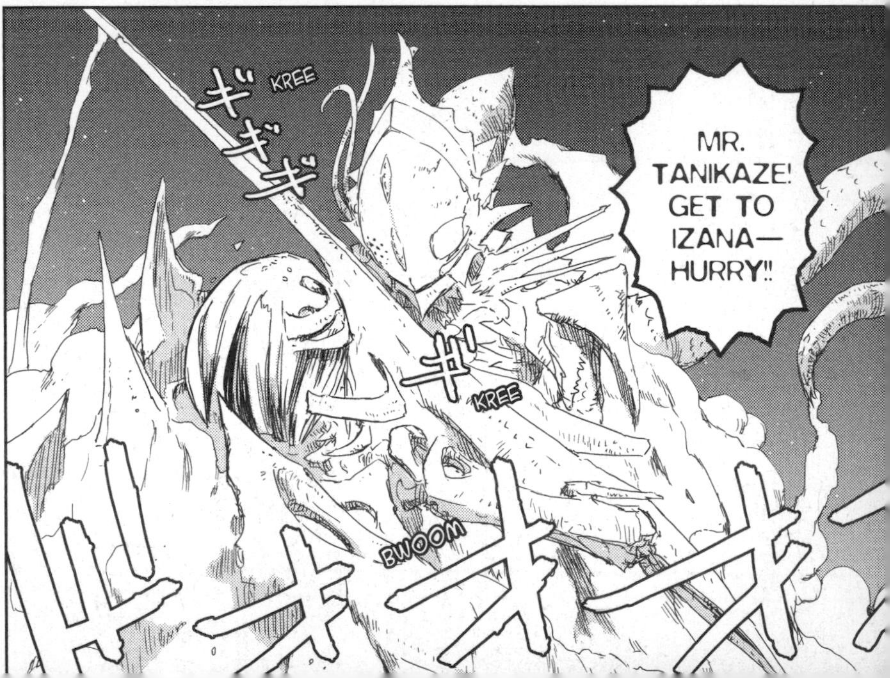
MR. TANIKAZE! GET TO IZANA— HURRY!!
KREE
KREE
BWOOM

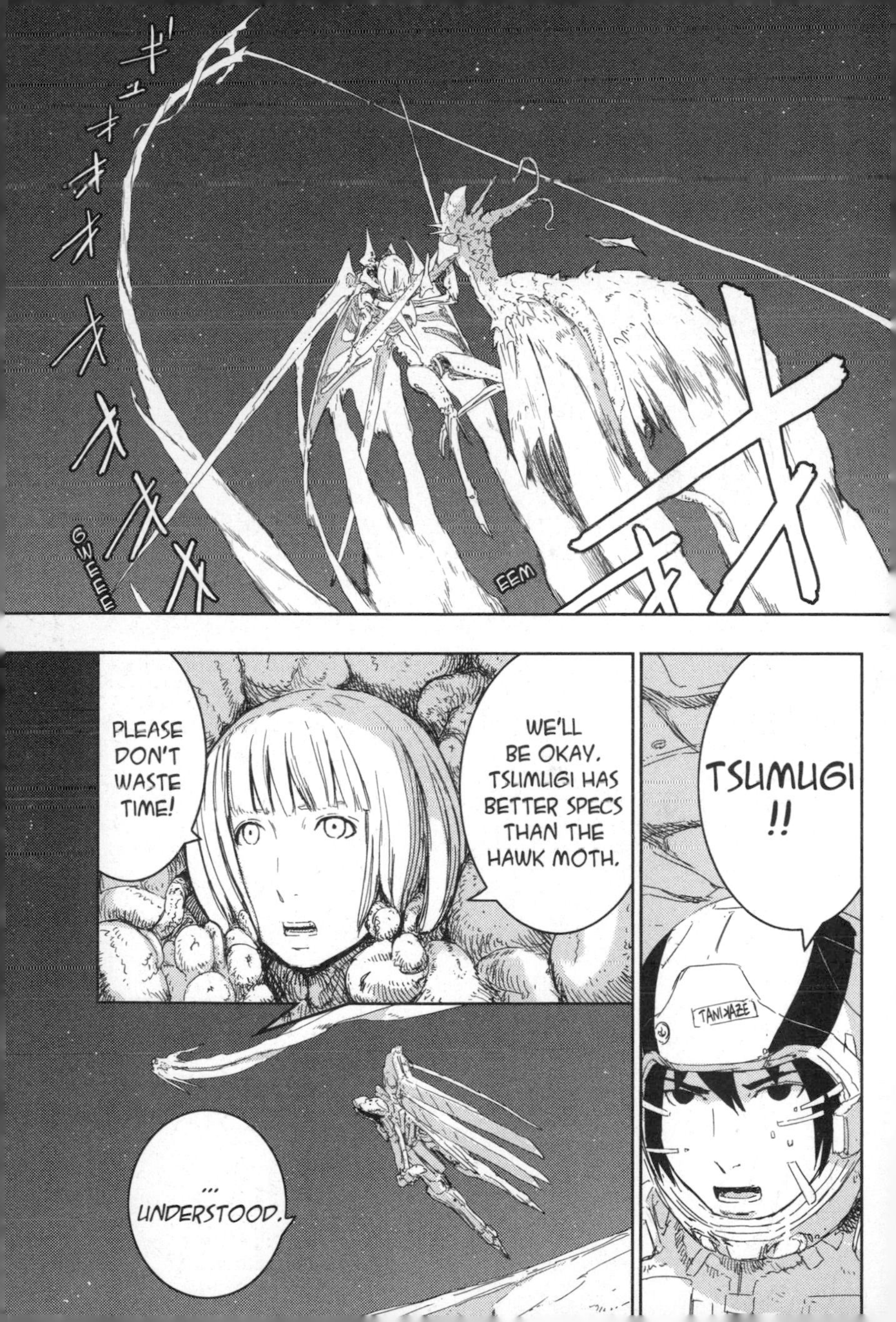
ギュオオオオオオオオオ
GWEEE
EEM
オオ
TSUMUGI !!
TANIKAZE
WE'LL BE OKAY. TSUMUGI HAS BETTER SPECS THAN THE HAWK MOTH.
PLEASE DON'T WASTE TIME!
... UNDERSTOOD.

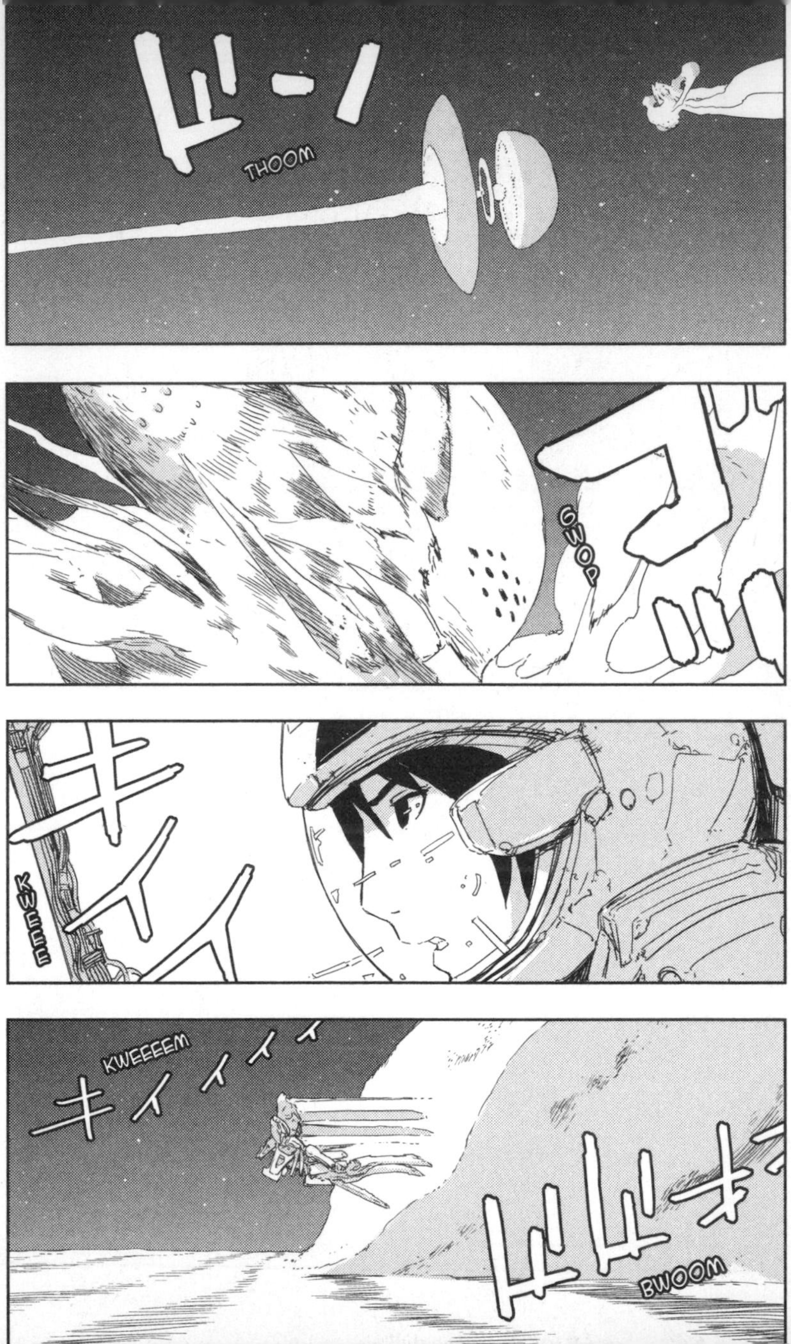

ドーン
THOOM
ゴッ
GWOP
キイイ
KWEEEE
キイイイイ
KWEEEEM
ドゥーオ
BWOOM

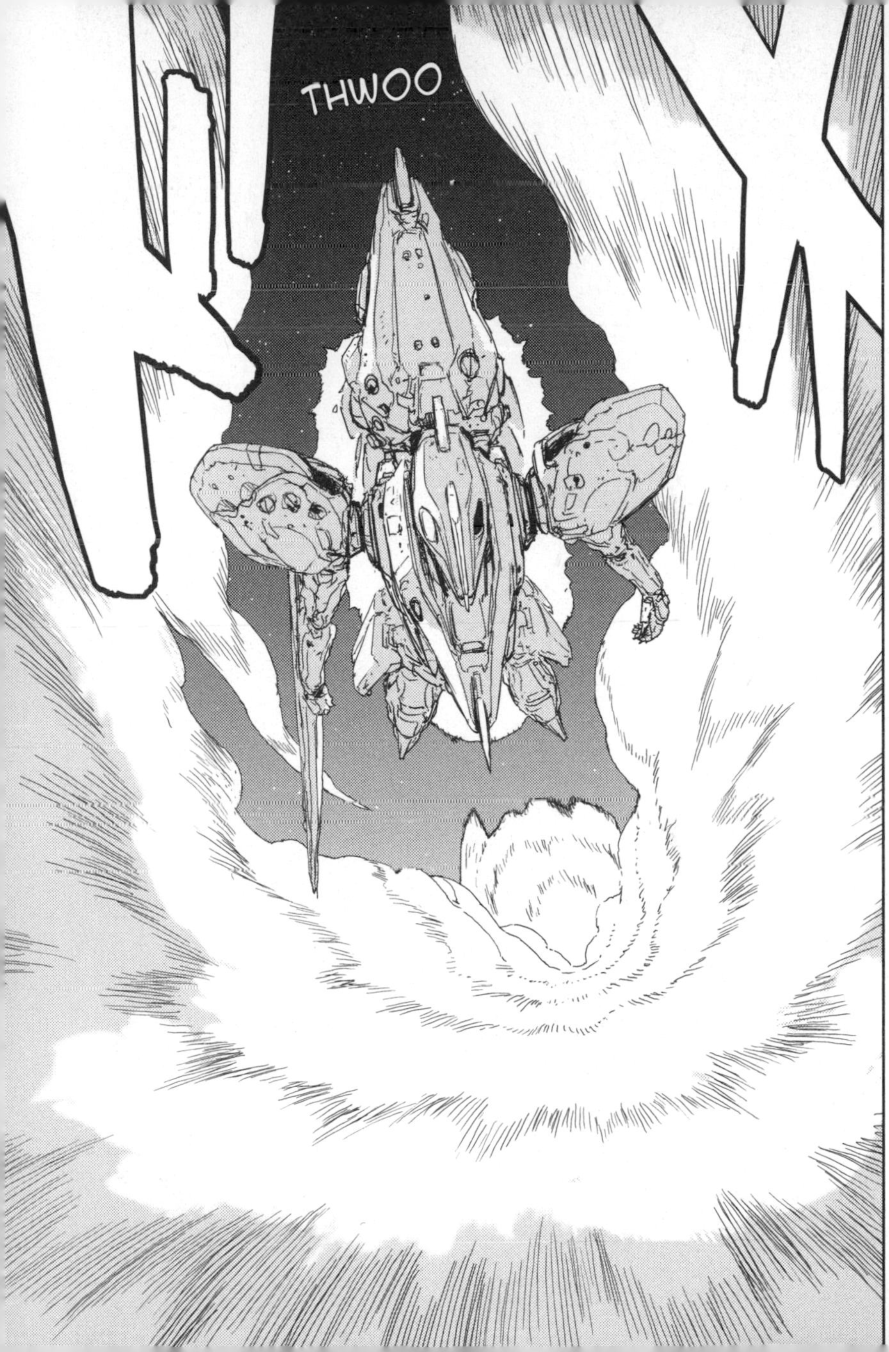
THWOO

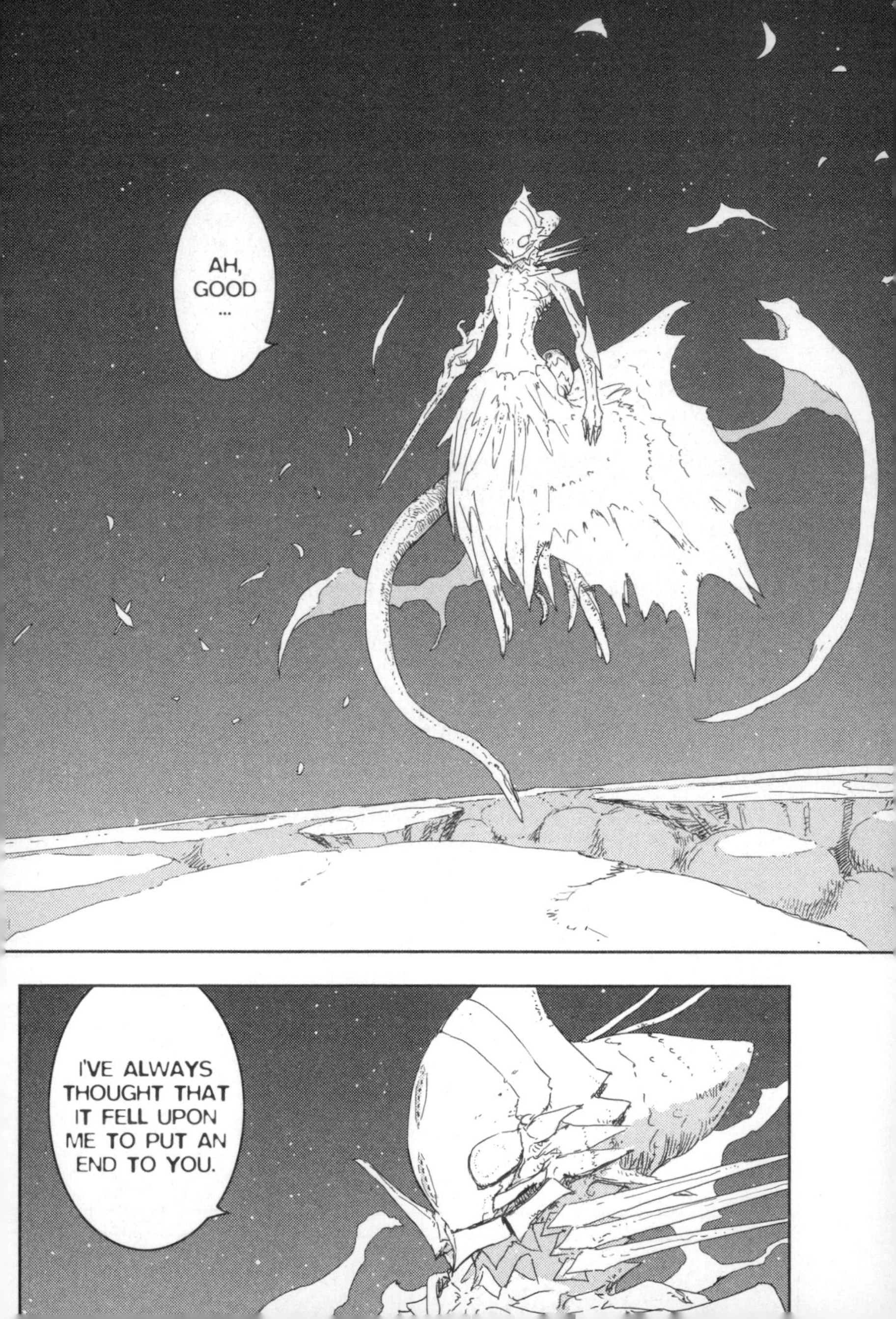
AH, GOOD ...
I'VE ALWAYS THOUGHT THAT IT FELL UPON ME TO PUT AN END TO YOU.

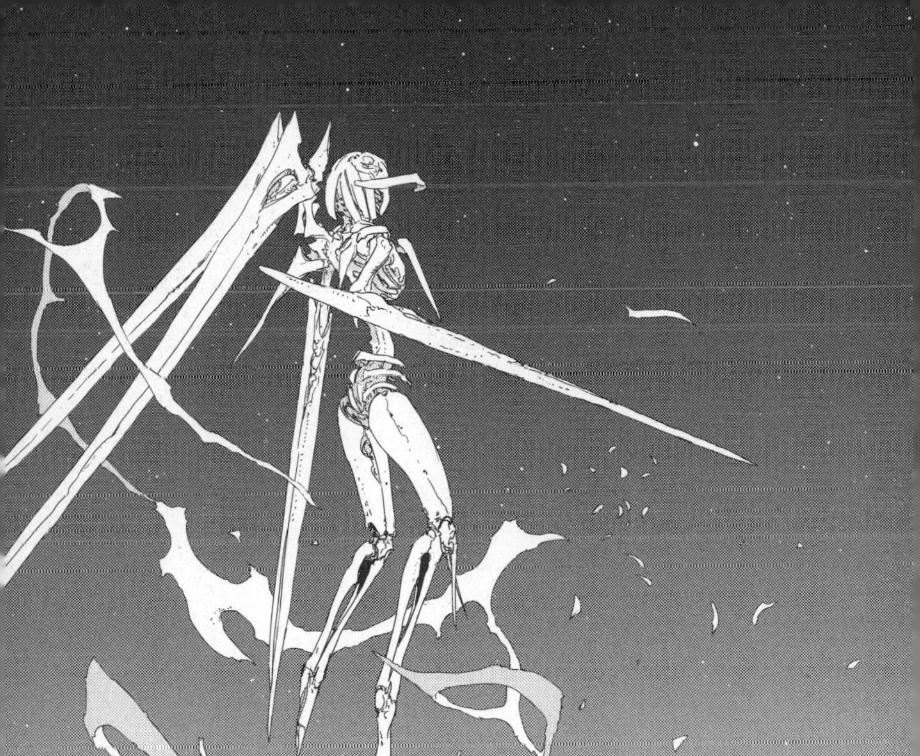

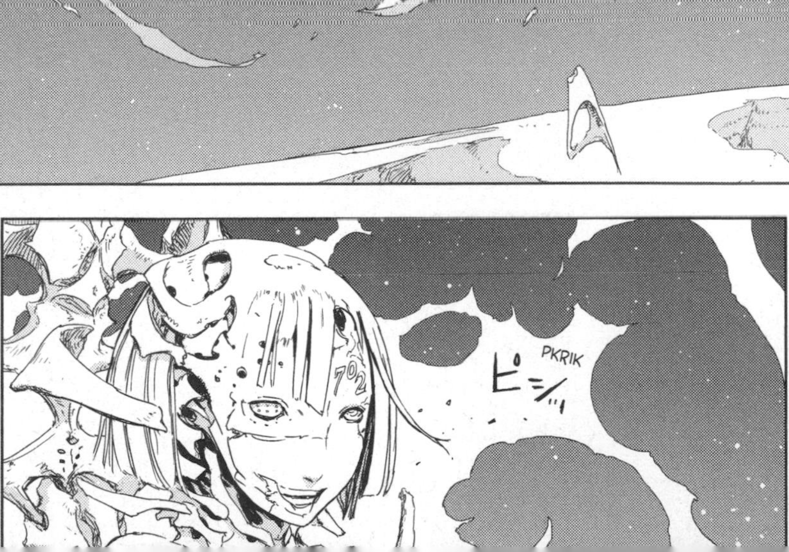
PKRIK
ピシッ

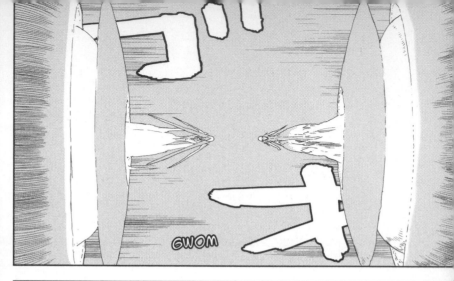

GWOM

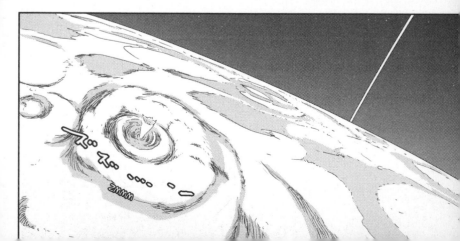

ZMMM

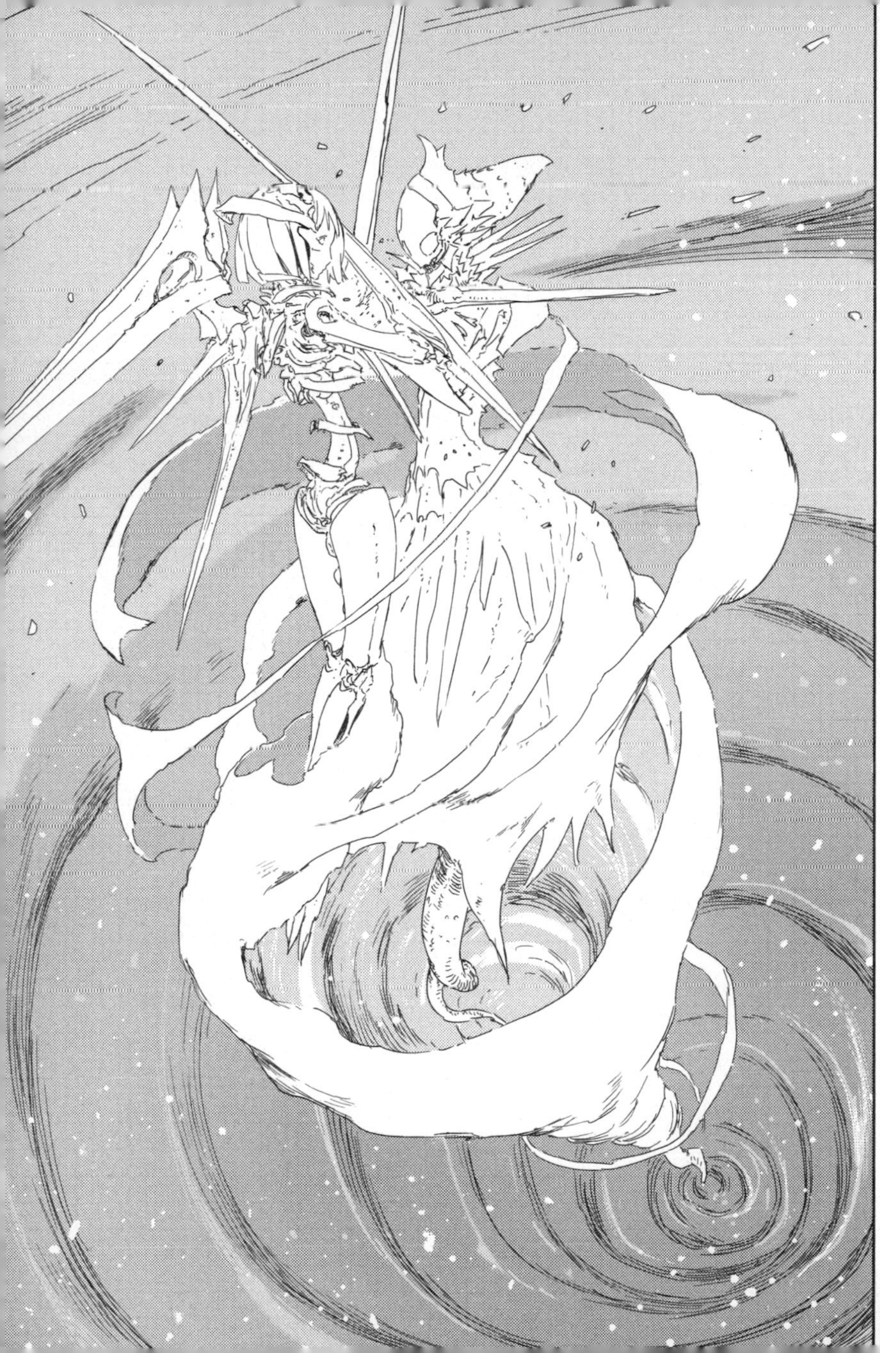

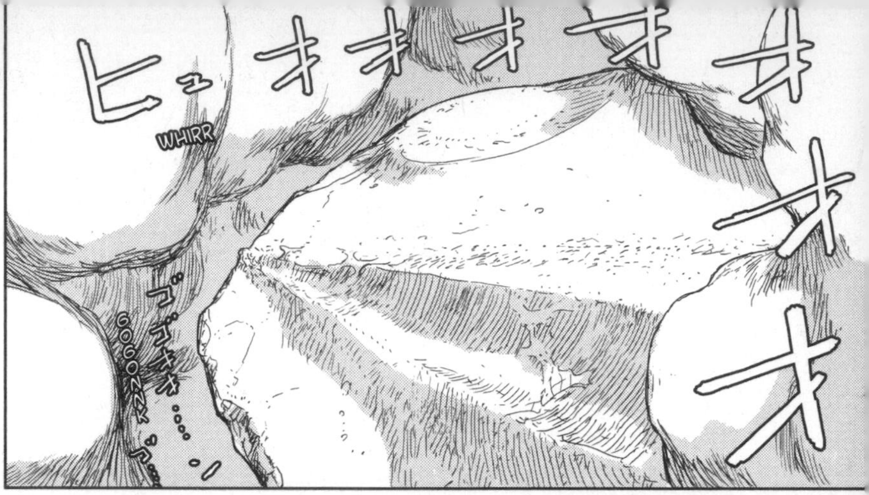
ヒュォォォォォォォォ
WHIRR
ゴゴオオ……
ゴ……
GOGONNK

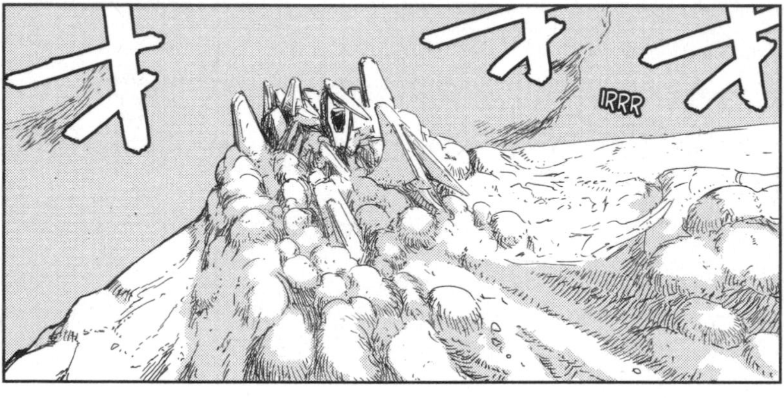
ォォォ
IRRR

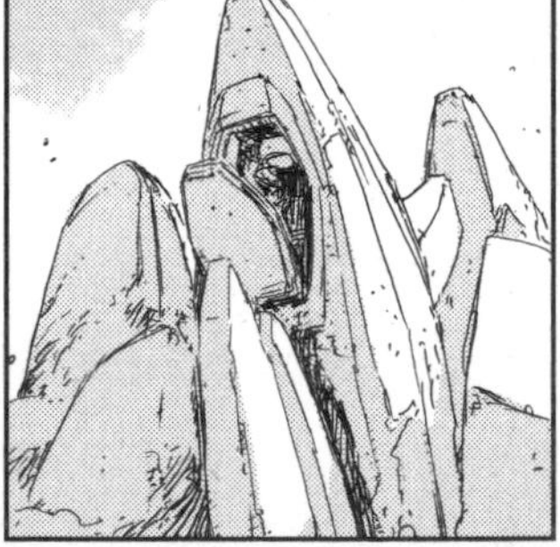

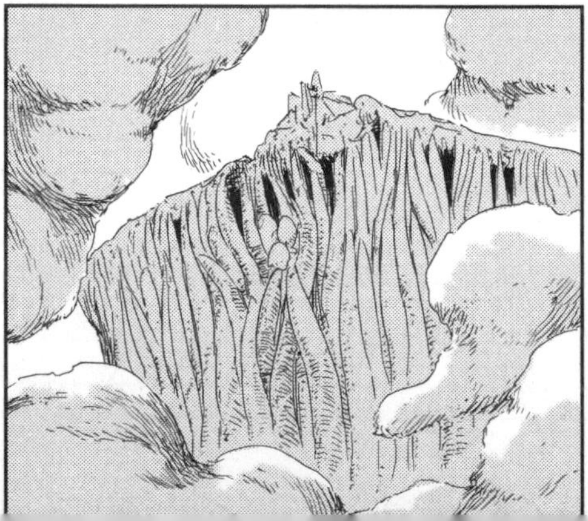

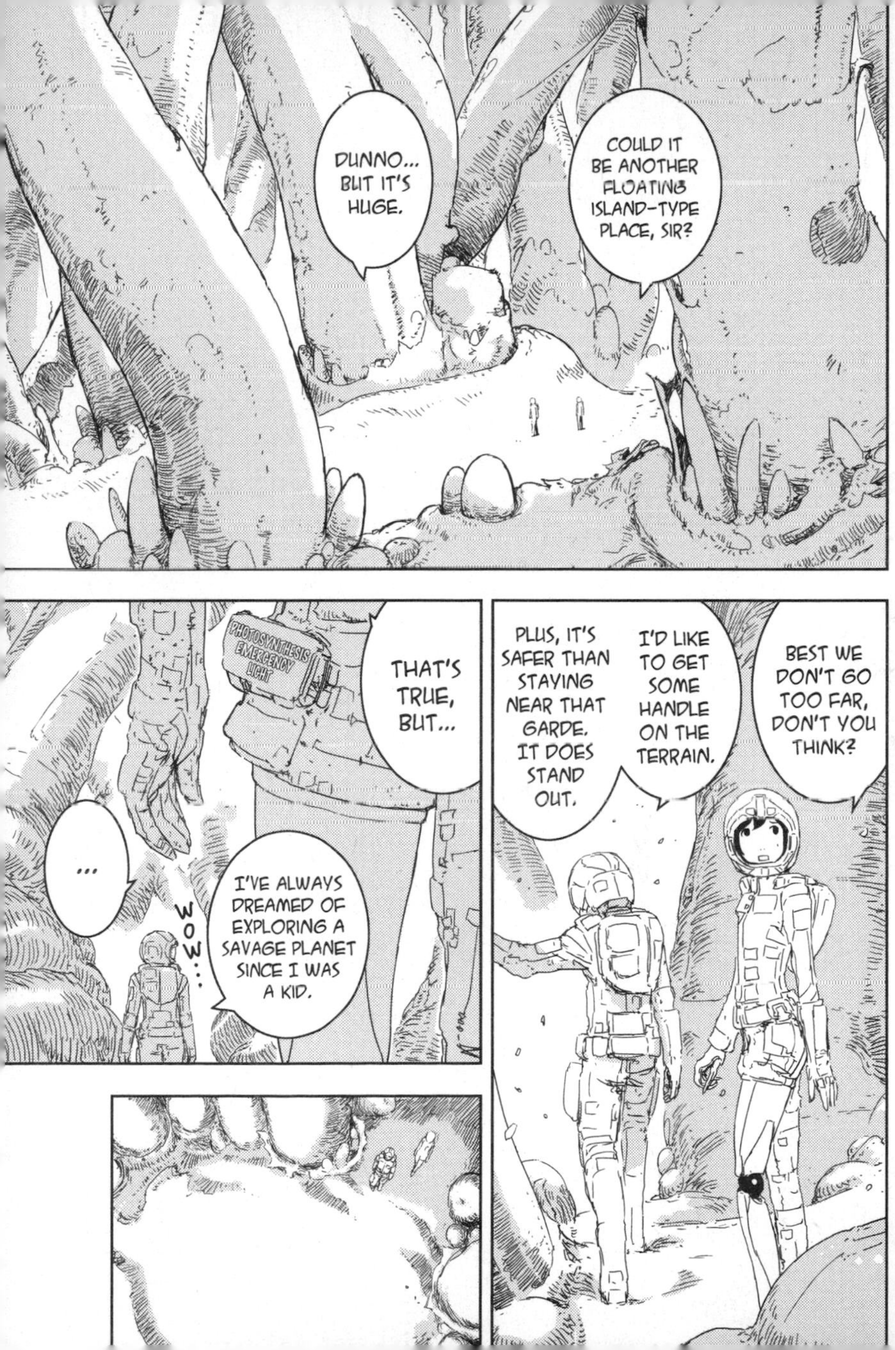
COULD IT BE ANOTHER FLOATING ISLAND-TYPE PLACE, SIR?
DUNNO... BUT IT'S HUGE.
BEST WE DON'T GO TOO FAR, DON'T YOU THINK?
I'D LIKE TO GET SOME HANDLE ON THE TERRAIN.
PLUS, IT'S SAFER THAN STAYING NEAR THAT GARDE. IT DOES STAND OUT.
PHOTOSYNTHESIS EMERGENCY LIGHT
THAT'S TRUE, BUT...
I'VE ALWAYS DREAMED OF EXPLORING A SAVAGE PLANET SINCE I WAS A KID.
WOW...
...

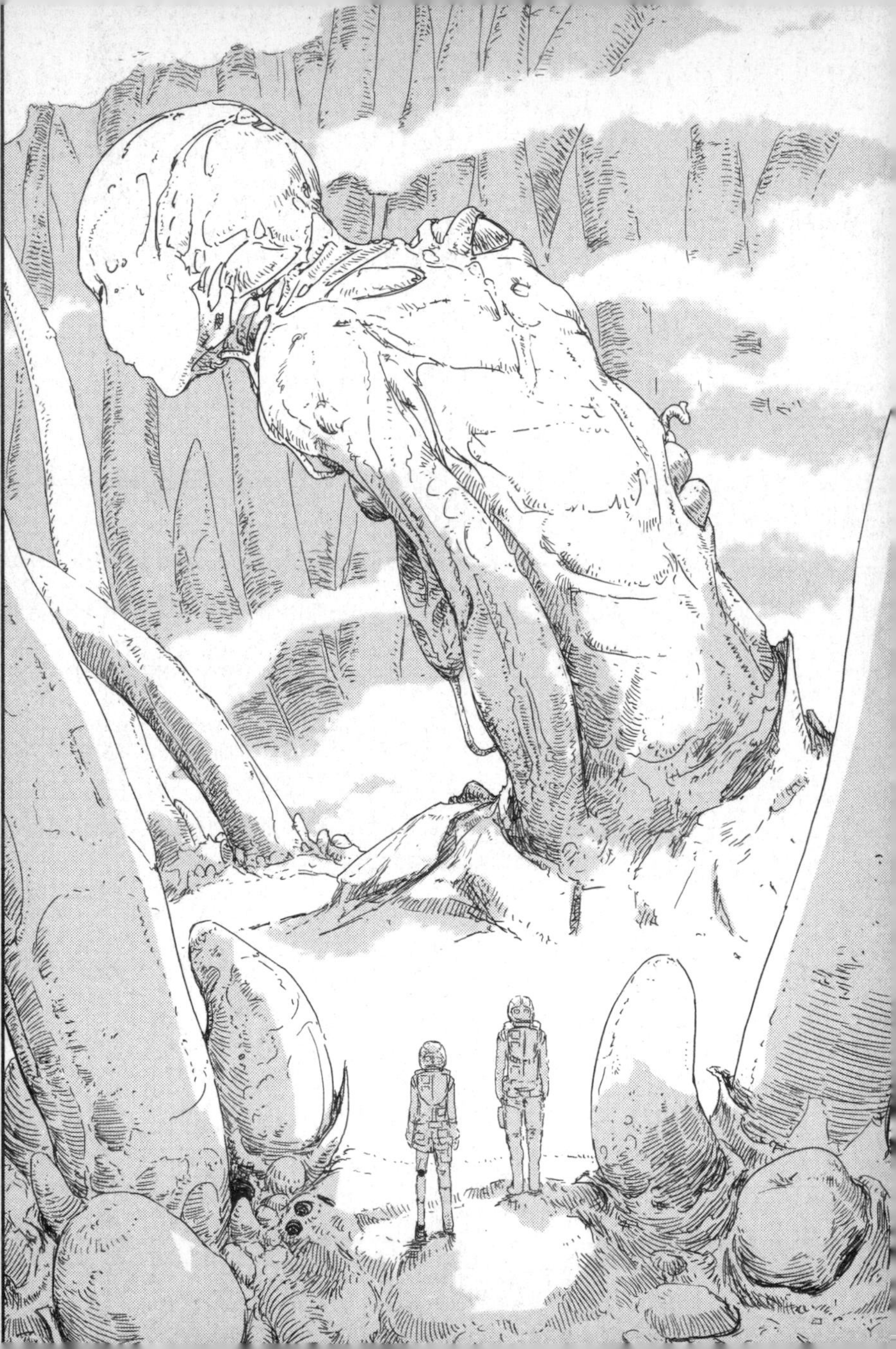

シドニアの騎士
KNIGHTS OF SIDONIA

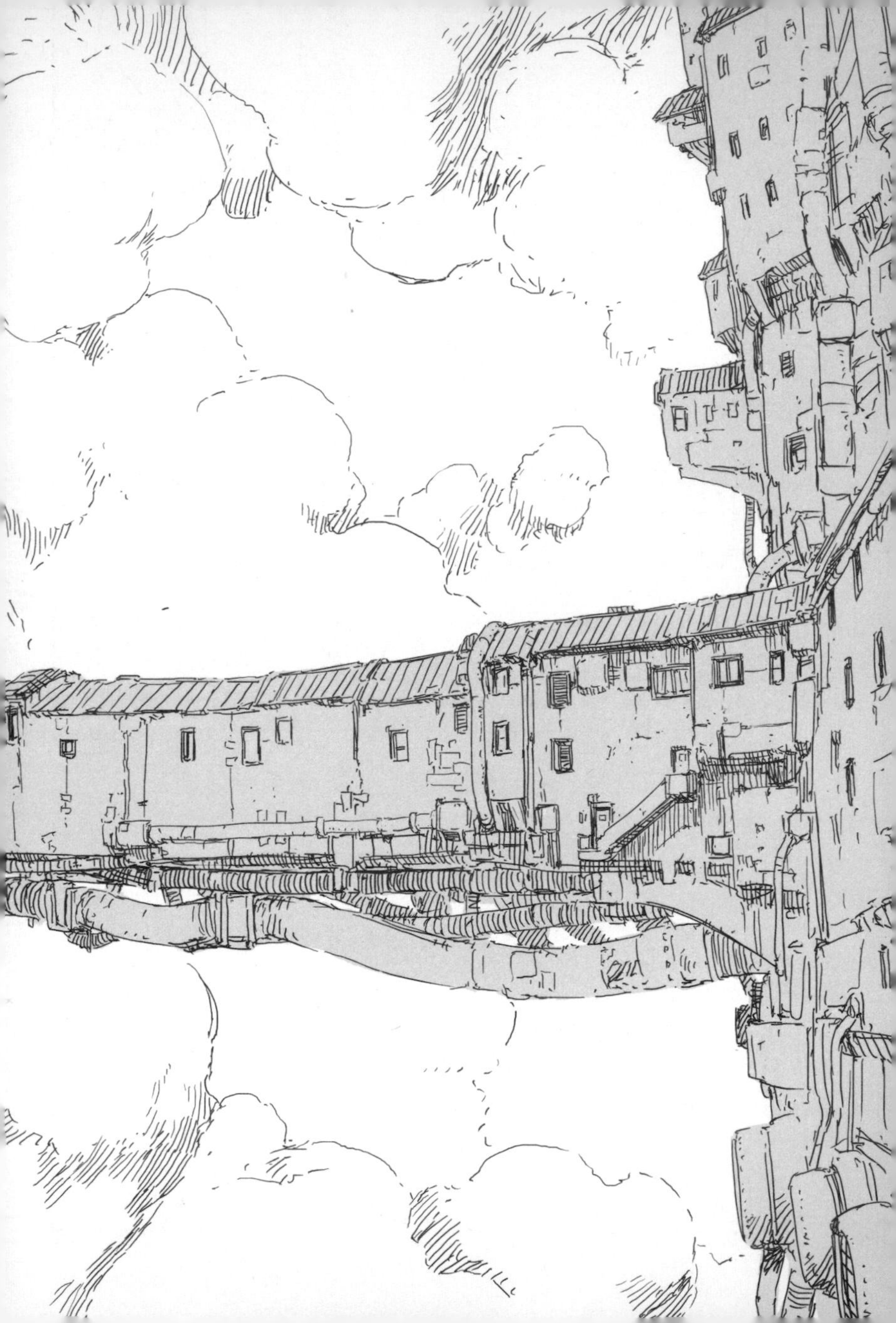

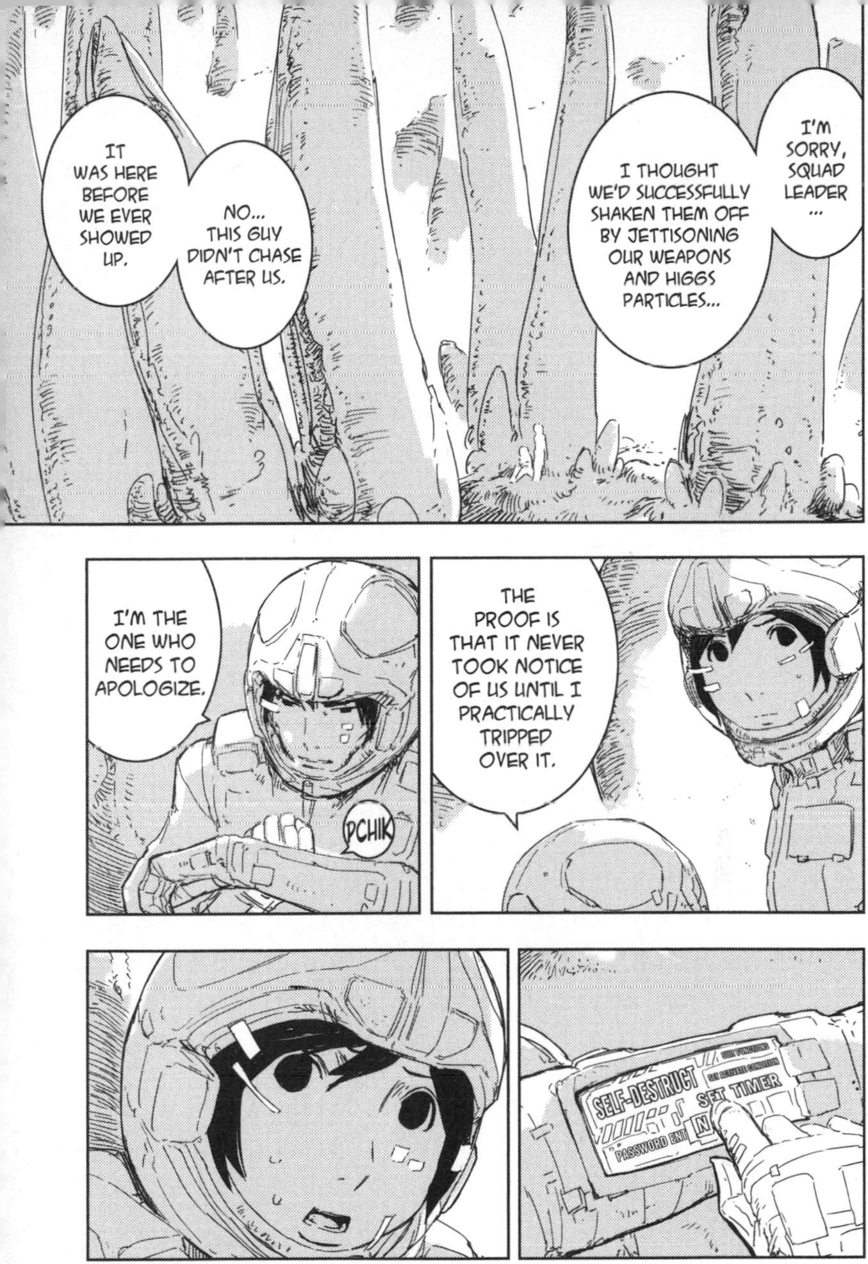
I'M SORRY, SQUAD LEADER...
I THOUGHT WE'D SUCCESSFULLY SHAKEN THEM OFF BY JETTISONING OUR WEAPONS AND HIGGS PARTICLES...
NO... THIS GUY DIDN'T CHASE AFTER US.
IT WAS HERE BEFORE WE EVER SHOWED UP.
THE PROOF IS THAT IT NEVER TOOK NOTICE OF US UNTIL I PRACTICALLY TRIPPED OVER IT.
I'M THE ONE WHO NEEDS TO APOLOGIZE.
PCHIK
SELF-DESTRUCT
SET TIMER
PASSWORD ENT

Chapter 41: Nagate Tanikaze's Land Battle

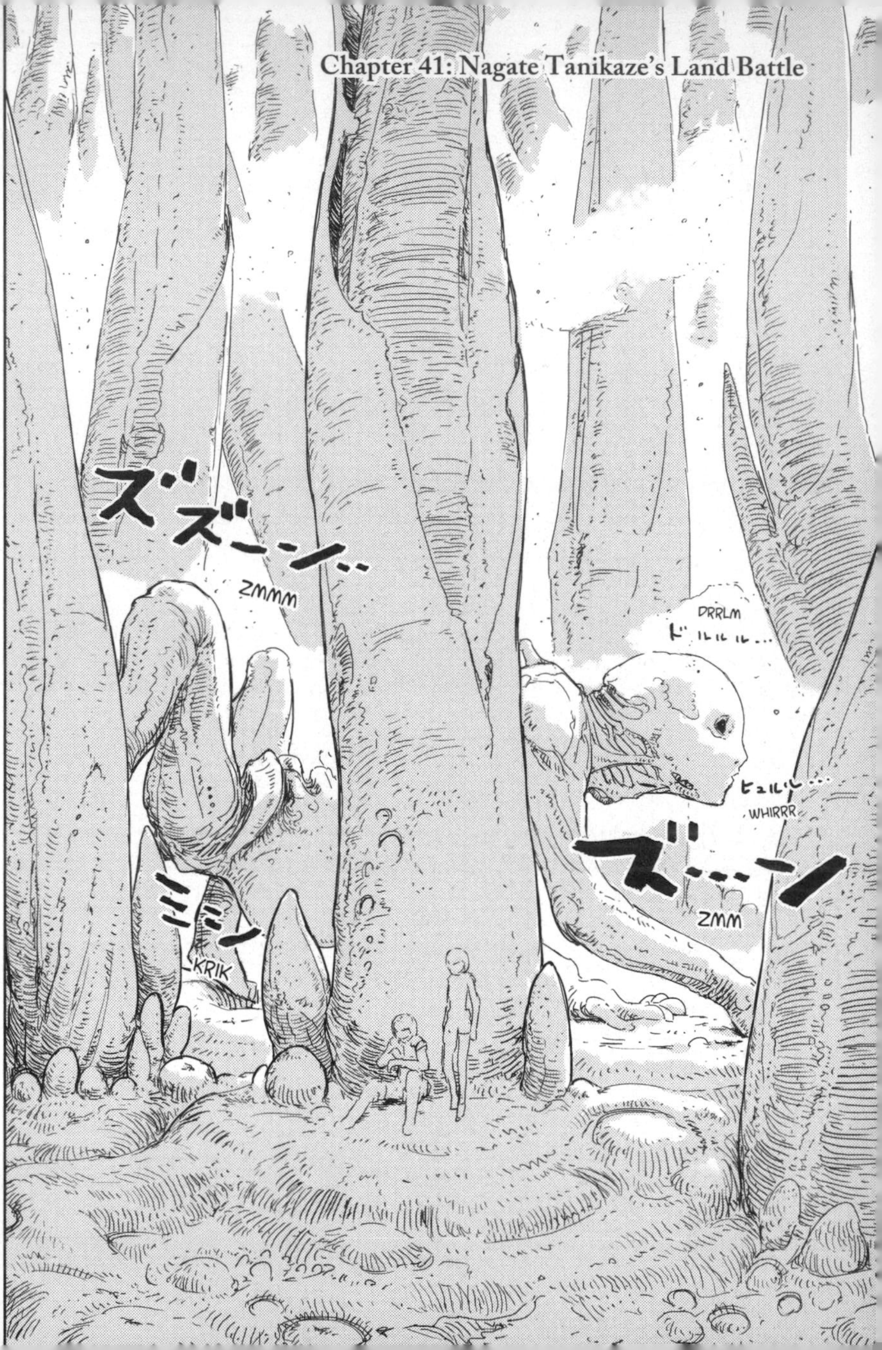
DRRLM
WHIRRR
ZMM
ZMMM
KRIK

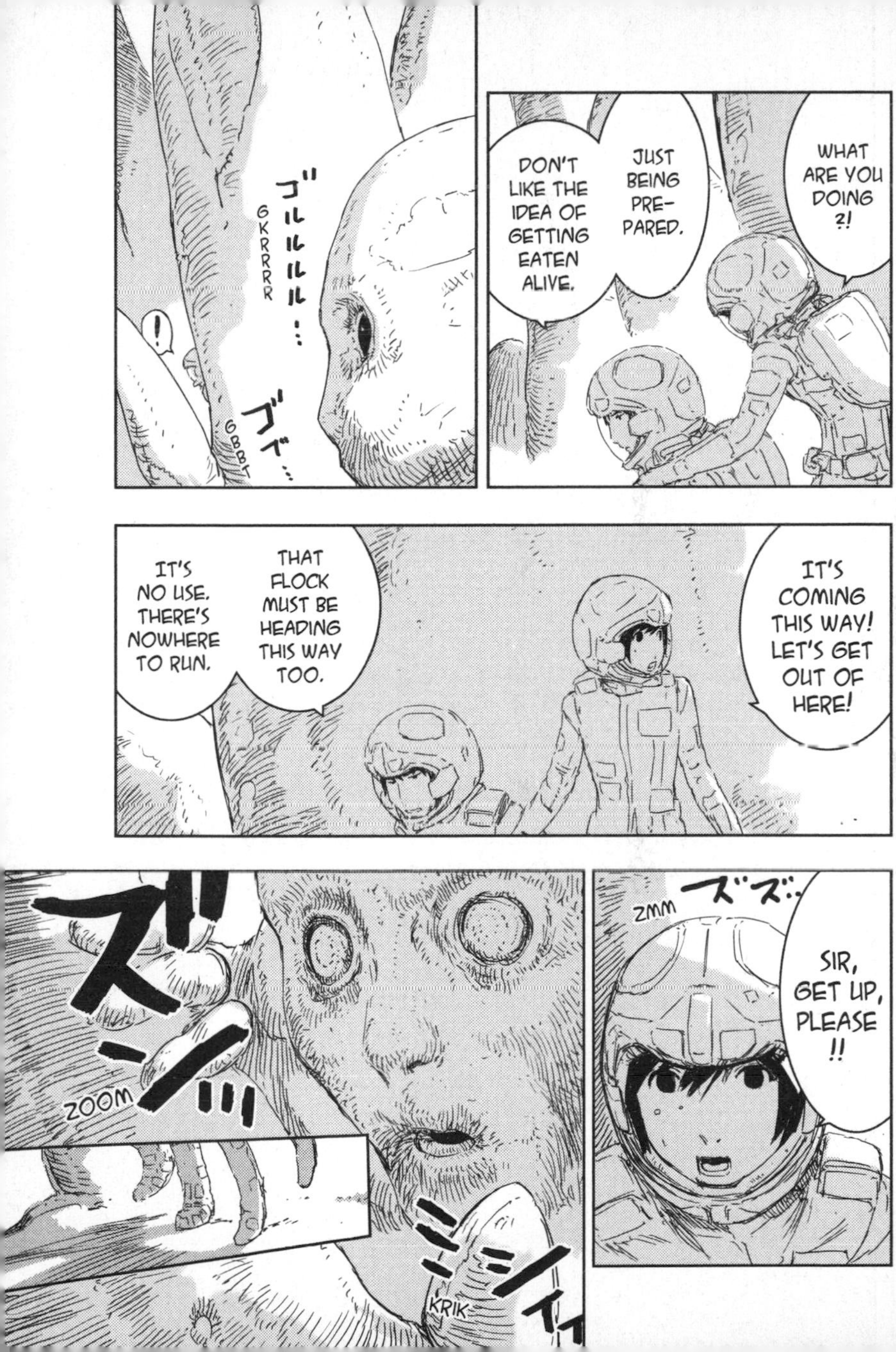
WHAT ARE YOU DOING ?!
JUST BEING PRE-PARED.
DON'T LIKE THE IDEA OF GETTING EATEN ALIVE.
ゴルルルル…
GKRRRR
!
ゴブ…
GBBT
IT'S COMING THIS WAY! LET'S GET OUT OF HERE!
THAT FLOCK MUST BE HEADING THIS WAY TOO.
IT'S NO USE. THERE'S NOWHERE TO RUN.
ズズ…
ZMM
SIR, GET UP, PLEASE !!
ズーッ
ZOOM
ミシィ
KRIK

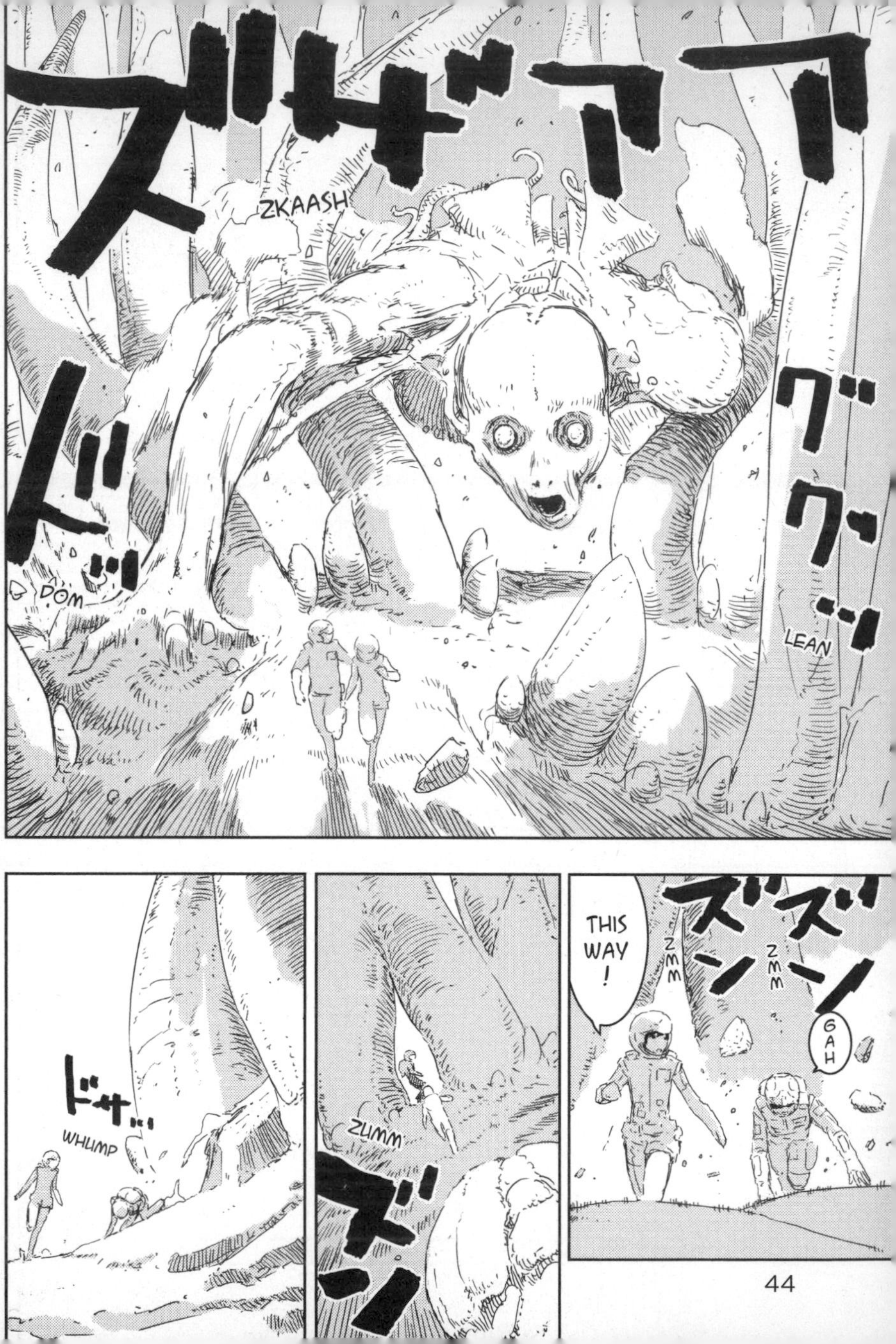
ZKAASH
LEAN
DOM
THIS WAY!
ZMM
ZMM
GAH
ZUMM
WHUMP

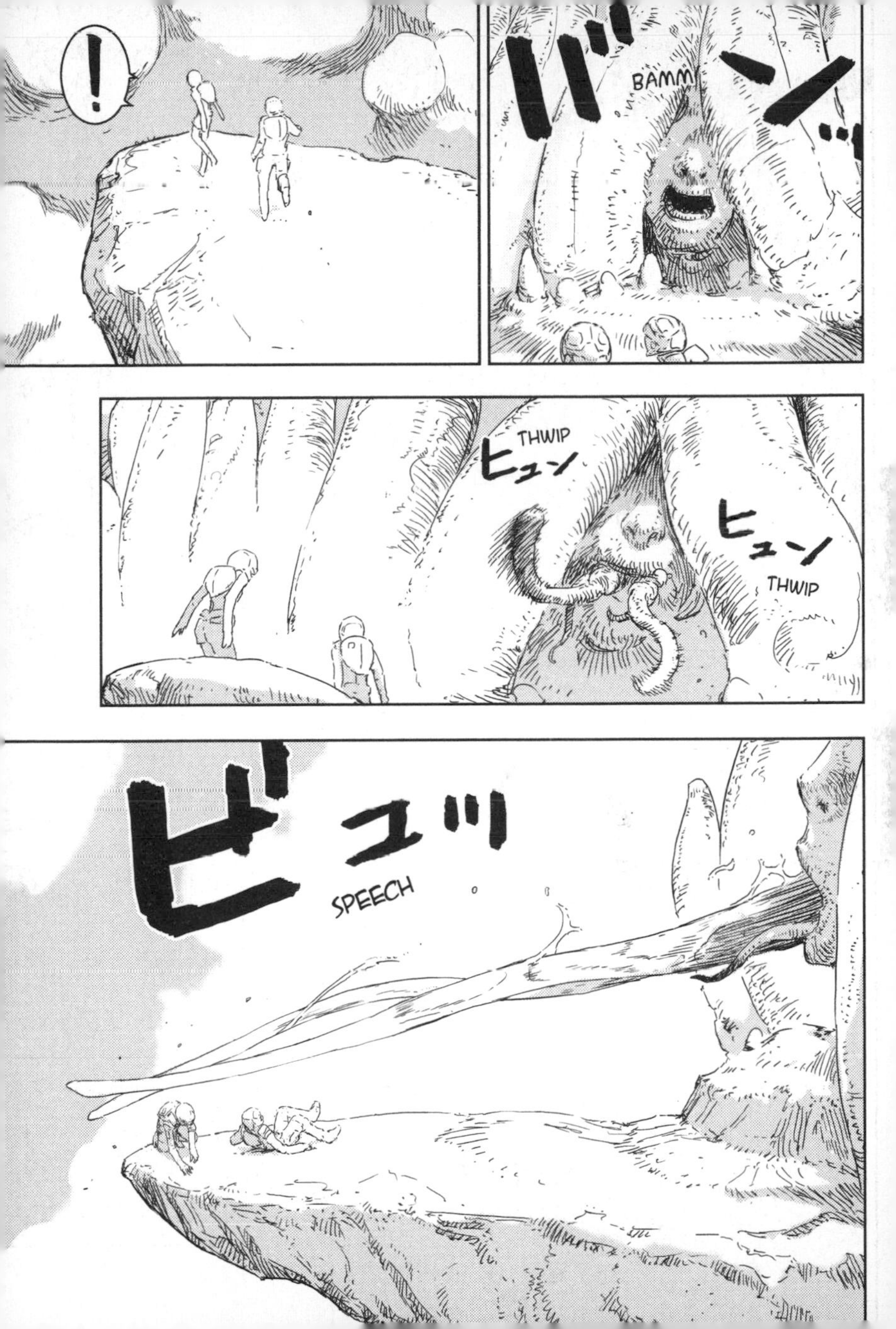

バン…
BAMM
!
ヒュン
THWIP
ヒュン
THWIP
ビュッ
SPEECH

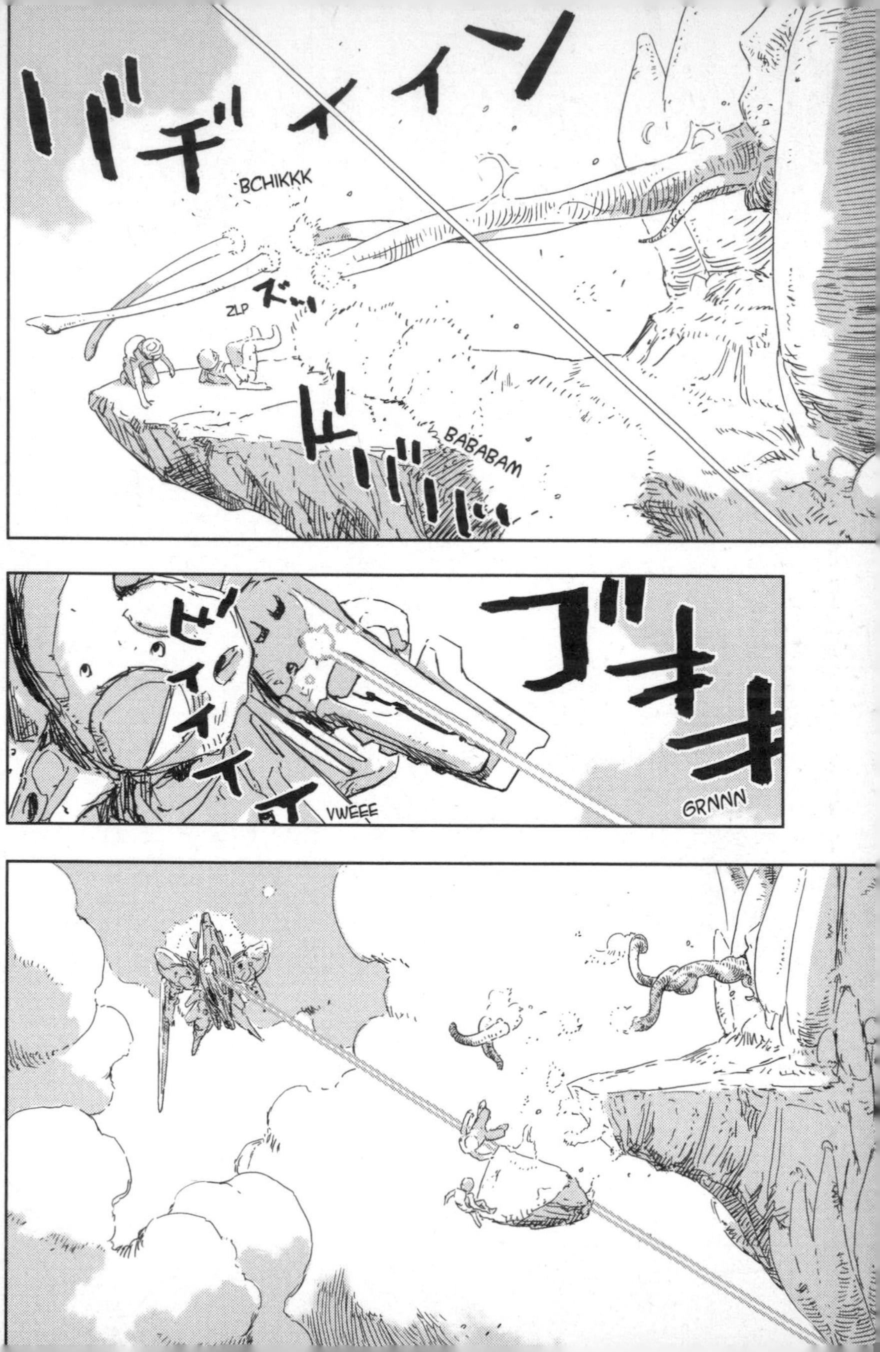
バヂィイン
BCHIKKK
ズッ
ZLP
BABABAM
ゴキキ
GRNNN
ビィイイイ
VWEEE

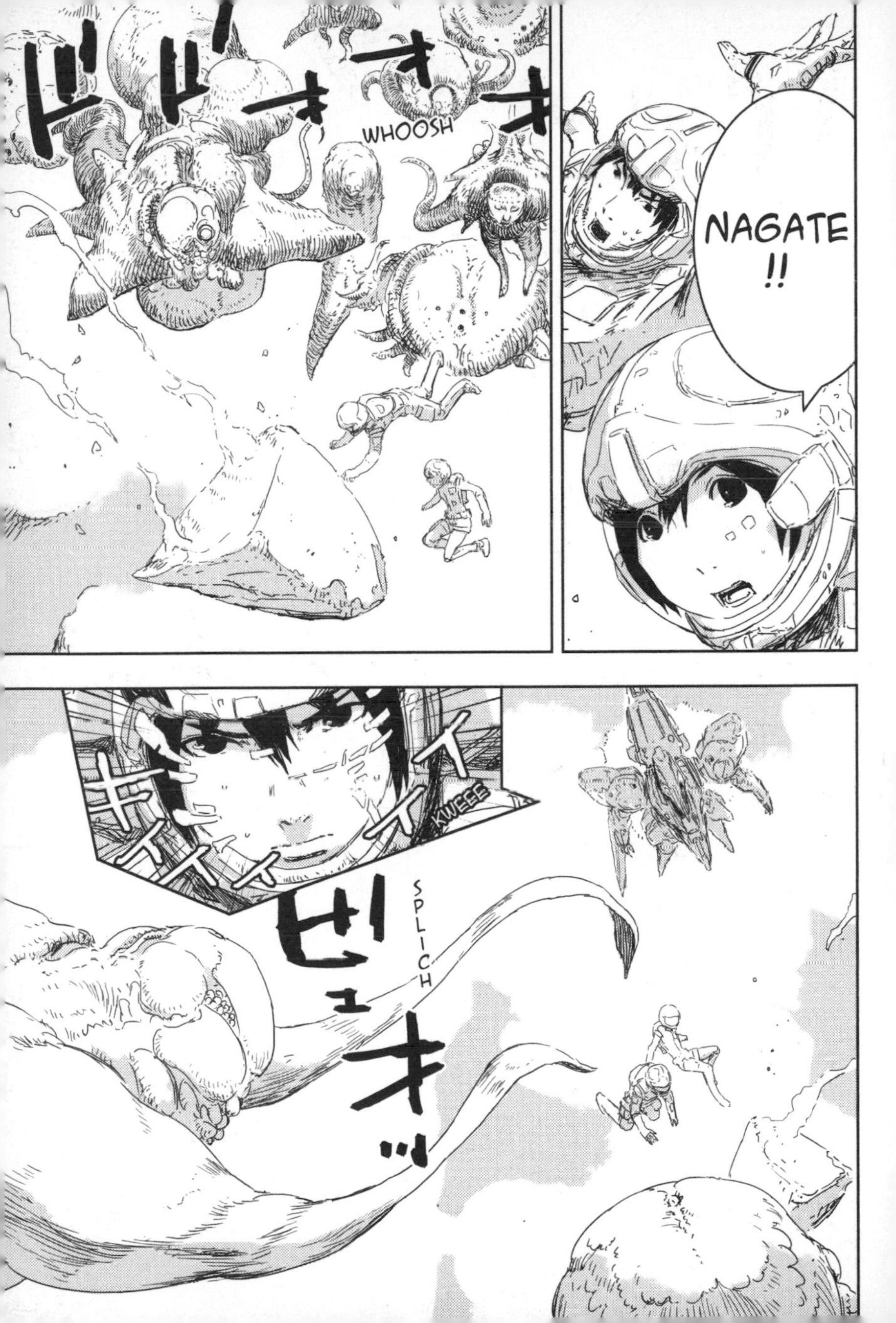
NAGATE !!
WHOOSH
KWEEE
SPLICH

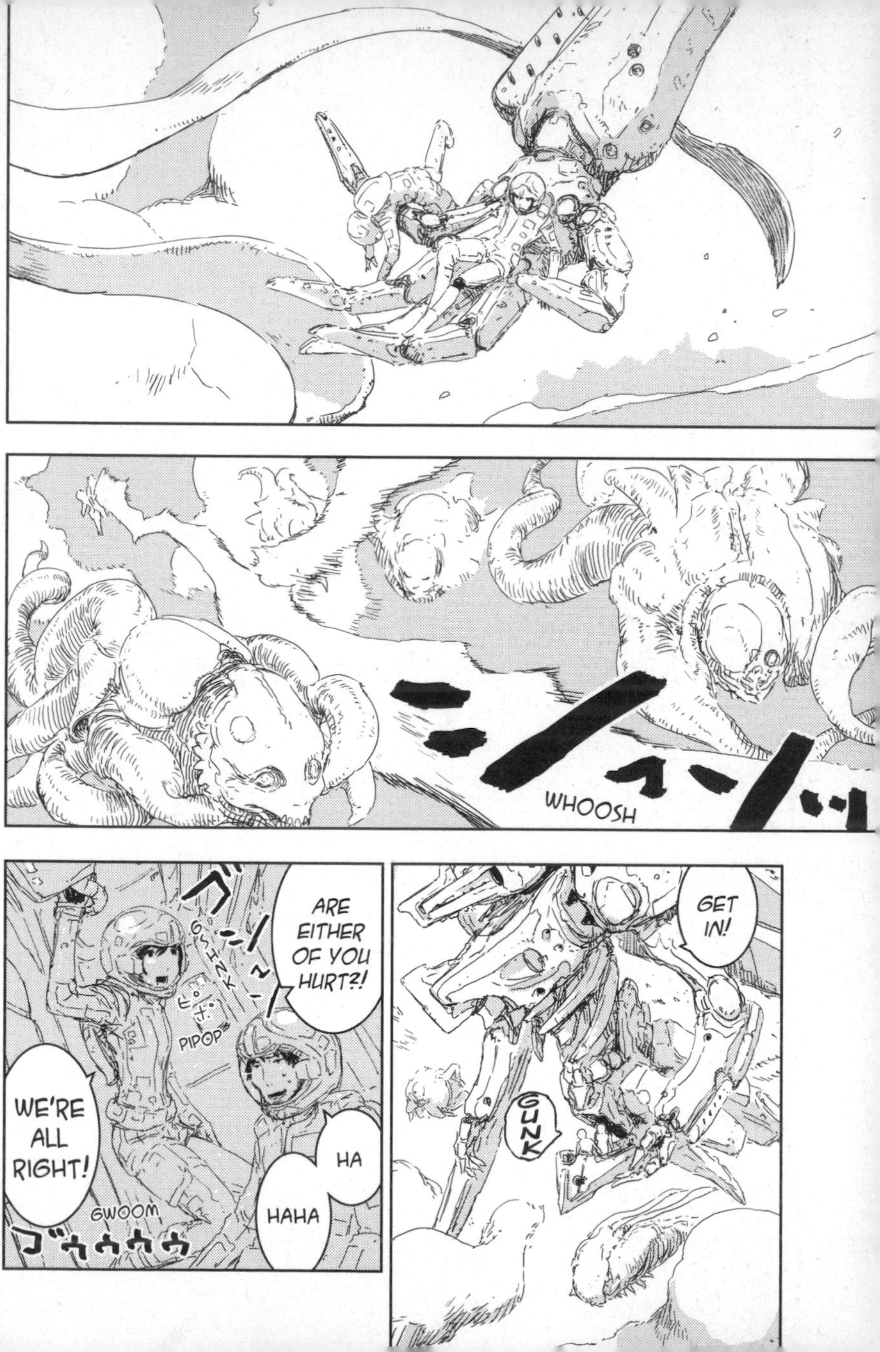
WHOOSH
GET IN!
GUNK
ARE EITHER OF YOU HURT?!
ピポ
PIPOP
HA
HAHA
WE'RE ALL RIGHT!
GWOOM

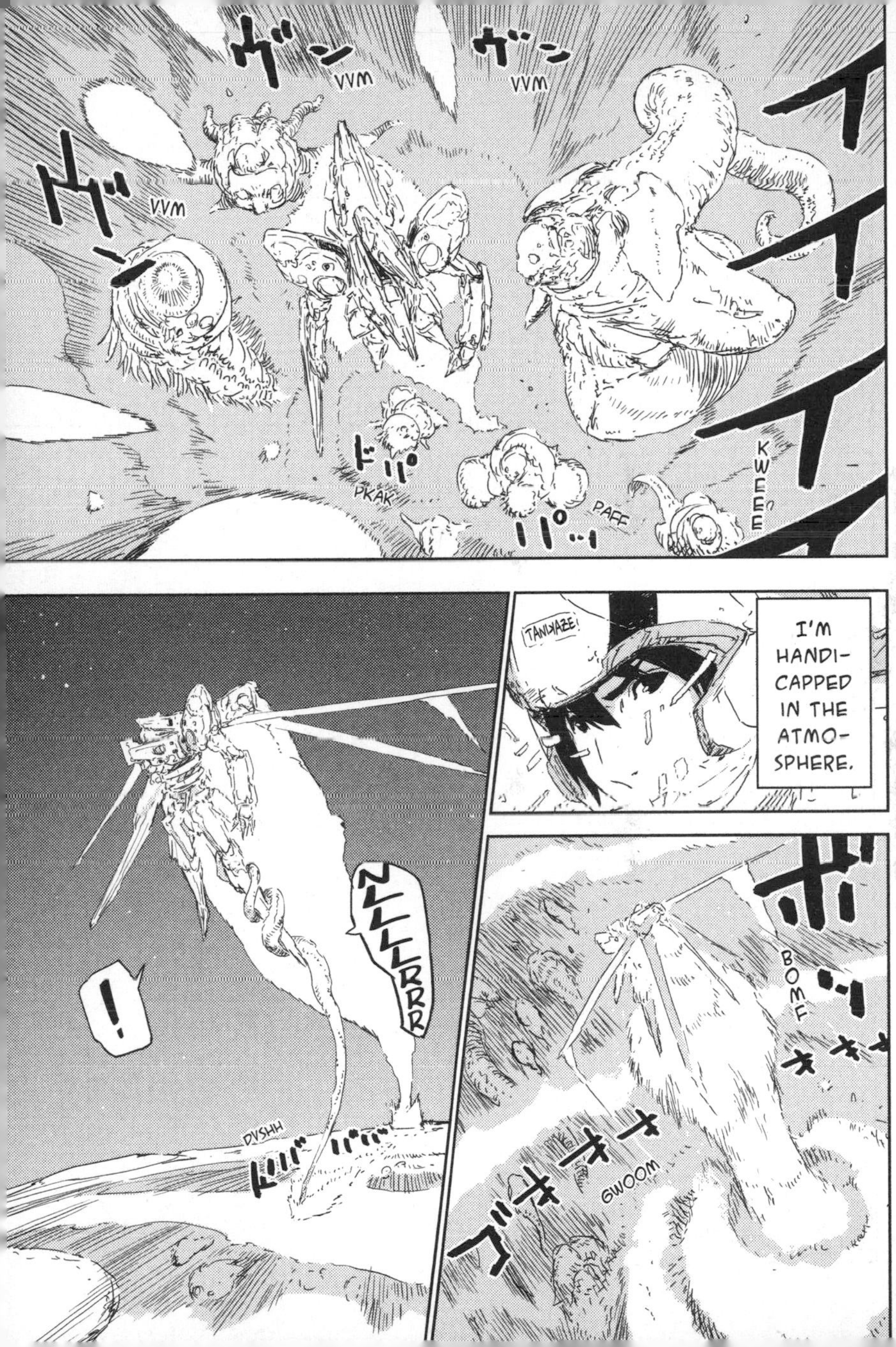
KWEEE
VVM
VVM
VVM
PAFF
PKAK
TANIKAZE
I'M HANDI-CAPPED IN THE ATMO-SPHERE.
BOMF
GWOOM
NLLLLRRR
!
DVSHH

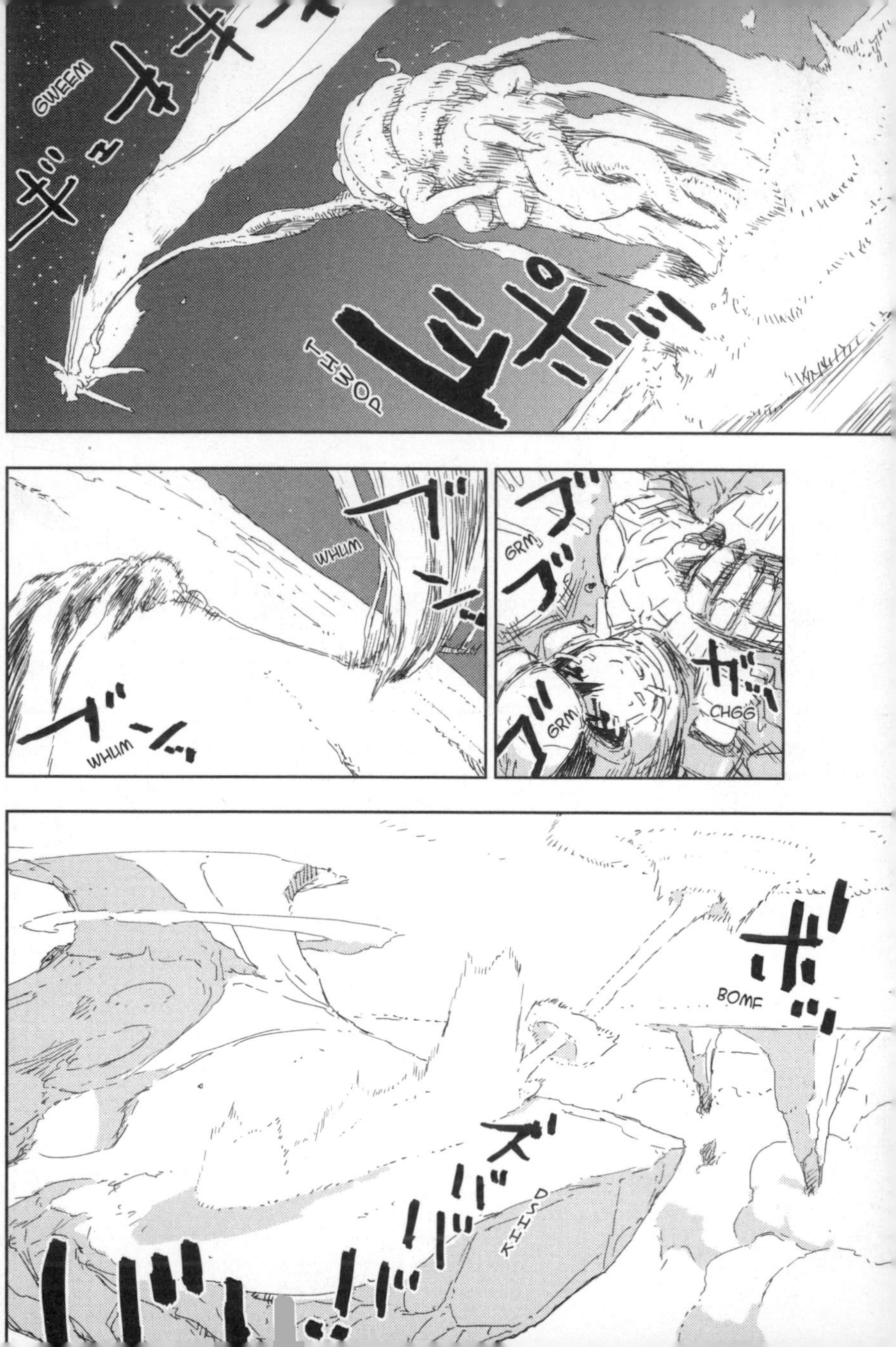
GWEEM
THWOP
GRM
GRM
CHGG
WHUM
WHUM
BOMF

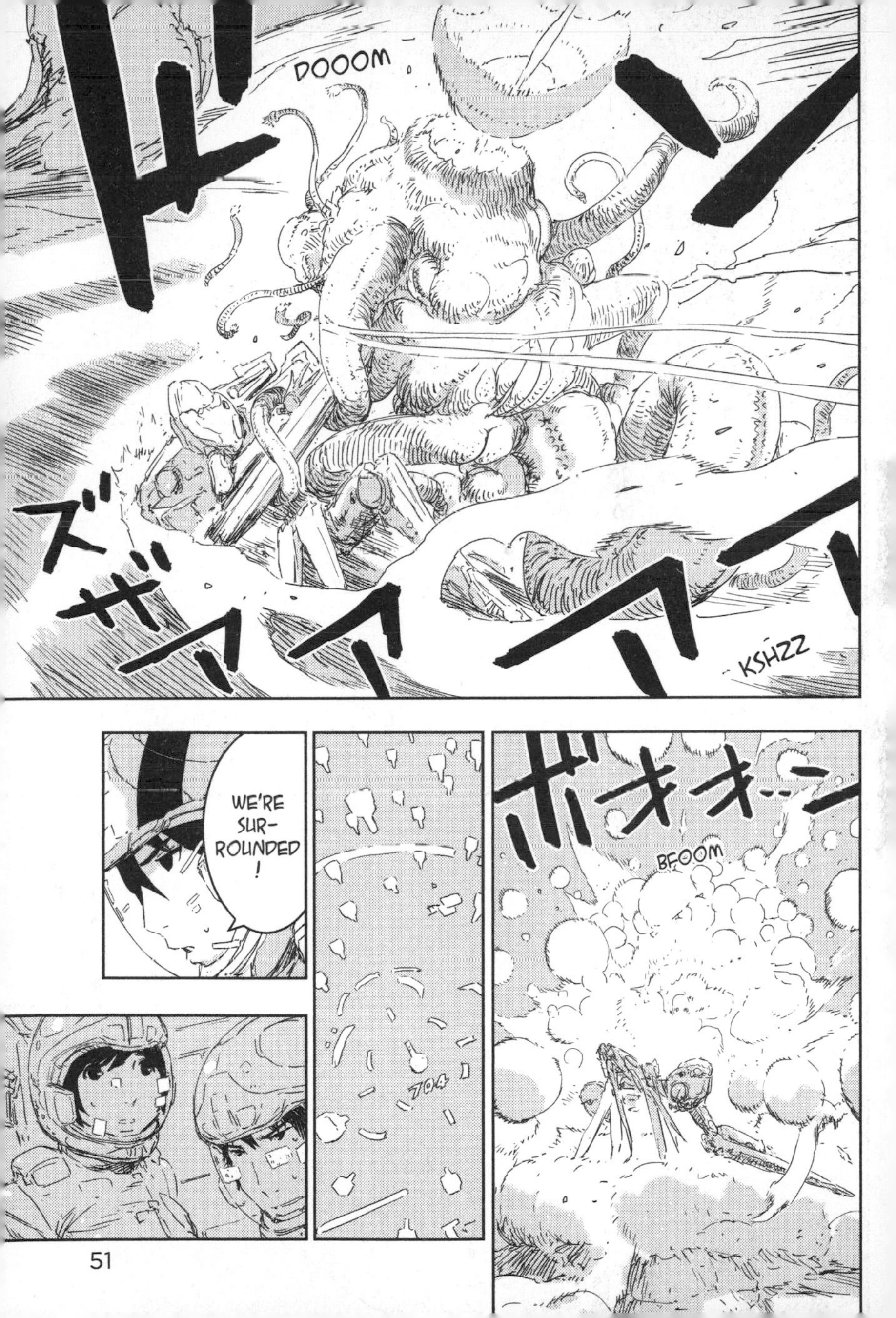
DOOOM
KSHZZ
BFOOM
704
WE'RE SUR-ROUNDED!

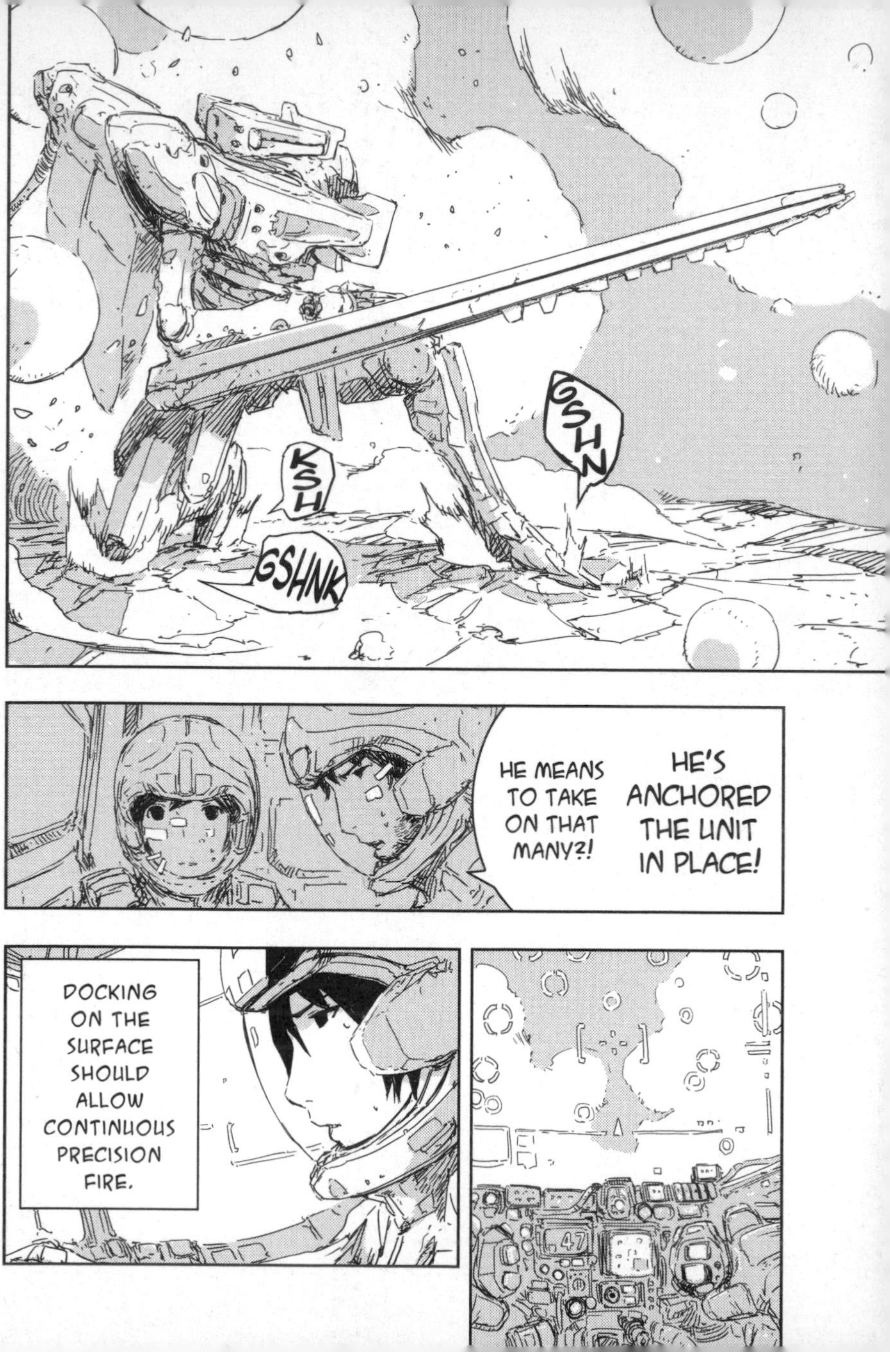
GSHN
KSH
GSHNK
HE'S ANCHORED THE UNIT IN PLACE!
HE MEANS TO TAKE ON THAT MANY?!
DOCKING ON THE SURFACE SHOULD ALLOW CONTINUOUS PRECISION FIRE.

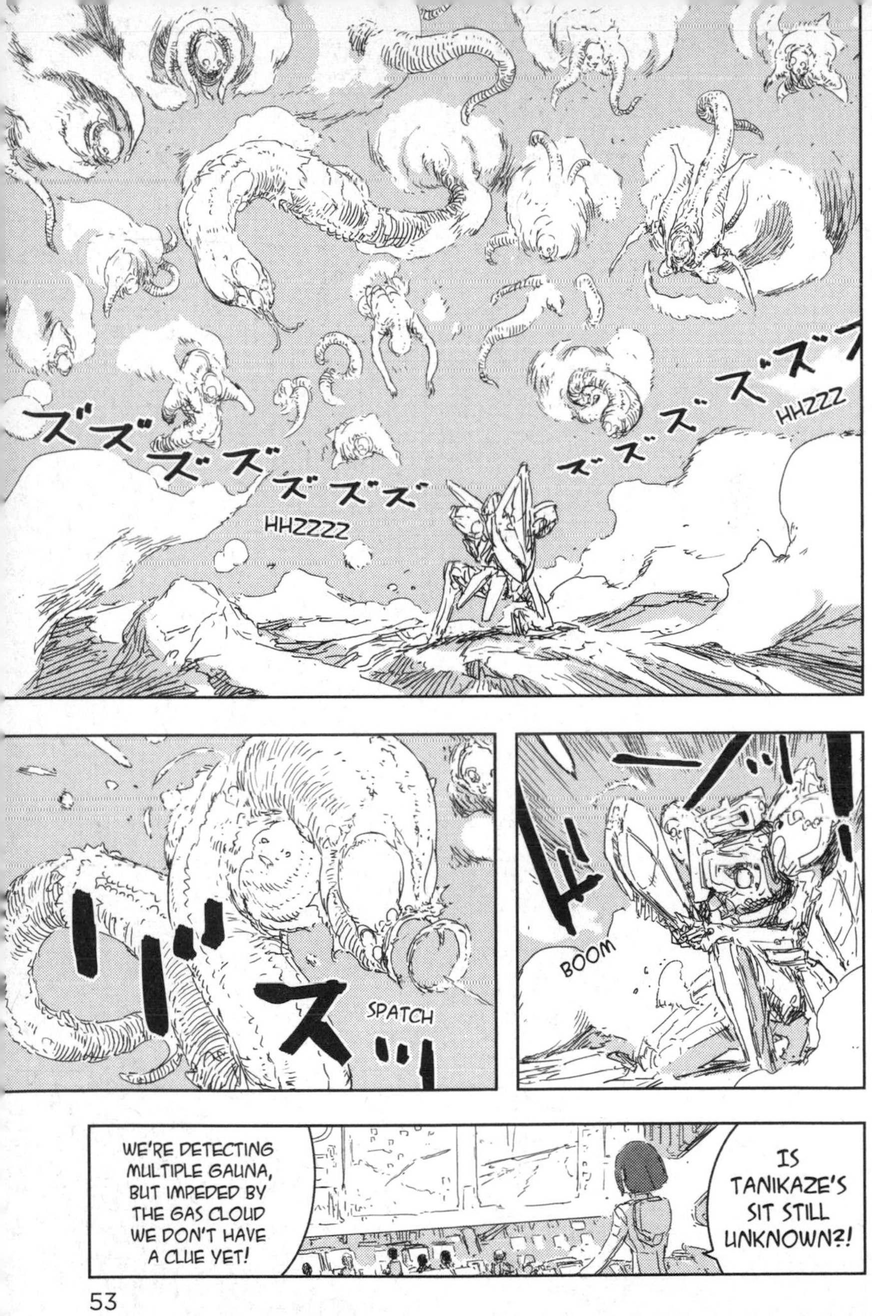
HHZZZ
HHZZZZ
BOOM
SPATCH
IS TANIKAZE'S SIT STILL UNKNOWN?!
WE'RE DETECTING MULTIPLE GAUNA, BUT IMPEDED BY THE GAS CLOUD WE DON'T HAVE A CLUE YET!

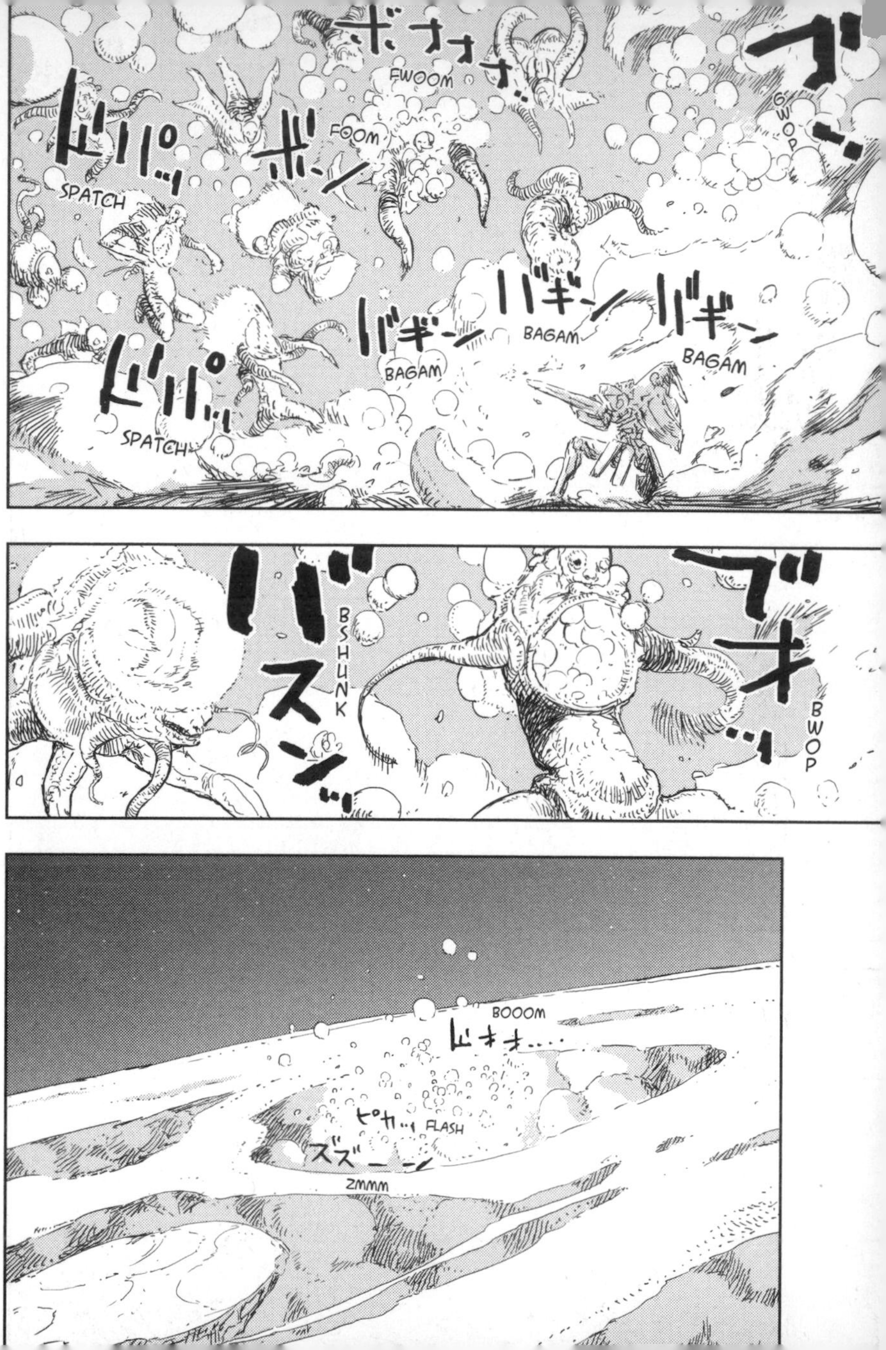
ゴッ
GWOP
ボオオォ
FWOOM
ボーン
FOOM
ドパッ
SPATCH
バギーン
BAGAM
バギーン
BAGAM
バギーン
BAGAM
ドパッ
SPATCH
ブオッ
BWOP
バスン
BSHUNK
ムオォ…
BOOOM
ピカッ
FLASH
ズズーン
ZMMM

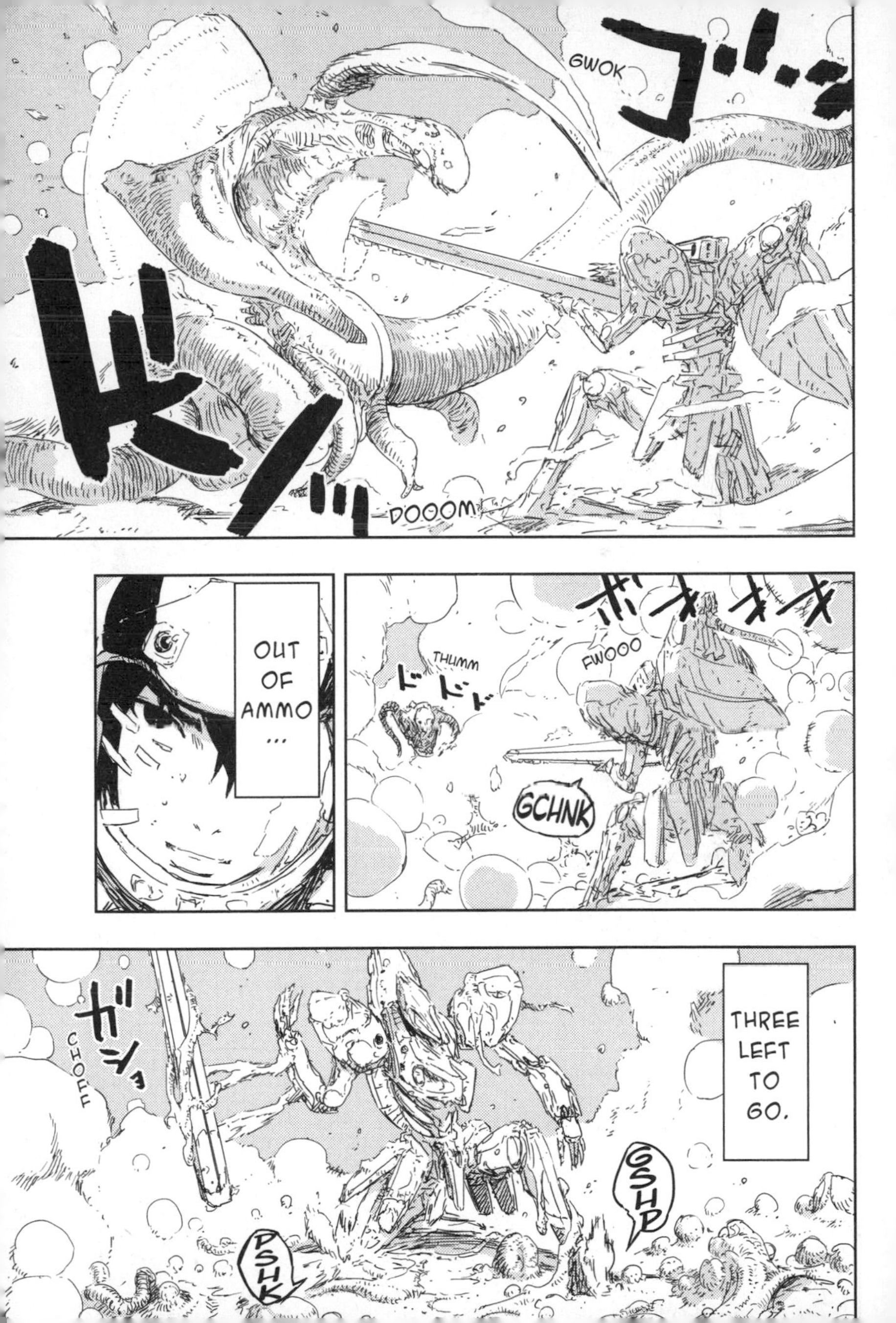
GWOK
DOOOM
FWOOO
THUMM
GCHNK
OUT OF AMMO...
THREE LEFT TO GO.
CHOFF
GSHP
PSHK

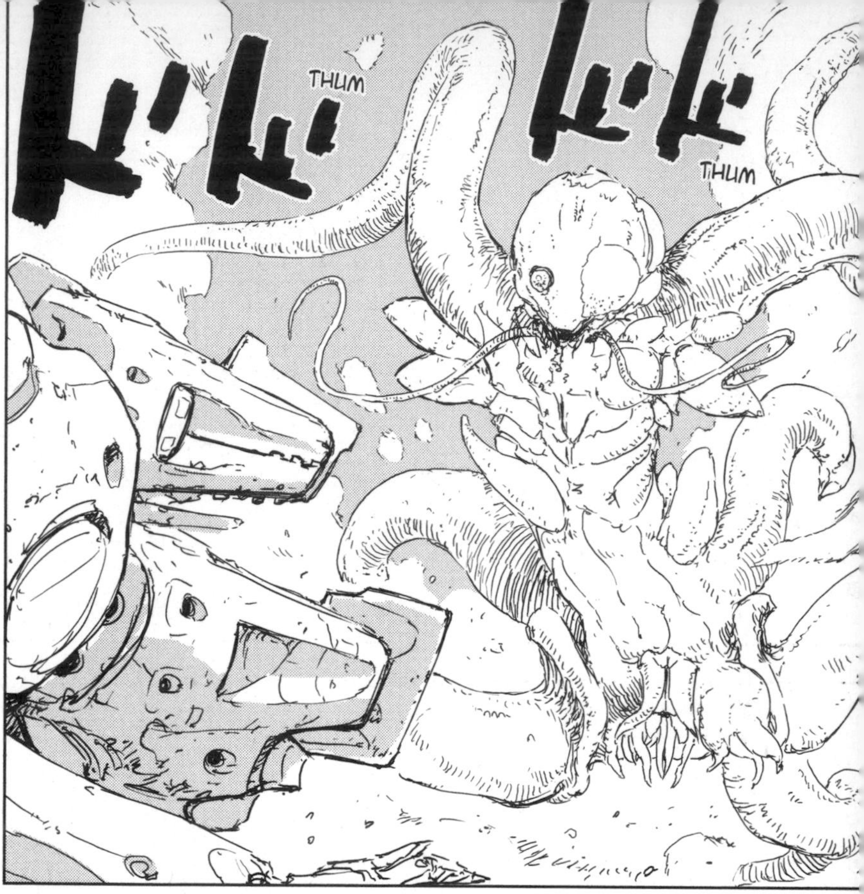
THUM
THUM
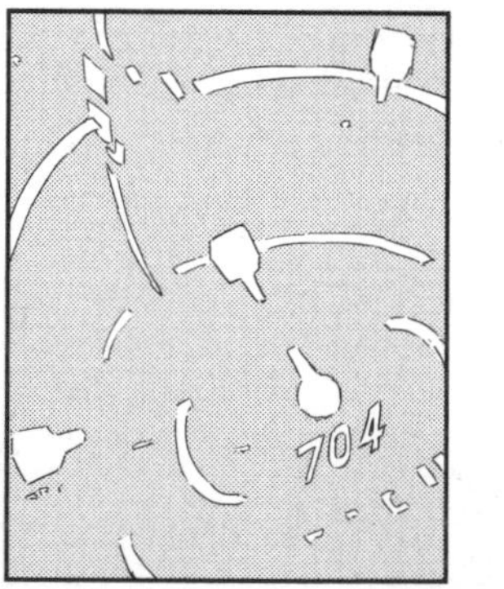
704
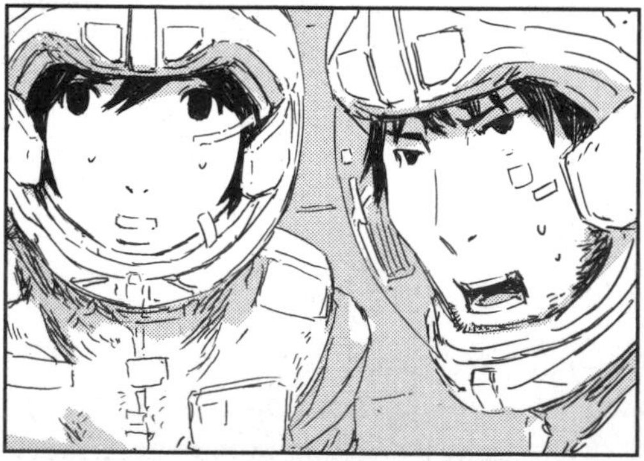

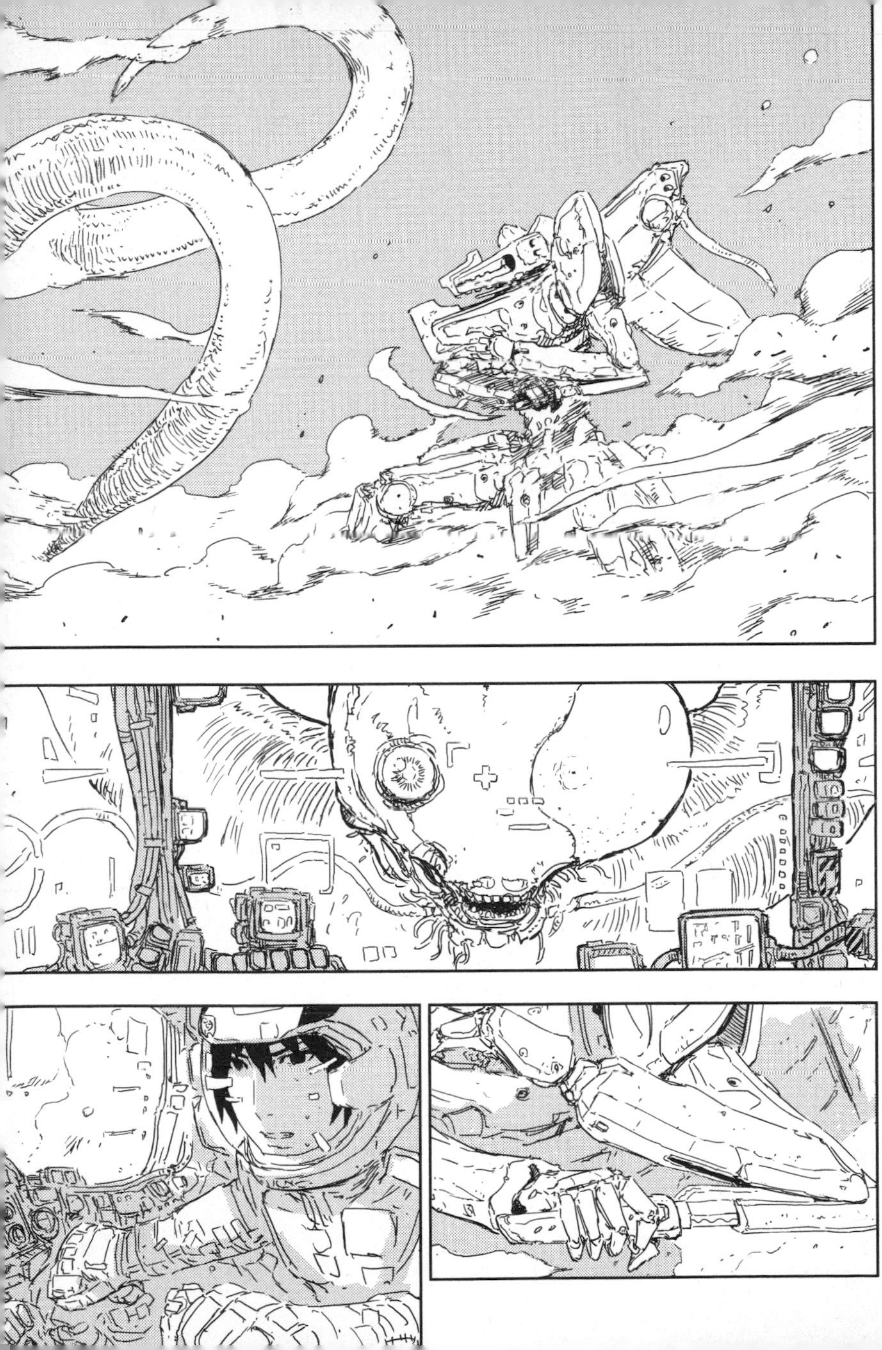

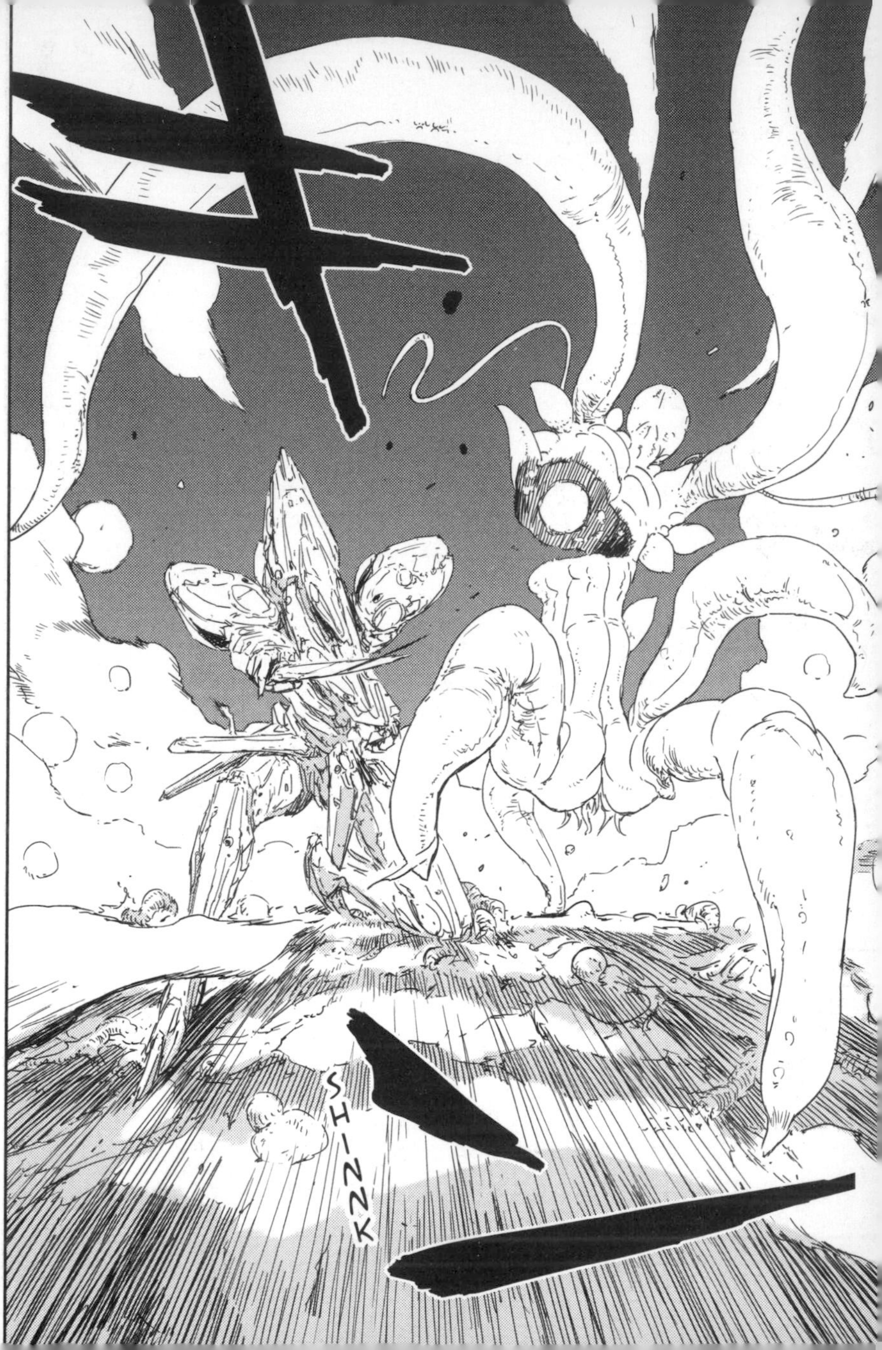
SHINNK

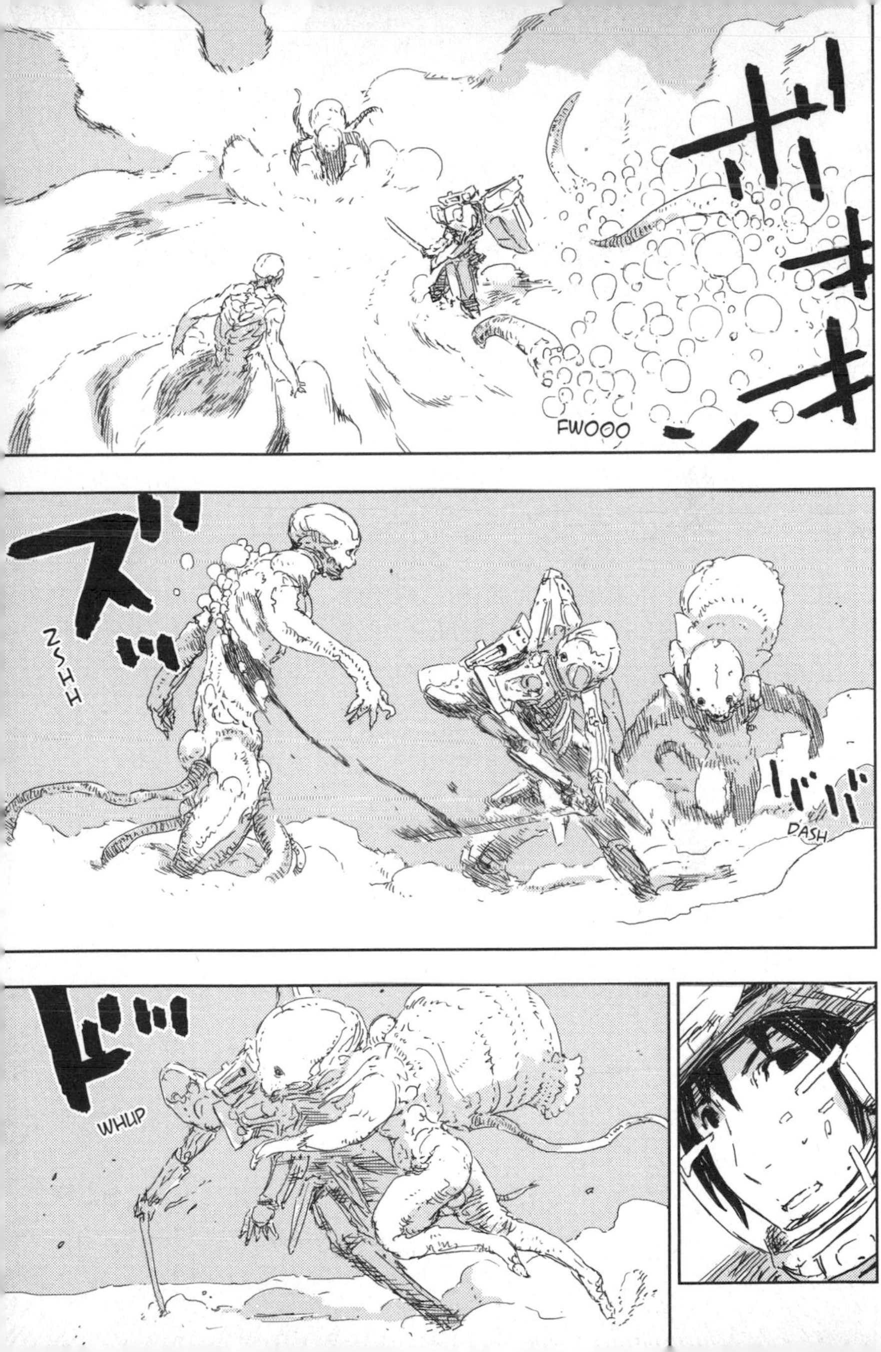
FWOOO
DASH
ZSHH
WHUP

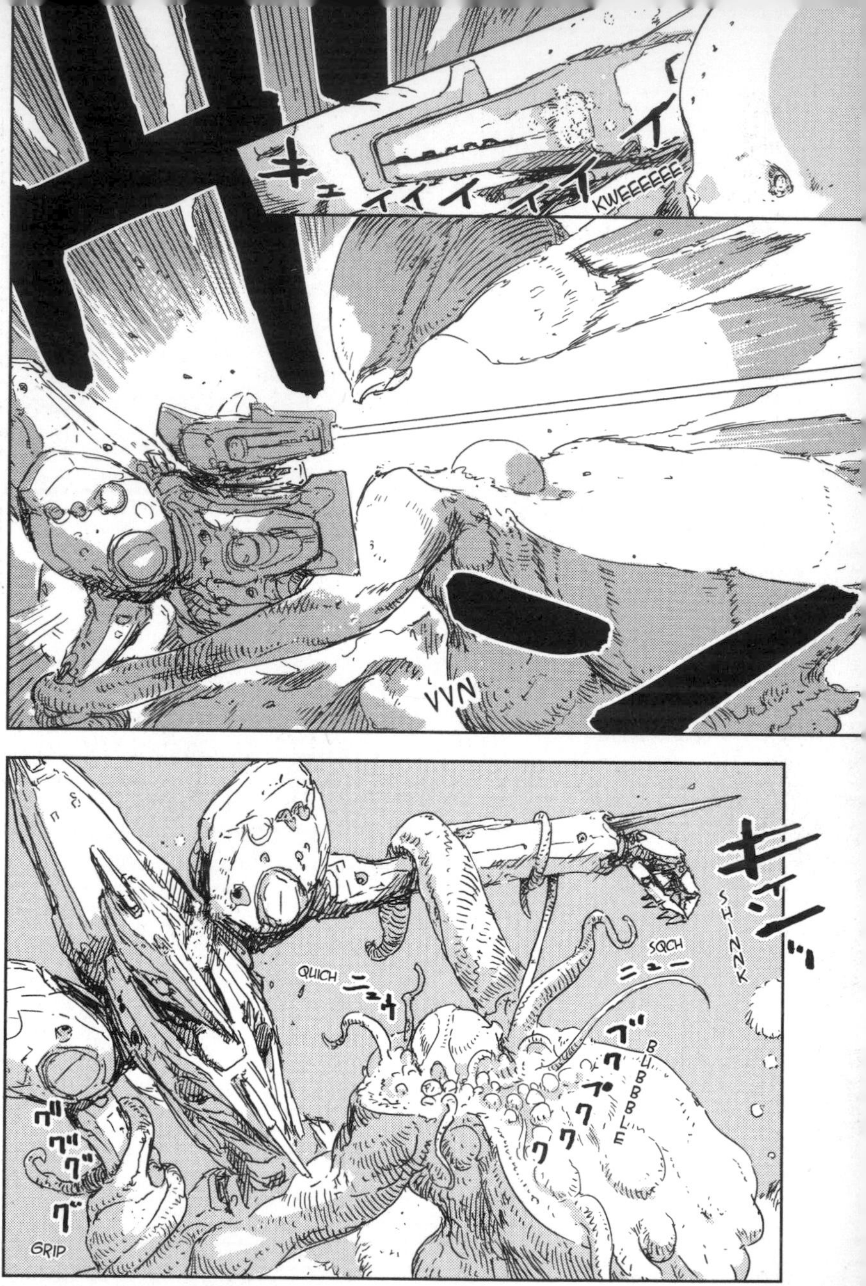
KWEEEEEEE
VVN
SHINNK
SQCH
BUBBBLE
QUICH
GRIP

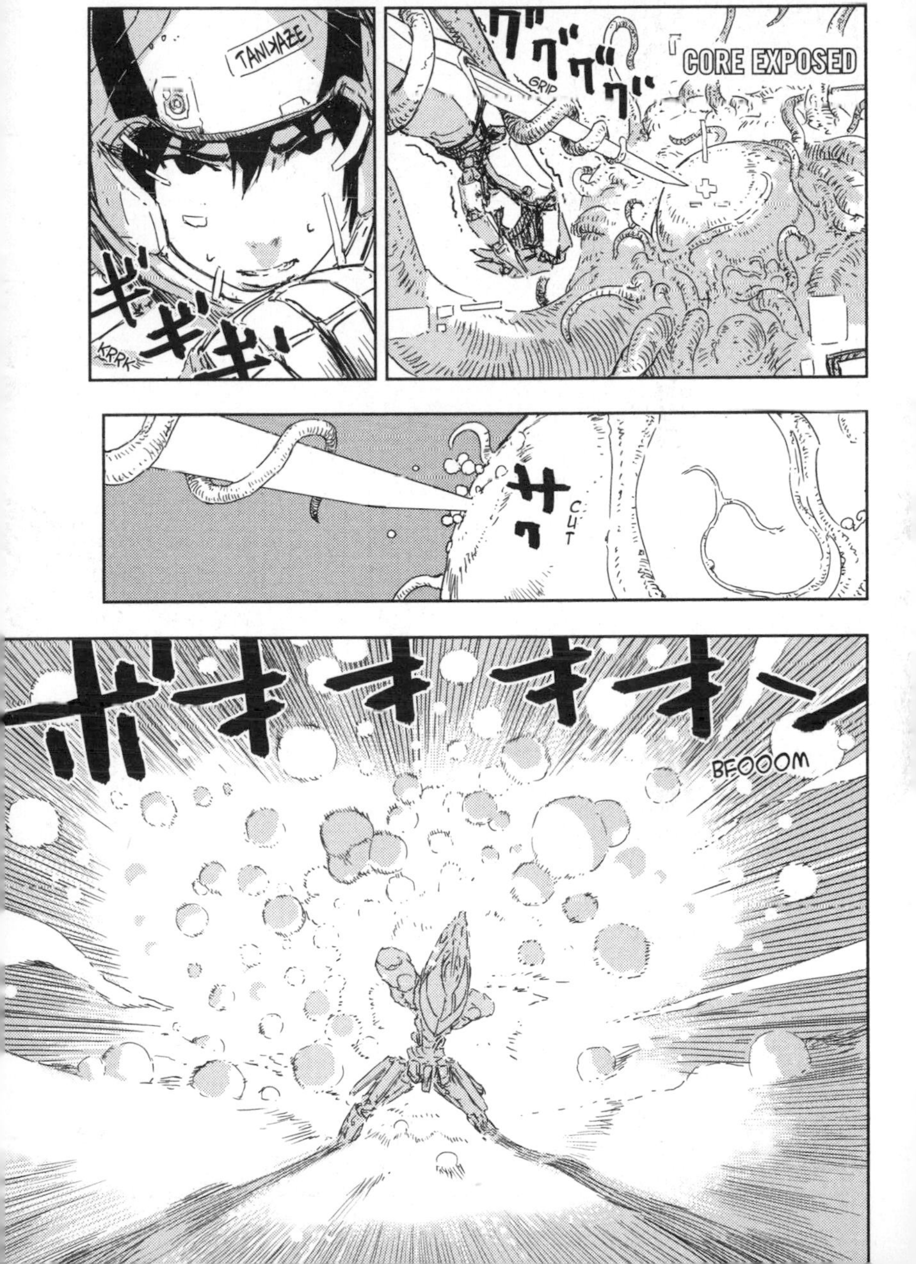
CORE EXPOSED
ググググ
GRIP
TANIKAZE
ギギギ
KRRK
サク
CUT
ボオオオン
BFOOOM

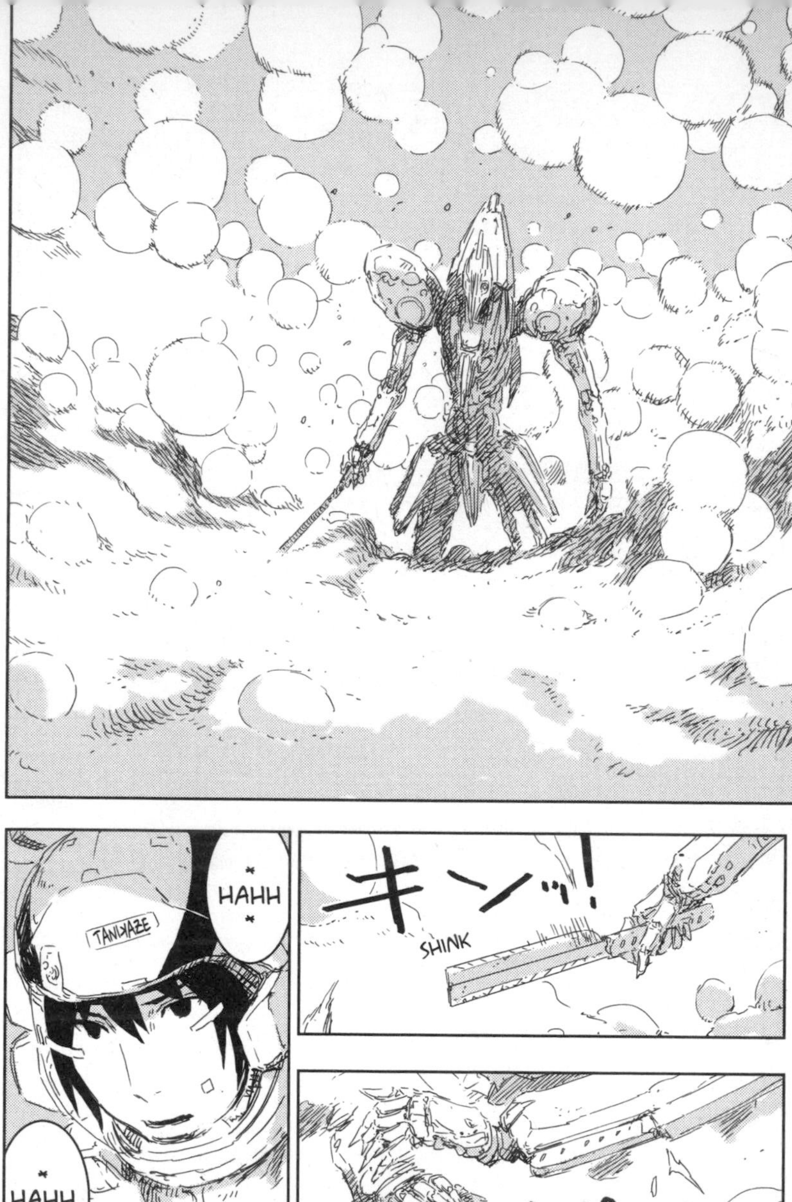
キンッ!
SHINK
パキーン
PCHIK
* HAHH *
TANIKAZE
* HAHH *

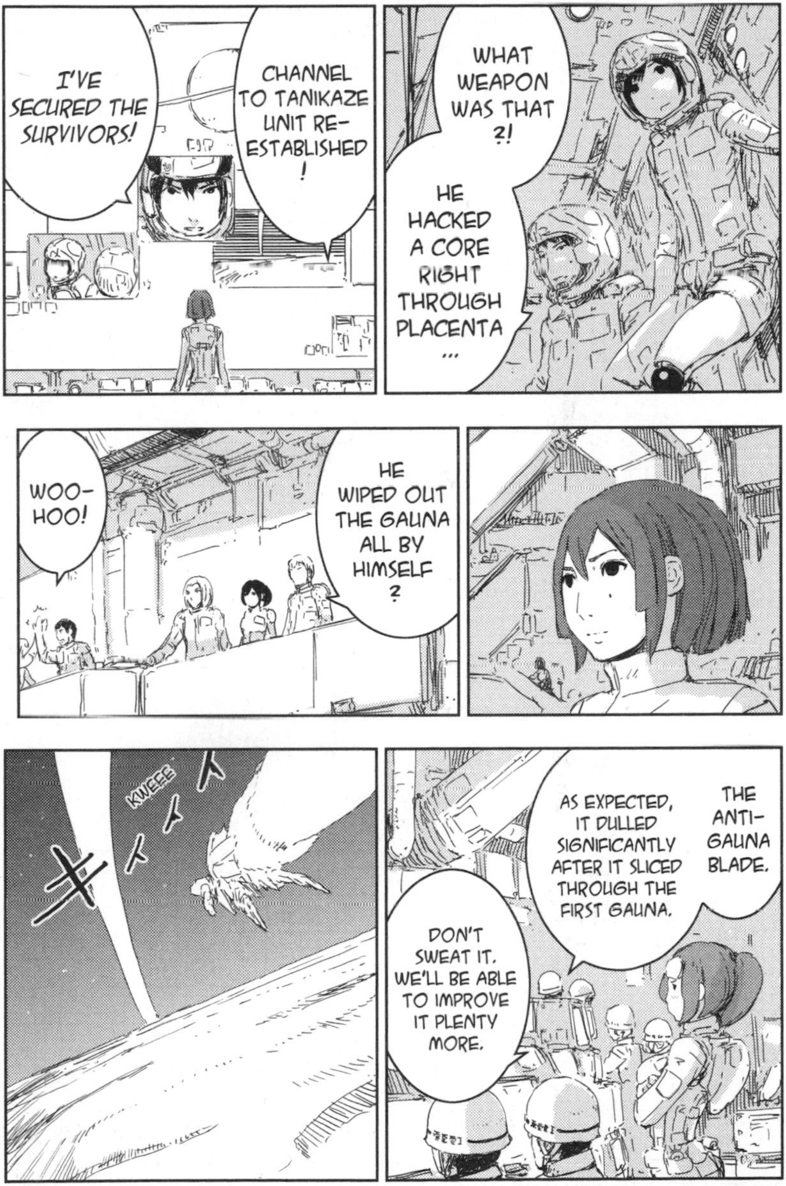
WHAT WEAPON WAS THAT ?!
HE HACKED A CORE RIGHT THROUGH PLACENTA ...
CHANNEL TO TANIKAZE UNIT RE-ESTABLISHED !
I'VE SECURED THE SURVIVORS!
HE WIPED OUT THE GAUNA ALL BY HIMSELF ?
WOO-HOO!
THE ANTI-GAUNA BLADE.
AS EXPECTED, IT DULLED SIGNIFICANTLY AFTER IT SLICED THROUGH THE FIRST GAUNA.
DON'T SWEAT IT. WE'LL BE ABLE TO IMPROVE IT PLENTY MORE.
KWEEE

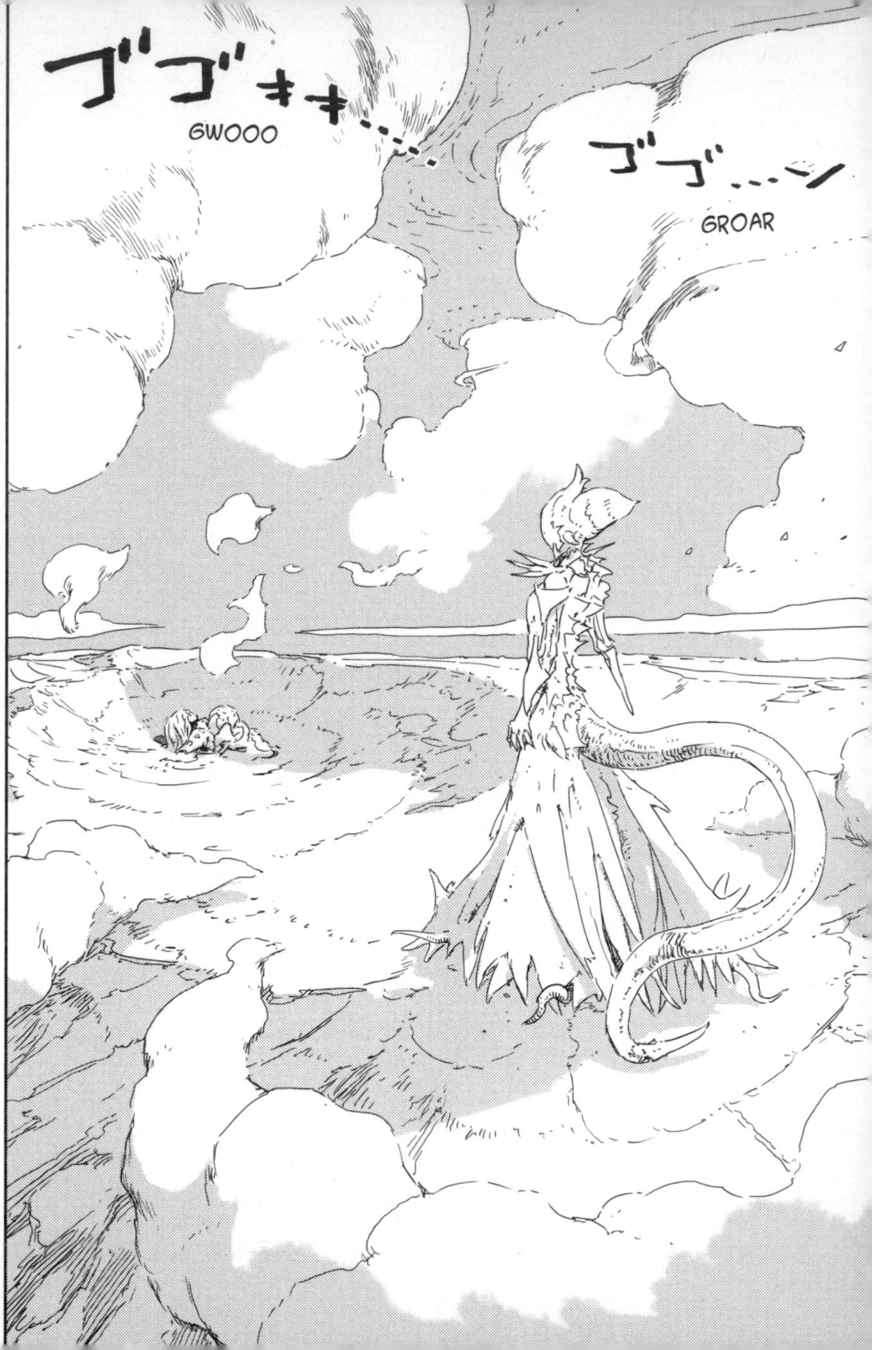
ゴゴォォ…
GWOOO
ゴゴ…ン
GROAR

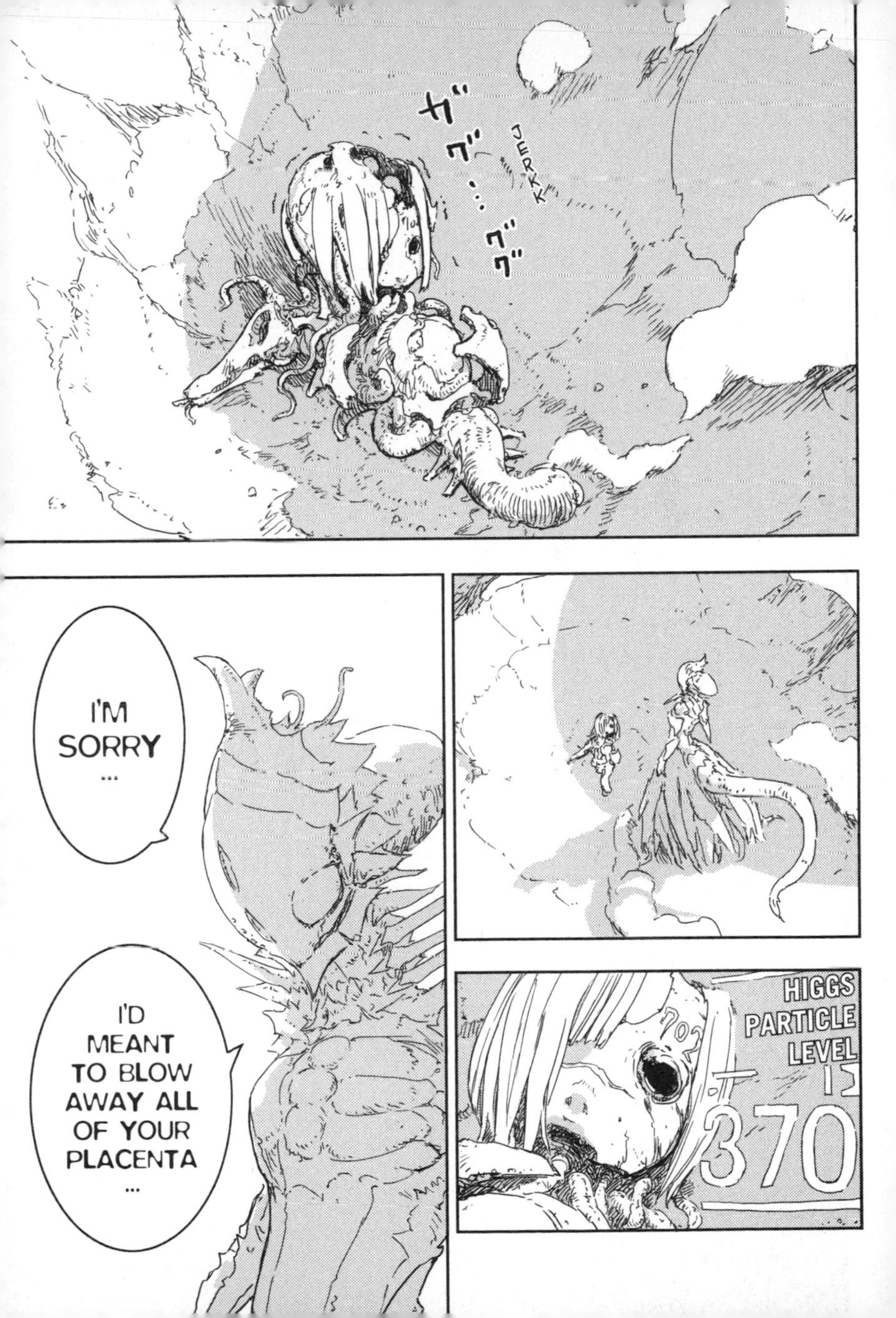
ガグ‥ググ
JERKK
HIGGS PARTICLE LEVEL
370
I'M SORRY ...
I'D MEANT TO BLOW AWAY ALL OF YOUR PLACENTA ...

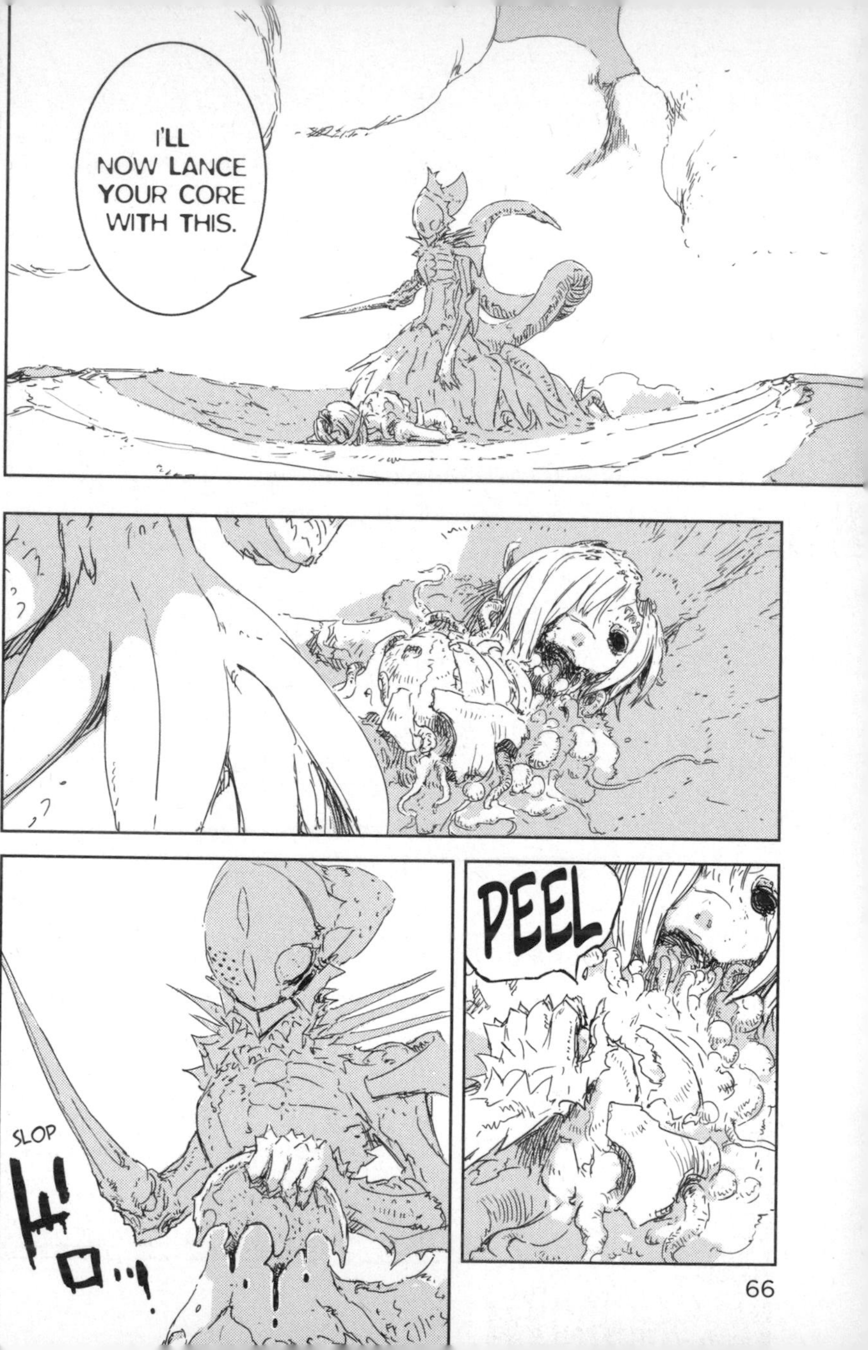
I'LL NOW LANCE YOUR CORE WITH THIS.
PEEL
SLOP
ドロ…

ズ ズ‥
ZLRR

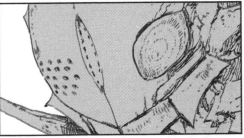

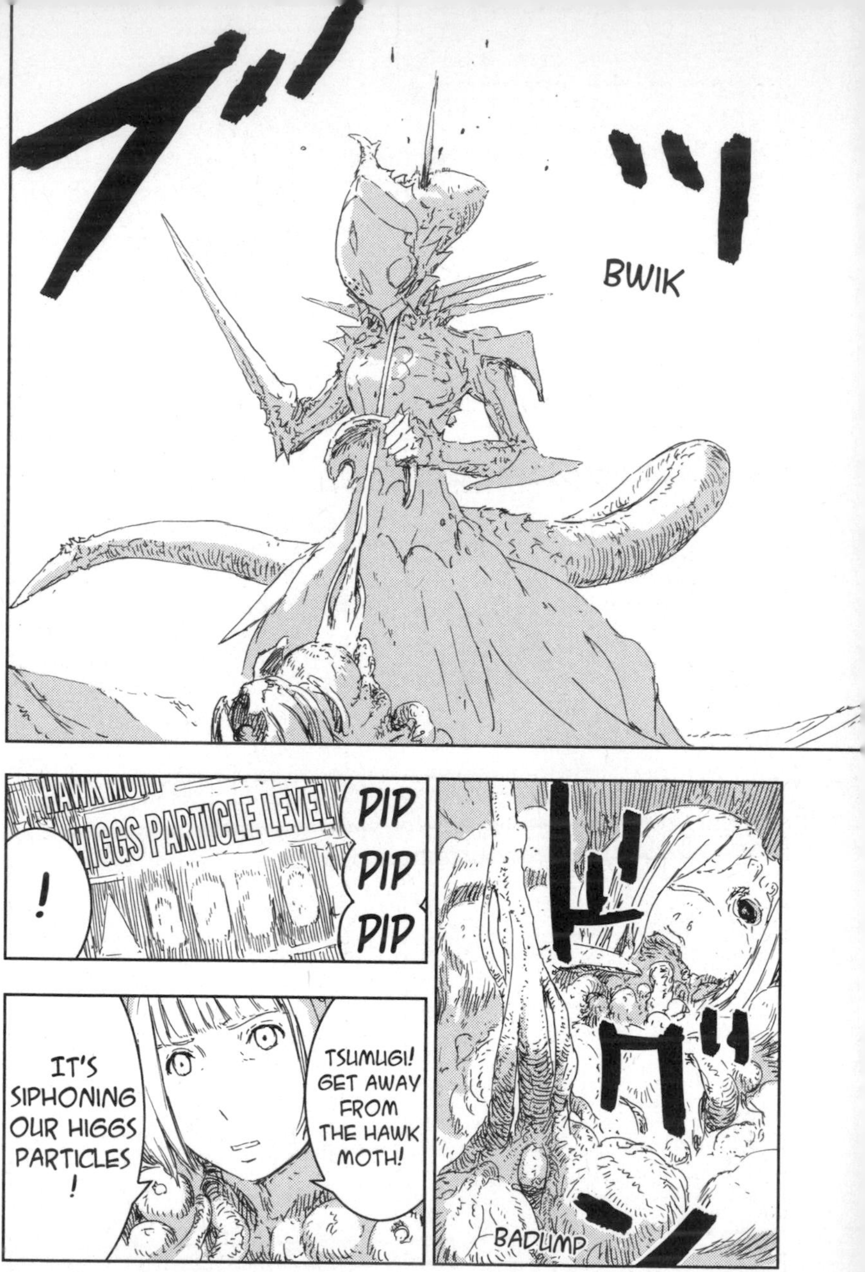
BWIK
BADUMP
HAWK MOTH
HIGGS PARTICLE LEVEL
PIP
PIP
PIP
!
TSUMUGI! GET AWAY FROM THE HAWK MOTH!
IT'S SIPHONING OUR HIGGS PARTICLES!

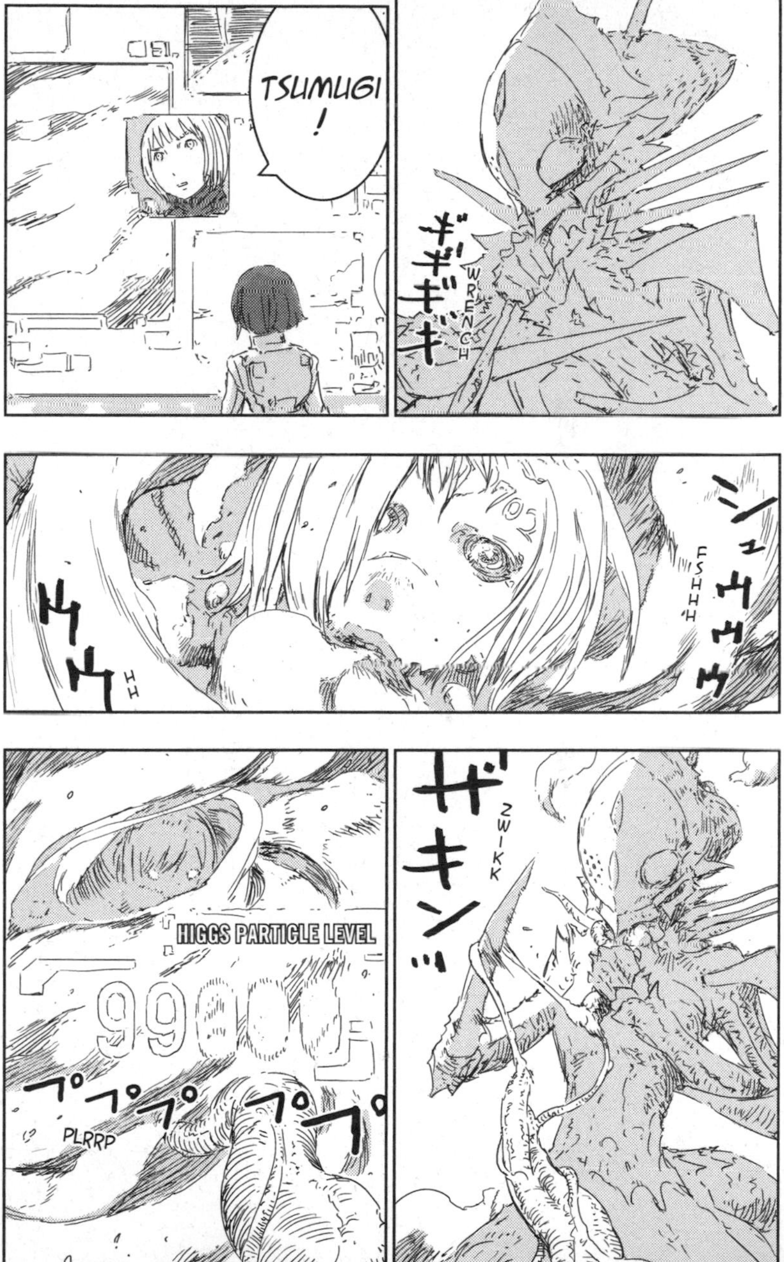
ギギギギ
WRENCH
TSUMUGI!
シュウウウウ
FSHHH
ムウ
HH
ザキンッ
ZWIKK
HIGGS PARTICLE LEVEL
ププププ
PLRRP

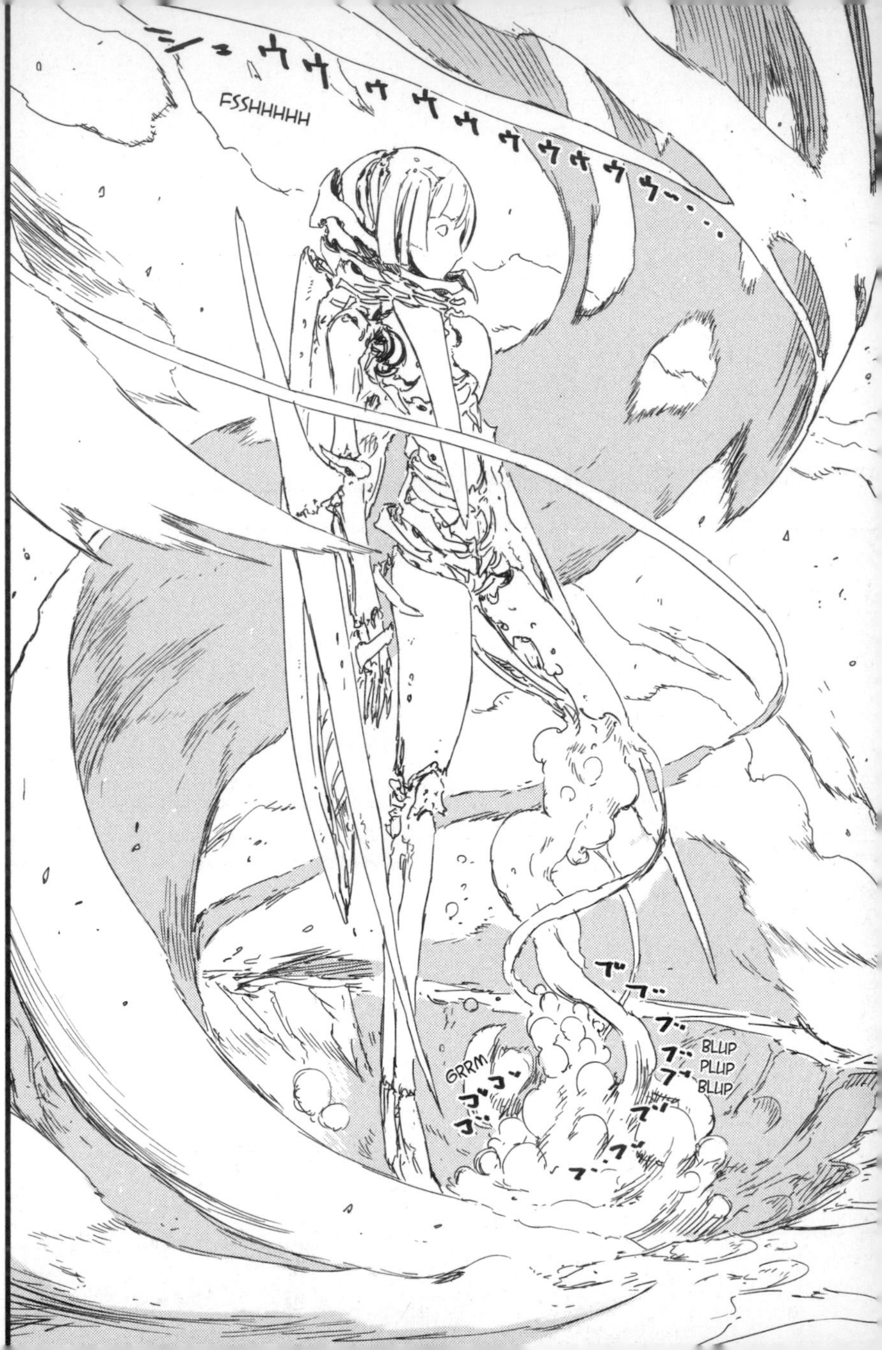
FSSHHHHH
BLUP
PLUP
BLUP
GRRM

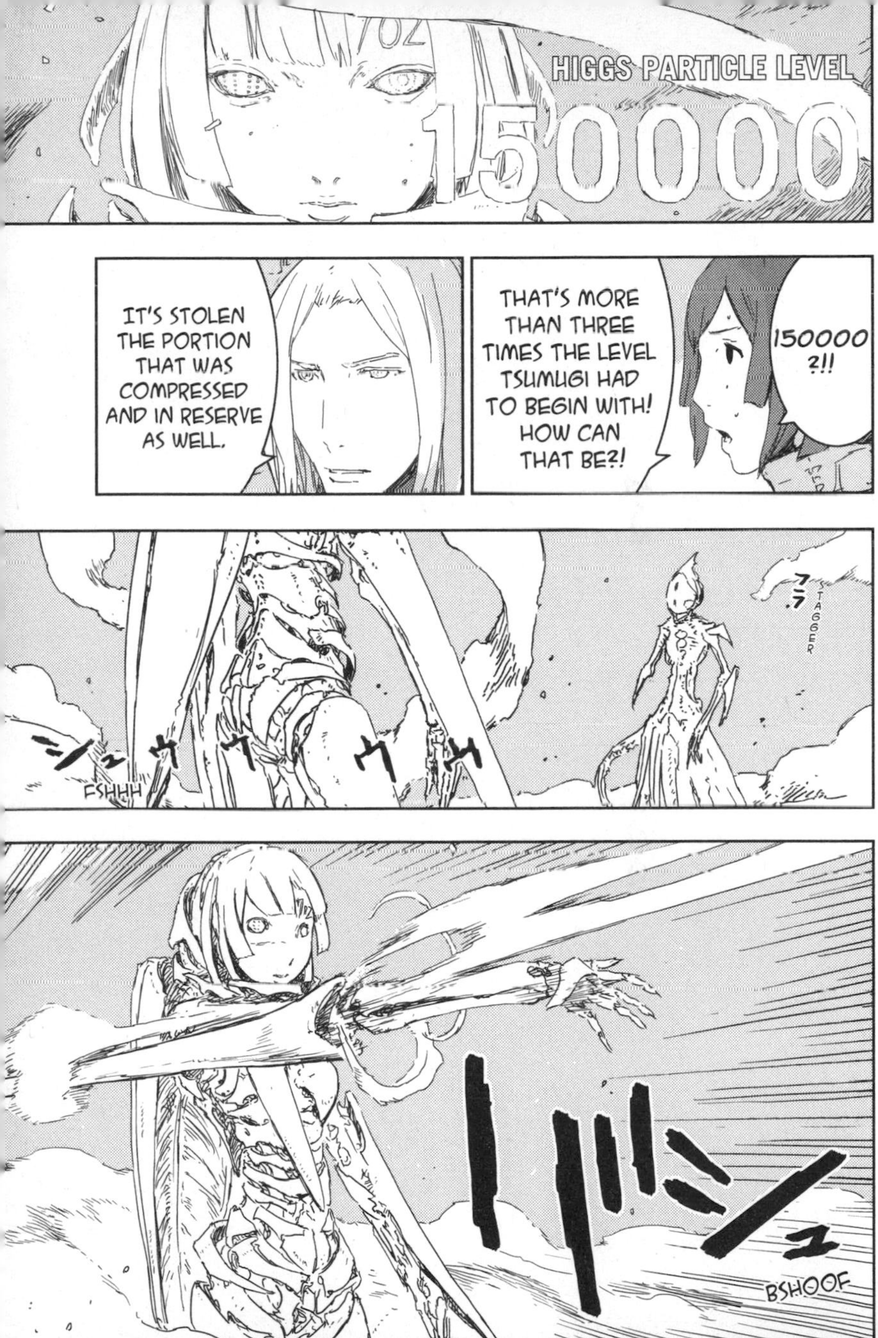
HIGGS PARTICLE LEVEL
150000
150000 ?!!
THAT'S MORE THAN THREE TIMES THE LEVEL TSUMUGI HAD TO BEGIN WITH! HOW CAN THAT BE?!
IT'S STOLEN THE PORTION THAT WAS COMPRESSED AND IN RESERVE AS WELL.
フラ
STAGGER
FSHHH
BSHOOF

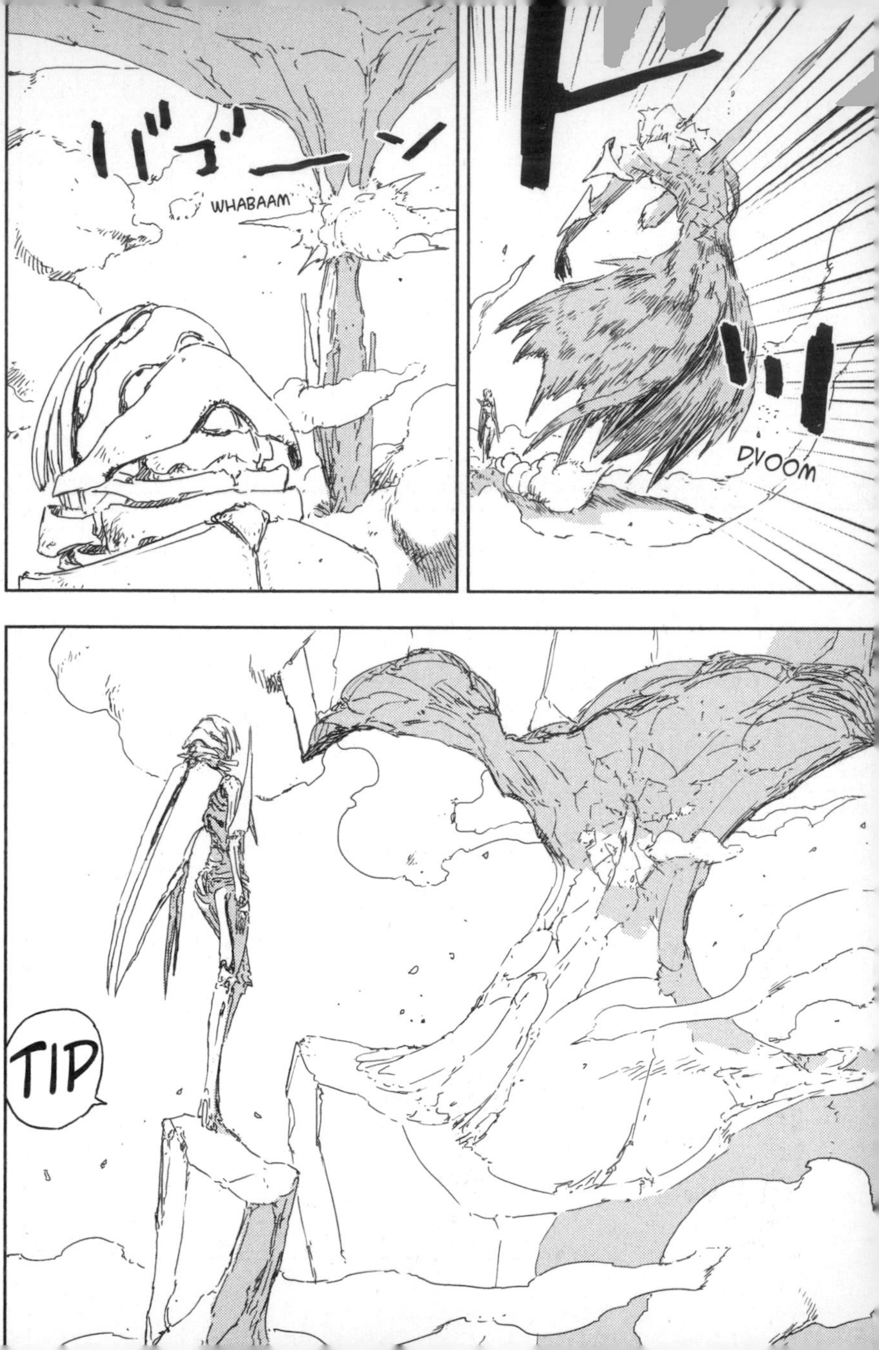
DVOOM
WHABAAM
TIP

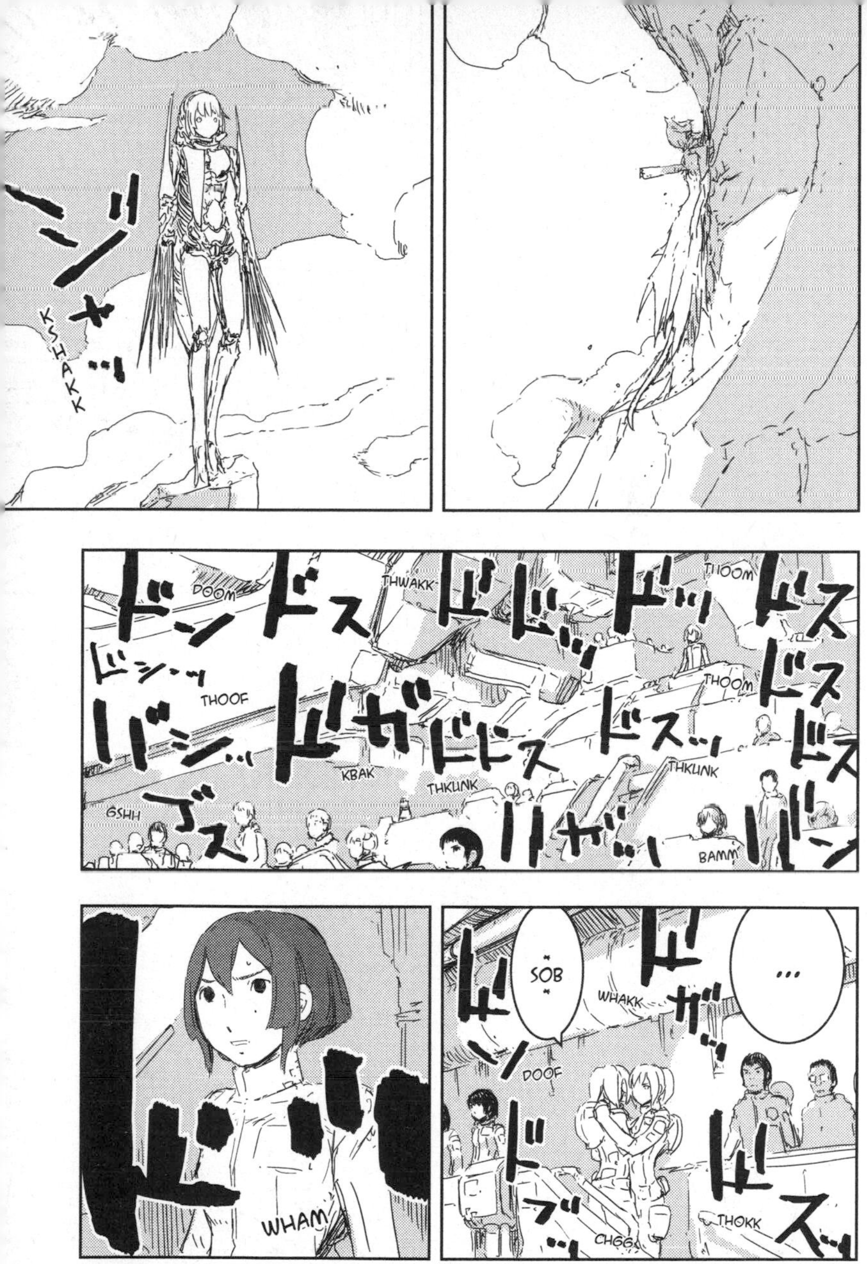
KSHAKK
THOOM
THWAKK
DOOM
THOOM
THOOF
THKUNK
KBAK
THKUNK
BAMM
GSHH
...
SOB
WHAKK
DOOF
THOKK
CHGG
WHAM

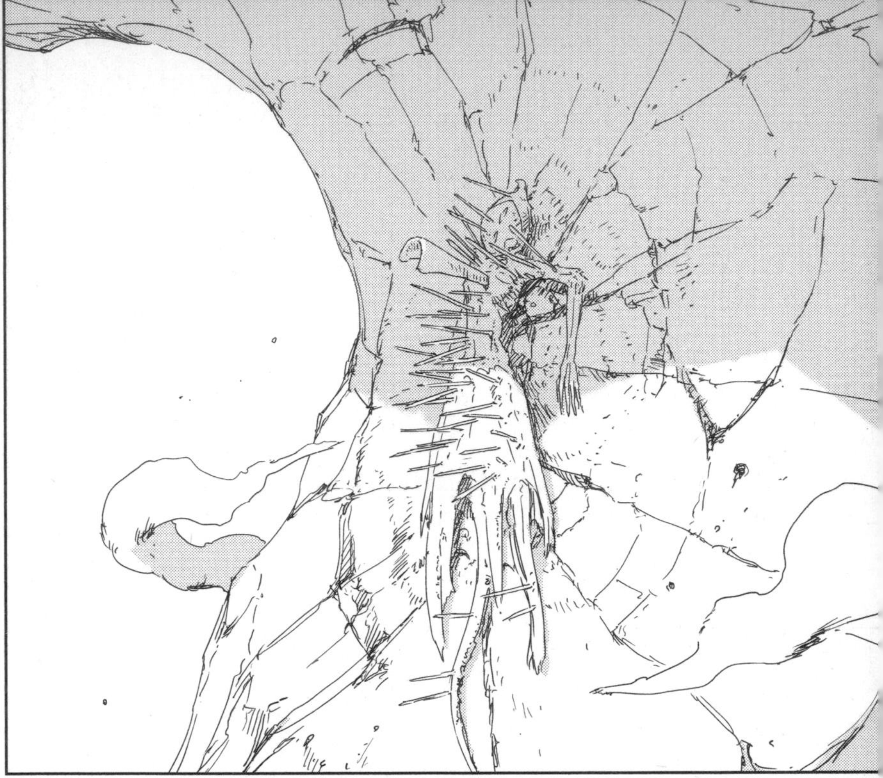

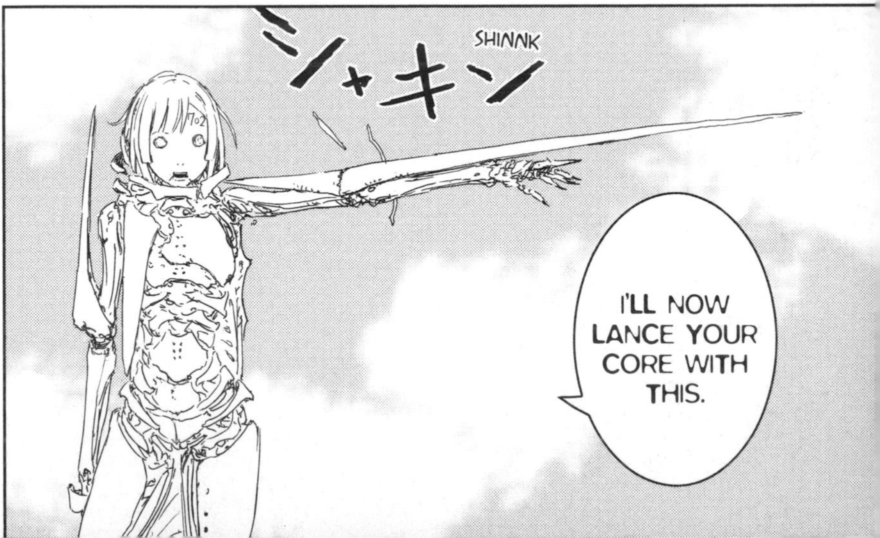
SHINNK
シャキン
I'LL NOW LANCE YOUR CORE WITH THIS.

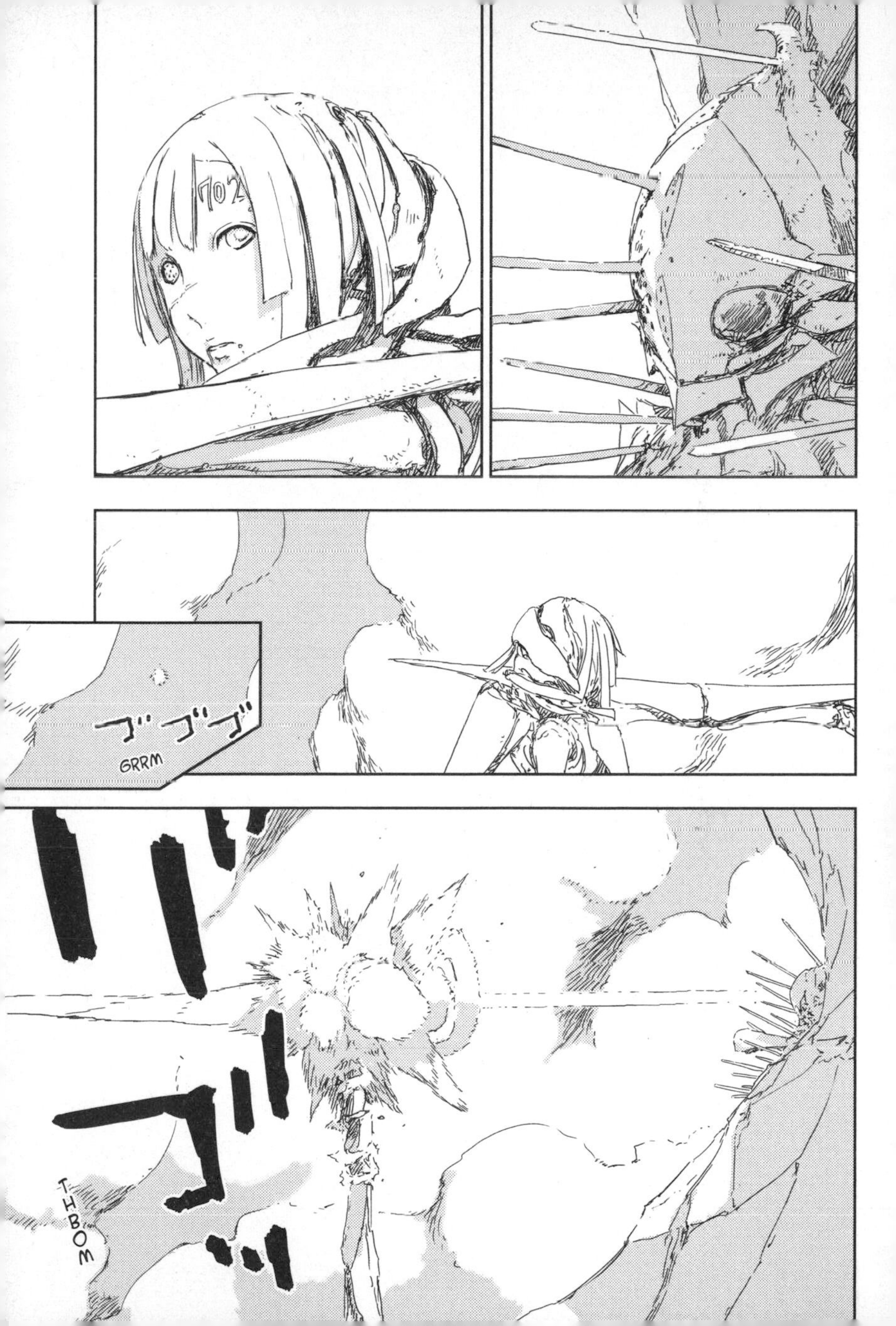
ゴゴゴ
GRRM
ゴッ
THBOM

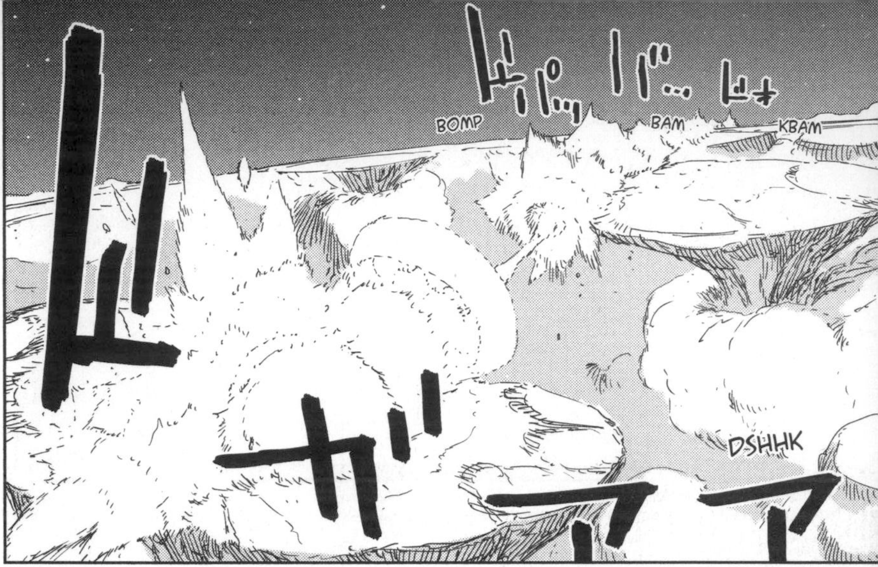
BOMP
BAM
KBAM
DSHHK
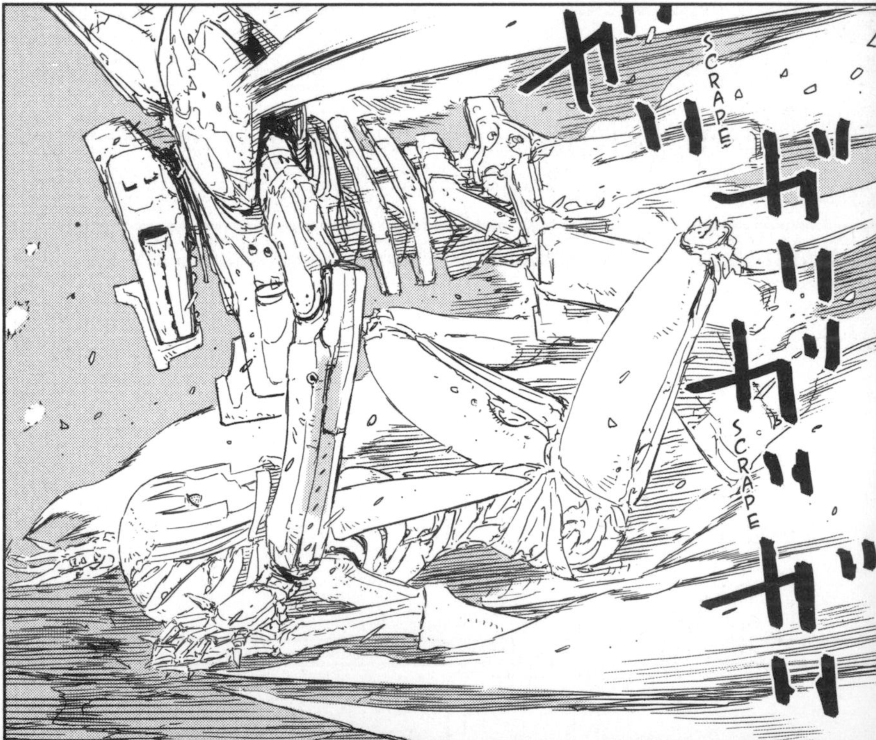
SCRAPE
SCRAPE

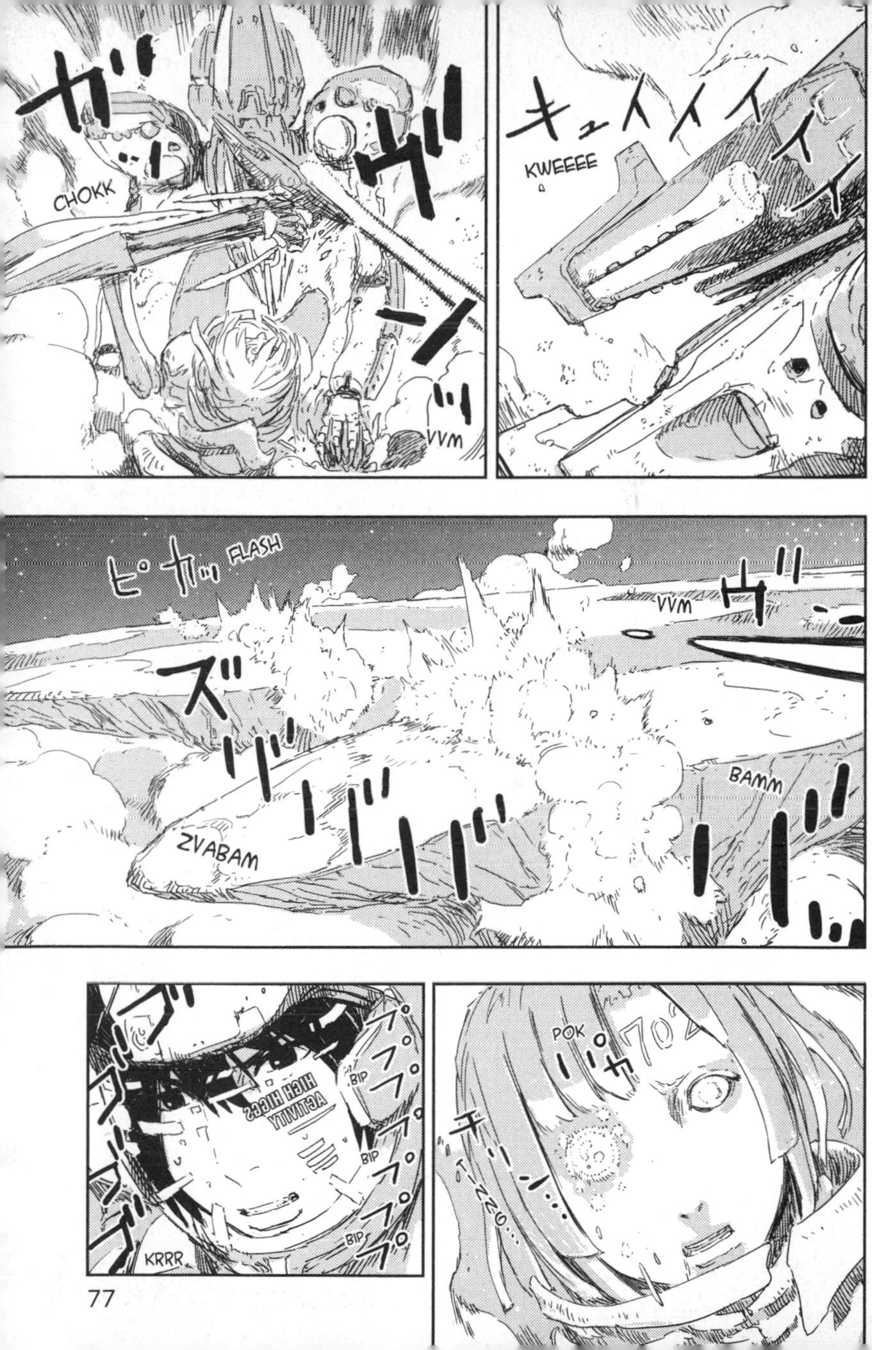
KWEEEE
CHOKK
VVM
VVM
FLASH
BAMM
ZVABAM
POK
T-ZZG...
HIGH HIGGS ACTIVITY
BIP
BIP
BIP
KRRR

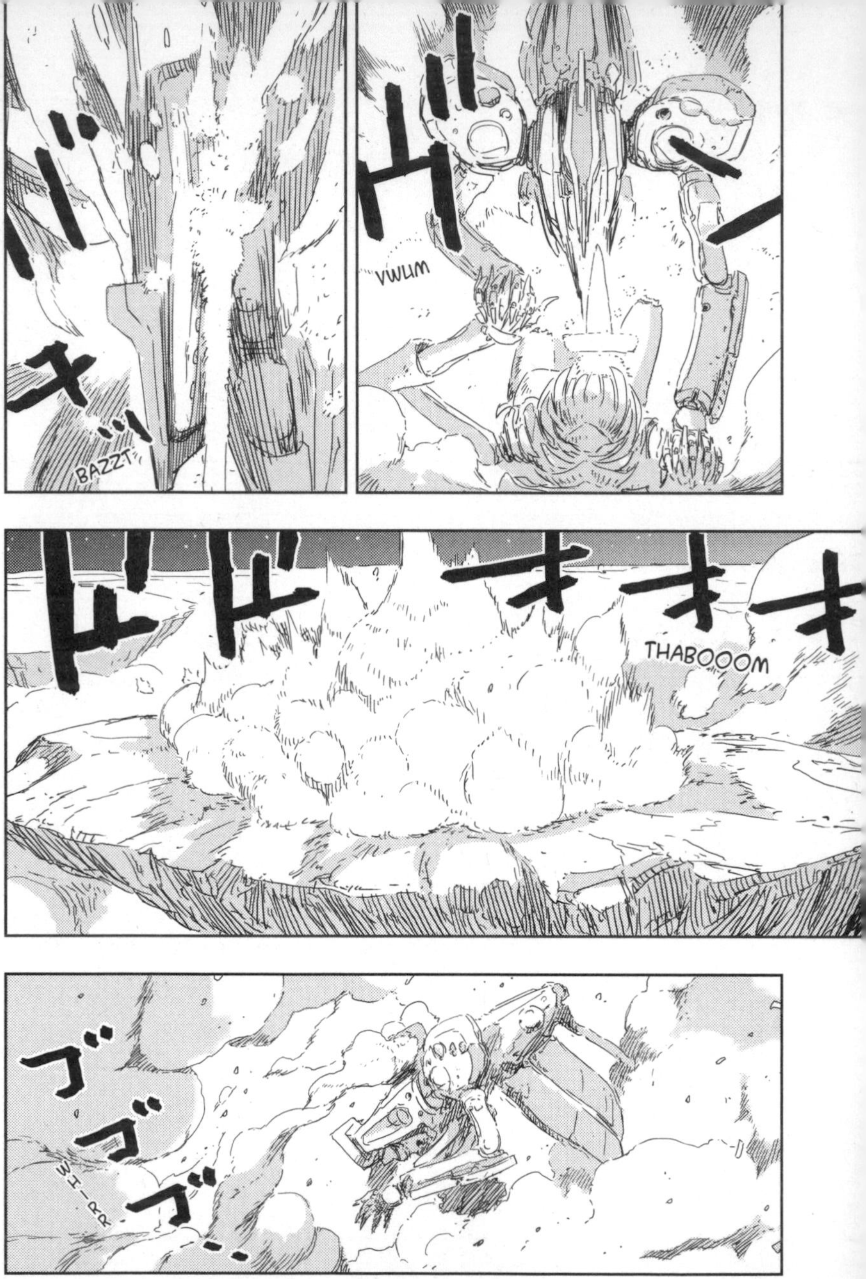
VWUM
BAZZT
THABOOOM
WHIRR

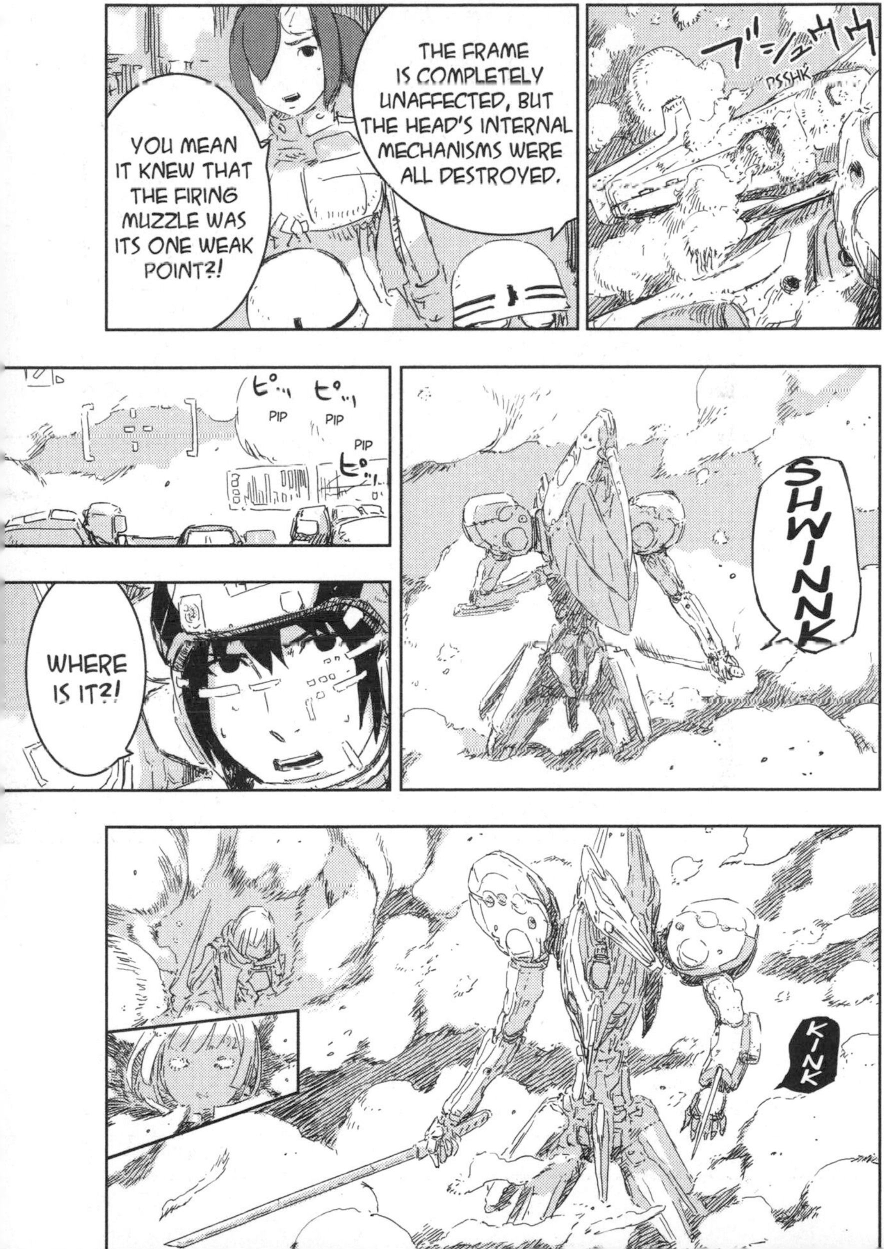
ブシュウウ
PSSHK
THE FRAME IS COMPLETELY UNAFFECTED, BUT THE HEAD'S INTERNAL MECHANISMS WERE ALL DESTROYED.
YOU MEAN IT KNEW THAT THE FIRING MUZZLE WAS ITS ONE WEAK POINT?!
SHWINNK
ピッ ピッ
PIP PIP
PIP
ピッ
WHERE IS IT?!
KINK

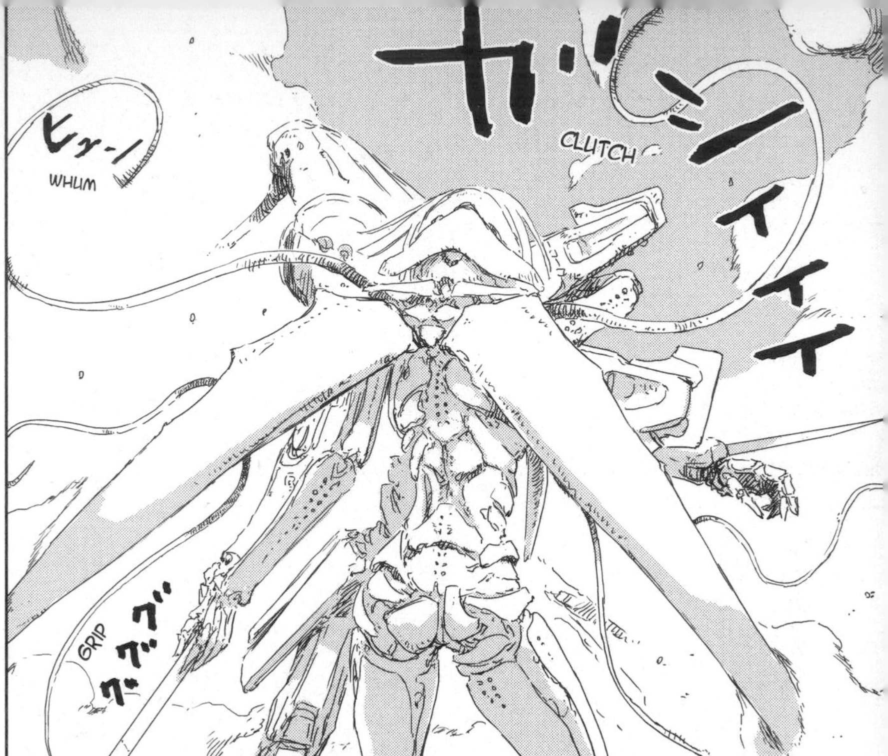
WHUM
CLUTCH
GRIP

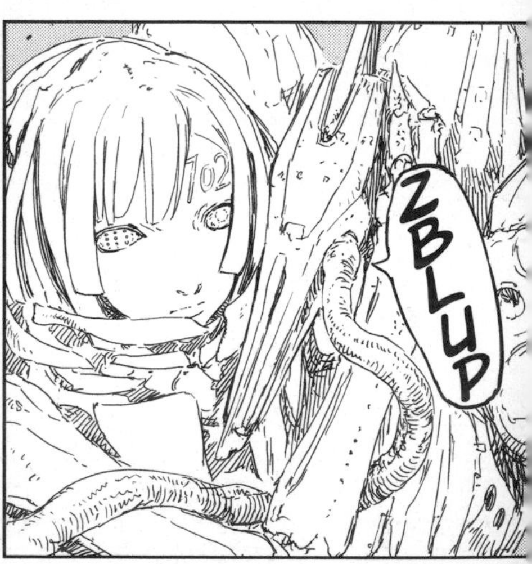
ZBLUP

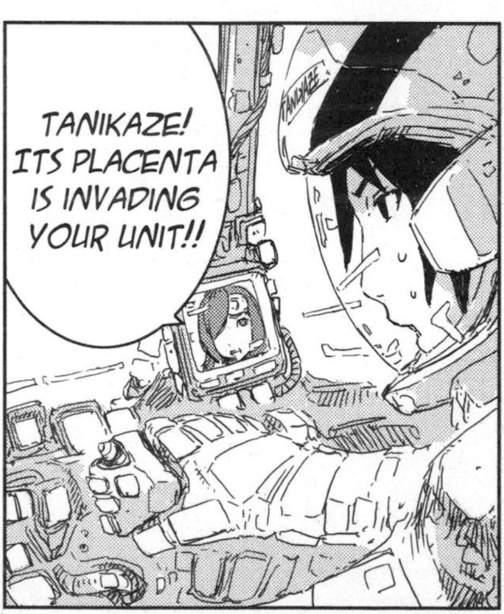
TANIKAZE! ITS PLACENTA IS INVADING YOUR UNIT!!

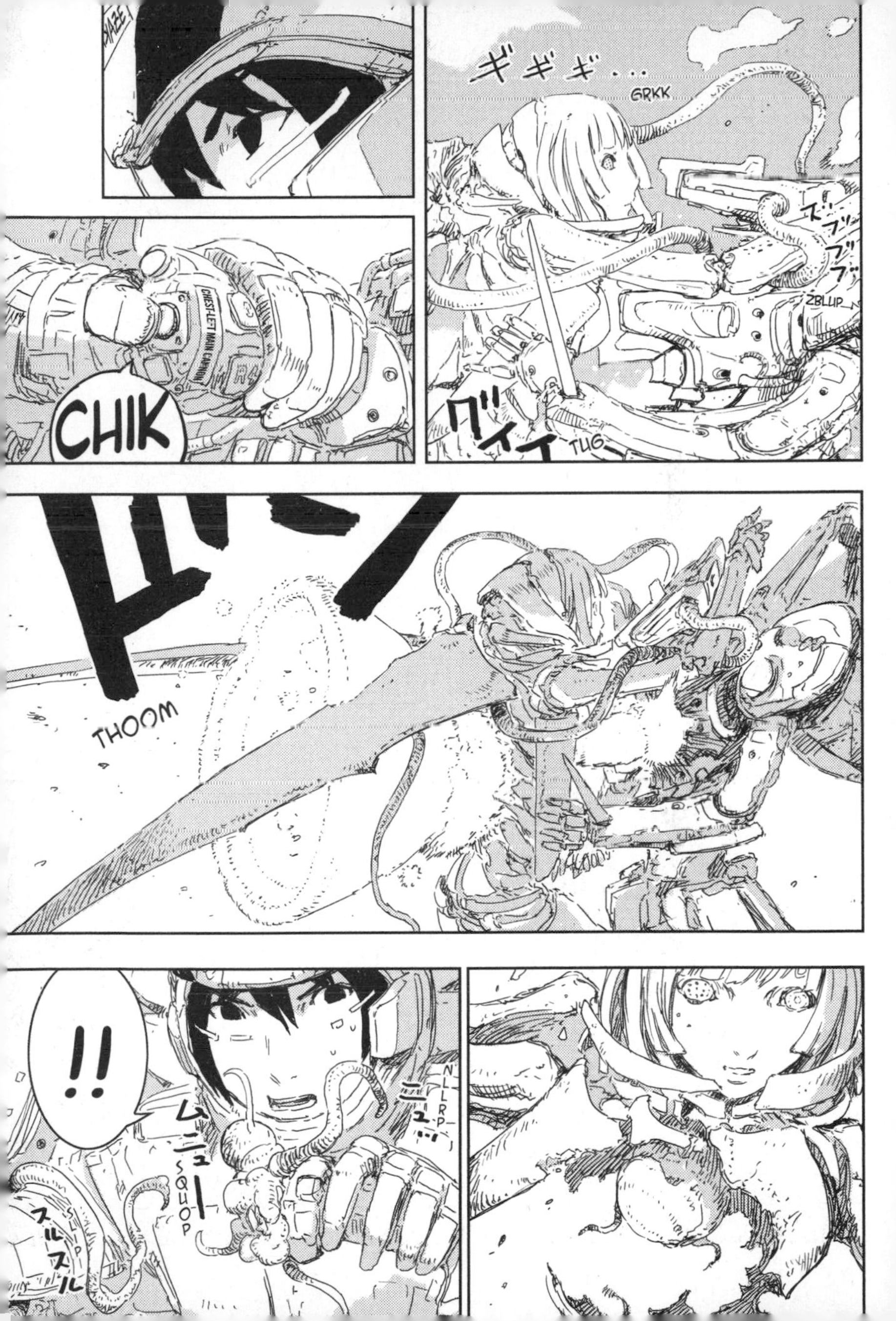
ギギギ...
GRKK
ズ!ブッブッブ
ZBLUP
グイイ
TUG—
CHEST-LET MAIN CANNON
CHIK
THOOM
!!
ニュ...
NLLRP...
ムニュー
SQUOP
スルスル
SLIP

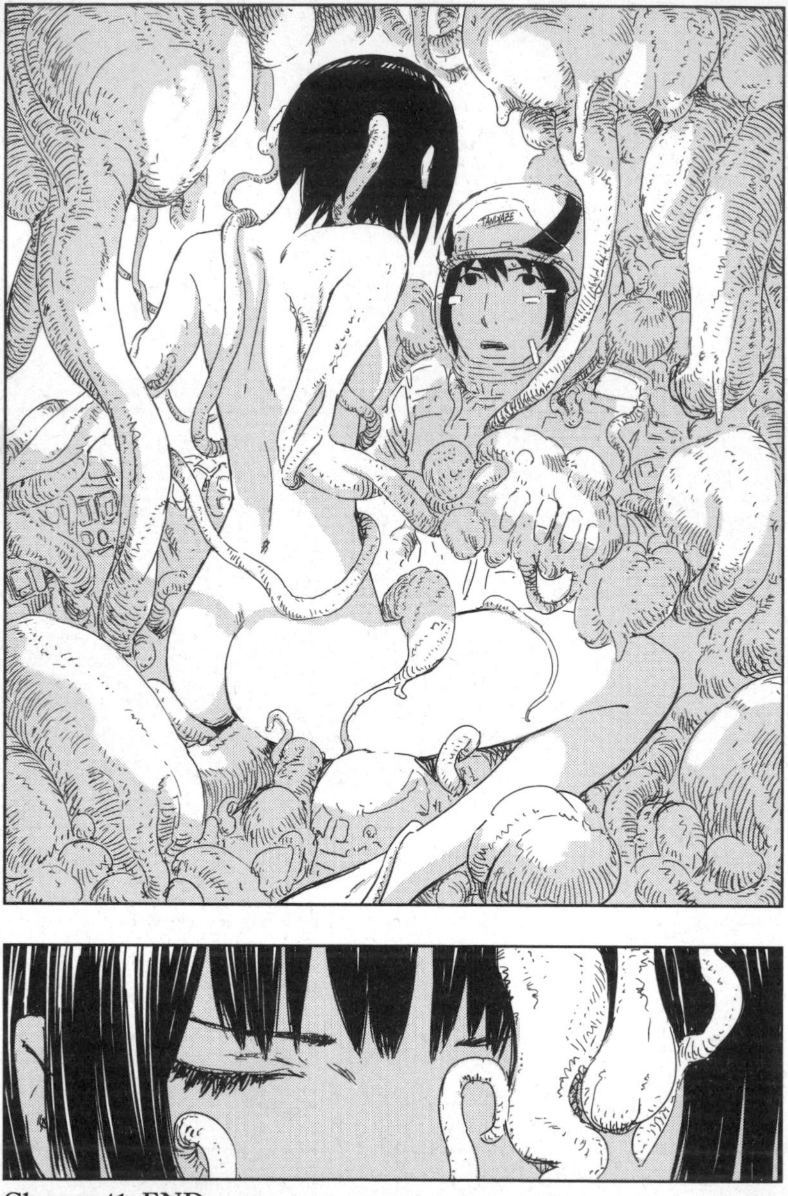

Chapter 41: END

シドニアの騎士

KNIGHTS OF SIDONIA

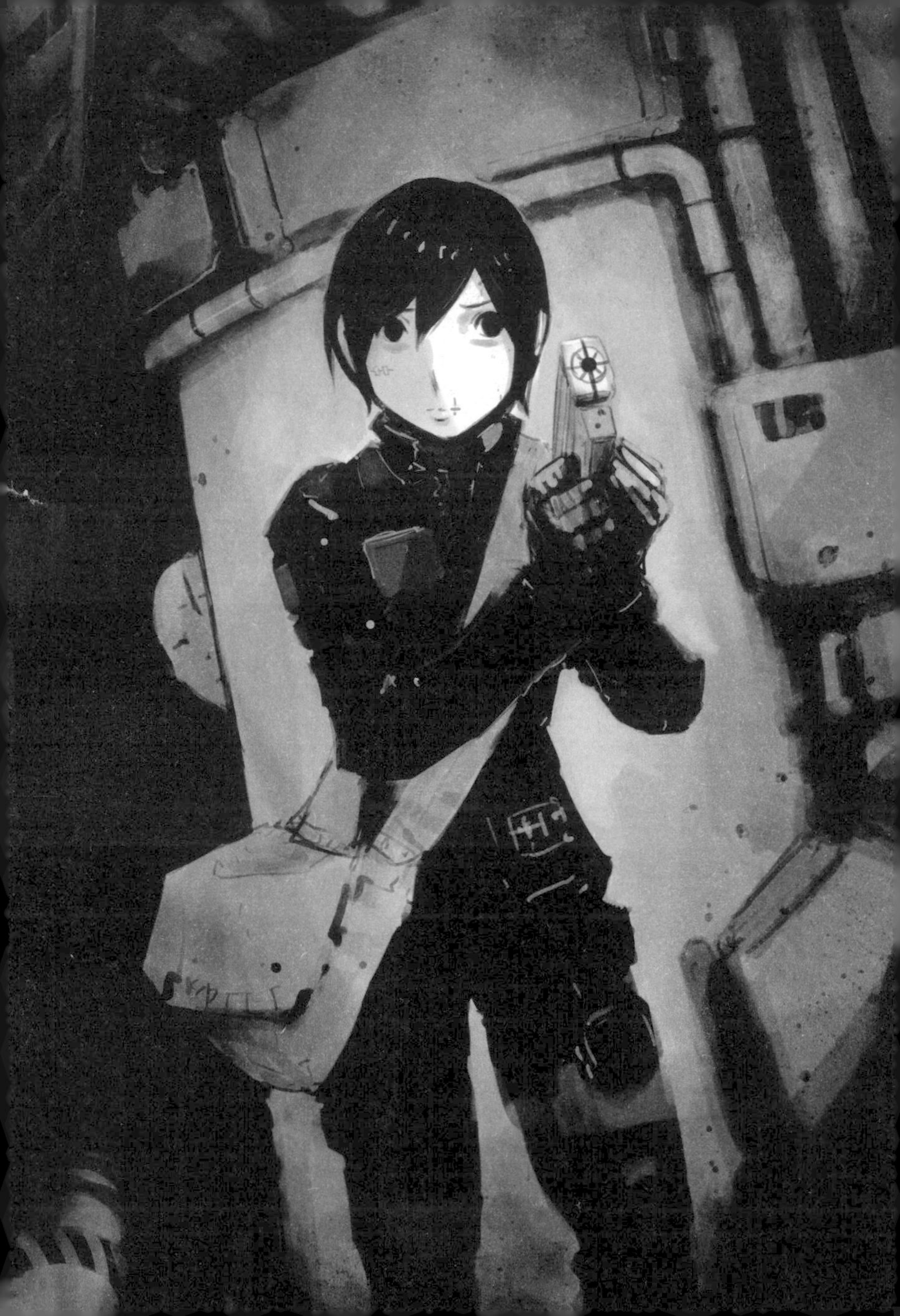

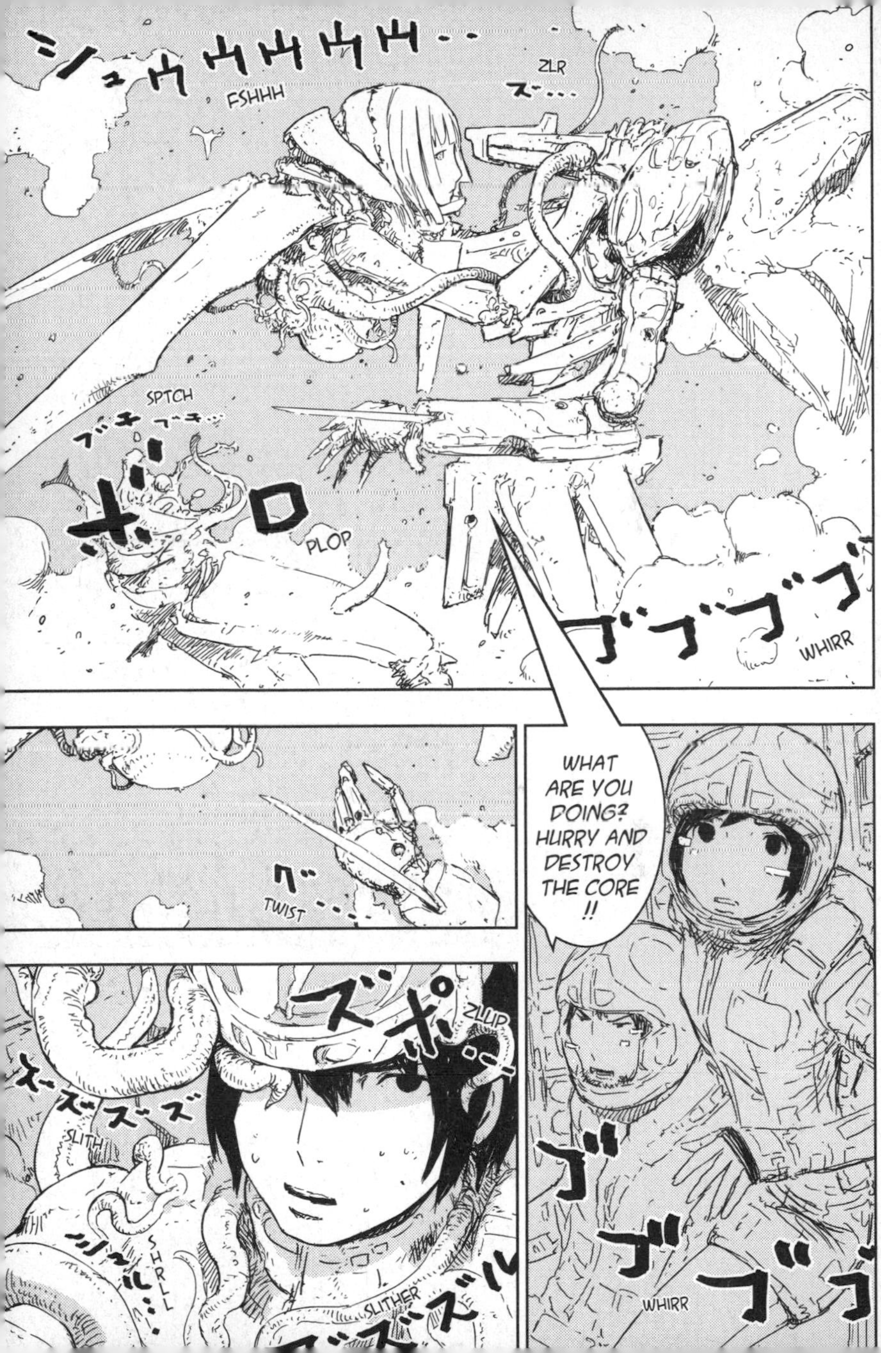
ZLR
FSHHH
WHIRR
PLOP
SPTCH
WHAT ARE YOU DOING? HURRY AND DESTROY THE CORE !!
WHIRR
TWIST
ZLUP
SLITH
SHRLL
SLITHER

Chapter 42: Shizuka Hoshijiro's Shape and Form

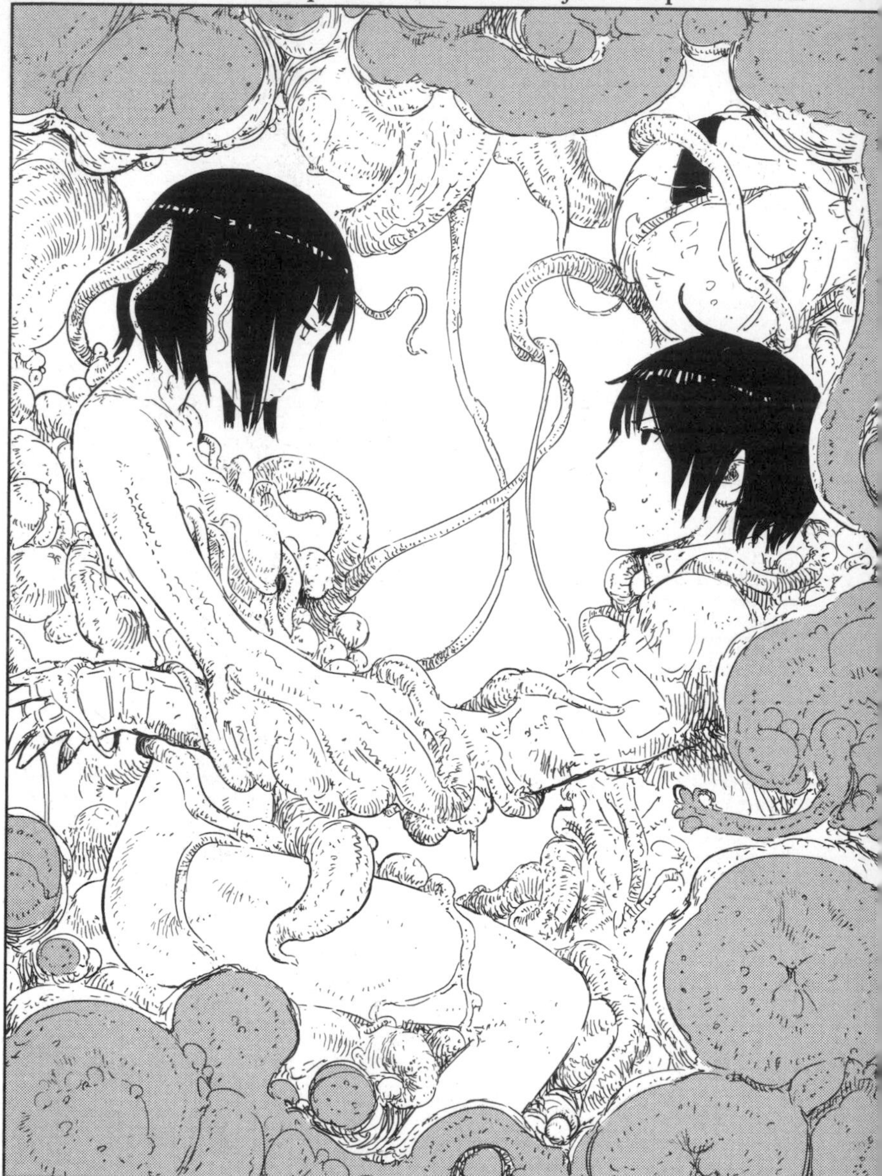

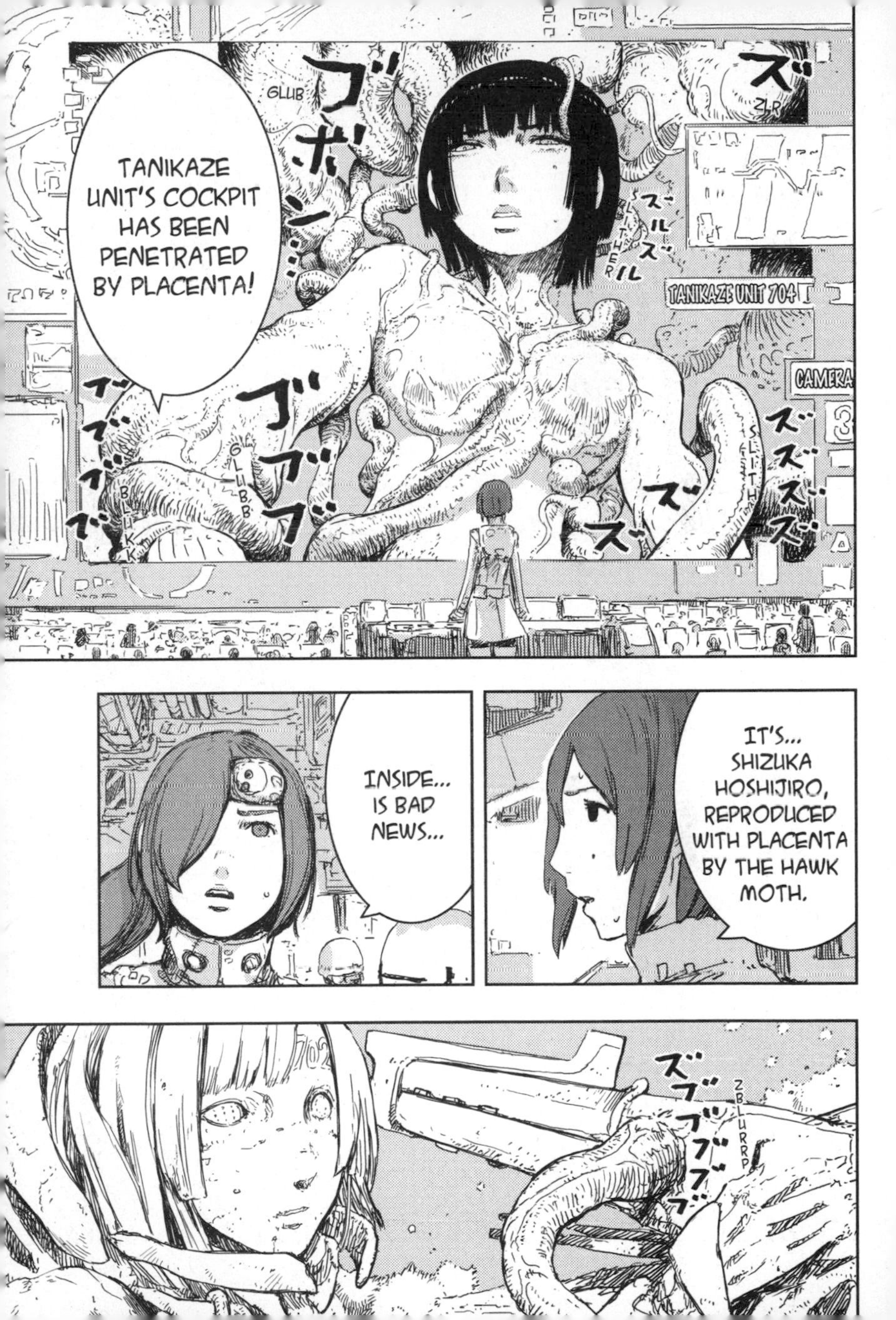
ズ
ZLR
TANIKAZE UNIT 704
CAMERA
3
ズルズル
SLITHER
ズズズズ
SLITH
ズズ
ゴボン
GLUB
TANIKAZE UNIT'S COCKPIT HAS BEEN PENETRATED BY PLACENTA!
ゴブブ
GLUBB
イブブブ
BLUKK
IT'S... SHIZUKA HOSHIJIRO, REPRODUCED WITH PLACENTA BY THE HAWK MOTH.
INSIDE... IS BAD NEWS...
ズブブブブ
ZBLURRP
702

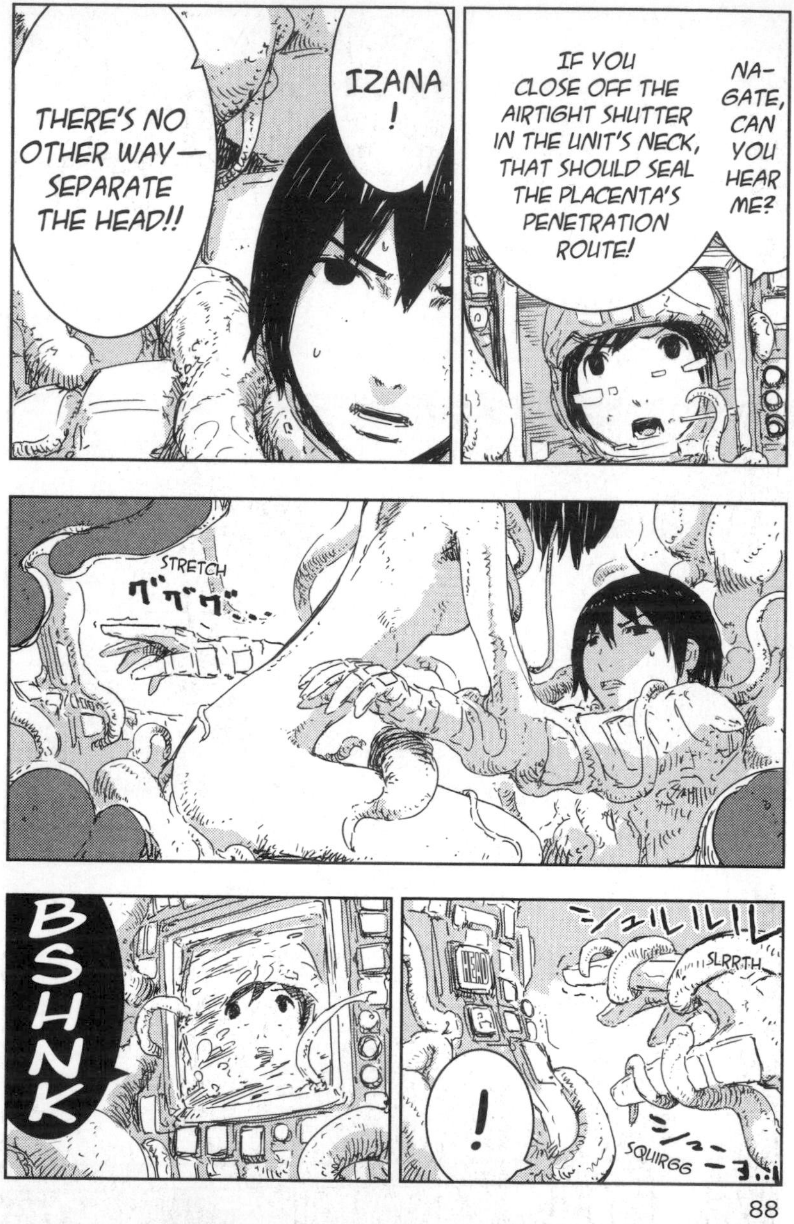

NA-GATE, CAN YOU HEAR ME?
IF YOU CLOSE OFF THE AIRTIGHT SHUTTER IN THE UNIT'S NECK, THAT SHOULD SEAL THE PLACENTA'S PENETRATION ROUTE!
IZANA!
THERE'S NO OTHER WAY—SEPARATE THE HEAD!!
STRETCH
ヴヴヴ…
シュルルルル
SLRRTH
HEAD
!
SQUIRGG
BSHNK

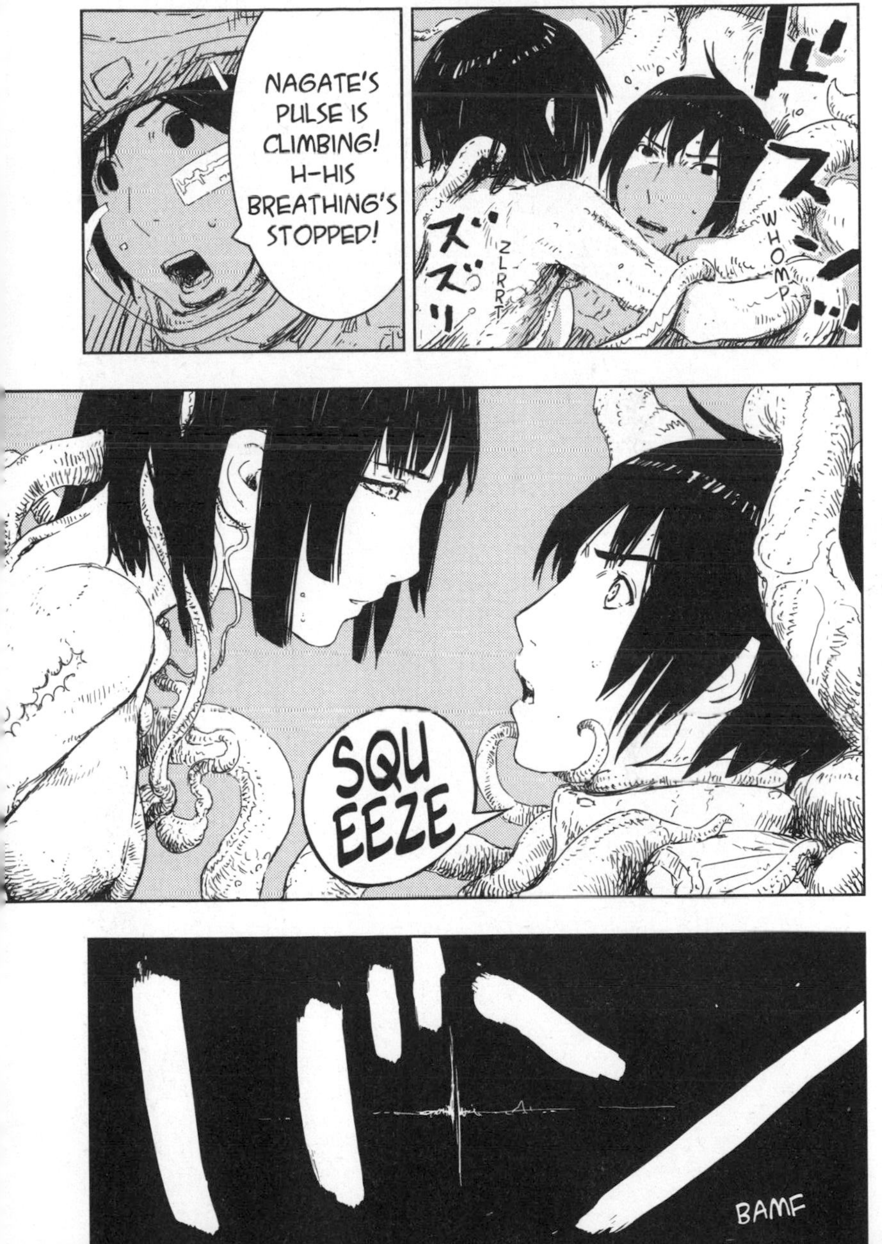
ドス…
WHOMP
ズズリ
ZLRRT
NAGATE'S PULSE IS CLIMBING! H-HIS BREATHING'S STOPPED!
SQUEEZE
BAMF

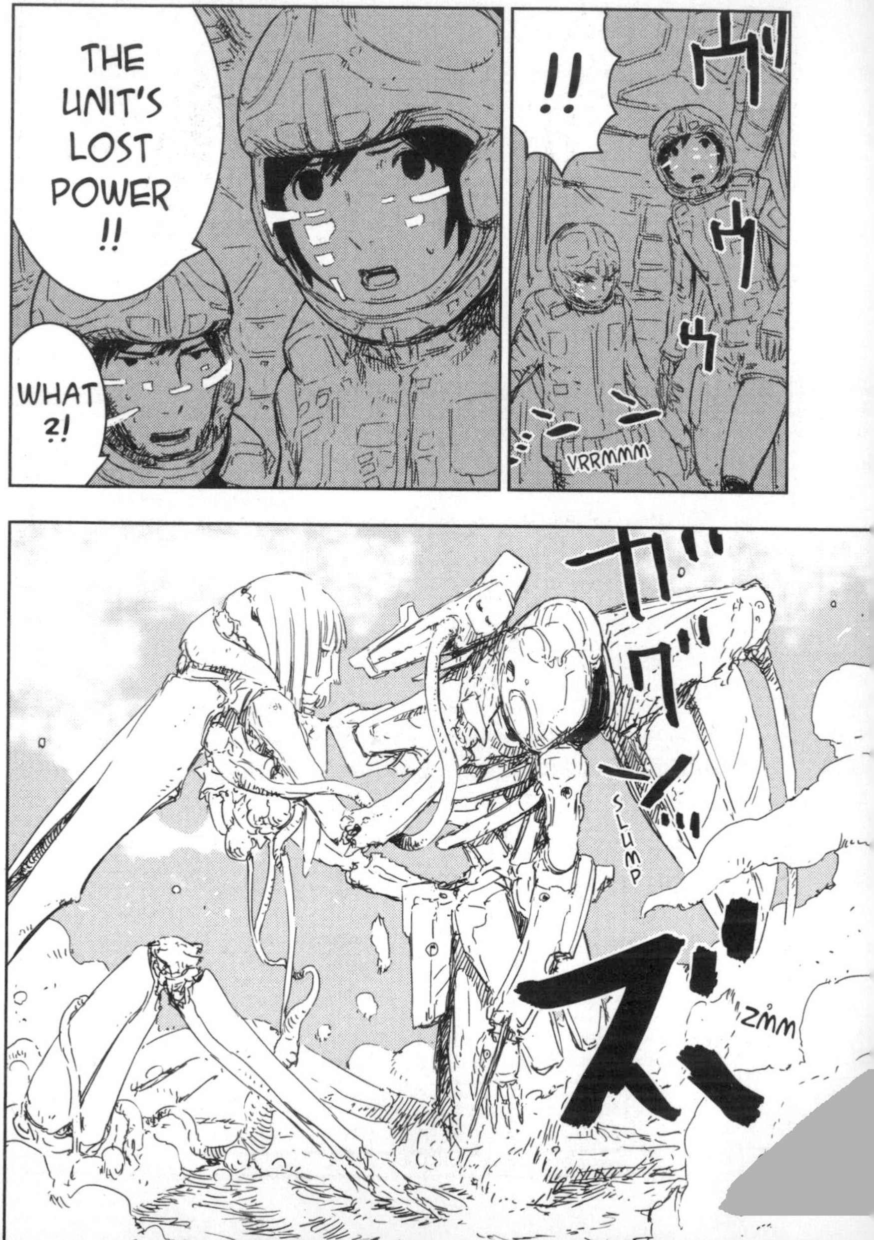
!!
VRRMMM
THE UNIT'S LOST POWER !!
WHAT ?!
SLUMP
ZMM

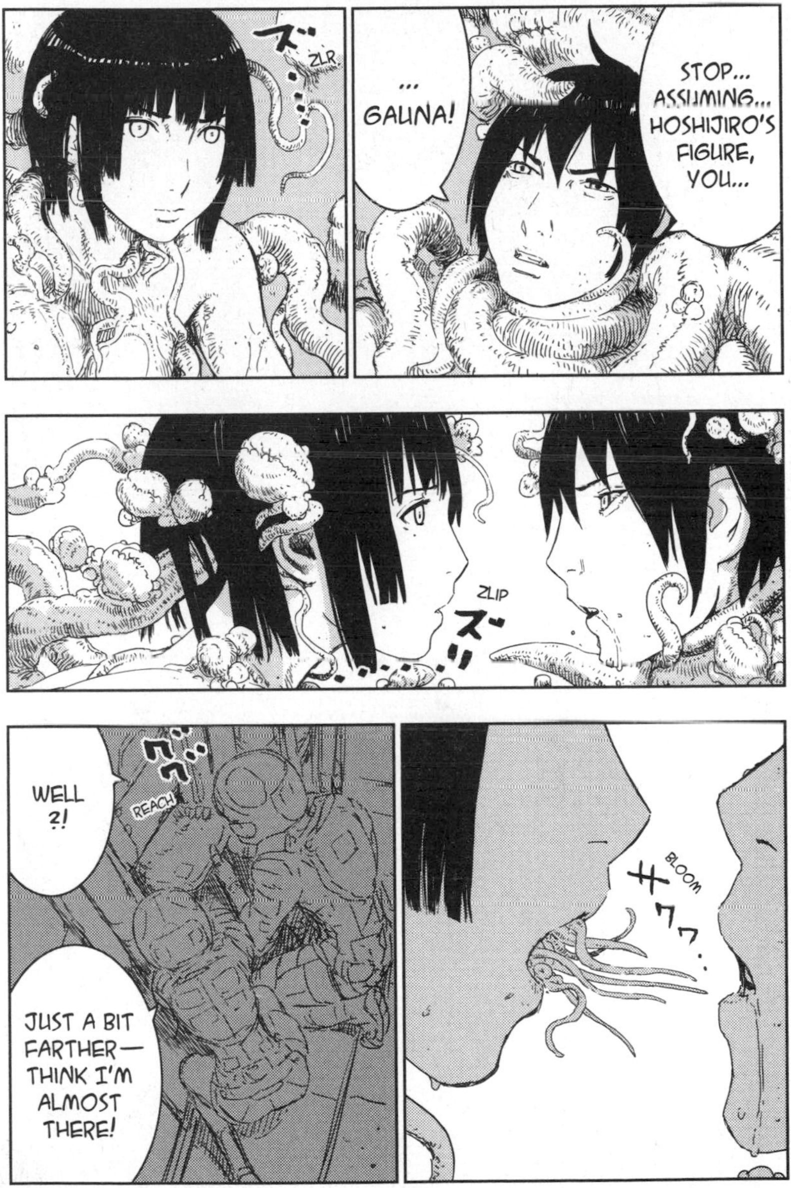
STOP... ASSUMING... HOSHIJIRO'S FIGURE, YOU...
... GAUNA!
ZLR
ZLIP
BLOOM
WELL ?!
REACH
JUST A BIT FARTHER— THINK I'M ALMOST THERE!

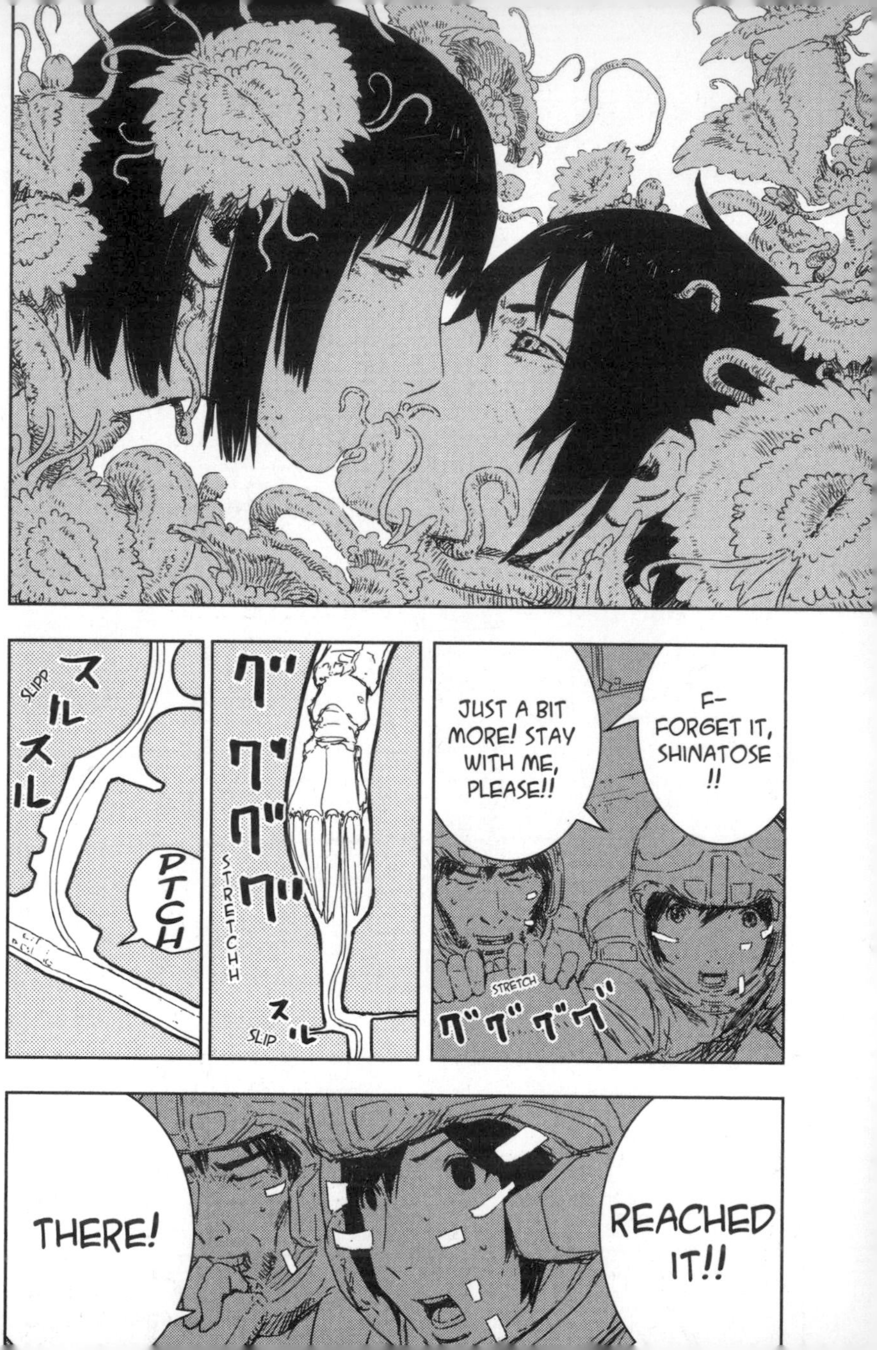
F- FORGET IT, SHINATOSE !!
JUST A BIT MORE! STAY WITH ME, PLEASE!!
STRETCH
ググググ
ググググ
STRETCHH
スル
SLIP
スルスル
SLIPP
PTCH
REACHED IT!!
THERE!

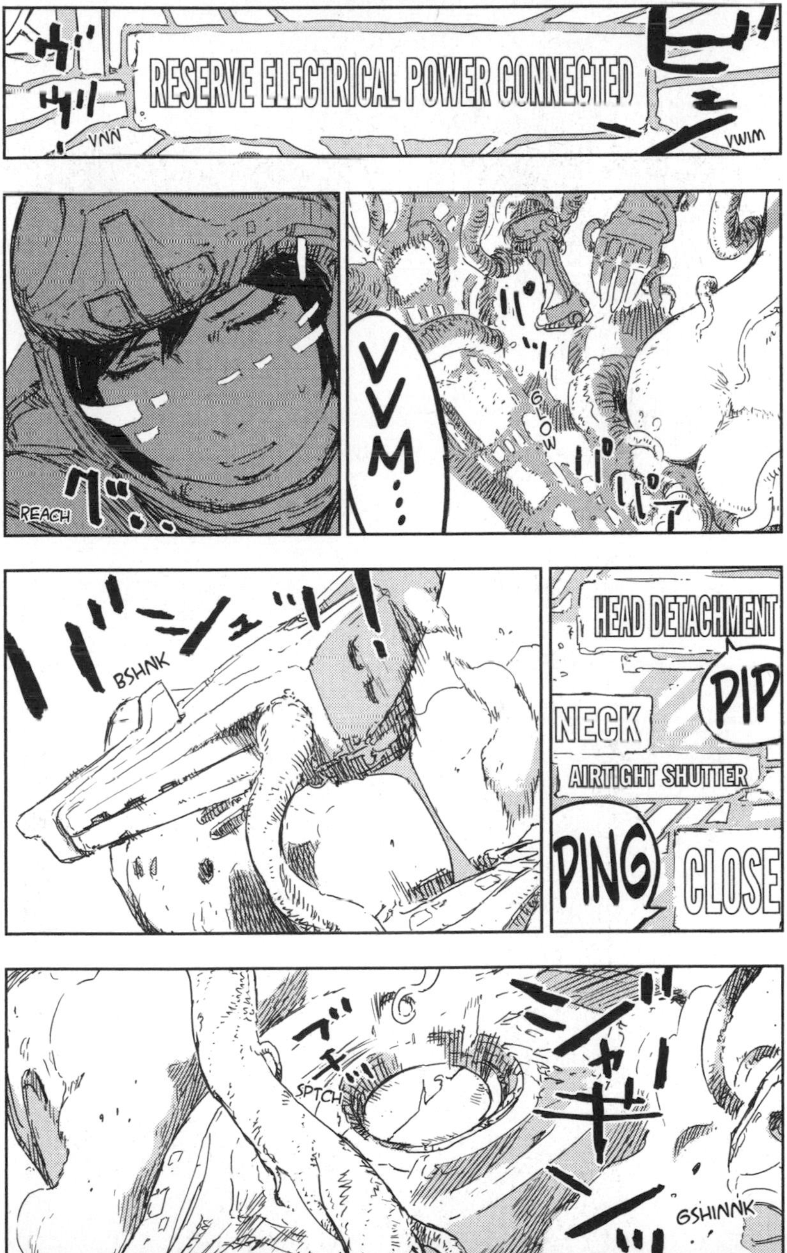
VWIM
RESERVE ELECTRICAL POWER CONNECTED
VNN
VVM...
GLOW
REACH
HEAD DETACHMENT
PIP
NECK
AIRTIGHT SHUTTER
PING
CLOSE
BSHNK
GSHINNK
SPTCH

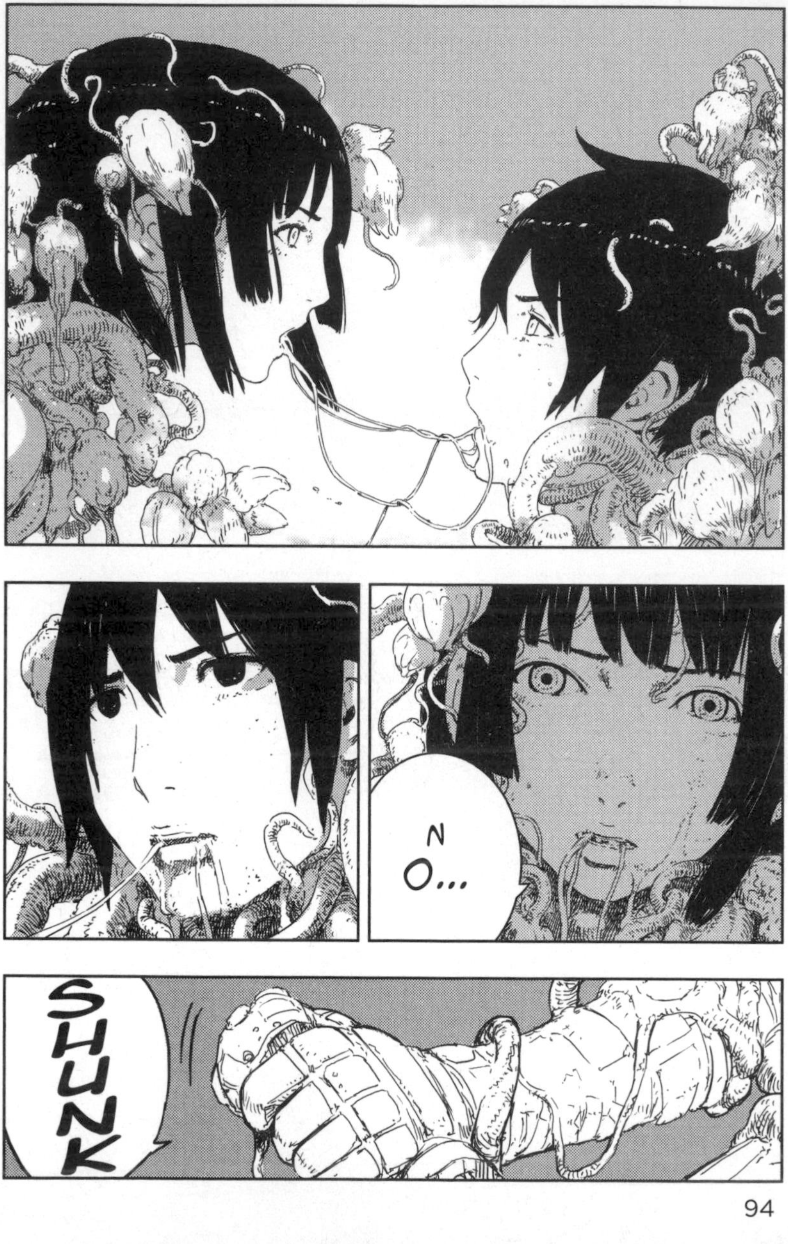
NO...
SHUNK

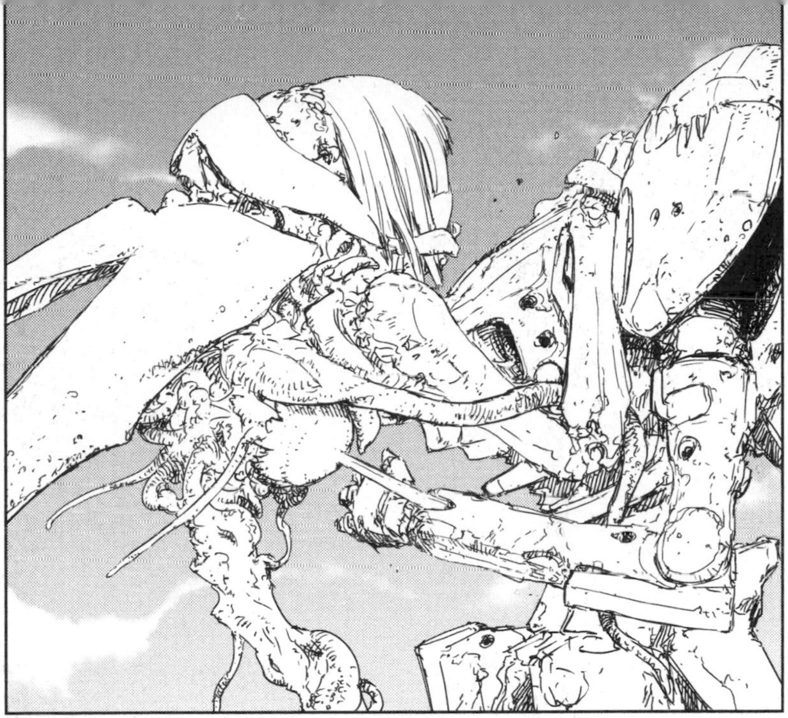

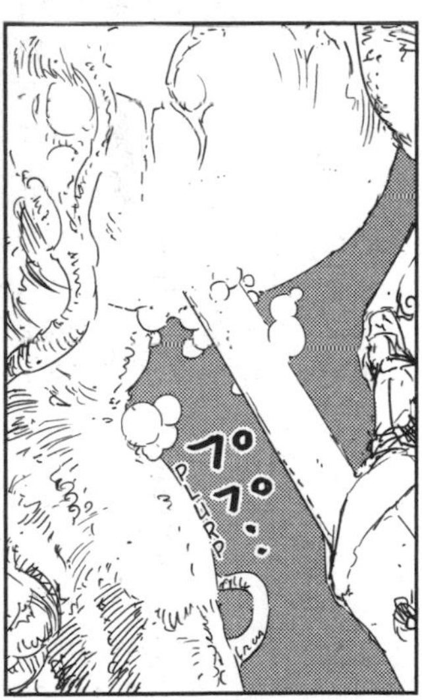
ペペ‥
PLURP

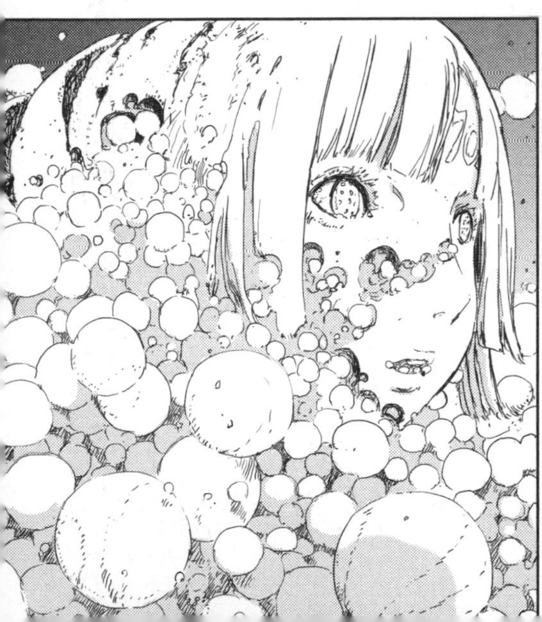

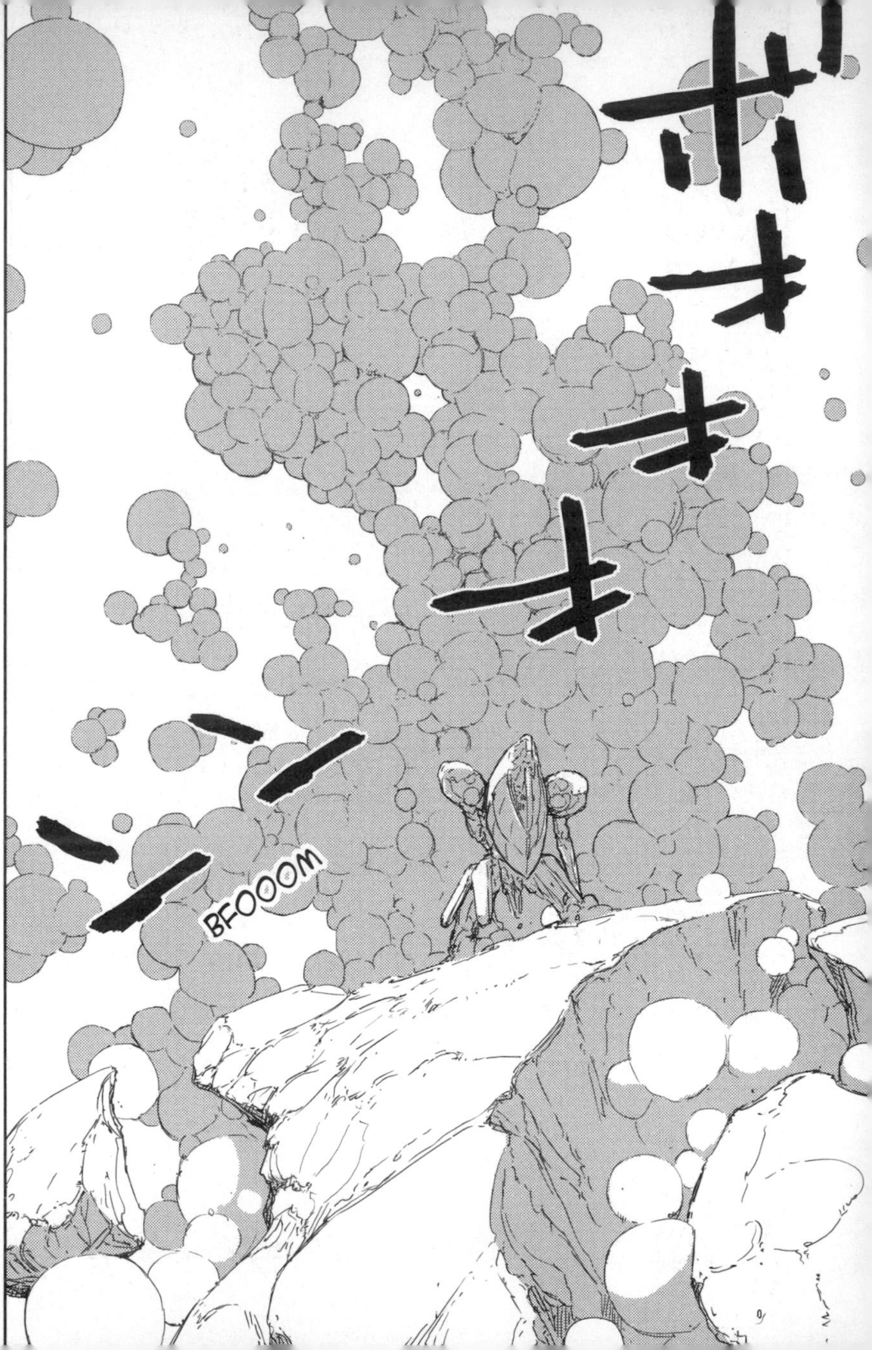
BFOOOM

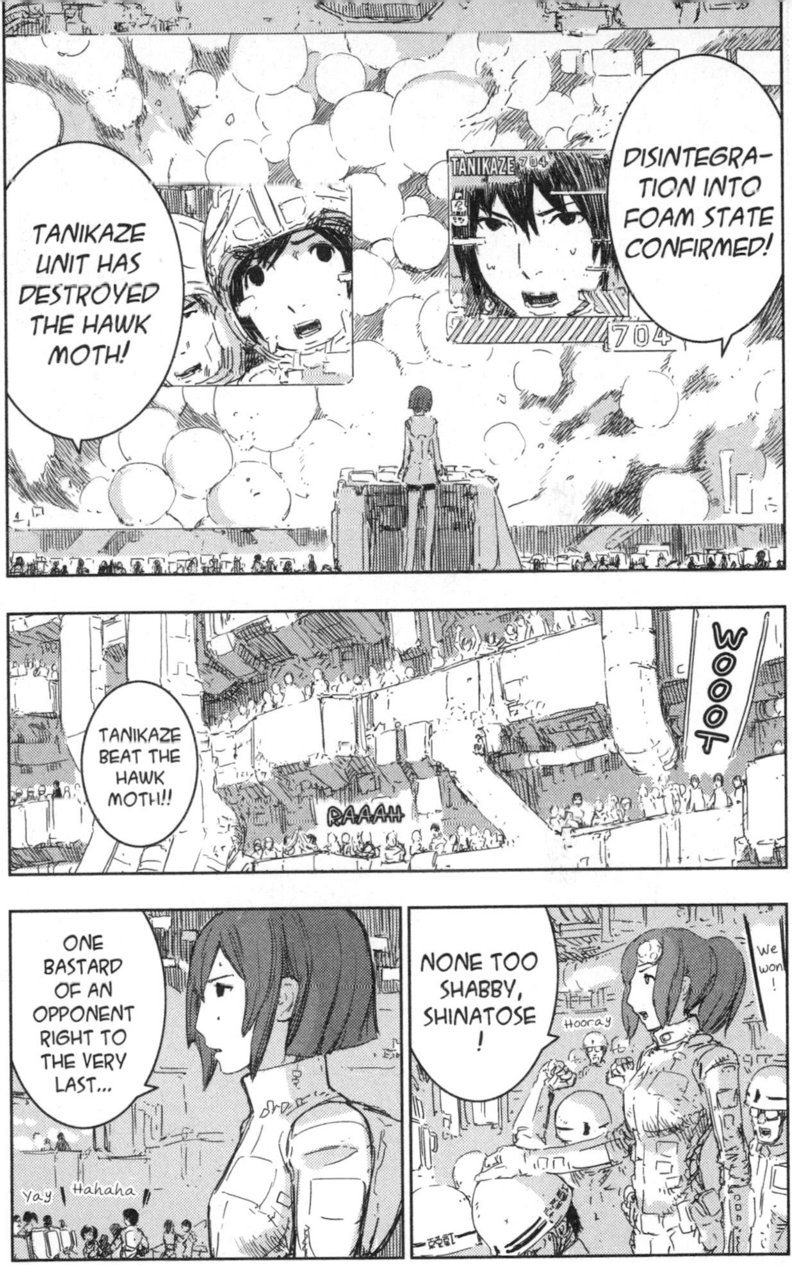
TANIKAZE 704
704
DISINTEGRATION INTO FOAM STATE CONFIRMED!
TANIKAZE UNIT HAS DESTROYED THE HAWK MOTH!
WOOOT
TANIKAZE BEAT THE HAWK MOTH!!
RAAAH
We won!
NONE TOO SHABBY, SHINATOSE!
Hooray
ONE BASTARD OF AN OPPONENT RIGHT TO THE VERY LAST...
Yay
Hahaha

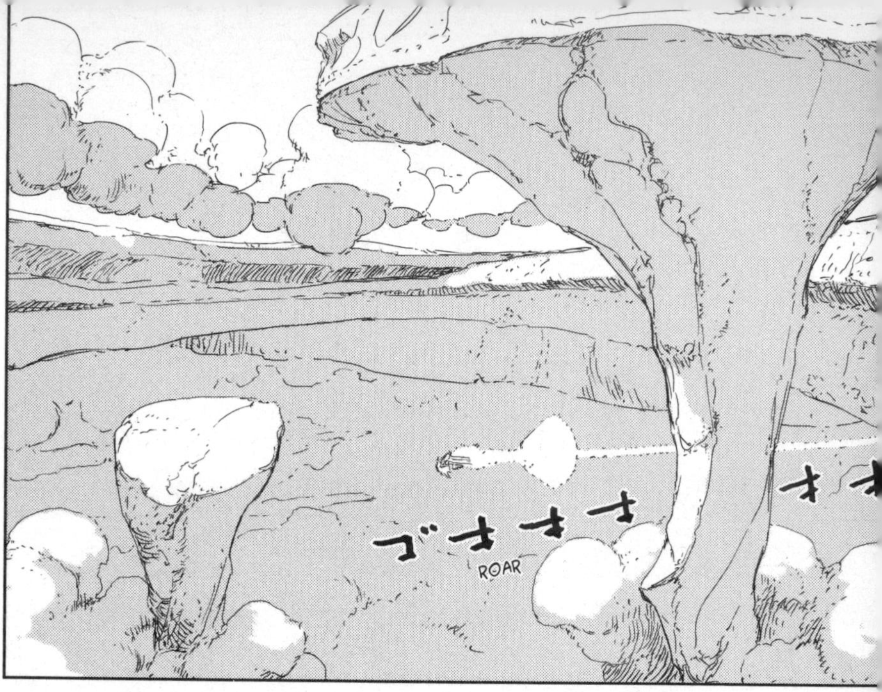
ゴォォォ
ROAR
ォォ
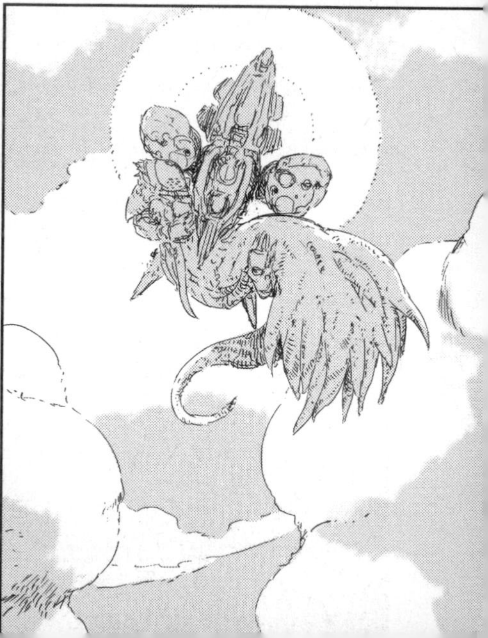
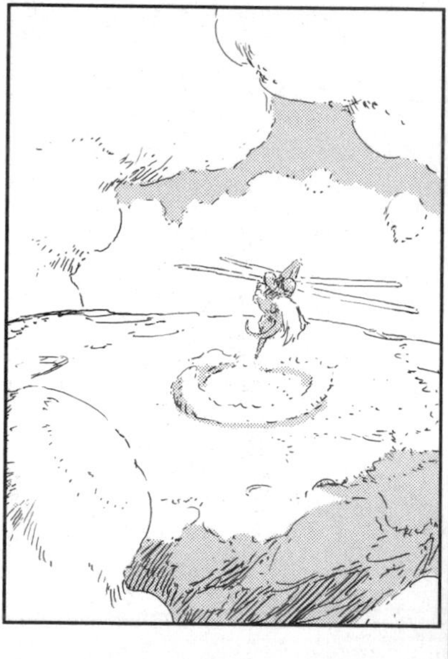

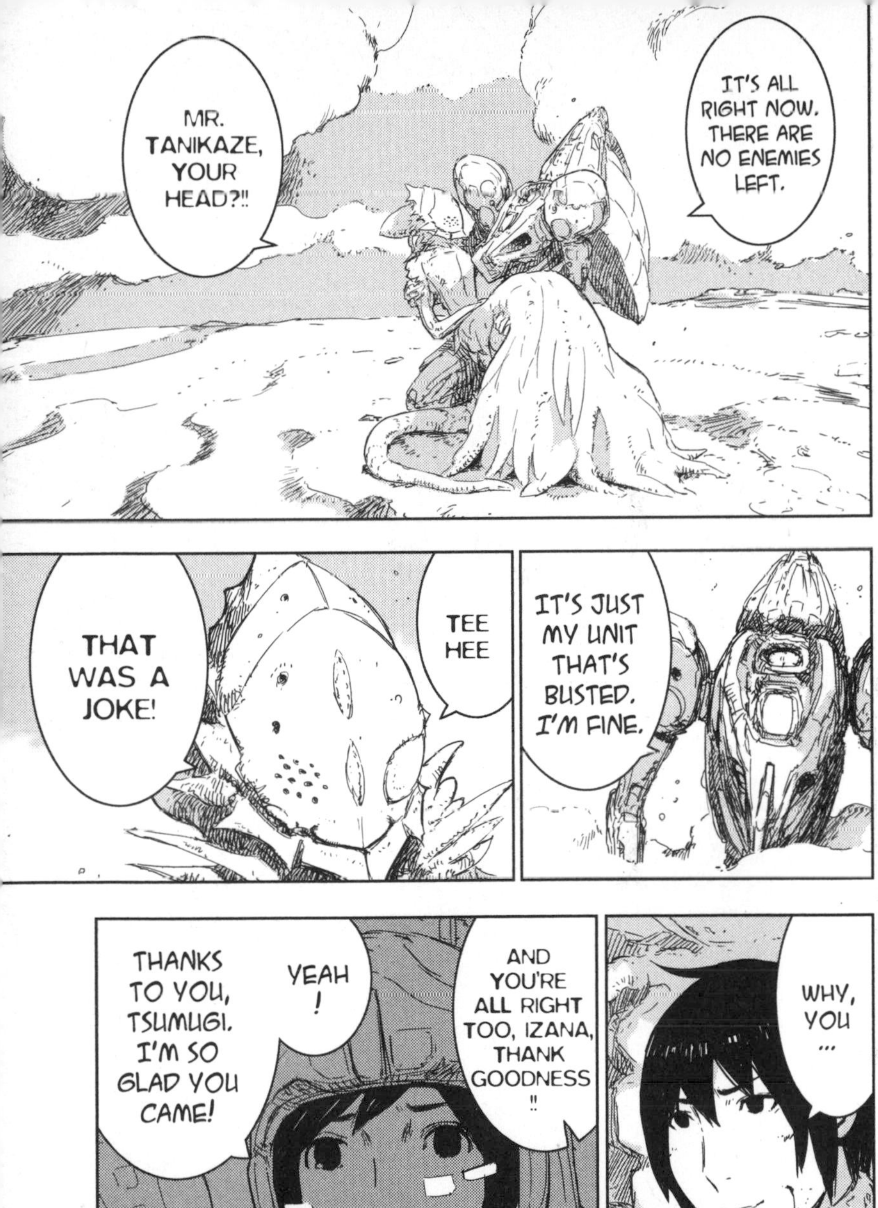
IT'S ALL RIGHT NOW. THERE ARE NO ENEMIES LEFT.
MR. TANIKAZE, YOUR HEAD?!!
IT'S JUST MY UNIT THAT'S BUSTED. I'M FINE.
TEE HEE
THAT WAS A JOKE!
WHY, YOU ...
AND YOU'RE ALL RIGHT TOO, IZANA, THANK GOODNESS !!
YEAH !
THANKS TO YOU, TSUMUGI. I'M SO GLAD YOU CAME!

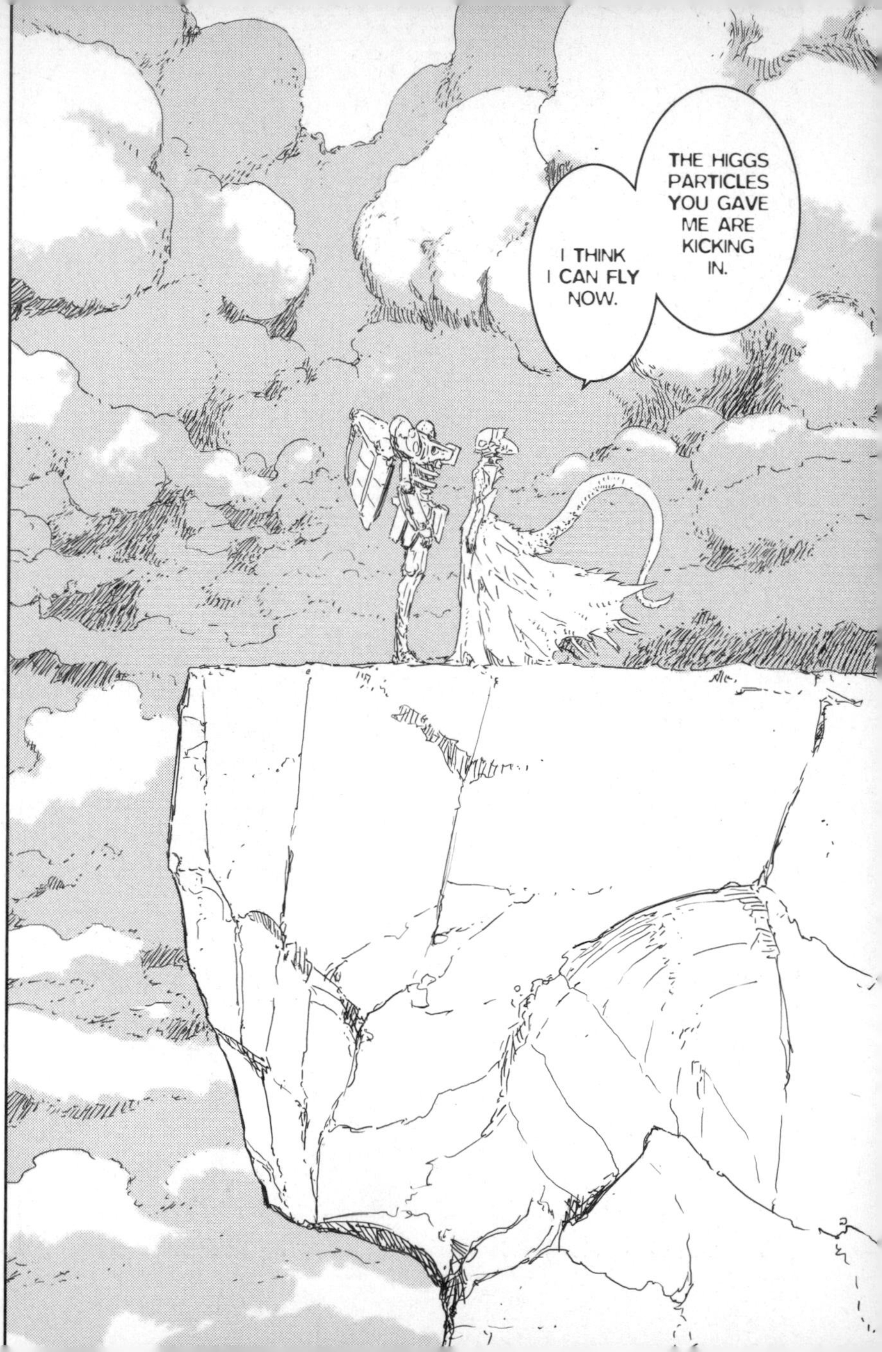
THE HIGGS PARTICLES YOU GAVE ME ARE KICKING IN.
I THINK I CAN FLY NOW.

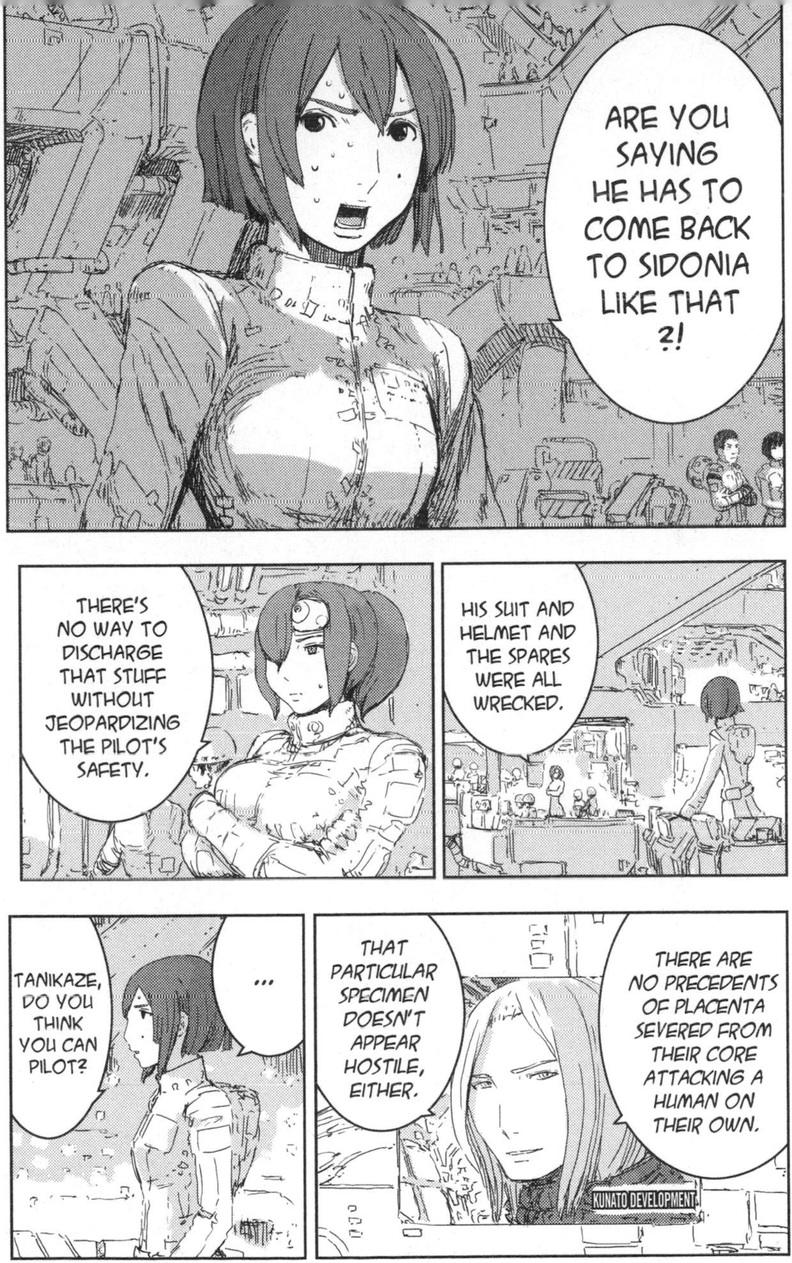
ARE YOU SAYING HE HAS TO COME BACK TO SIDONIA LIKE THAT ?!
HIS SUIT AND HELMET AND THE SPARES WERE ALL WRECKED.
THERE'S NO WAY TO DISCHARGE THAT STUFF WITHOUT JEOPARDIZING THE PILOT'S SAFETY.
THERE ARE NO PRECEDENTS OF PLACENTA SEVERED FROM THEIR CORE ATTACKING A HUMAN ON THEIR OWN.
THAT PARTICULAR SPECIMEN DOESN'T APPEAR HOSTILE, EITHER.
KUNATO DEVELOPMENT
...
TANIKAZE, DO YOU THINK YOU CAN PILOT?

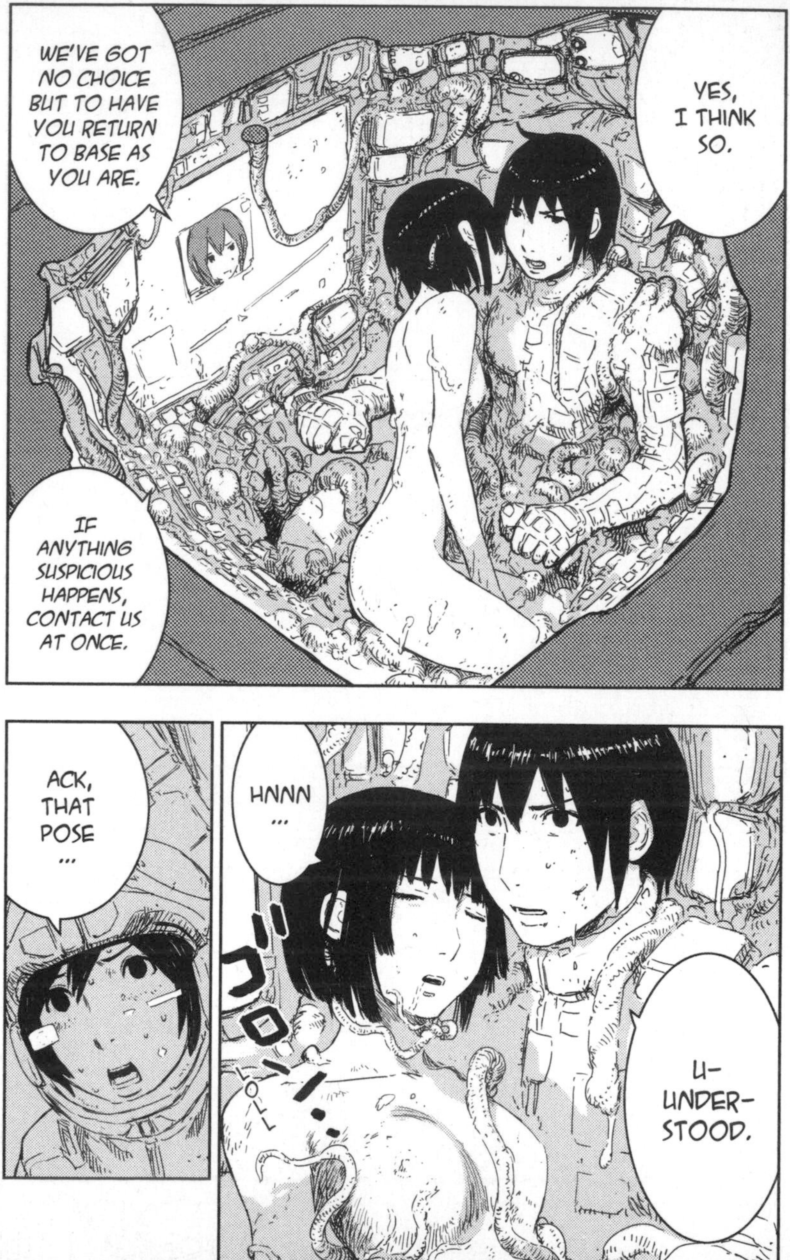
YES, I THINK SO.
WE'VE GOT NO CHOICE BUT TO HAVE YOU RETURN TO BASE AS YOU ARE.
IF ANYTHING SUSPICIOUS HAPPENS, CONTACT US AT ONCE.
HNNN...
U-UNDERSTOOD.
ROLL
ACK, THAT POSE...

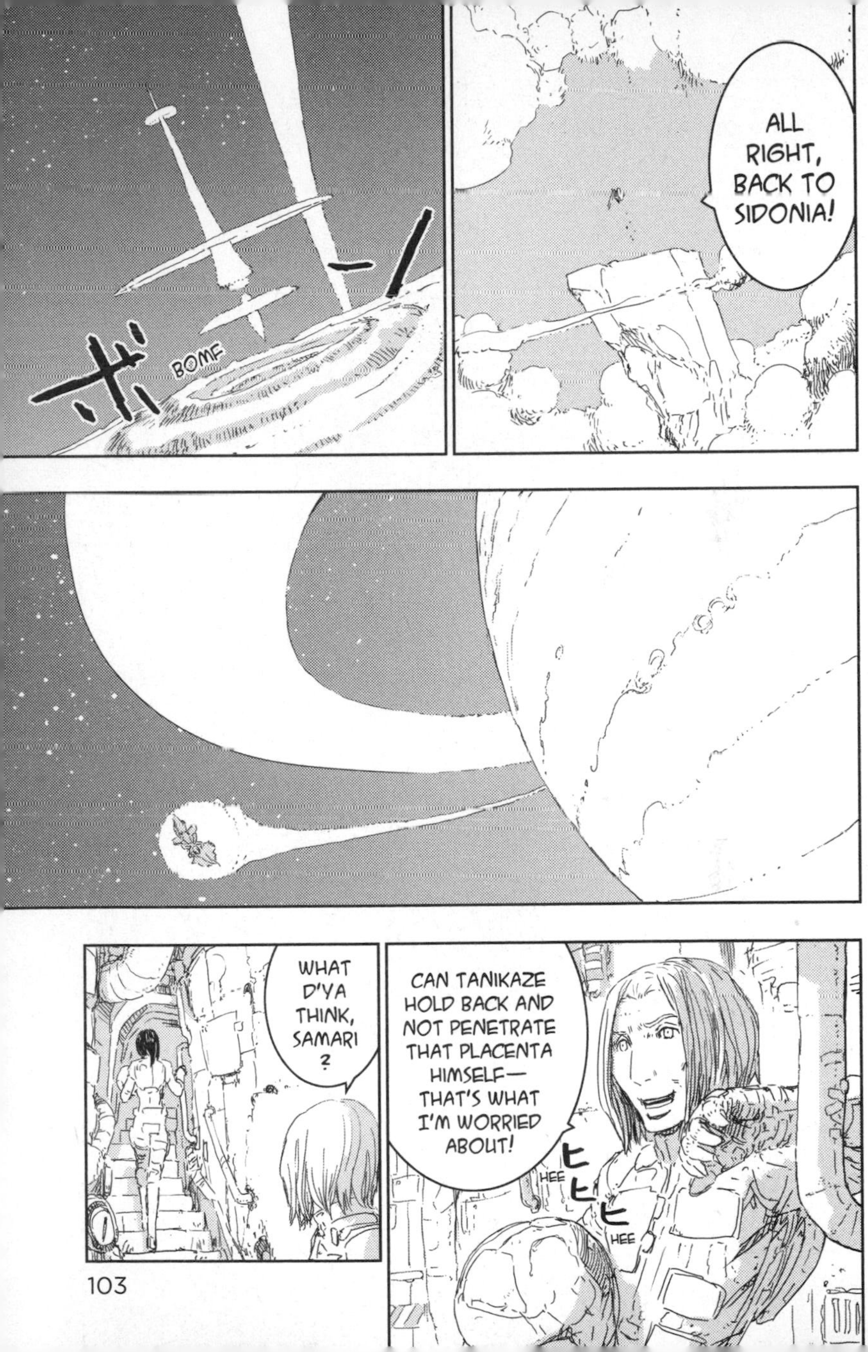
ALL RIGHT, BACK TO SIDONIA!
ボ
BOMF
CAN TANIKAZE HOLD BACK AND NOT PENETRATE THAT PLACENTA HIMSELF—THAT'S WHAT I'M WORRIED ABOUT!
ヒ
HEE
ヒ
ヒ
HEE
WHAT D'YA THINK, SAMARI?

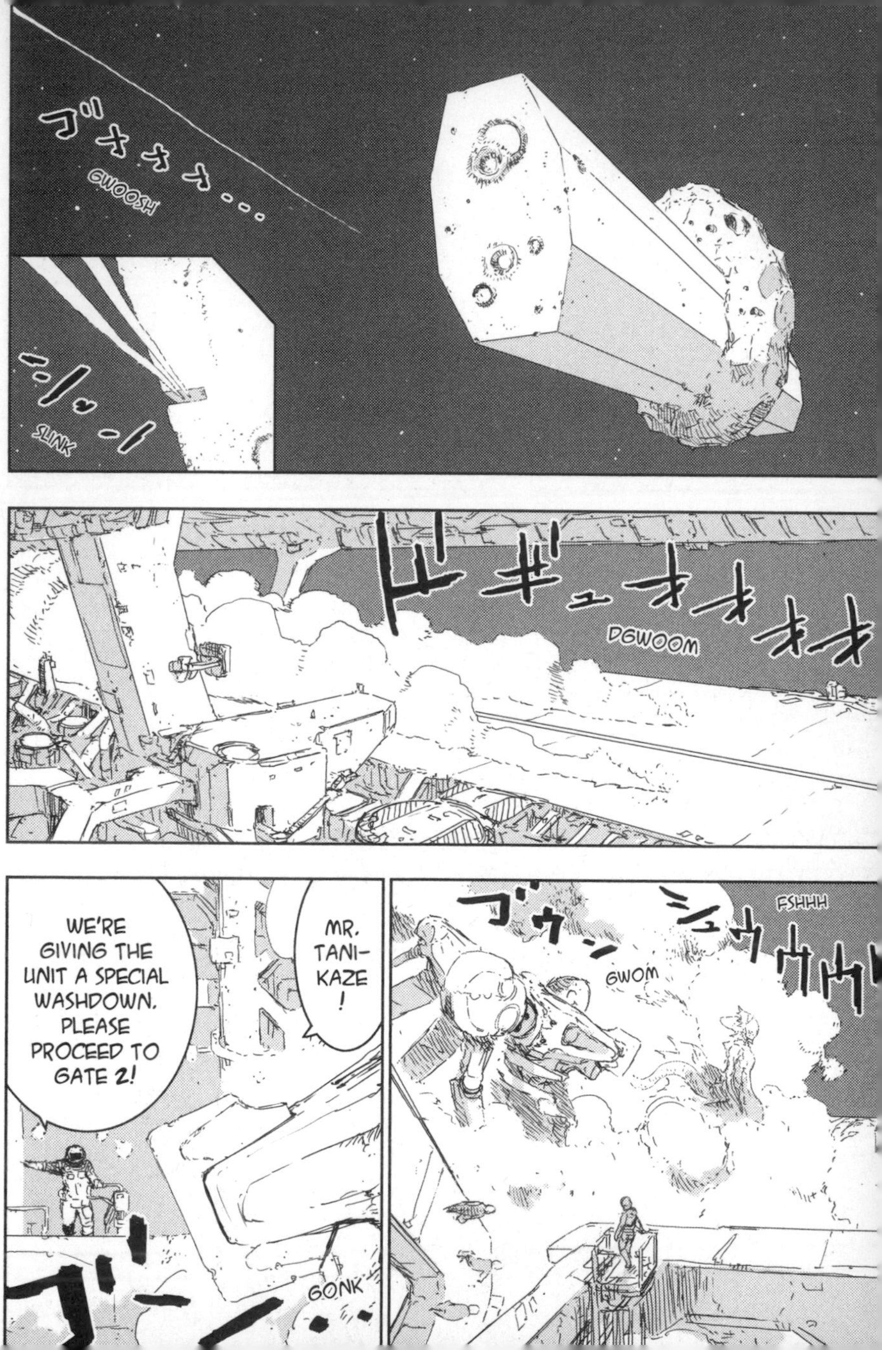
GWOOSH
SLINK
DGWOOM
FSHHH
GWOM
MR. TANI-KAZE!
WE'RE GIVING THE UNIT A SPECIAL WASHDOWN. PLEASE PROCEED TO GATE 2!
GONK

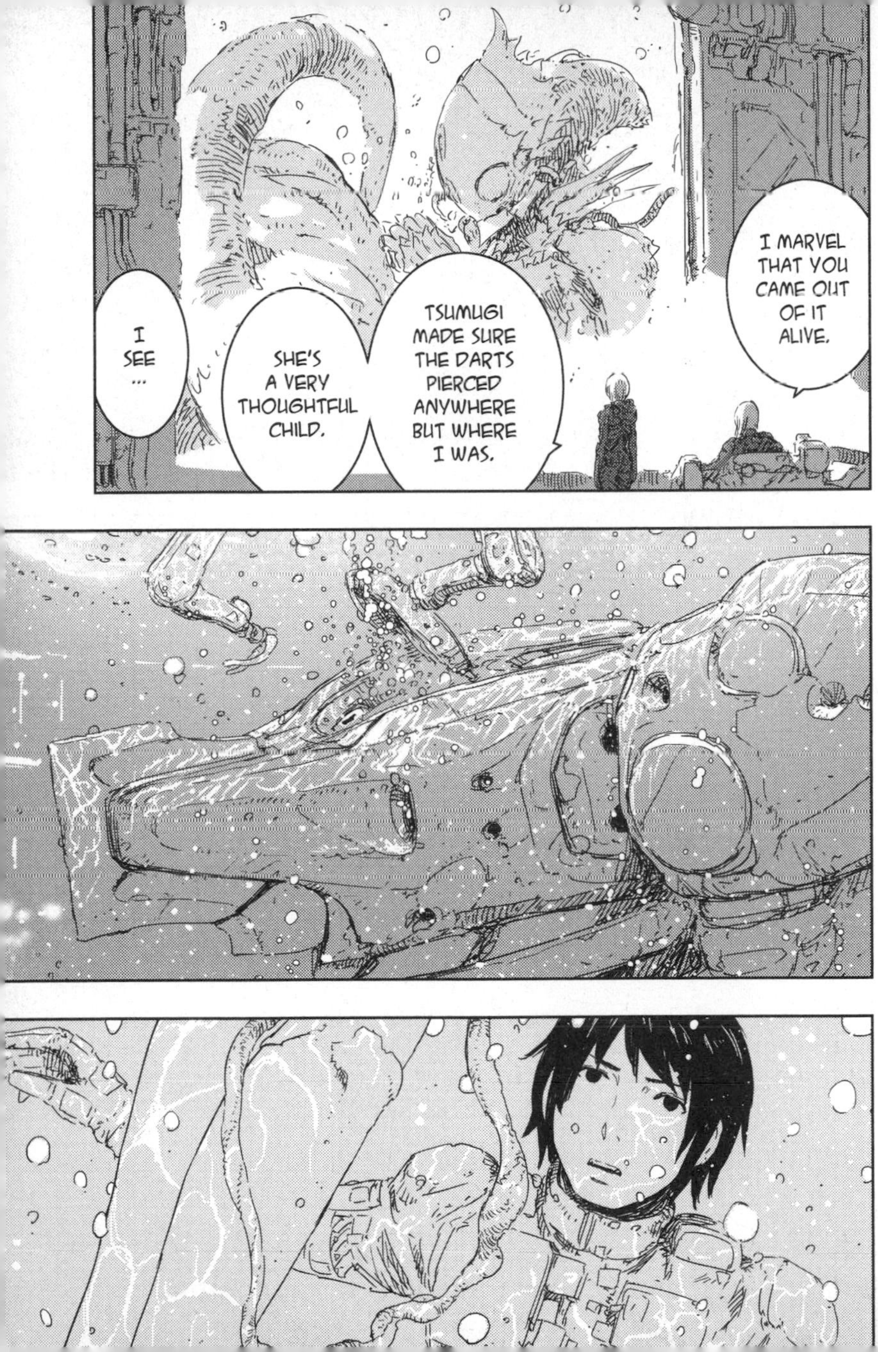
I MARVEL THAT YOU CAME OUT OF IT ALIVE.
TSUMUGI MADE SURE THE DARTS PIERCED ANYWHERE BUT WHERE I WAS.
SHE'S A VERY THOUGHTFUL CHILD.
I SEE ...

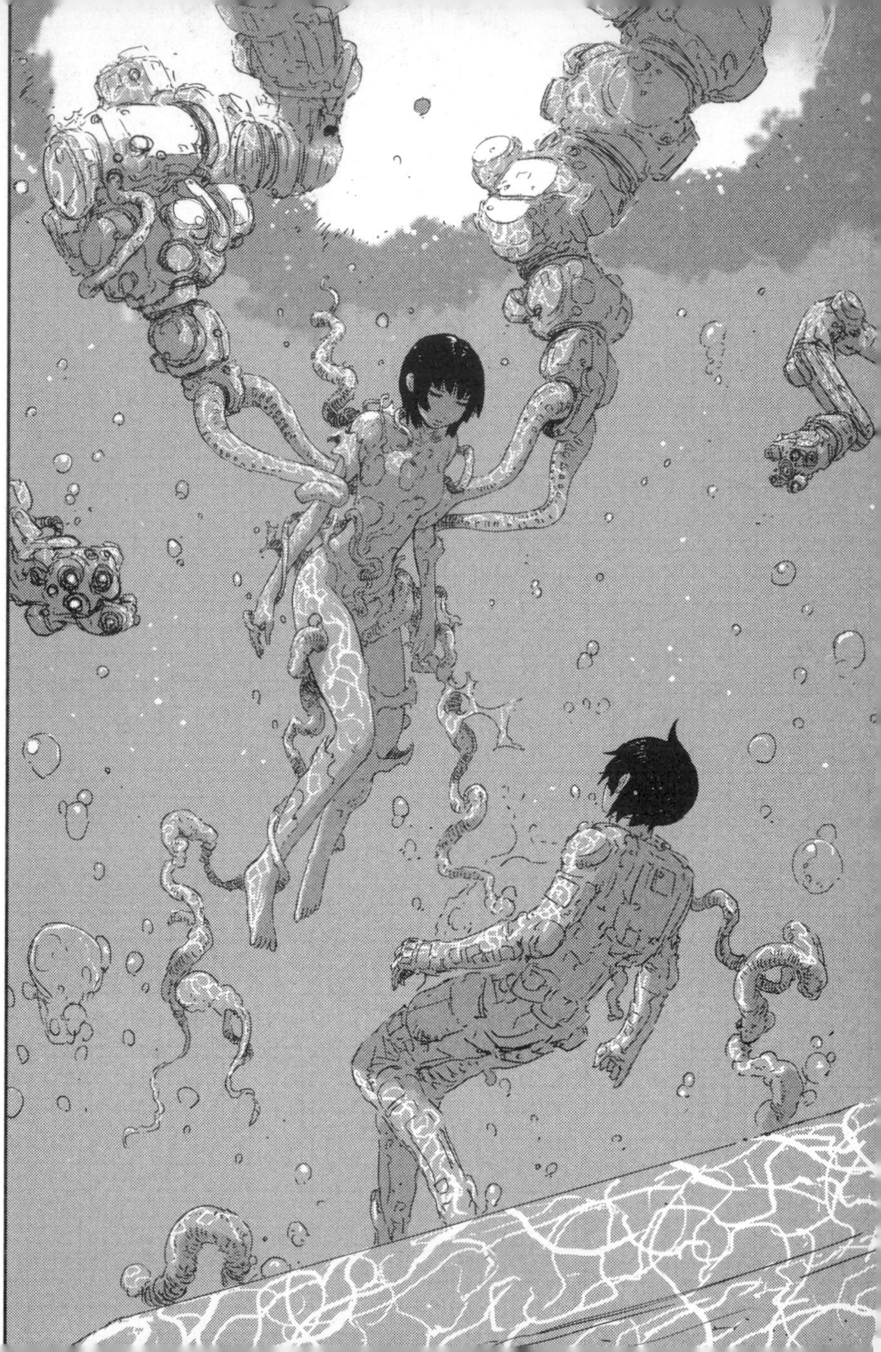

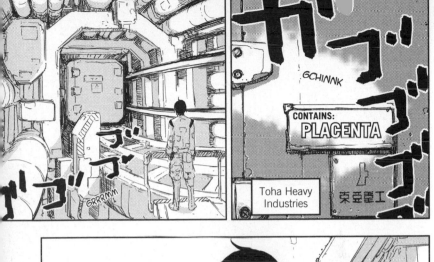

GCHINNK

CONTAINS:
PLACENTA

Toha Heavy
Industries

東亞重工

GRRRMM

HOSHI-
JIRO...

...

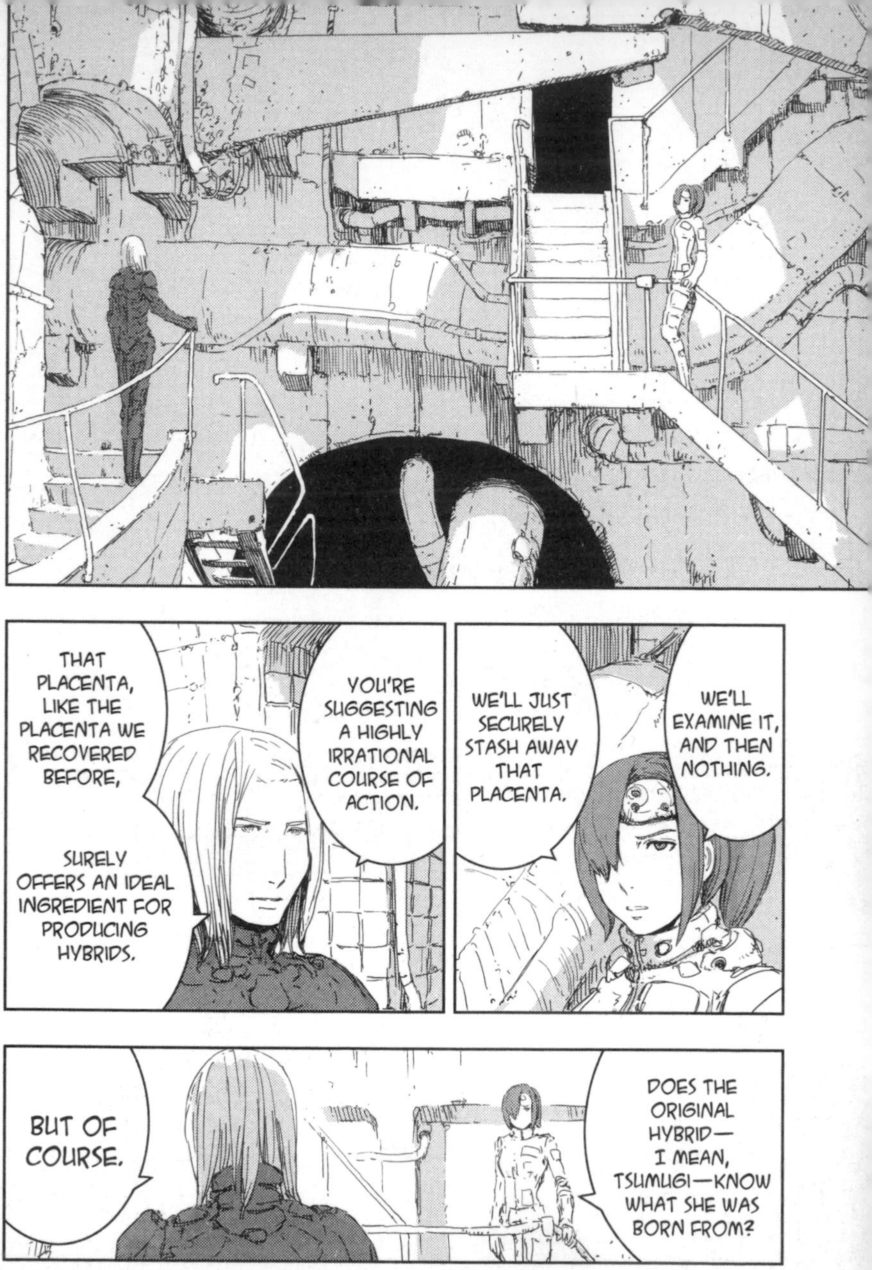
WE'LL EXAMINE IT, AND THEN NOTHING.
WE'LL JUST SECURELY STASH AWAY THAT PLACENTA.
YOU'RE SUGGESTING A HIGHLY IRRATIONAL COURSE OF ACTION.
THAT PLACENTA, LIKE THE PLACENTA WE RECOVERED BEFORE,
SURELY OFFERS AN IDEAL INGREDIENT FOR PRODUCING HYBRIDS.
DOES THE ORIGINAL HYBRID— I MEAN, TSUMUGI—KNOW WHAT SHE WAS BORN FROM?
BUT OF COURSE.

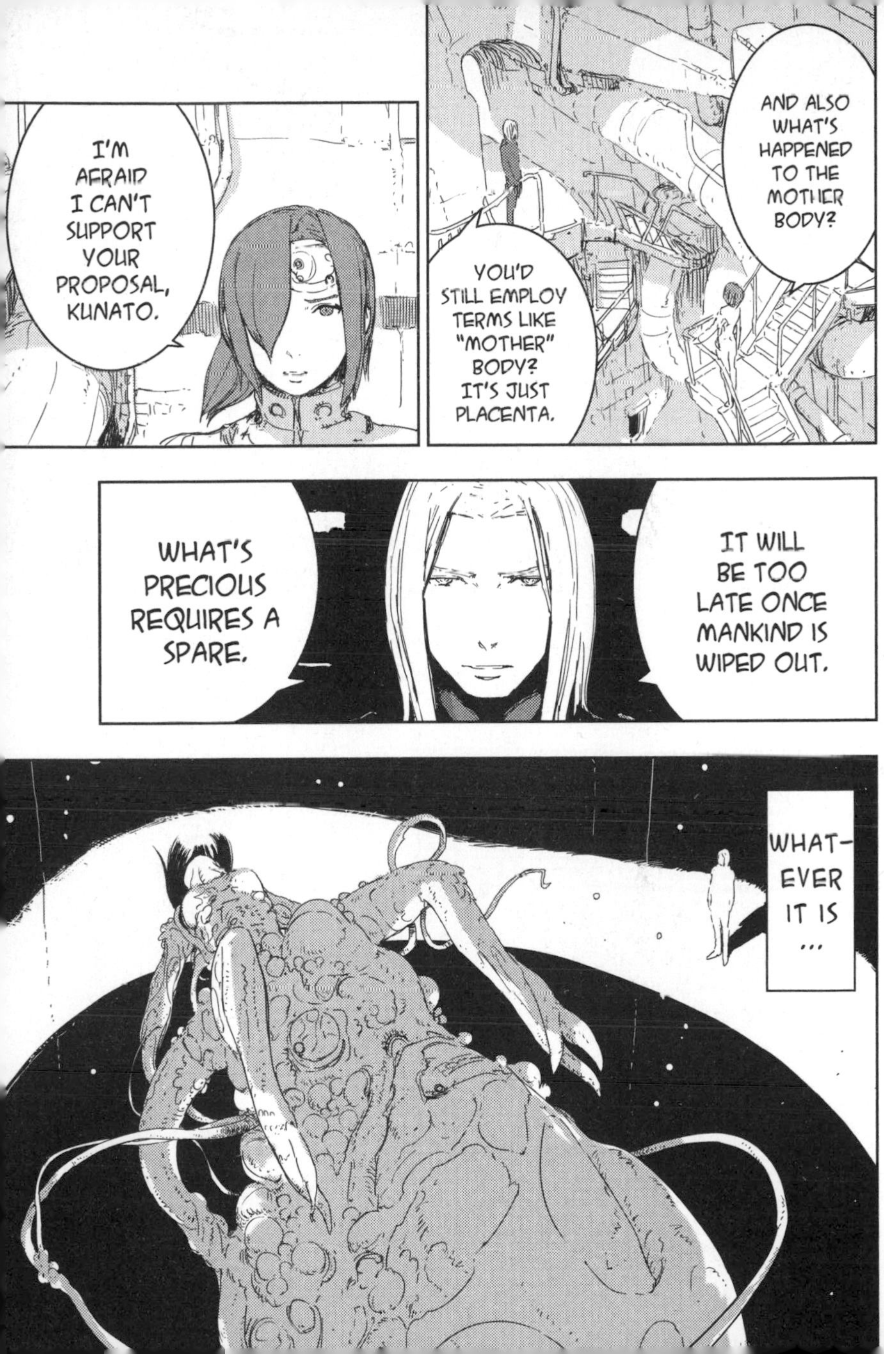
AND ALSO WHAT'S HAPPENED TO THE MOTHER BODY?
YOU'D STILL EMPLOY TERMS LIKE "MOTHER" BODY? IT'S JUST PLACENTA.
I'M AFRAID I CAN'T SUPPORT YOUR PROPOSAL, KUNATO.
IT WILL BE TOO LATE ONCE MANKIND IS WIPED OUT.
WHAT'S PRECIOUS REQUIRES A SPARE.
WHAT-EVER IT IS ...

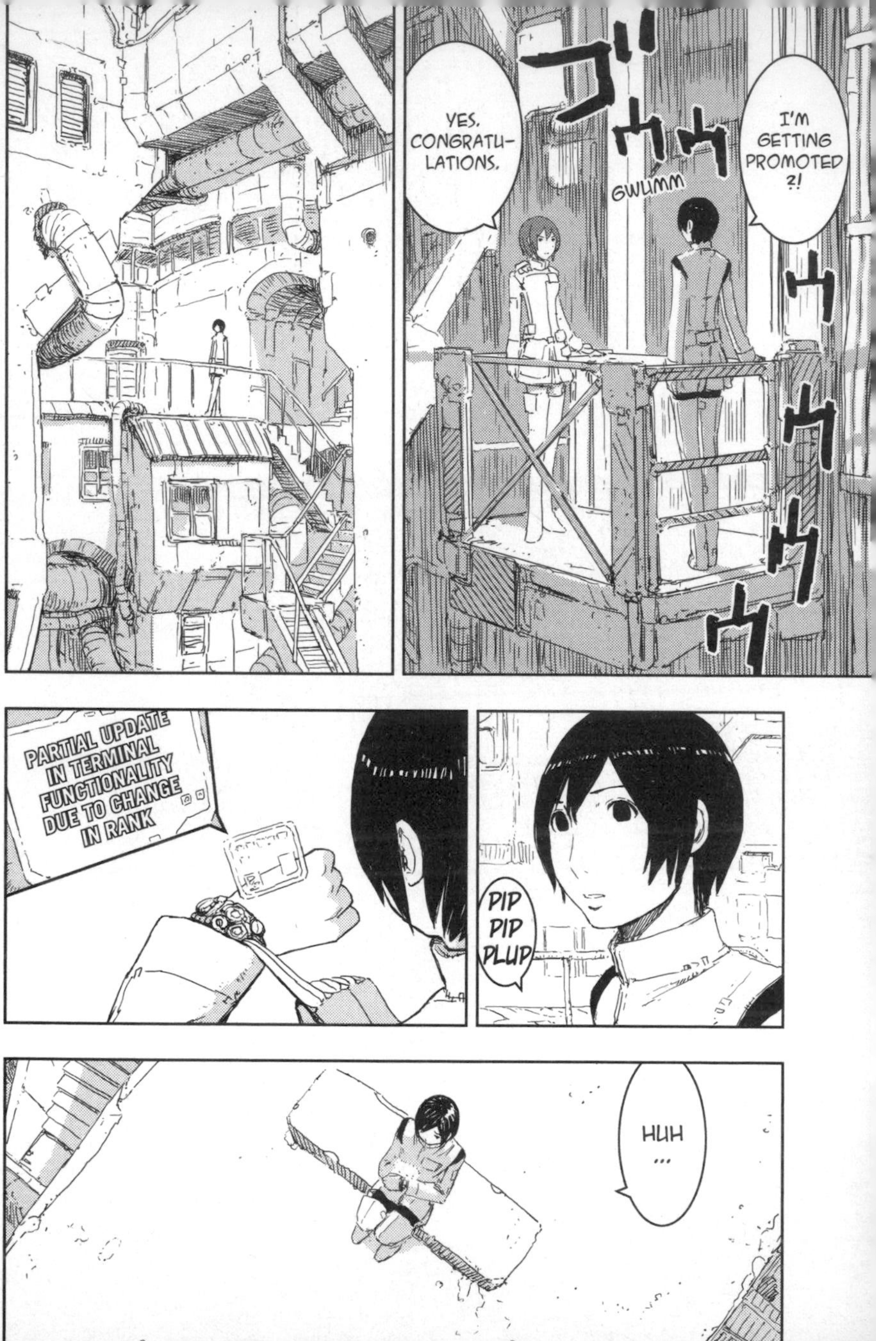
I'M GETTING PROMOTED ?!
GWUMM
YES. CONGRATULATIONS.
PIP PIP PLUP
PARTIAL UPDATE IN TERMINAL FUNCTIONALITY DUE TO CHANGE IN RANK
HUH ...

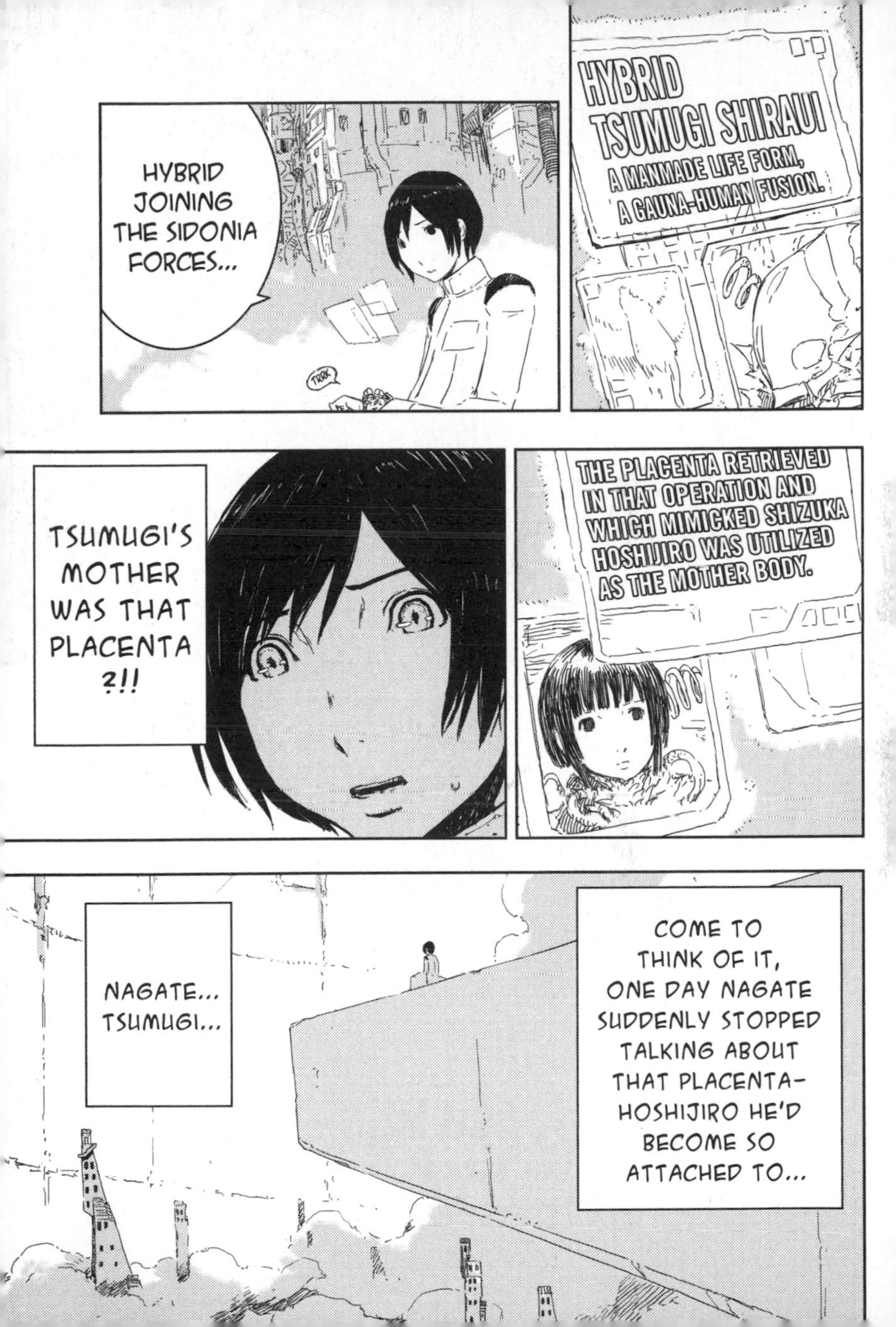
HYBRID
TSUMUGI SHIRAUI
A MANMADE LIFE FORM, A GAUNA-HUMAN FUSION.
HYBRID JOINING THE SIDONIA FORCES...
TRKK
THE PLACENTA RETRIEVED IN THAT OPERATION AND WHICH MIMICKED SHIZUKA HOSHIJIRO WAS UTILIZED AS THE MOTHER BODY.
TSUMUGI'S MOTHER WAS THAT PLACENTA ?!!
COME TO THINK OF IT, ONE DAY NAGATE SUDDENLY STOPPED TALKING ABOUT THAT PLACENTA-HOSHIJIRO HE'D BECOME SO ATTACHED TO...
NAGATE... TSUMUGI...

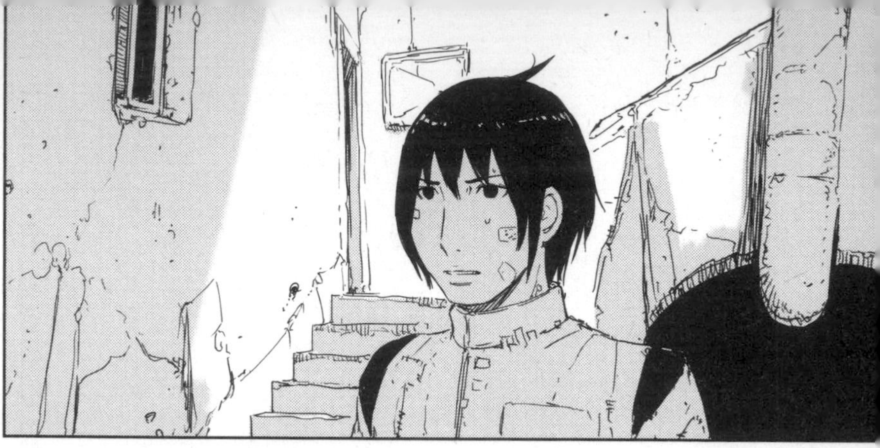

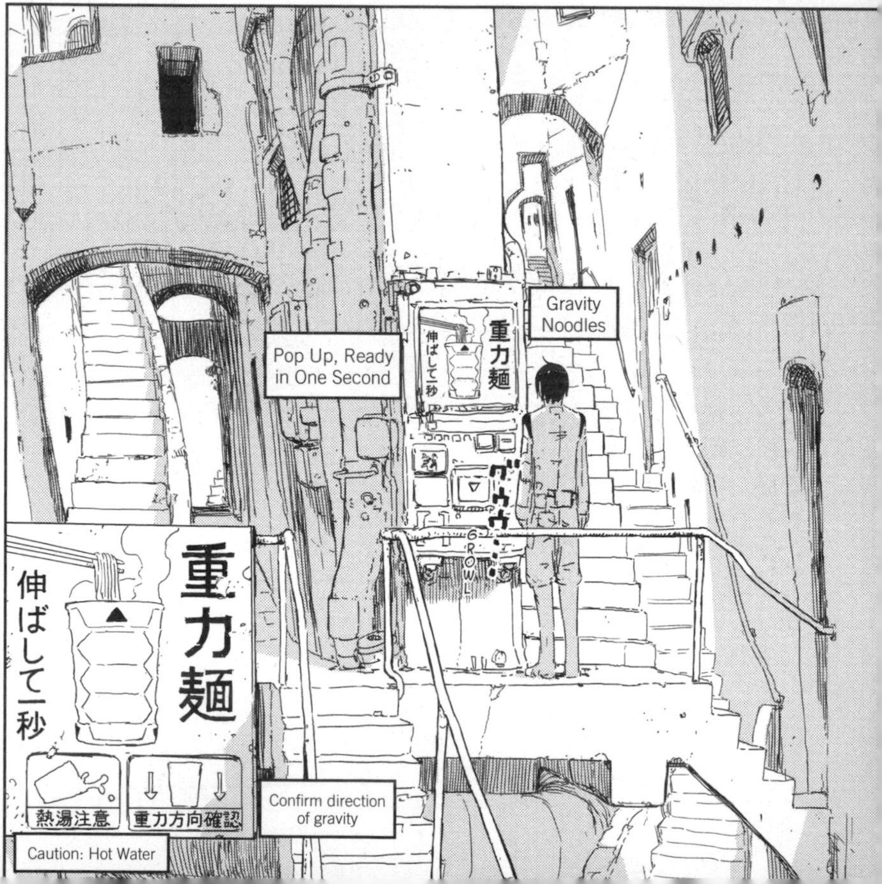
Gravity Noodles
重力麺
伸ばして一秒
Pop Up, Ready in One Second
グウウ…
GROWL
重力麺
伸ばして一秒
熱湯注意
重力方向確認
Confirm direction of gravity
Caution: Hot Water

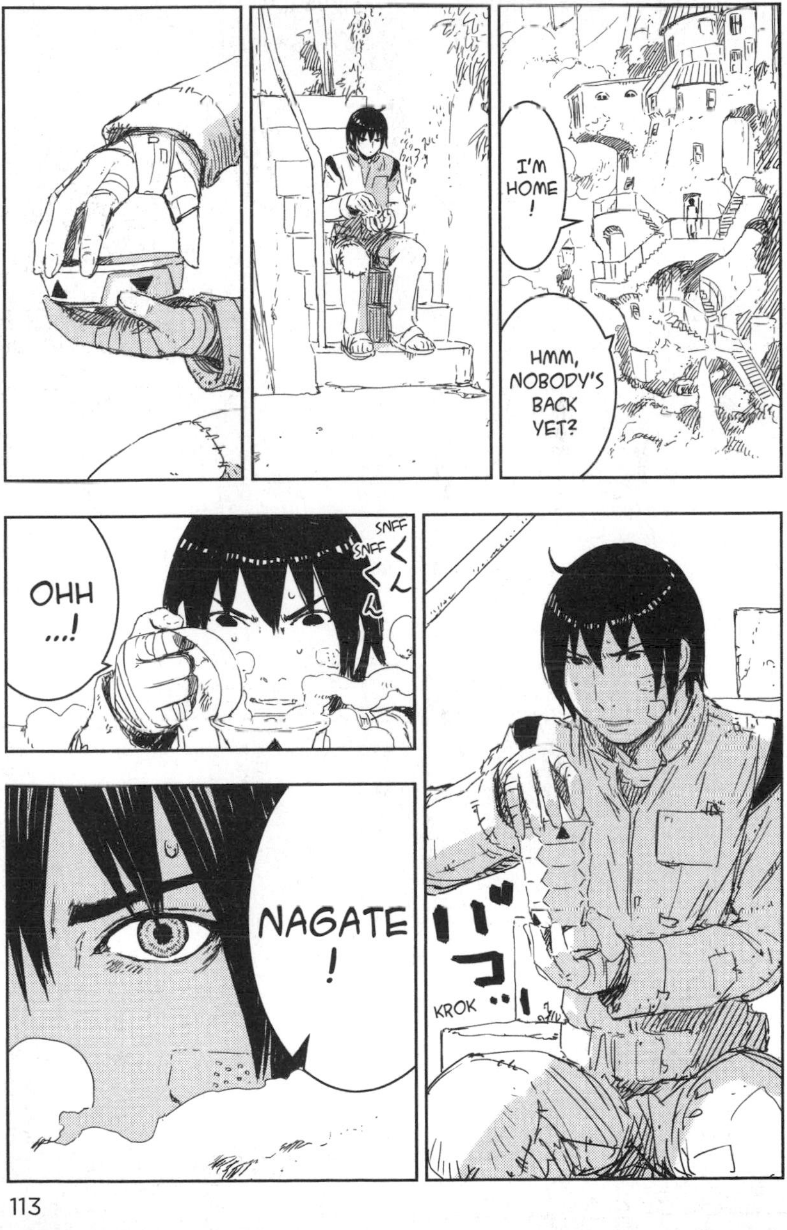
I'M HOME!
HMM, NOBODY'S BACK YET?
KROK
SNFF SNFF
くんくん
OHH ...!
NAGATE!

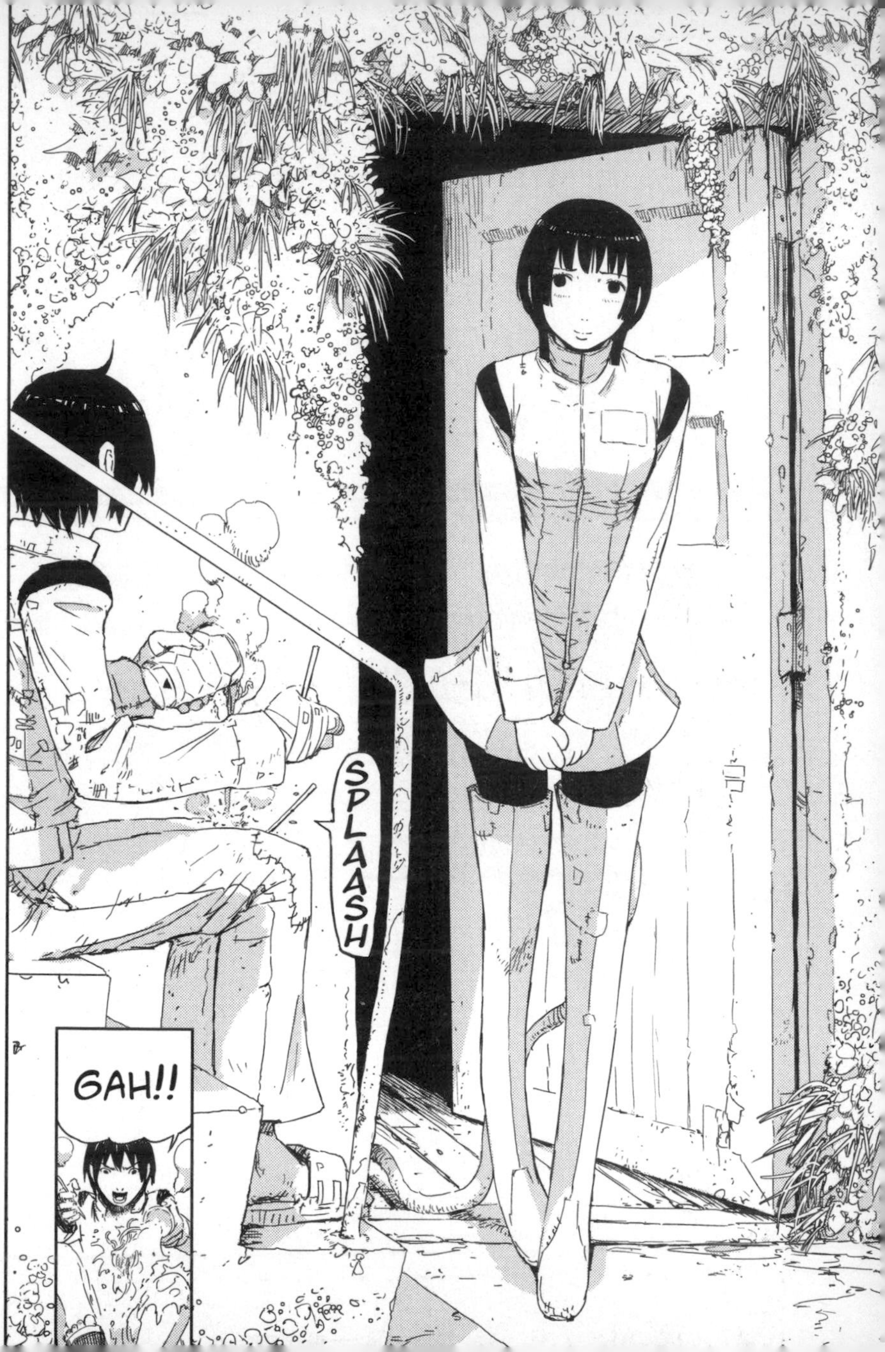
SPLAASH
GAH!!

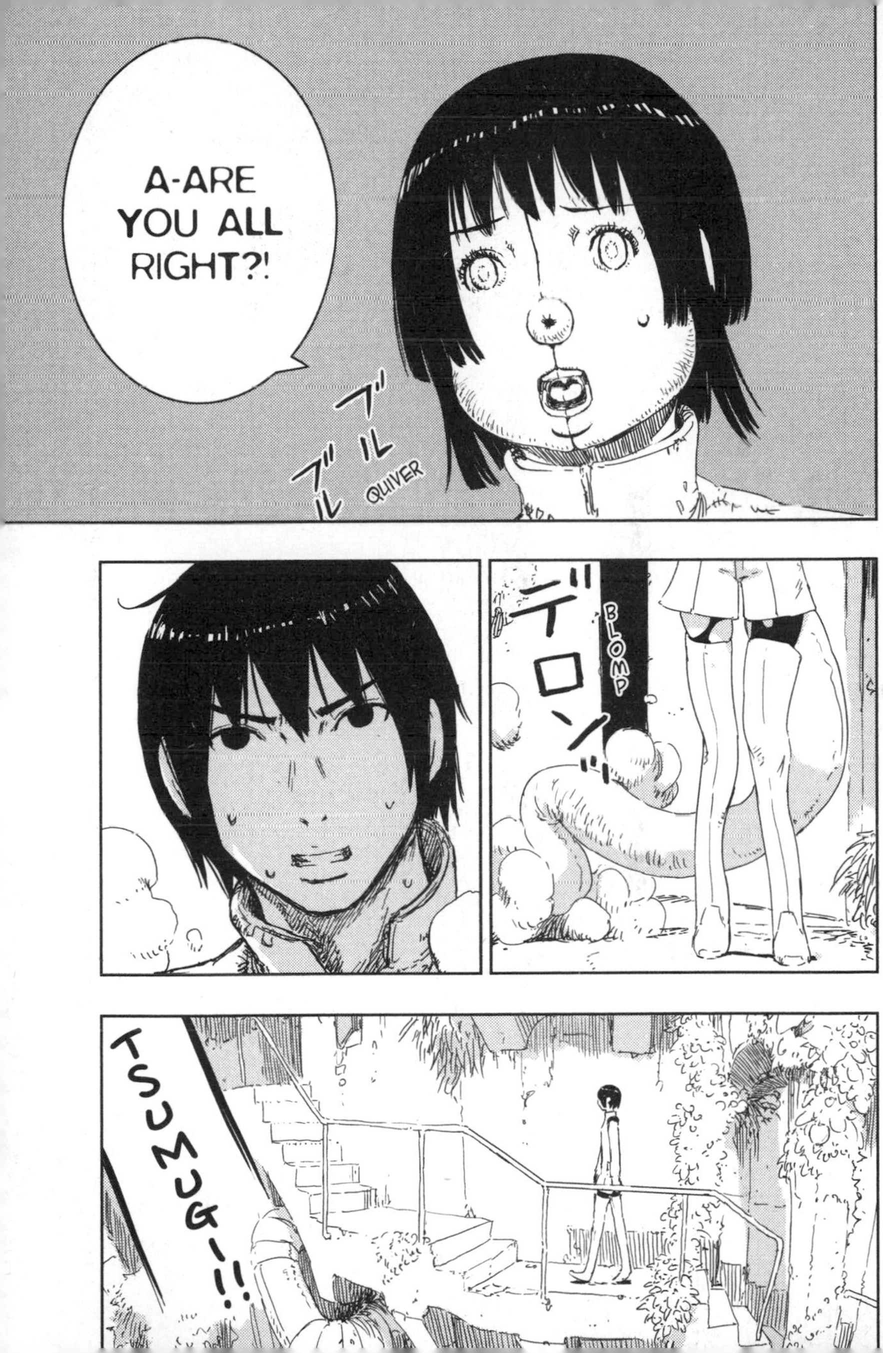
A-ARE YOU ALL RIGHT?!
ブルブル
QUIVER
デロン
BLOMP
TSUMUGI!!

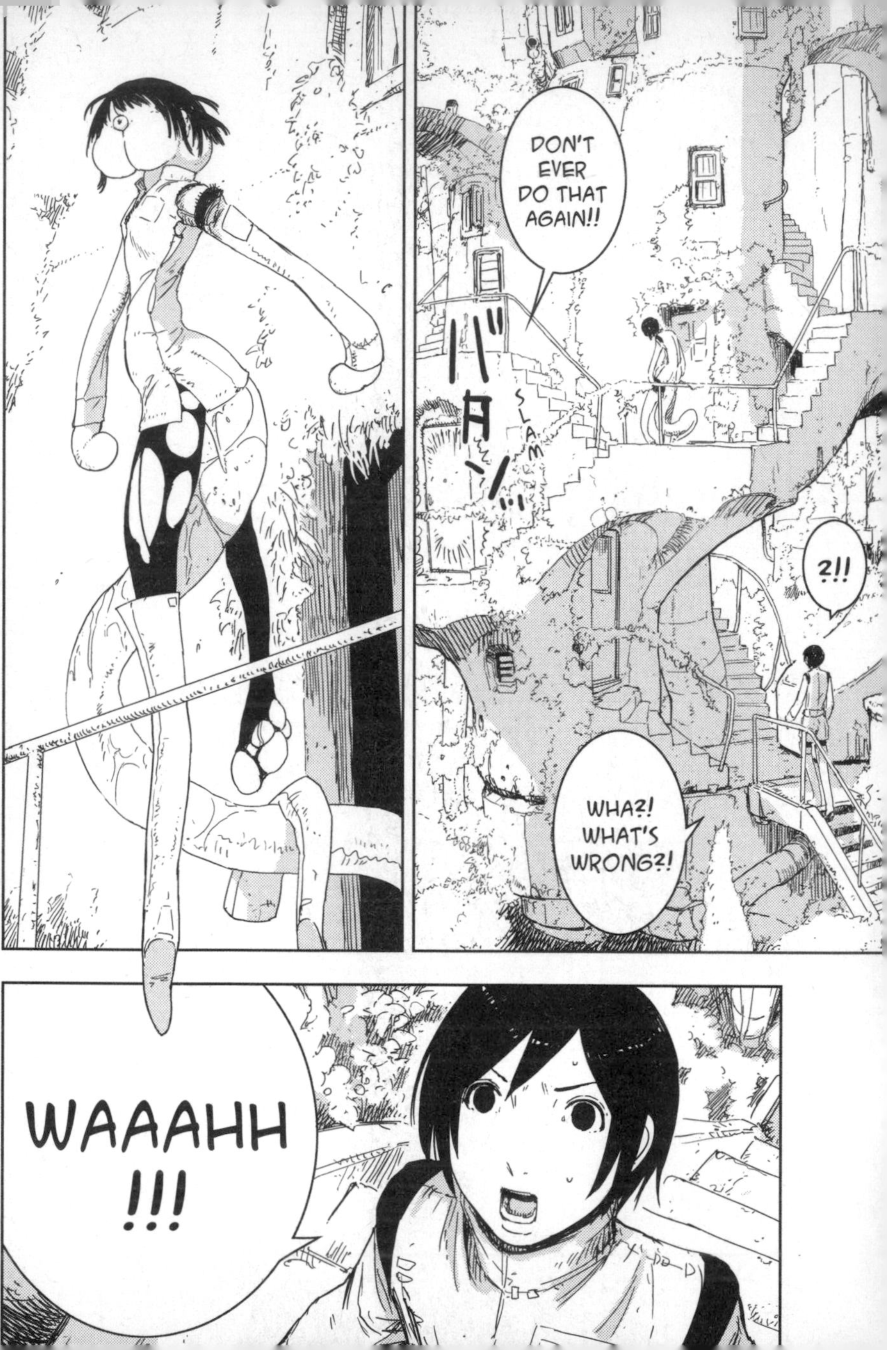
DON'T EVER DO THAT AGAIN!!
SLAM
?!!
WHA?! WHAT'S WRONG?!
WAAAHH !!!

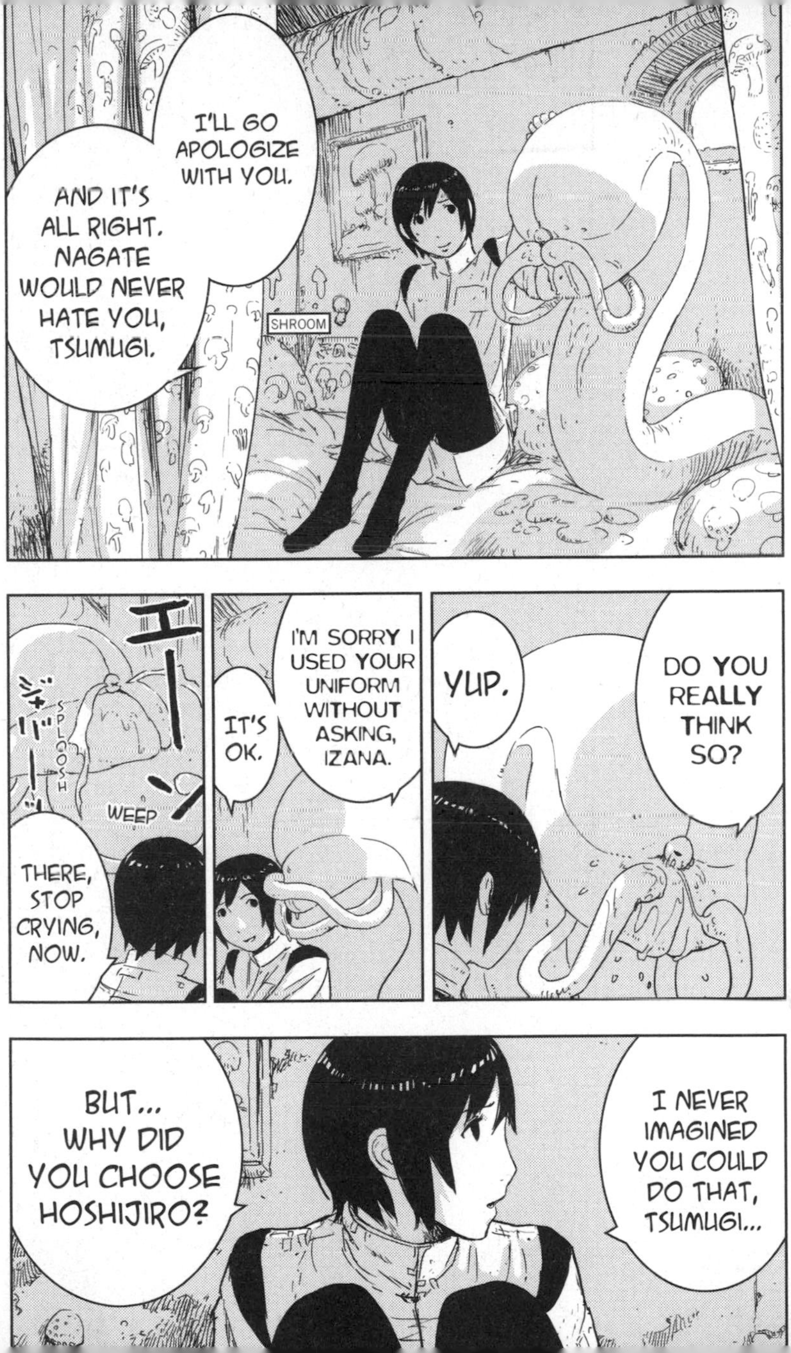
I'LL GO APOLOGIZE WITH YOU.
AND IT'S ALL RIGHT. NAGATE WOULD NEVER HATE YOU, TSUMUGI.
SHROOM
DO YOU REALLY THINK SO?
YUP.
I'M SORRY I USED YOUR UNIFORM WITHOUT ASKING, IZANA.
IT'S OK.
エーン
WEEP
ジャバー
SPLGOSH
THERE, STOP CRYING, NOW.
I NEVER IMAGINED YOU COULD DO THAT, TSUMUGI...
BUT... WHY DID YOU CHOOSE HOSHIJIRO?

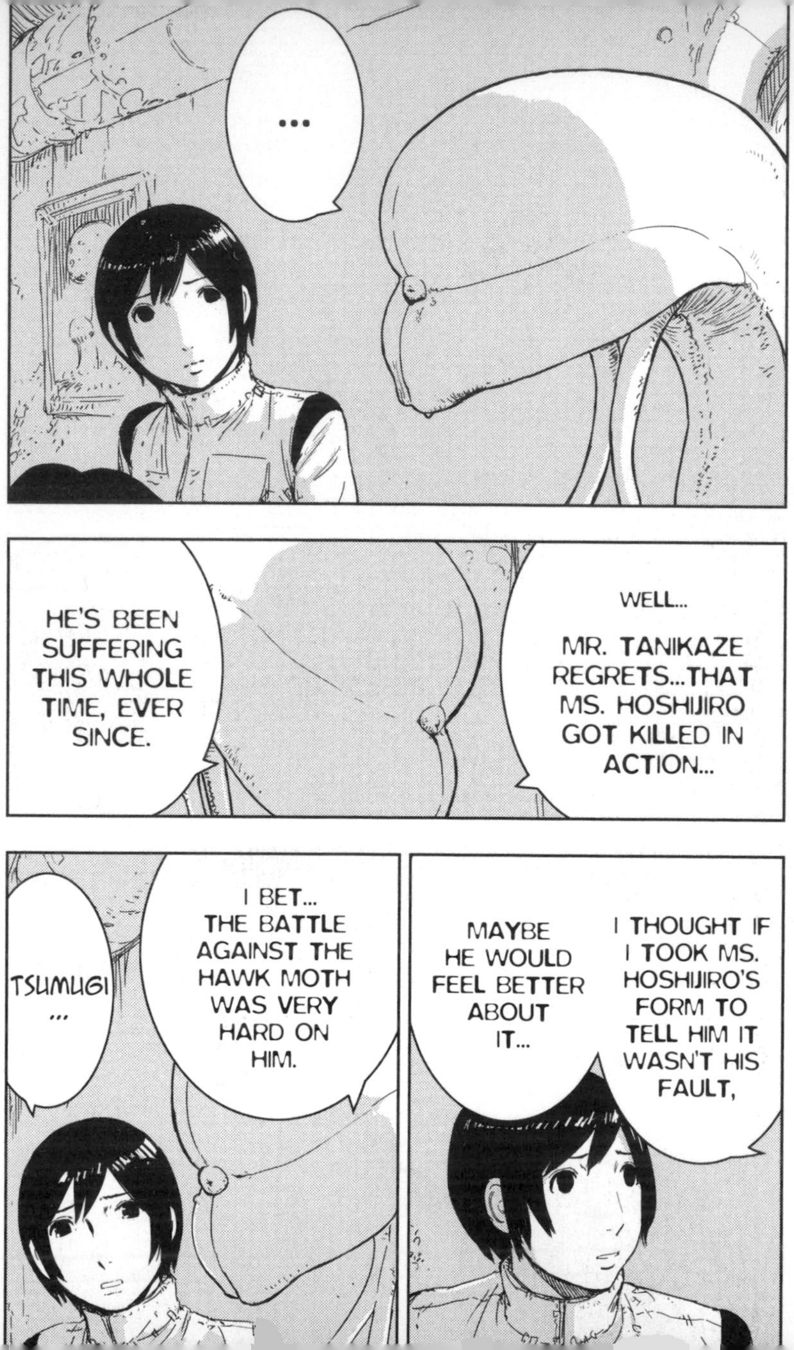
...
WELL...
MR. TANIKAZE REGRETS...THAT MS. HOSHIJIRO GOT KILLED IN ACTION...
HE'S BEEN SUFFERING THIS WHOLE TIME, EVER SINCE.
I THOUGHT IF I TOOK MS. HOSHIJIRO'S FORM TO TELL HIM IT WASN'T HIS FAULT,
MAYBE HE WOULD FEEL BETTER ABOUT IT...
I BET... THE BATTLE AGAINST THE HAWK MOTH WAS VERY HARD ON HIM.
TSUMUGI ...

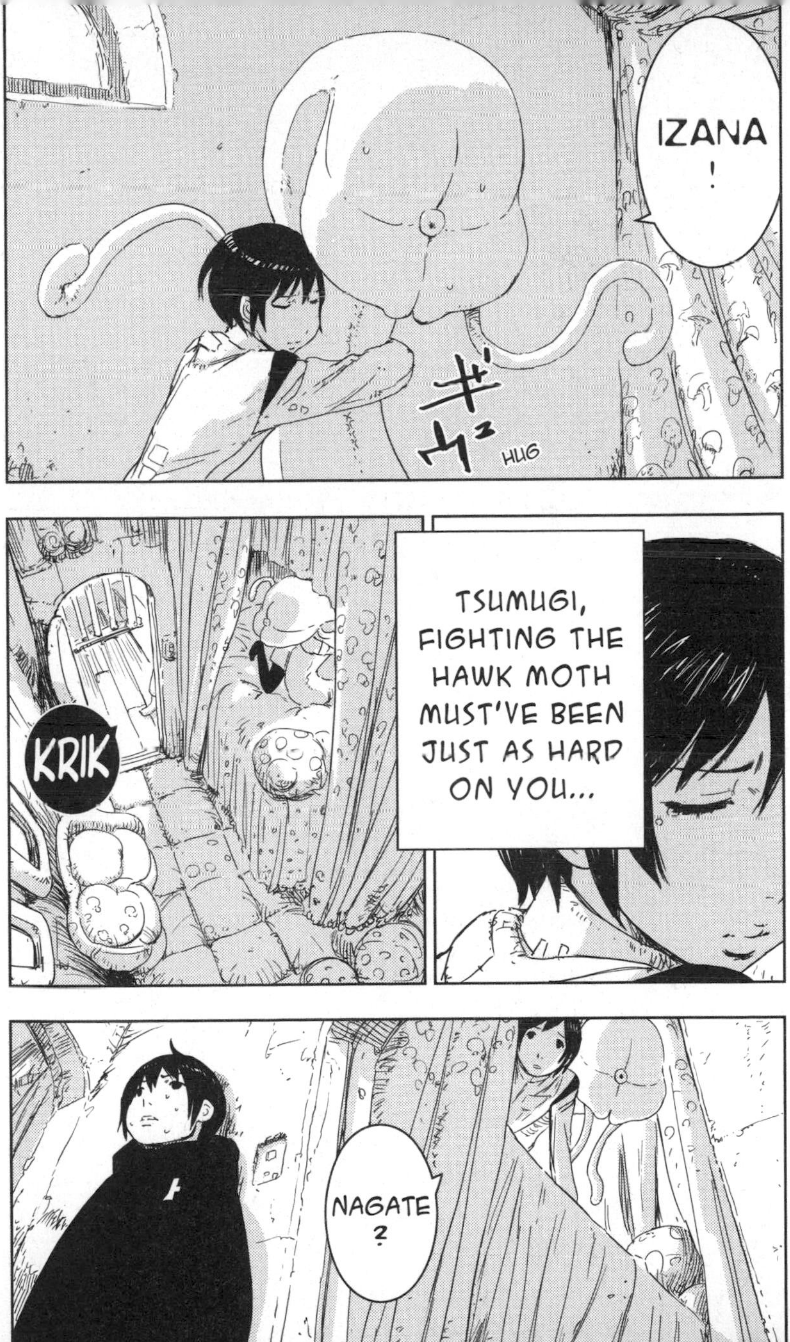
IZANA!
ギュ
HUG
TSUMUGI, FIGHTING THE HAWK MOTH MUST'VE BEEN JUST AS HARD ON YOU...
KRIK
NAGATE?

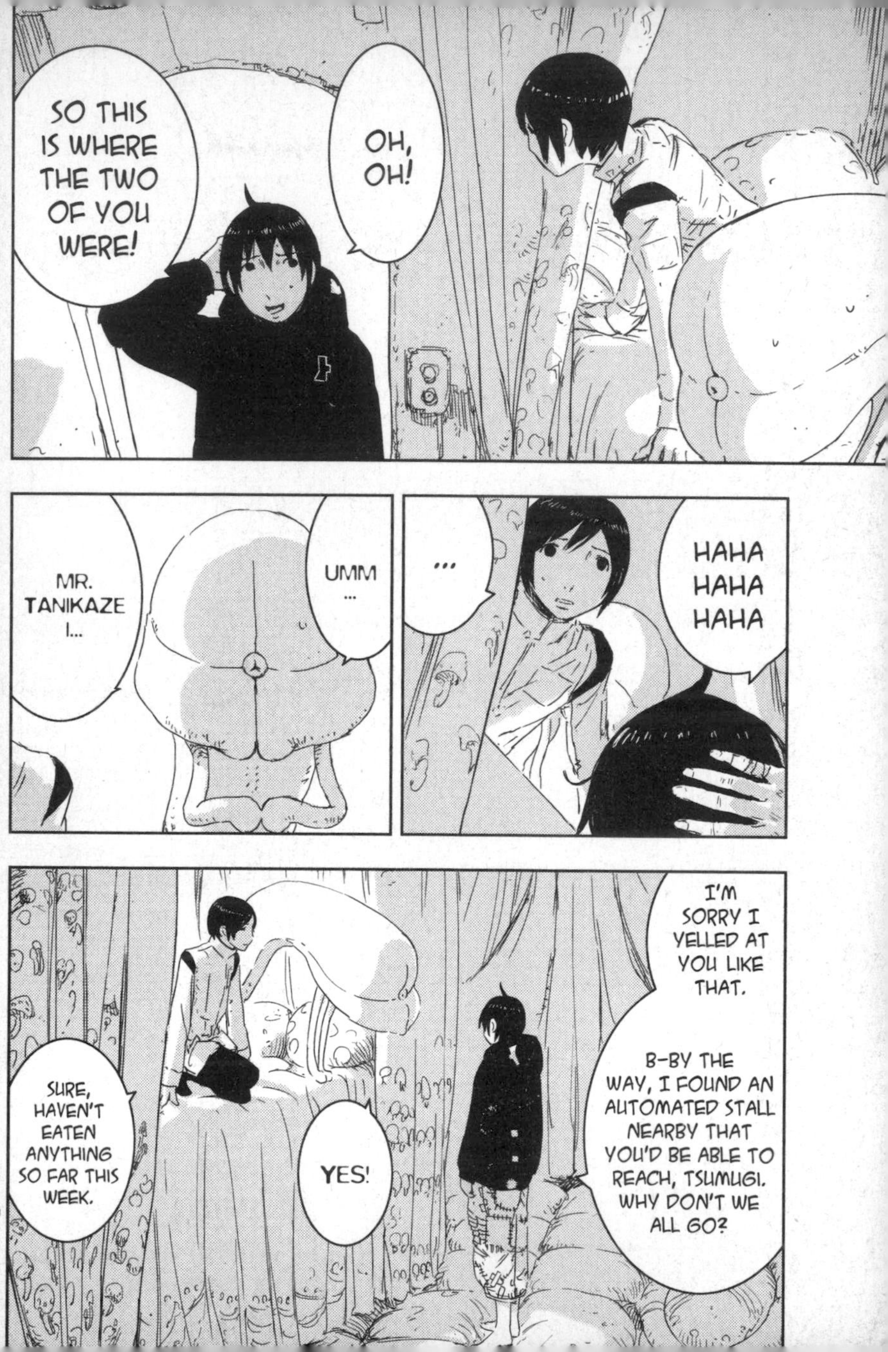
OH, OH!
SO THIS IS WHERE THE TWO OF YOU WERE!
HAHA HAHA HAHA
...
UMM ...
MR. TANIKAZE I...
I'M SORRY I YELLED AT YOU LIKE THAT.
B-BY THE WAY, I FOUND AN AUTOMATED STALL NEARBY THAT YOU'D BE ABLE TO REACH, TSUMUGI. WHY DON'T WE ALL GO?
YES!
SURE, HAVEN'T EATEN ANYTHING SO FAR THIS WEEK.

Chapter 42: END

シドニアの騎士
KNIGHTS OF SIDONIA

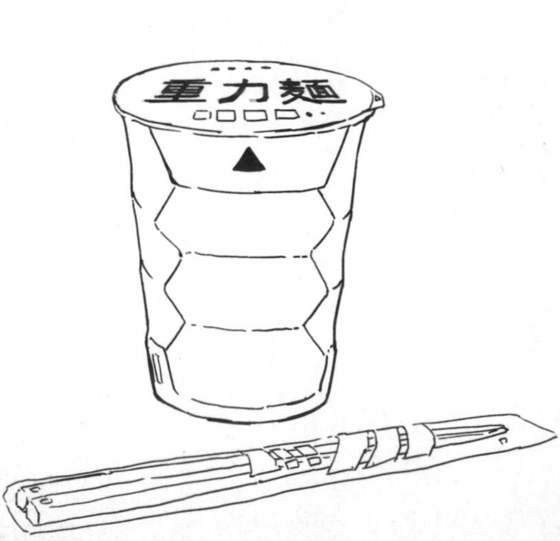
重力麺

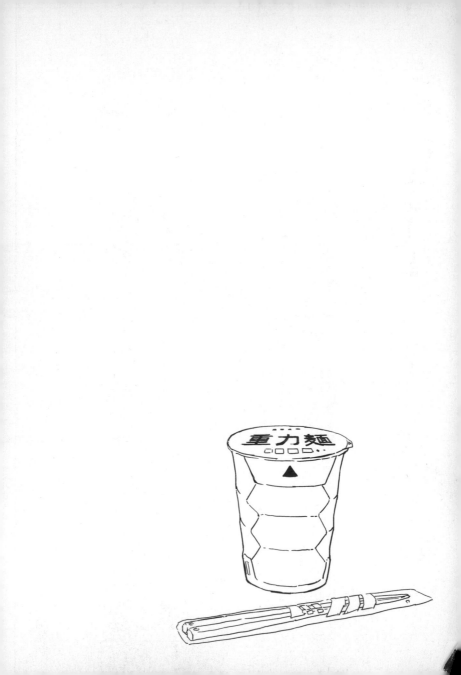

Chapter 43: Pilot Tsuruuchi's Blues

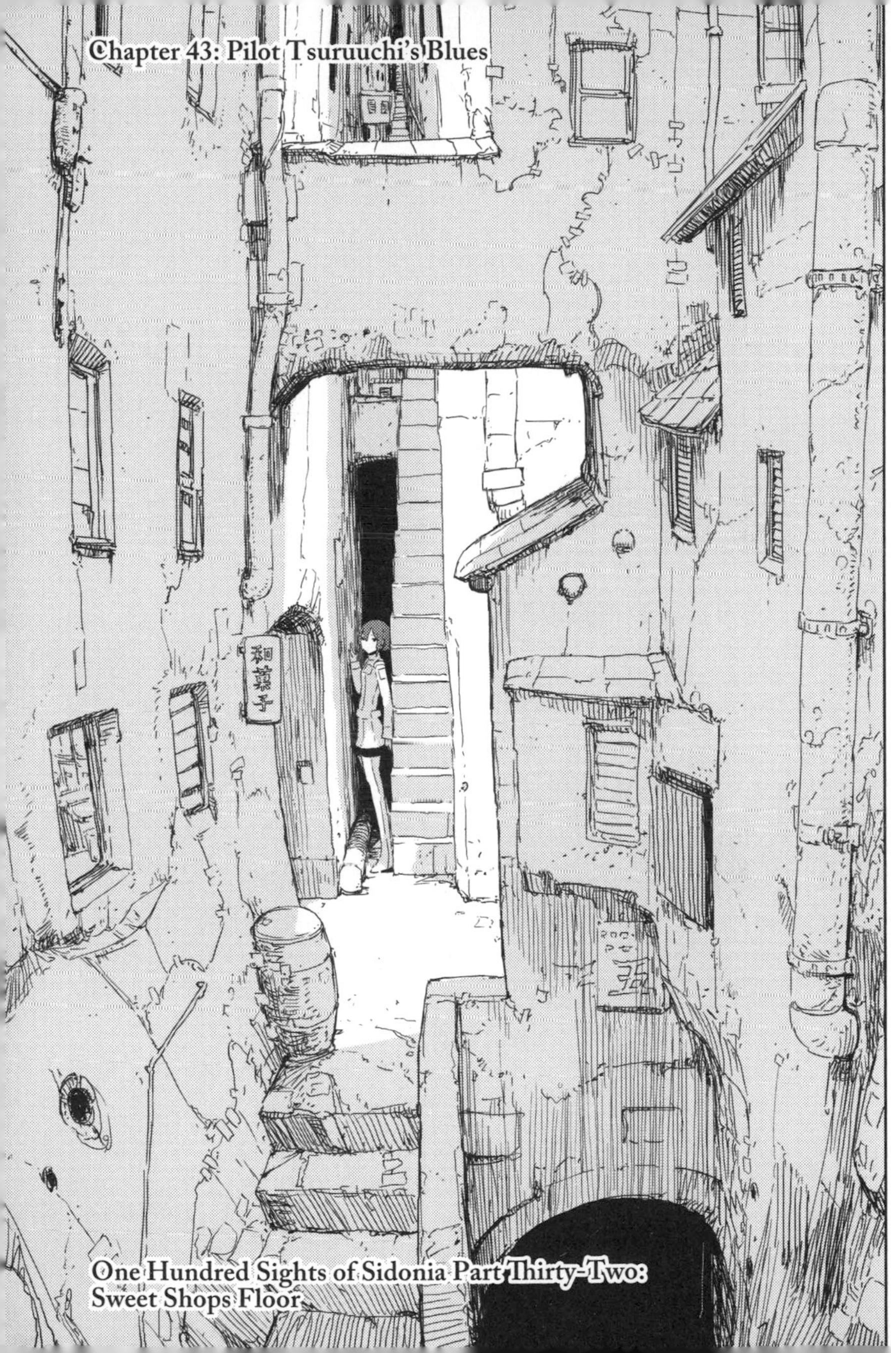
和菓子

One Hundred Sights of Sidonia Part Thirty-Two:
Sweet Shops Floor

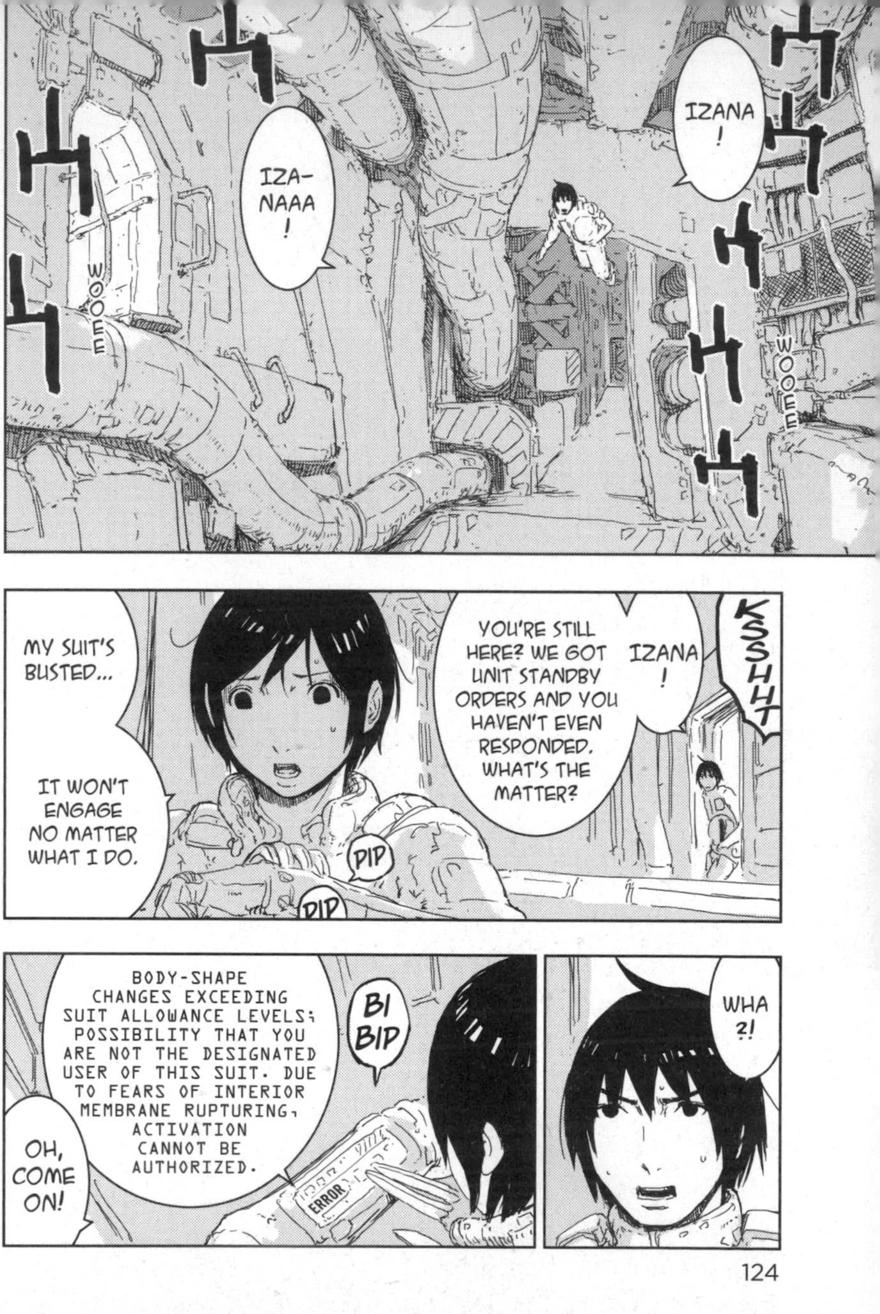
IZANA!
WOOEE
IZA-NAAA!
WOOEE
KSSHHT
IZANA!
YOU'RE STILL HERE? WE GOT UNIT STANDBY ORDERS AND YOU HAVEN'T EVEN RESPONDED. WHAT'S THE MATTER?
MY SUIT'S BUSTED...
IT WON'T ENGAGE NO MATTER WHAT I DO.
PIP
PIP
WHA?!
BI BIP
BODY-SHAPE CHANGES EXCEEDING SUIT ALLOWANCE LEVELS; POSSIBILITY THAT YOU ARE NOT THE DESIGNATED USER OF THIS SUIT. DUE TO FEARS OF INTERIOR MEMBRANE RUPTURING, ACTIVATION CANNOT BE AUTHORIZED.
ERROR
OH, COME ON!

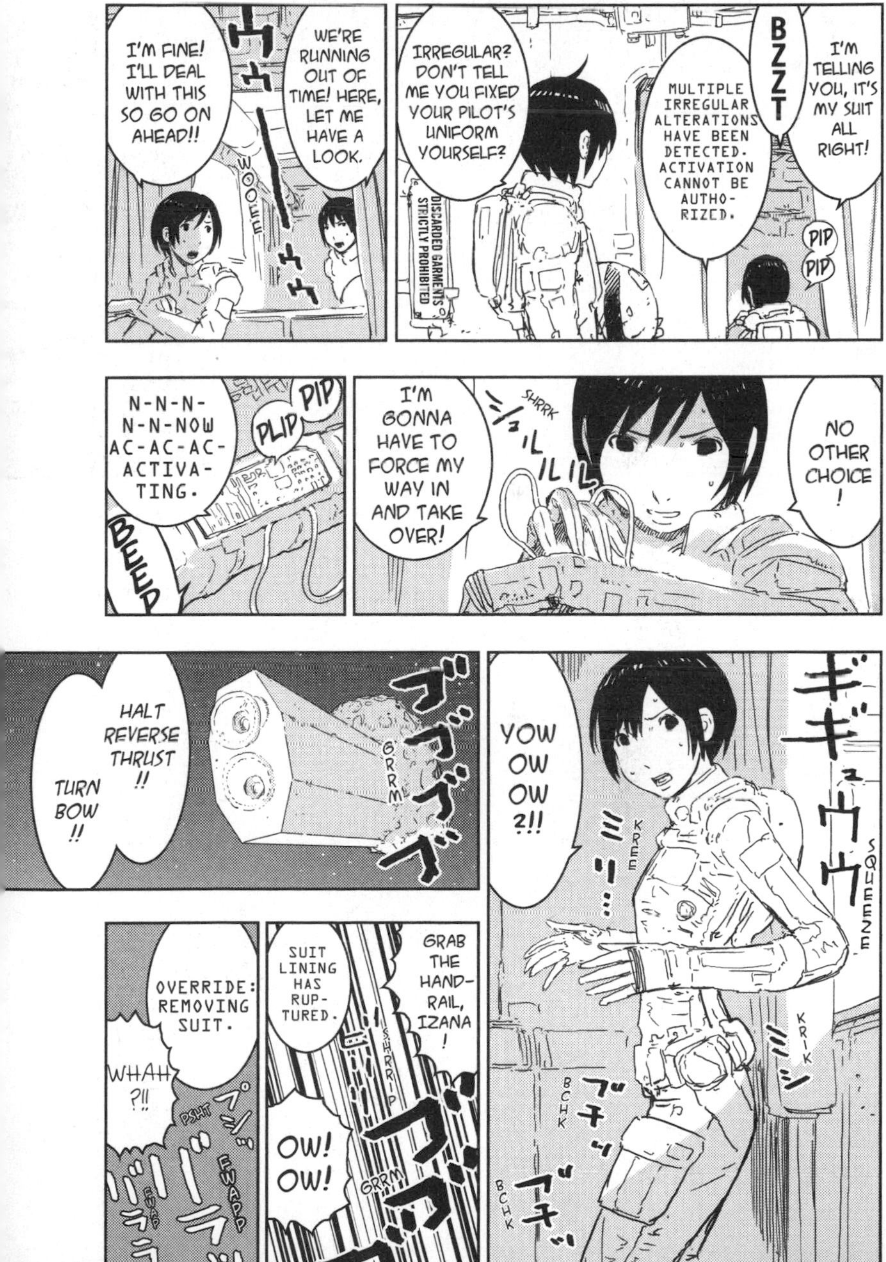
I'M TELLING YOU, IT'S MY SUIT ALL RIGHT!
BZZT
MULTIPLE IRREGULAR ALTERATIONS HAVE BEEN DETECTED. ACTIVATION CANNOT BE AUTHORIZED.
PIP PIP
IRREGULAR? DON'T TELL ME YOU FIXED YOUR PILOT'S UNIFORM YOURSELF?
DISCARDED GARMENTS STRICTLY PROHIBITED
WE'RE RUNNING OUT OF TIME! HERE, LET ME HAVE A LOOK.
WOOEE
I'M FINE! I'LL DEAL WITH THIS SO GO ON AHEAD!!
NO OTHER CHOICE!
SHRRK
I'M GONNA HAVE TO FORCE MY WAY IN AND TAKE OVER!
PIP
PLIP
N-N-N-N-N-NOW AC-AC-AC-ACTIVATING.
BEEEP
YOW OW OW?!!
KREE
SQUEEZE
KRIK
BCHK
BCHK
GRRM
HALT REVERSE THRUST!!
TURN BOW!!
GRAB THE HANDRAIL, IZANA!
SUIT LINING HAS RUPTURED.
SHRRIP
OW! OW!
GRRM
OVERRIDE: REMOVING SUIT.
WHAH?!!
PSHT
FWAPP
FWAP

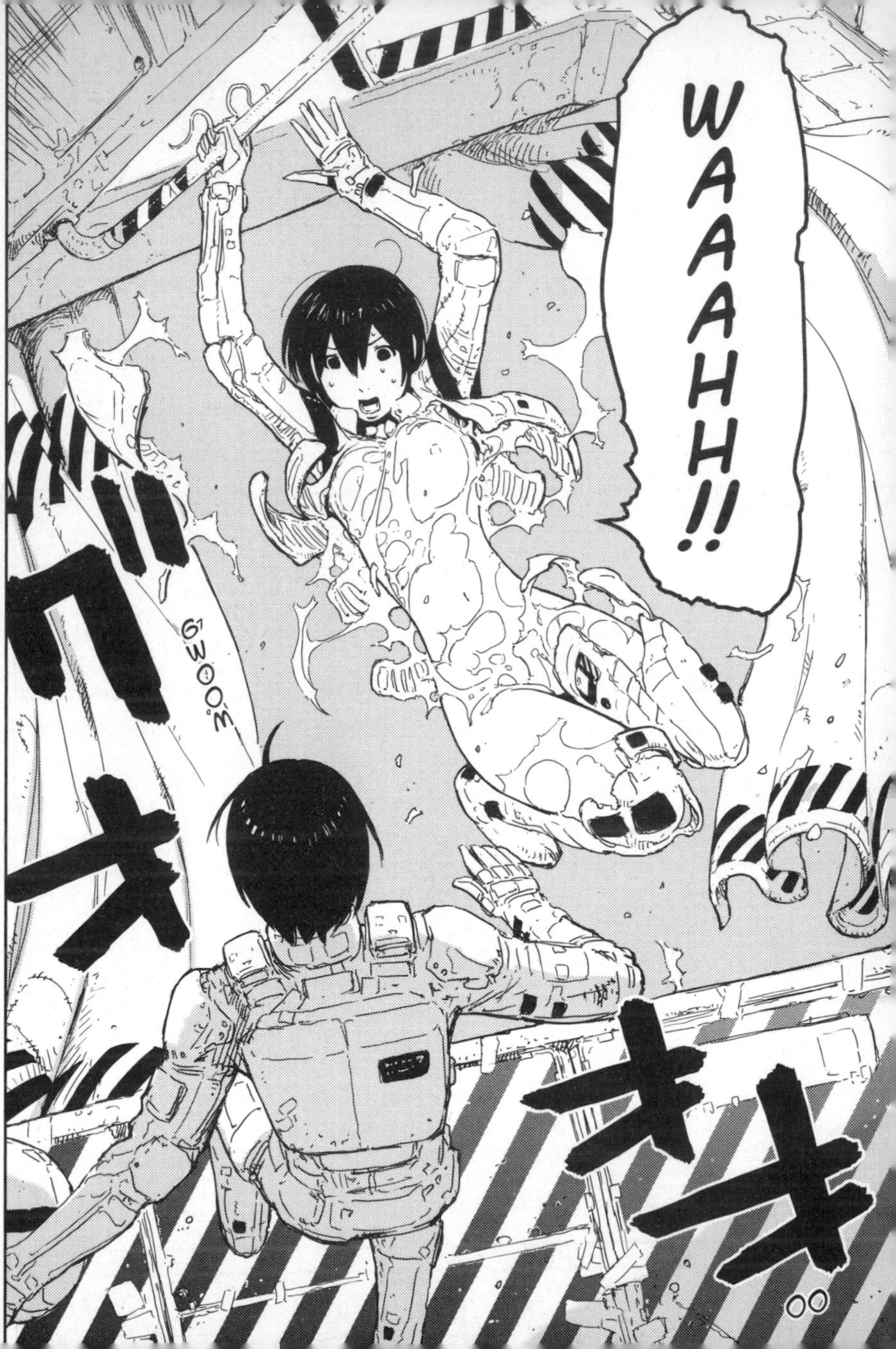
WAAAAHH!!
GWOOM

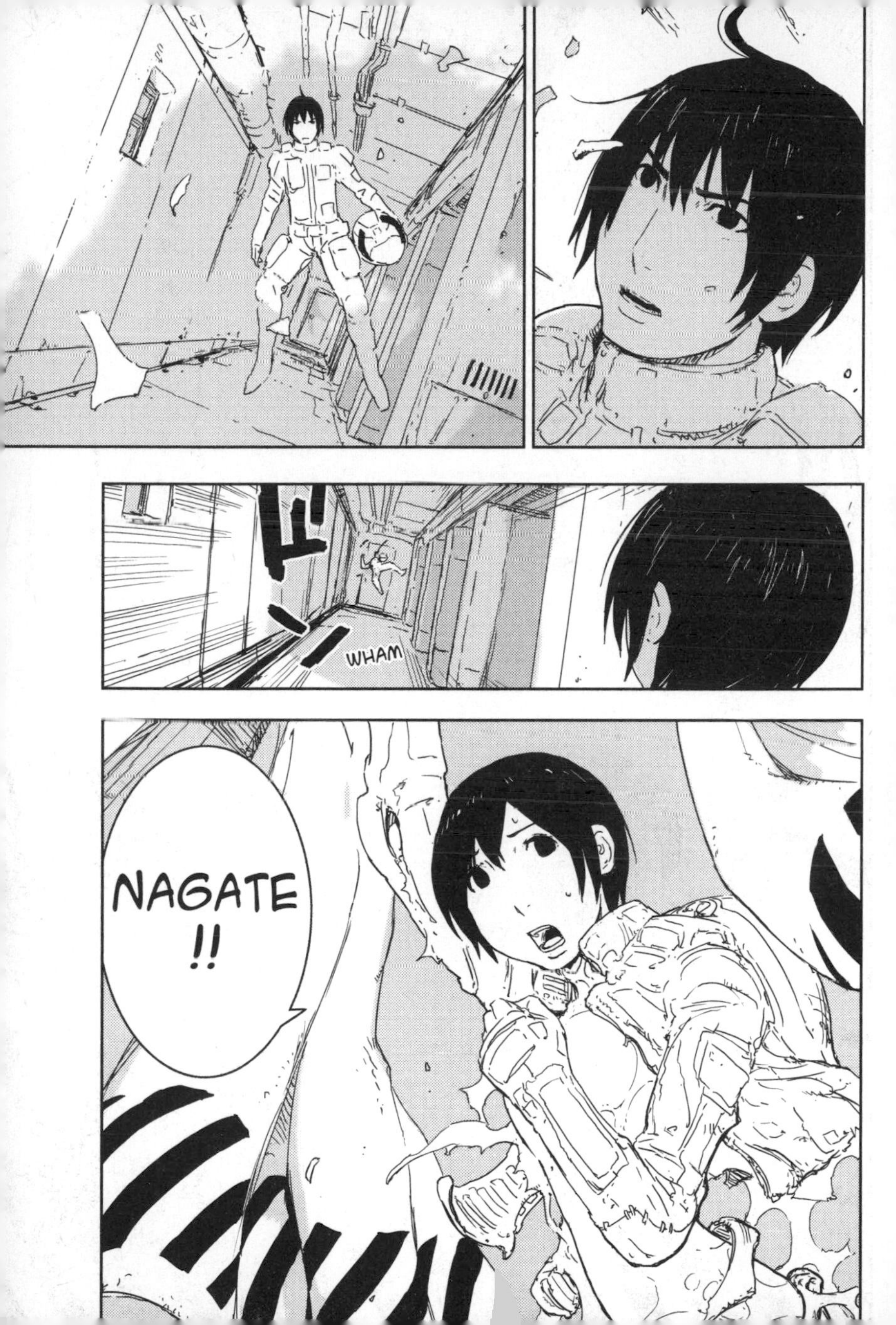
WHAM
NAGATE !!

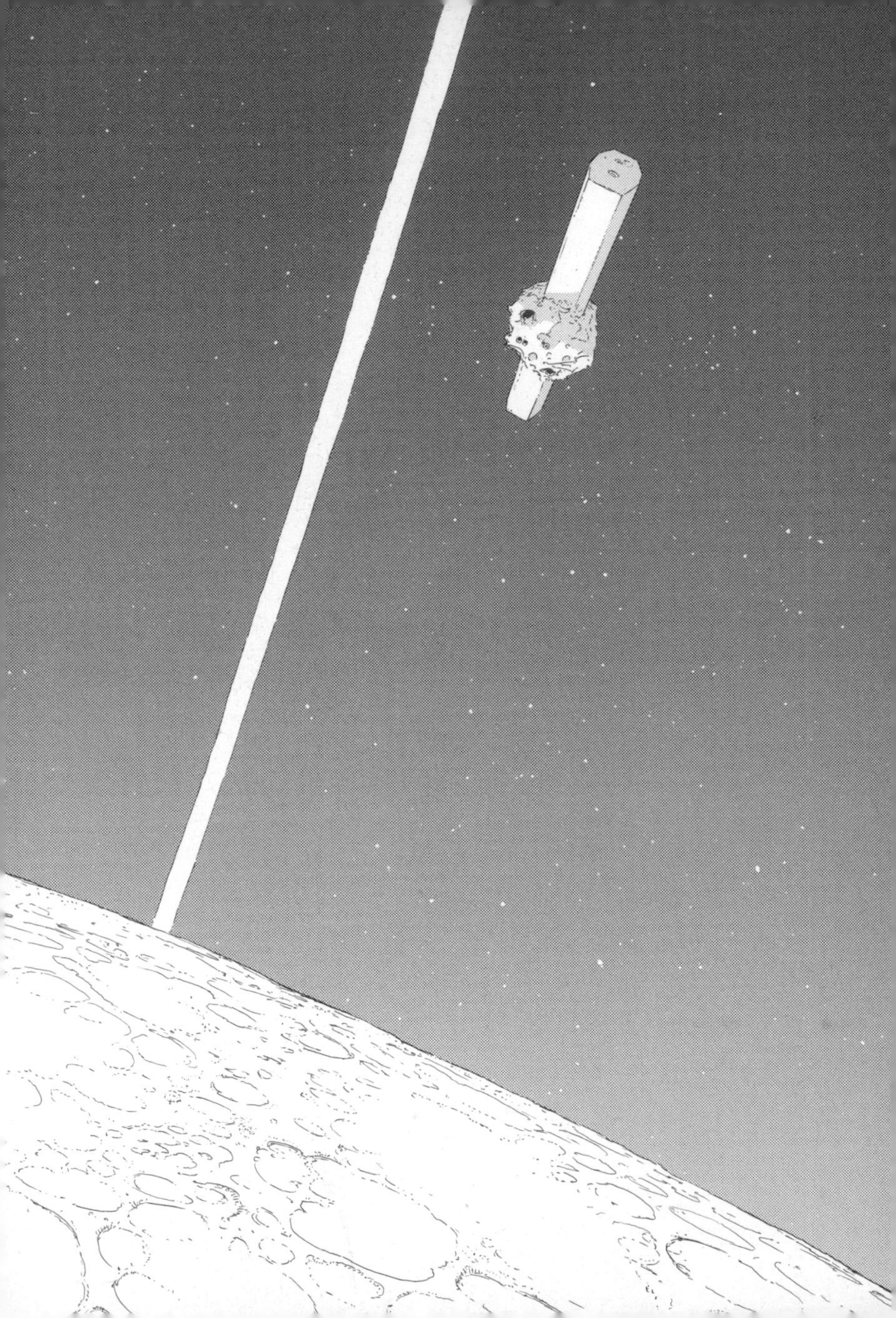

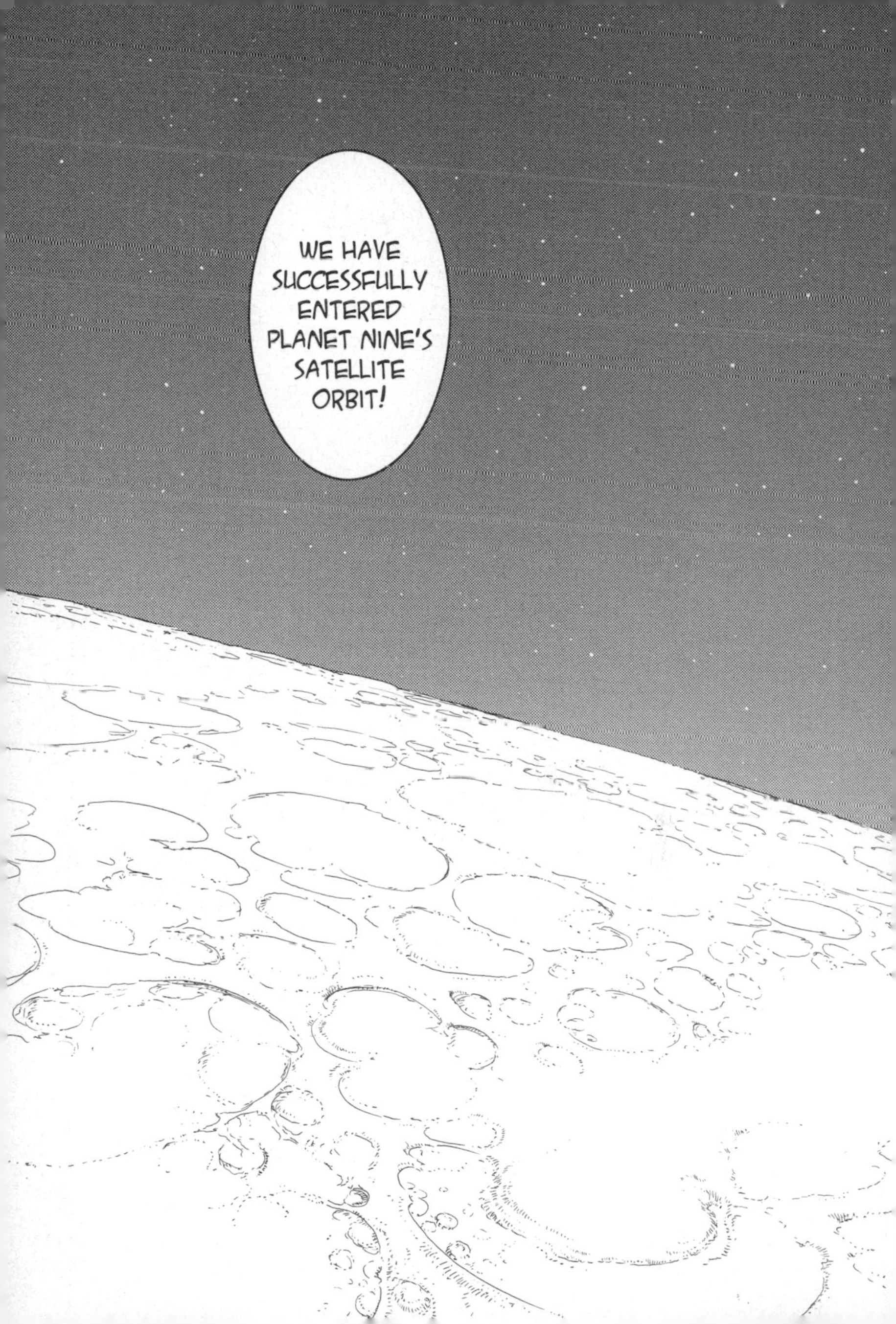
WE HAVE SUCCESSFULLY ENTERED PLANET NINE'S SATELLITE ORBIT!

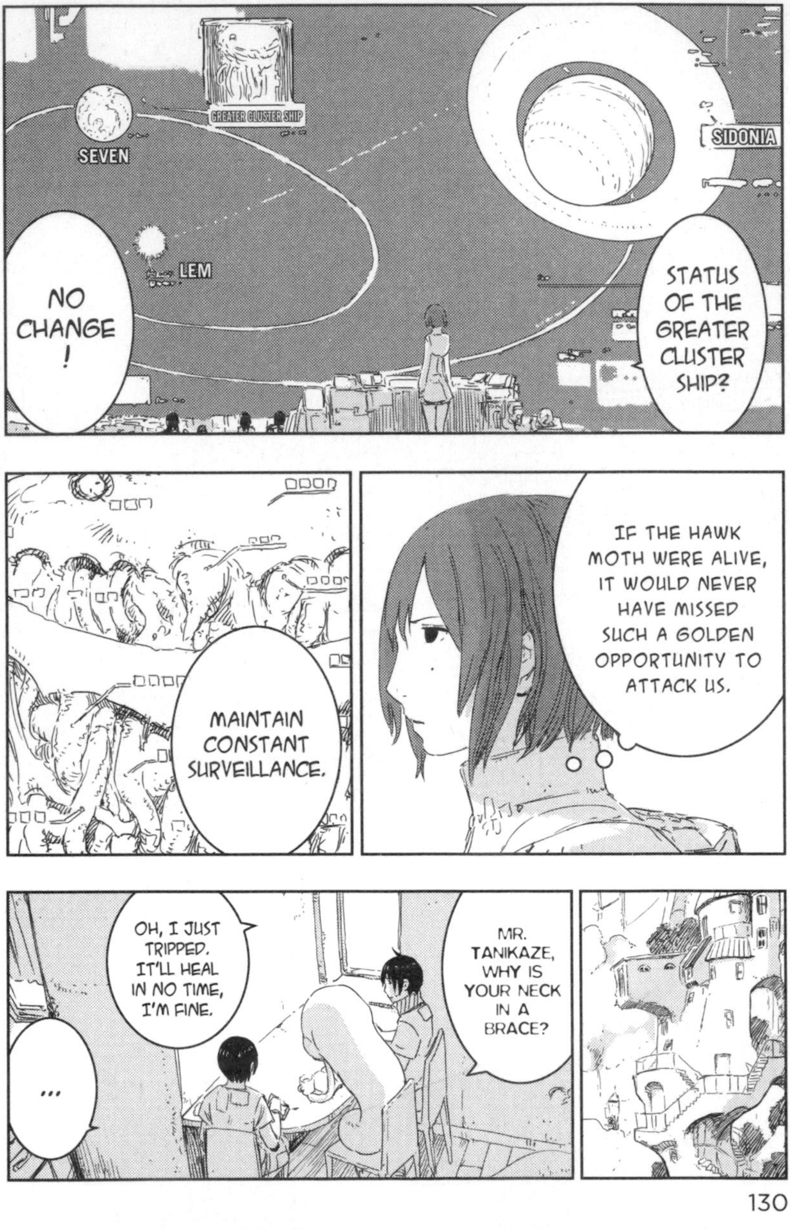
SIDONIA
GREATER CLUSTER SHIP
SEVEN
STATUS OF THE GREATER CLUSTER SHIP?
LEM
NO CHANGE!
IF THE HAWK MOTH WERE ALIVE, IT WOULD NEVER HAVE MISSED SUCH A GOLDEN OPPORTUNITY TO ATTACK US.
MAINTAIN CONSTANT SURVEILLANCE.
MR. TANIKAZE, WHY IS YOUR NECK IN A BRACE?
OH, I JUST TRIPPED. IT'LL HEAL IN NO TIME, I'M FINE.
...

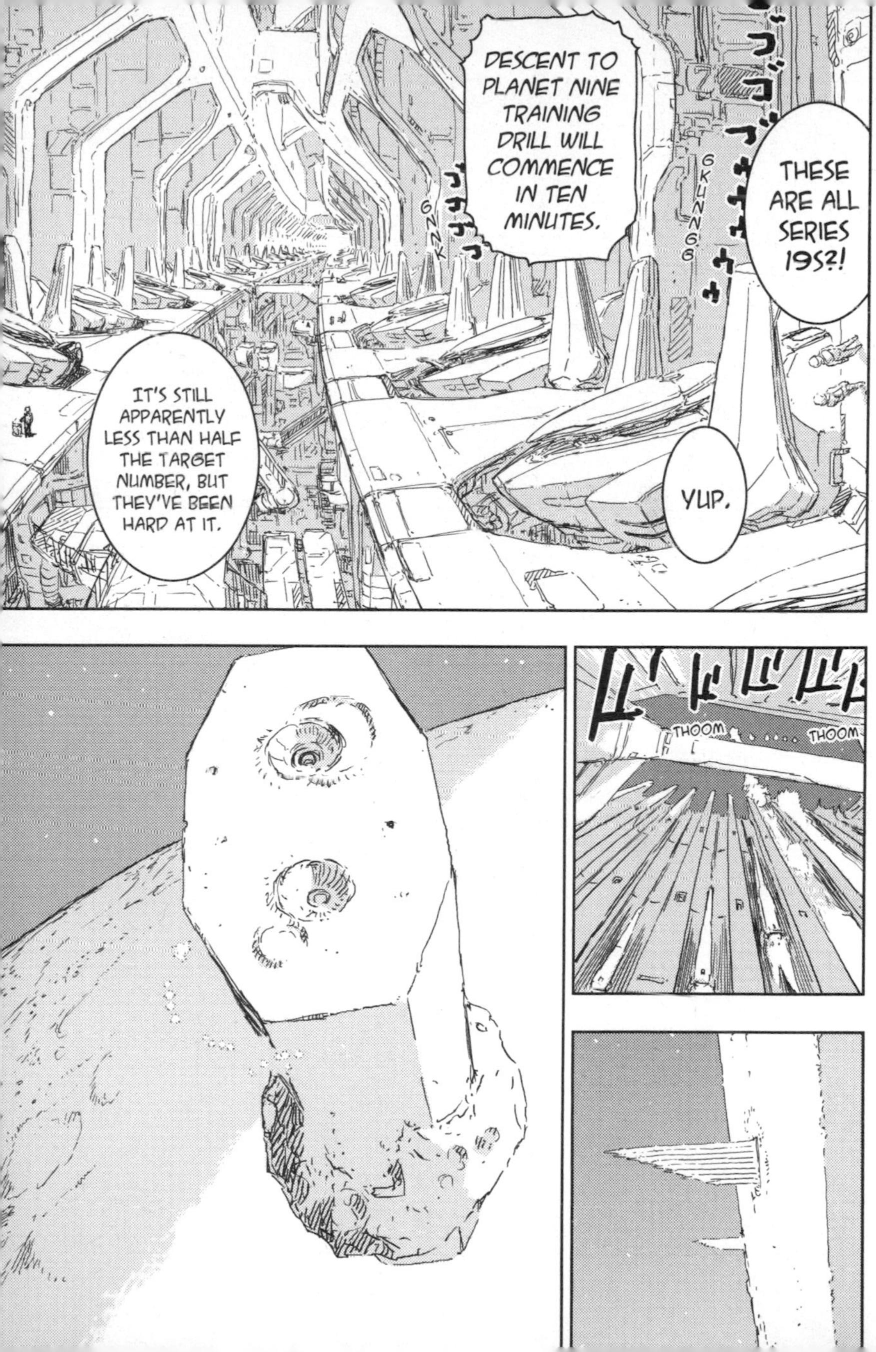
DESCENT TO PLANET NINE TRAINING DRILL WILL COMMENCE IN TEN MINUTES.
GKUNNGG
GNNK
THESE ARE ALL SERIES 19S?!
YUP.
IT'S STILL APPARENTLY LESS THAN HALF THE TARGET NUMBER, BUT THEY'VE BEEN HARD AT IT.
THOOM
THOOM

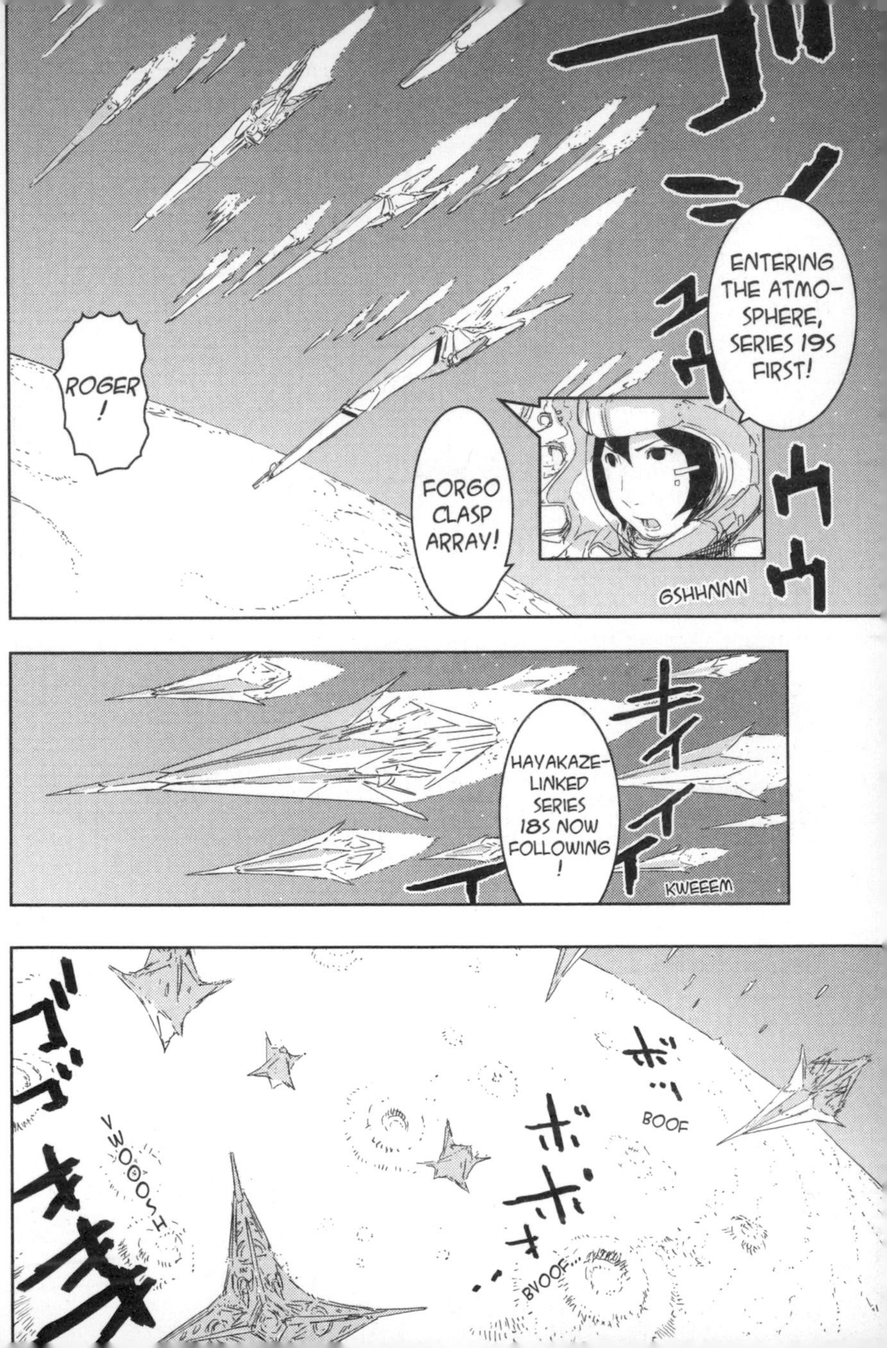
ENTERING THE ATMO-SPHERE, SERIES 19S FIRST!
FORGO CLASP ARRAY!
GSHHNNN
ROGER!
HAYAKAZE-LINKED SERIES 18S NOW FOLLOWING!
KWEEEM
BOOF
BVOOF...
VWOOOSH

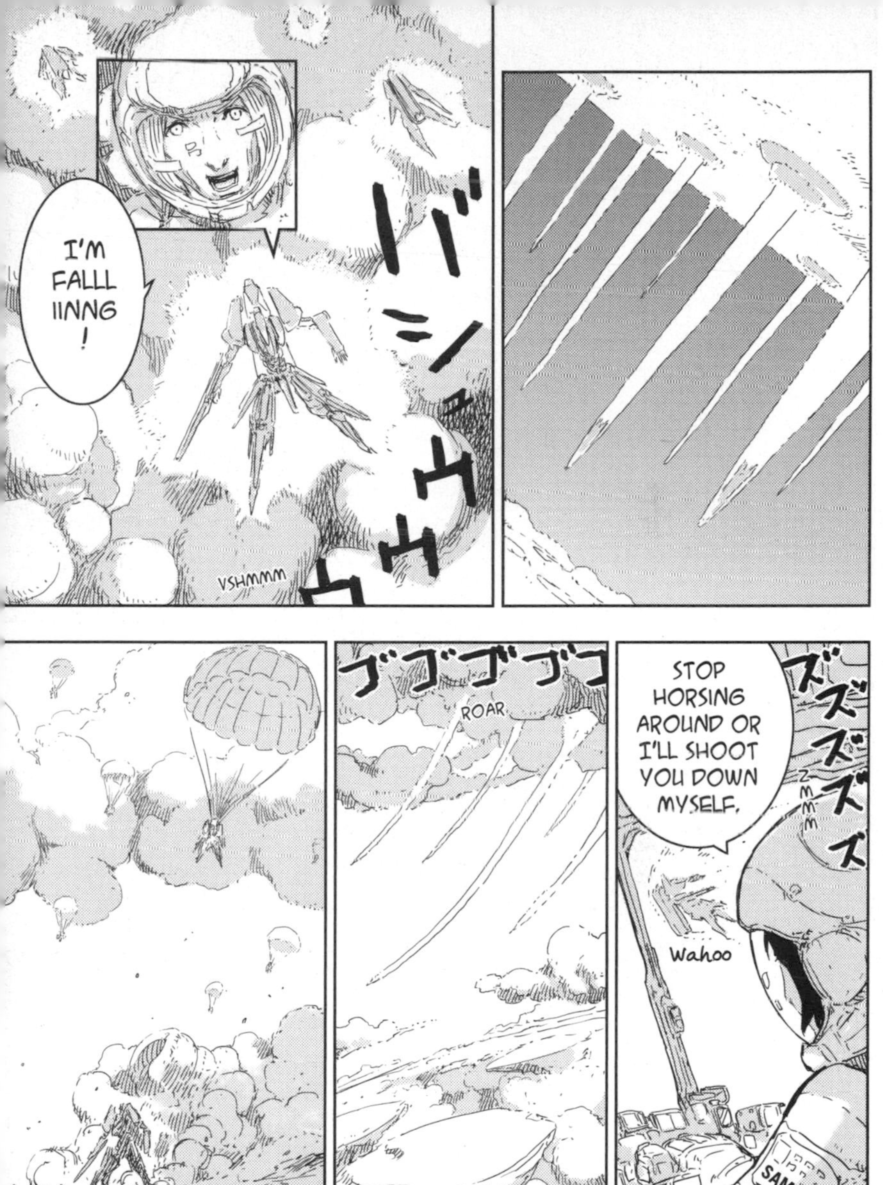
I'M FALLL IINNG!
VSHMMM
STOP HORSING AROUND OR I'LL SHOOT YOU DOWN MYSELF.
ZMMM
Wahoo
SAMARI
ROAR

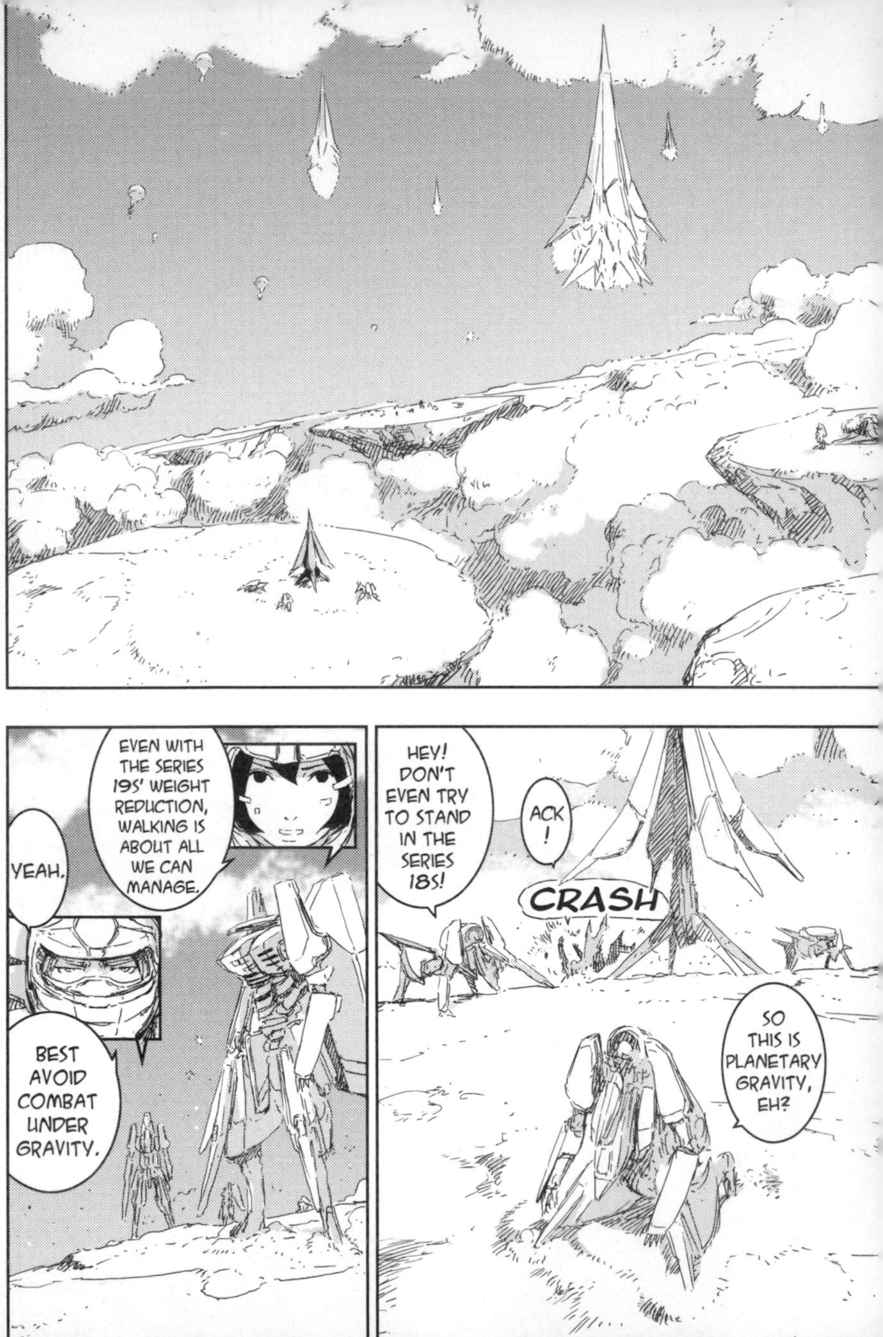
HEY! DON'T EVEN TRY TO STAND IN THE SERIES 18S!
ACK!
CRASH
SO THIS IS PLANETARY GRAVITY, EH?
EVEN WITH THE SERIES 19S' WEIGHT REDUCTION, WALKING IS ABOUT ALL WE CAN MANAGE.
YEAH.
BEST AVOID COMBAT UNDER GRAVITY.

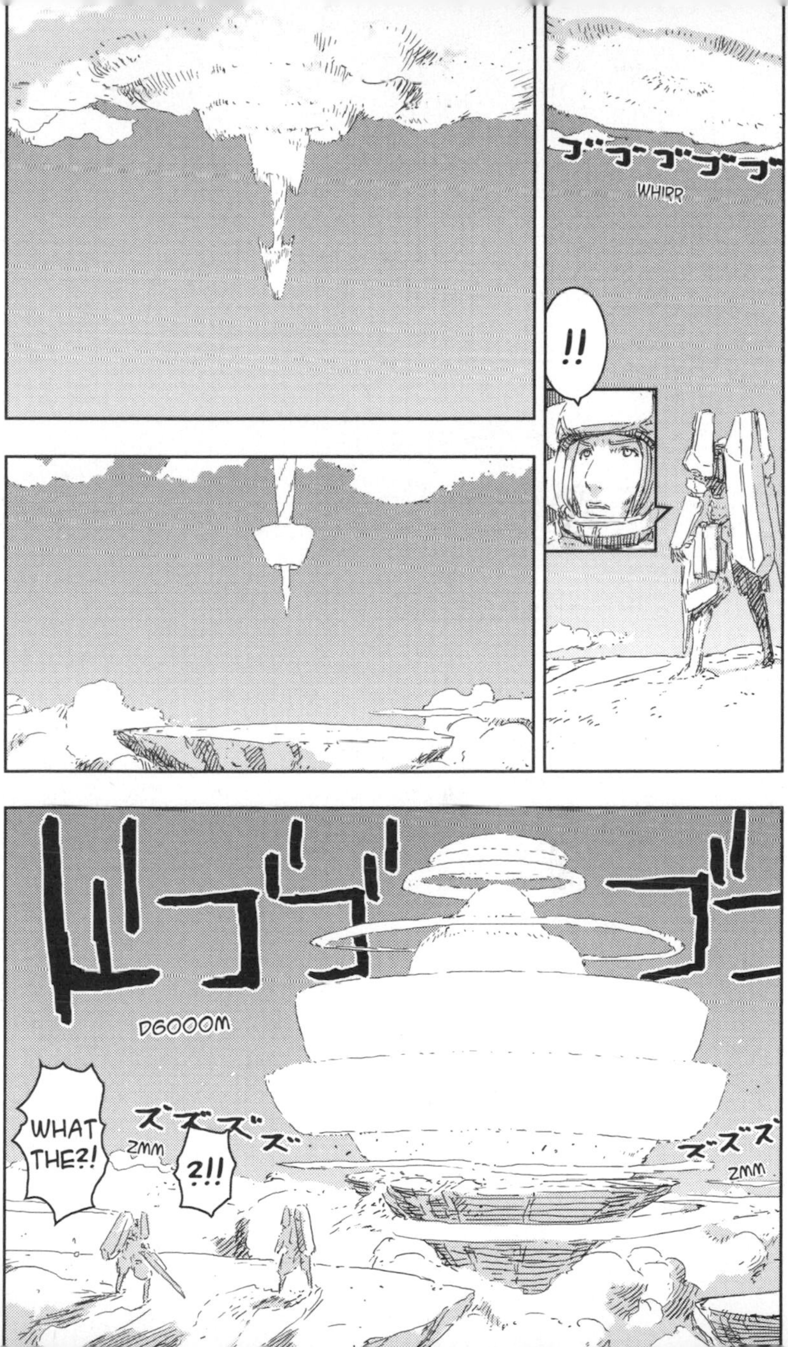
ゴゴゴゴゴ
WHIRR
!!
ドゴゴゴー
DGOOOM
ズズズ
ZMM
?!!
ズズズズ
ZMM
WHAT THE?!

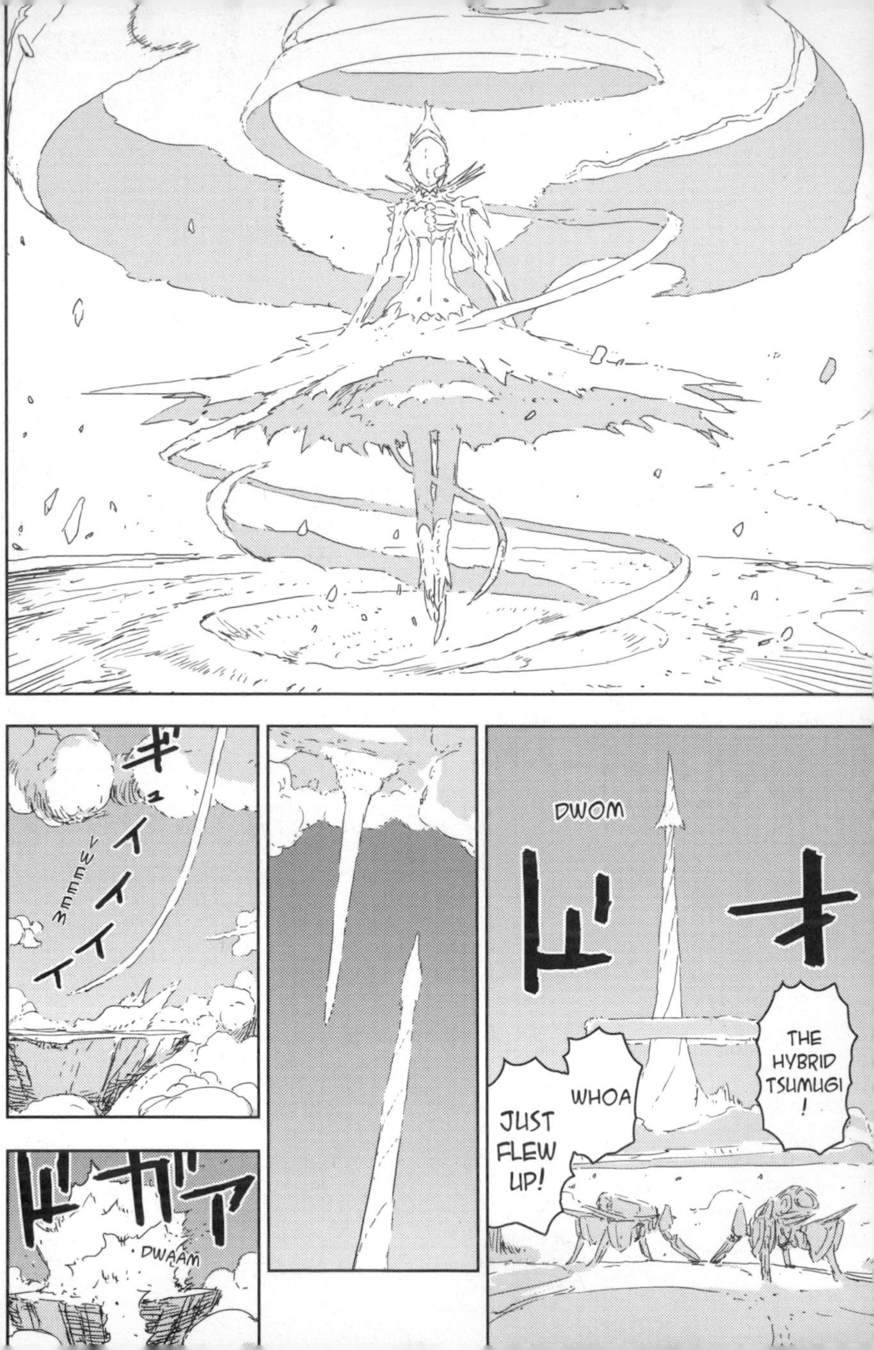
DWOM
ドオ
THE HYBRID TSUMUGI!
WHOA
JUST FLEW UP!
ギュイイイイ
VWEEEEW
ドガァ
DWAAM

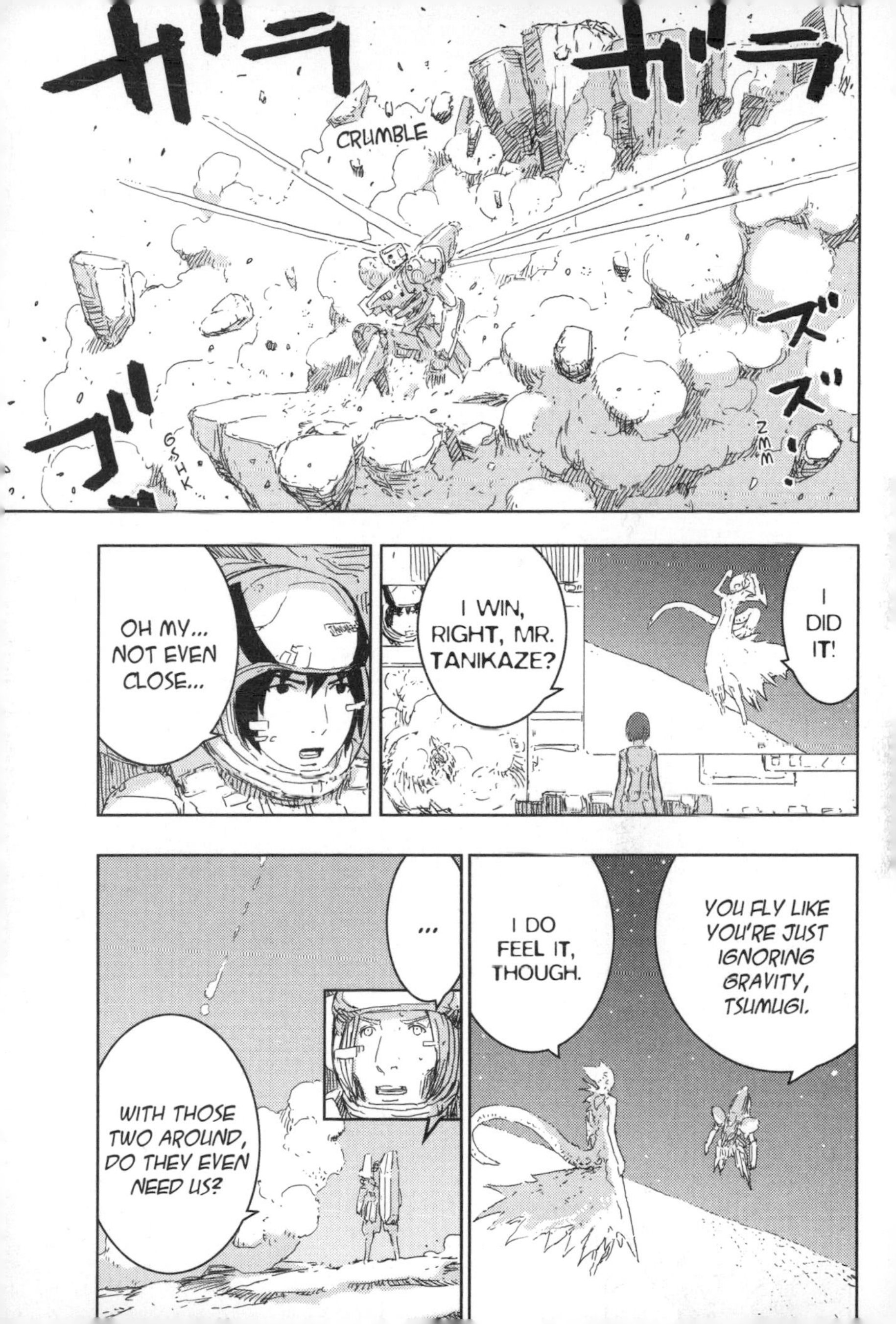
ガラ
ガラ
CRUMBLE
ズズ
ZMM
ゴ
GSHK...
I DID IT!
I WIN, RIGHT, MR. TANIKAZE?
OH MY... NOT EVEN CLOSE...
YOU FLY LIKE YOU'RE JUST IGNORING GRAVITY, TSUMUGI.
I DO FEEL IT, THOUGH.
...
WITH THOSE TWO AROUND, DO THEY EVEN NEED US?

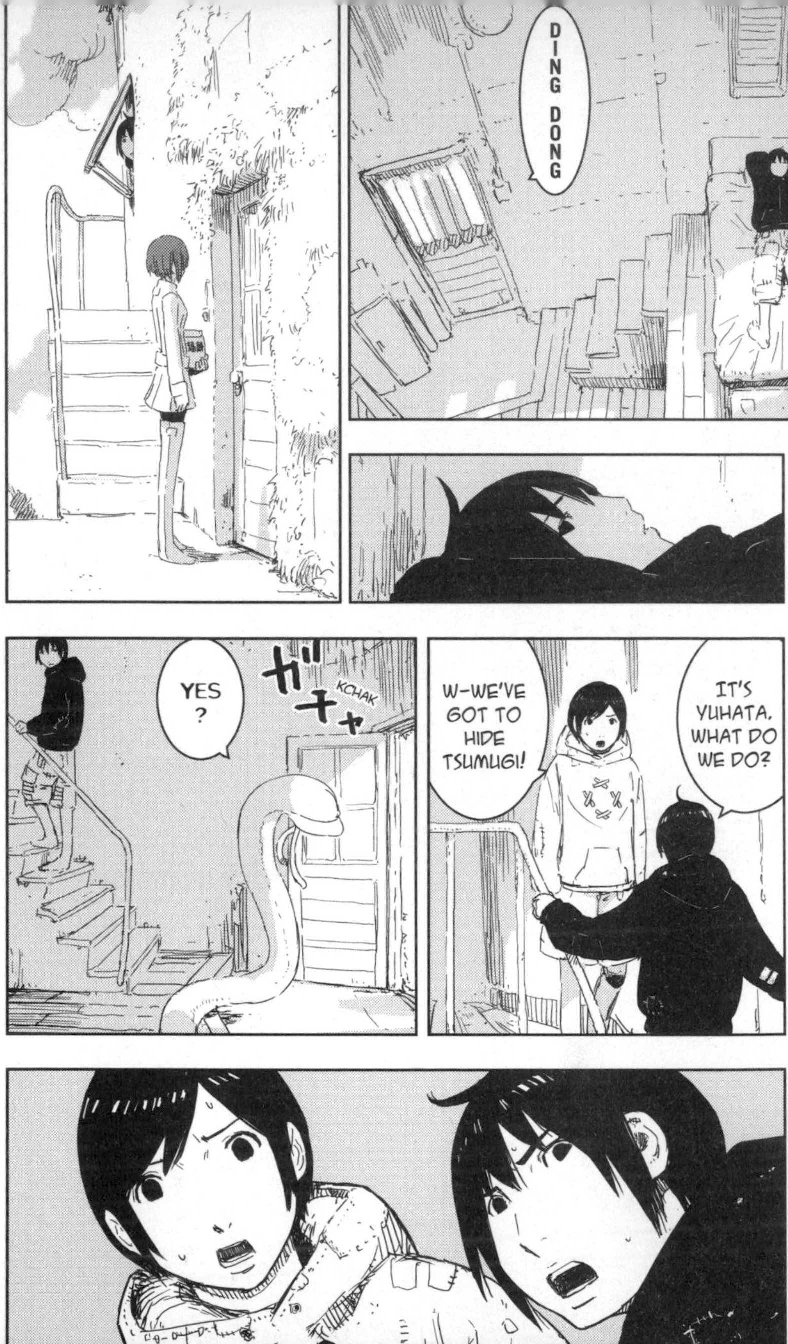
DING DONG
IT'S YUHATA. WHAT DO WE DO?
W-WE'VE GOT TO HIDE TSUMUGI!
ガチャ
KCHAK
YES?

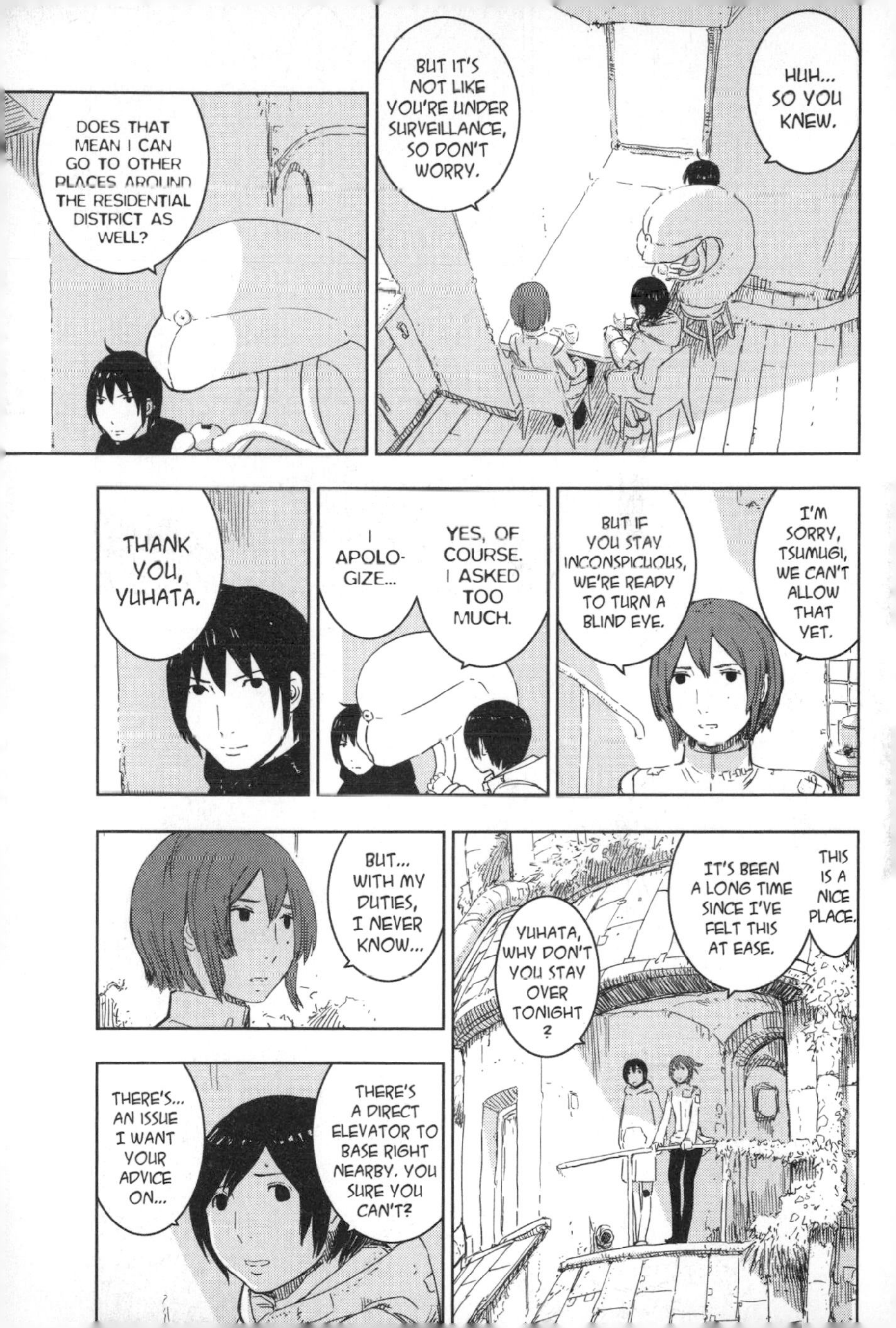
HUH... SO YOU KNEW.
BUT IT'S NOT LIKE YOU'RE UNDER SURVEILLANCE, SO DON'T WORRY.
DOES THAT MEAN I CAN GO TO OTHER PLACES AROUND THE RESIDENTIAL DISTRICT AS WELL?
I'M SORRY, TSUMUGI, WE CAN'T ALLOW THAT YET.
BUT IF YOU STAY INCONSPICUOUS, WE'RE READY TO TURN A BLIND EYE.
YES, OF COURSE. I ASKED TOO MUCH.
I APOLOGIZE...
THANK YOU, YUHATA.
THIS IS A NICE PLACE.
IT'S BEEN A LONG TIME SINCE I'VE FELT THIS AT EASE.
YUHATA, WHY DON'T YOU STAY OVER TONIGHT?
BUT... WITH MY DUTIES, I NEVER KNOW...
THERE'S A DIRECT ELEVATOR TO BASE RIGHT NEARBY. YOU SURE YOU CAN'T?
THERE'S... AN ISSUE I WANT YOUR ADVICE ON...

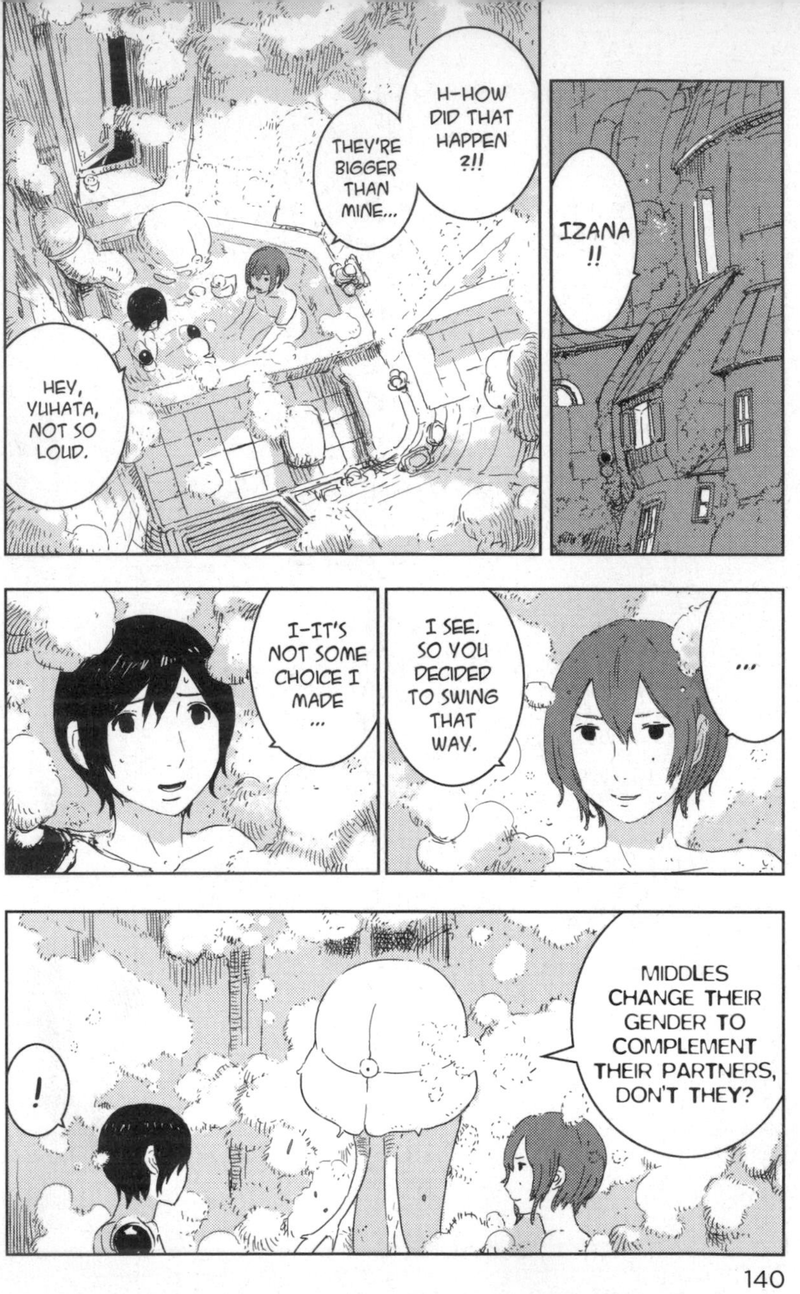
IZANA!!
H-HOW DID THAT HAPPEN?!!
THEY'RE BIGGER THAN MINE...
HEY, YUHATA, NOT SO LOUD.
...
I SEE. SO YOU DECIDED TO SWING THAT WAY.
I-IT'S NOT SOME CHOICE I MADE...
MIDDLES CHANGE THEIR GENDER TO COMPLEMENT THEIR PARTNERS, DON'T THEY?
!

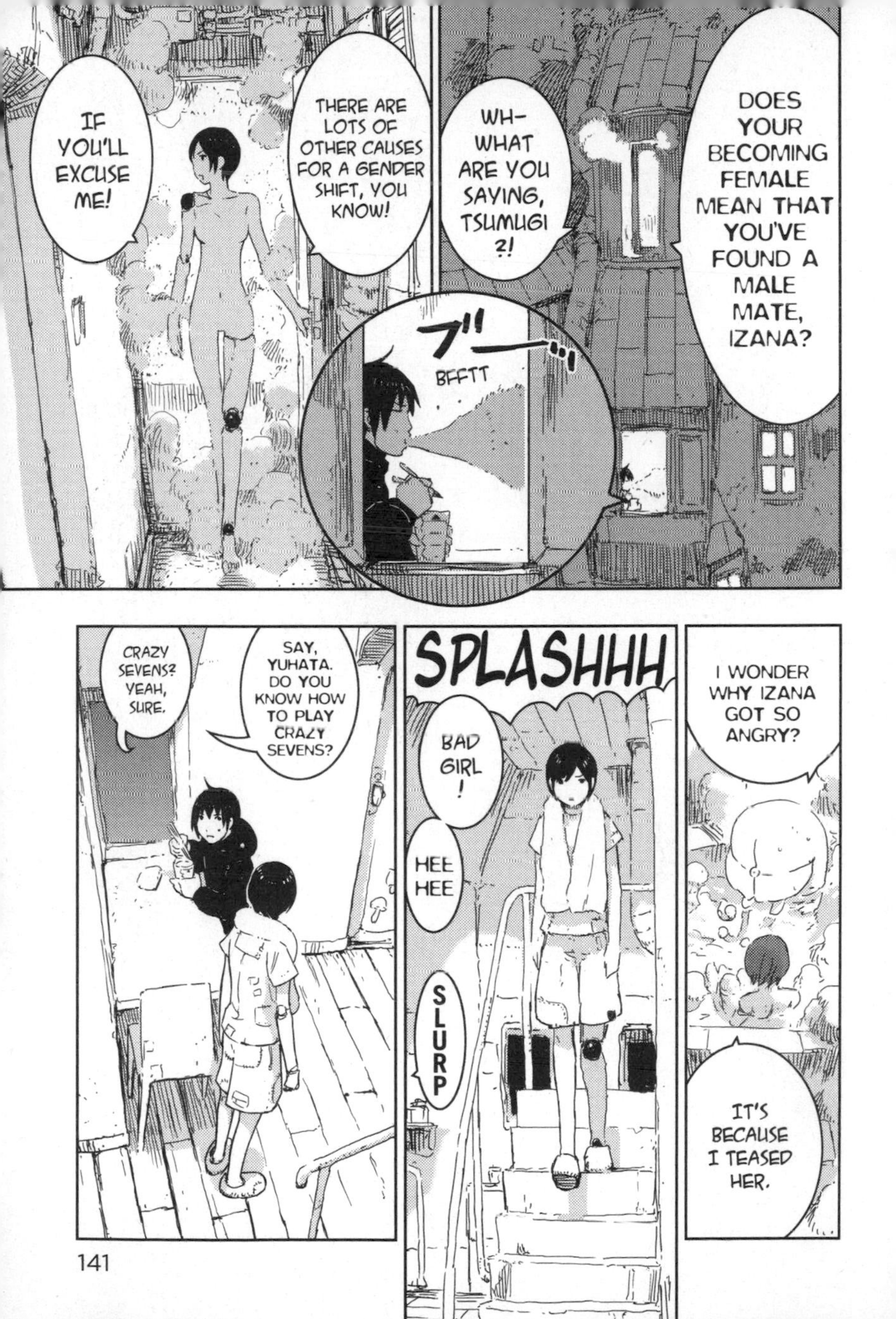
DOES YOUR BECOMING FEMALE MEAN THAT YOU'VE FOUND A MALE MATE, IZANA?
WH-WHAT ARE YOU SAYING, TSUMUGI?!
BFFTT
THERE ARE LOTS OF OTHER CAUSES FOR A GENDER SHIFT, YOU KNOW!
IF YOU'LL EXCUSE ME!
I WONDER WHY IZANA GOT SO ANGRY?
IT'S BECAUSE I TEASED HER.
SPLASHHH
BAD GIRL!
HEE HEE
SLURP
SAY, YUHATA. DO YOU KNOW HOW TO PLAY CRAZY SEVENS?
CRAZY SEVENS? YEAH, SURE.

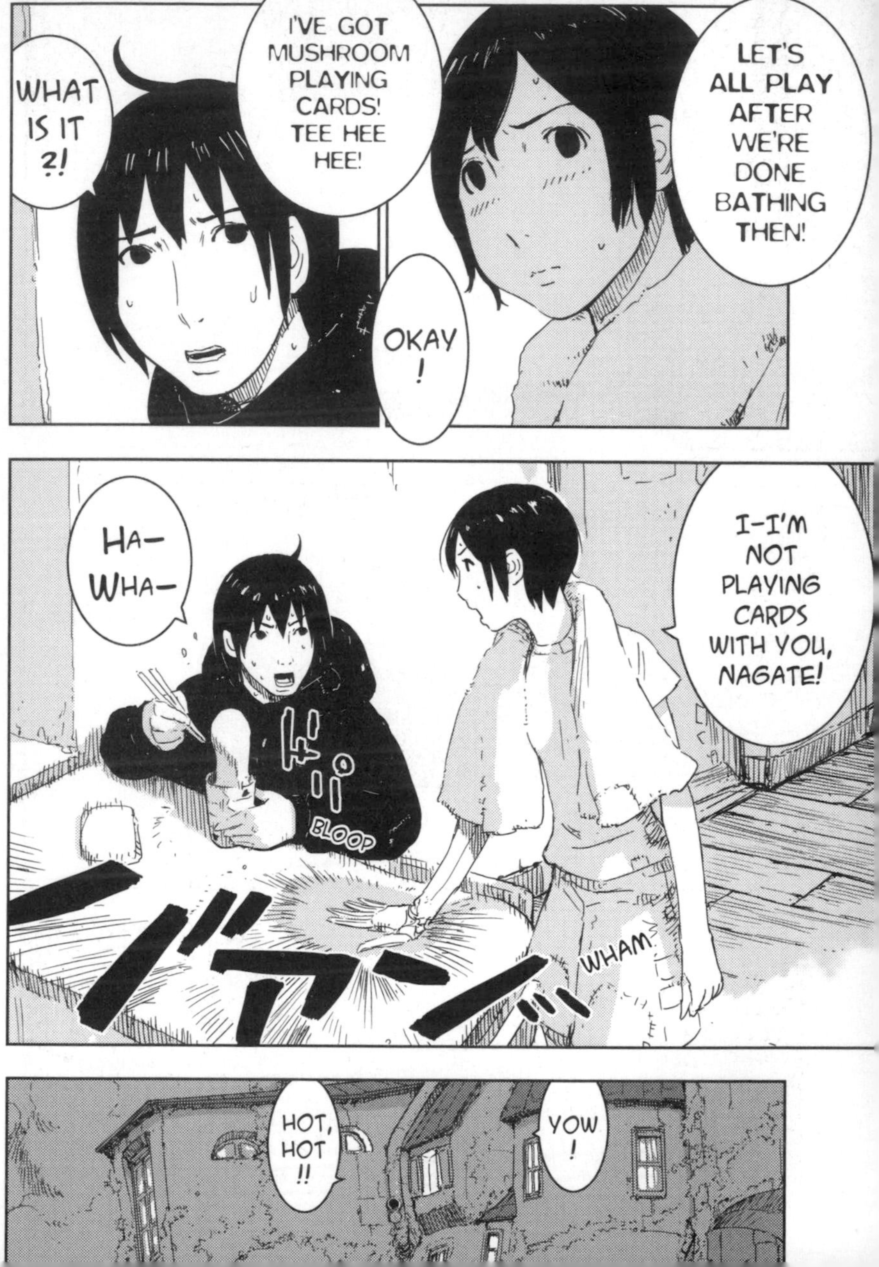
LET'S ALL PLAY AFTER WE'RE DONE BATHING THEN!
I'VE GOT MUSHROOM PLAYING CARDS! TEE HEE HEE!
WHAT IS IT ?!
OKAY !
I-I'M NOT PLAYING CARDS WITH YOU, NAGATE!
WHAM
BLOOP
HA- WHA-
YOW !
HOT, HOT !!

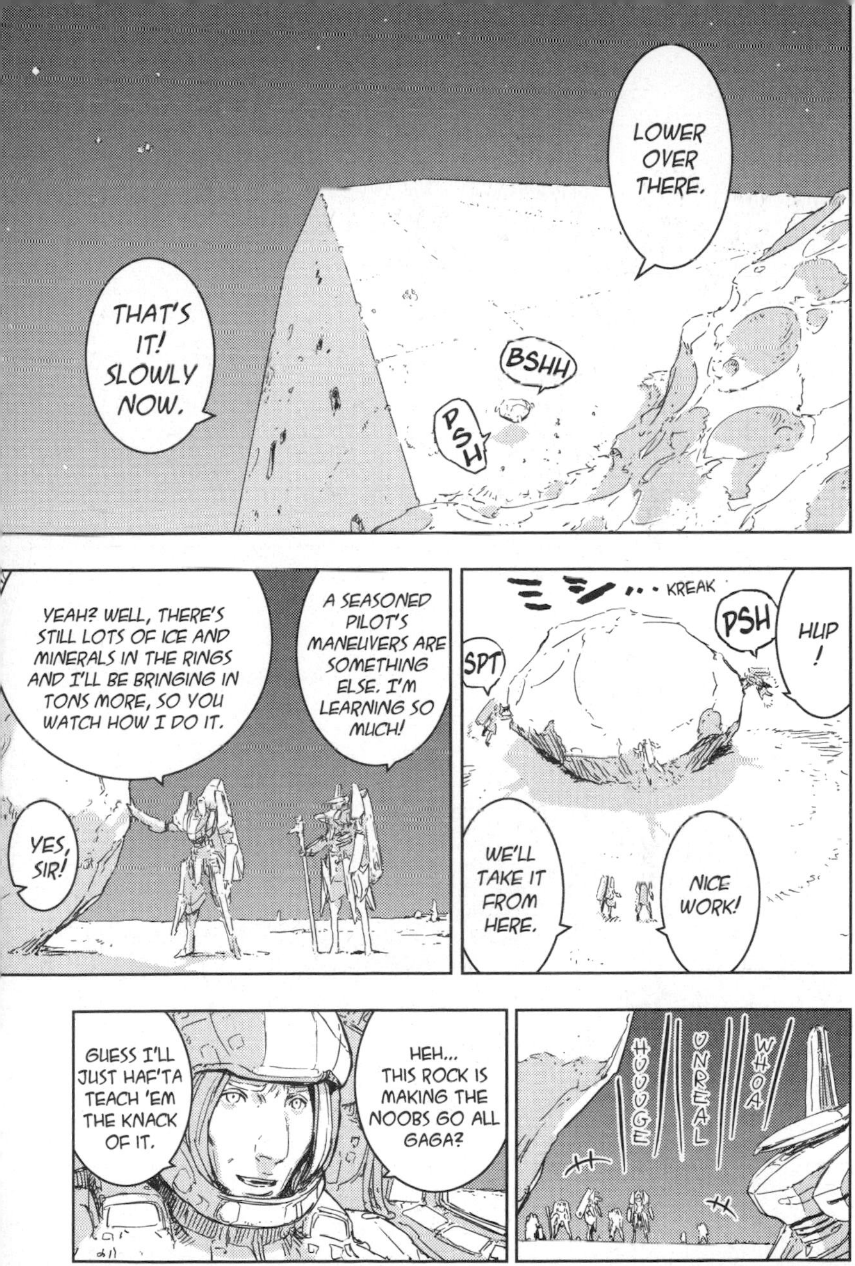
LOWER OVER THERE.
BSHH
PSH
THAT'S IT! SLOWLY NOW.
KREAK
HUP!
PSH
SPT
NICE WORK!
WE'LL TAKE IT FROM HERE.
A SEASONED PILOT'S MANEUVERS ARE SOMETHING ELSE. I'M LEARNING SO MUCH!
YEAH? WELL, THERE'S STILL LOTS OF ICE AND MINERALS IN THE RINGS AND I'LL BE BRINGING IN TONS MORE, SO YOU WATCH HOW I DO IT.
YES, SIR!
WHOA
UNREAL
HUUUGE
HEH... THIS ROCK IS MAKING THE NOOBS GO ALL GAGA?
GUESS I'LL JUST HAF'TA TEACH 'EM THE KNACK OF IT.

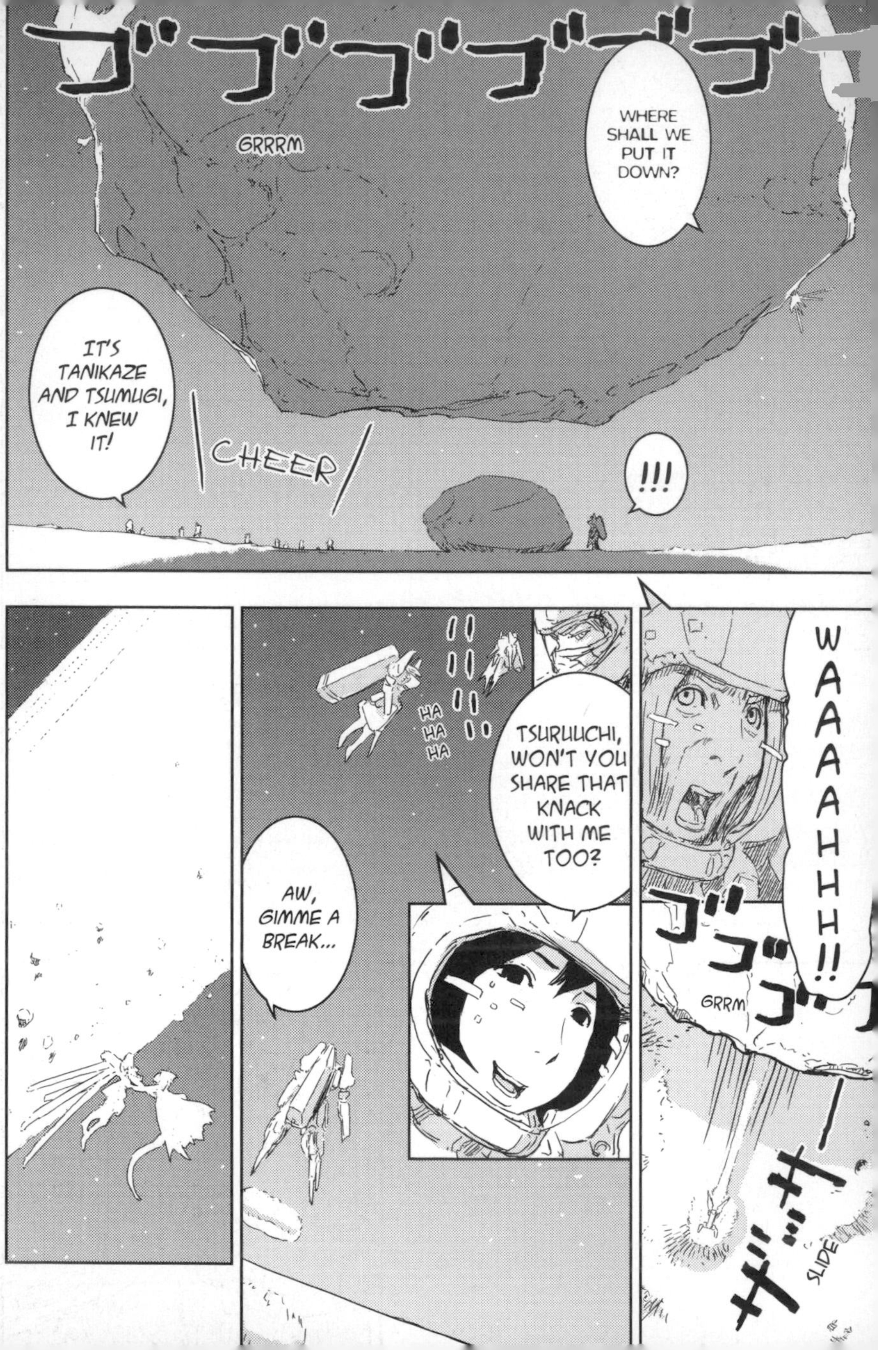
ゴゴゴゴゴ
WHERE SHALL WE PUT IT DOWN?
GRRRM
!!!
CHEER
IT'S TANIKAZE AND TSUMUGI, I KNEW IT!
WAAAAAHHHH!!
ゴゴゴ
GRRM
SLIDE
HA HA HA
TSURUUCHI, WON'T YOU SHARE THAT KNACK WITH ME TOO?
AW, GIMME A BREAK...

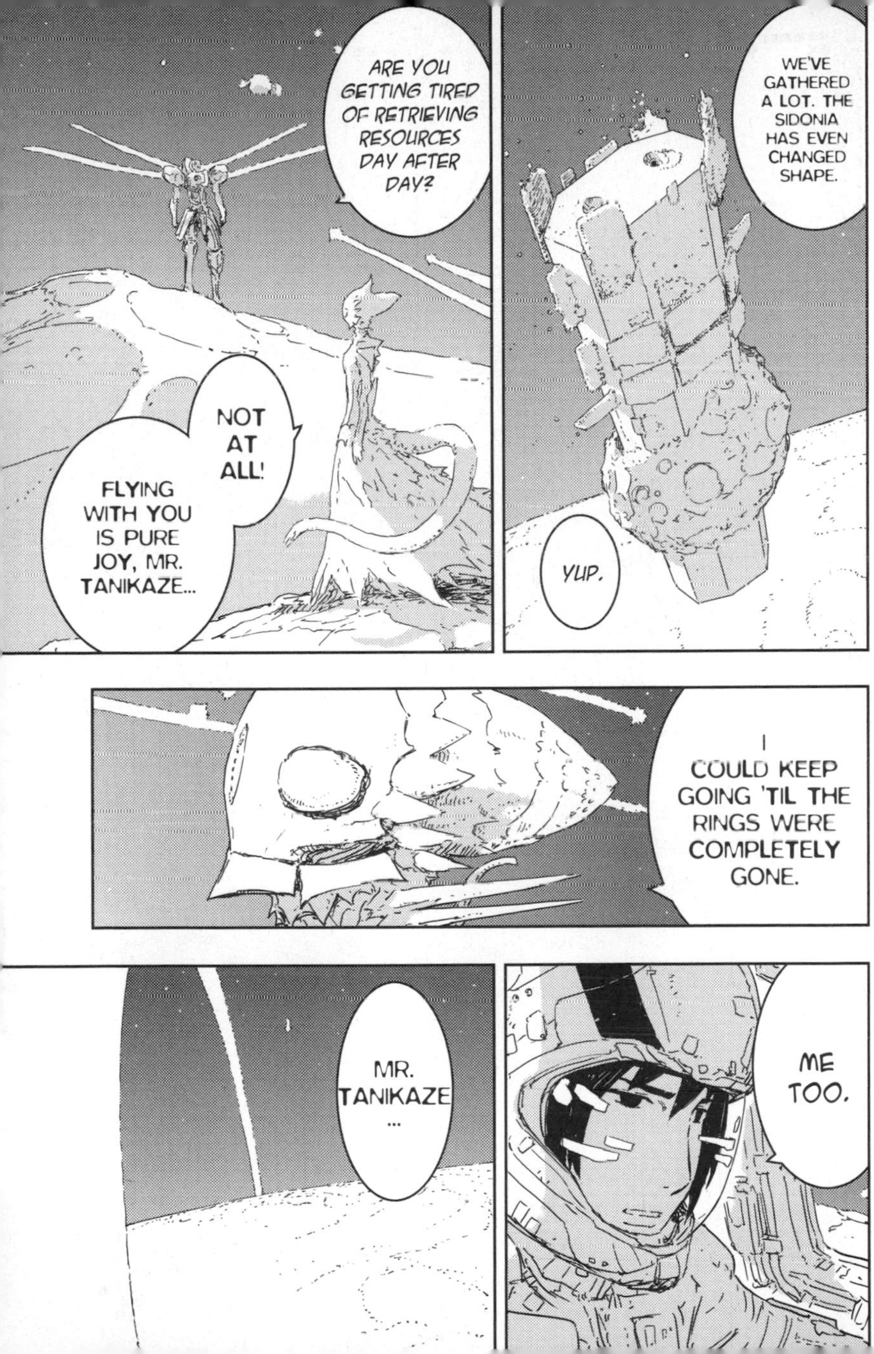
WE'VE GATHERED A LOT. THE SIDONIA HAS EVEN CHANGED SHAPE.
YUP.
ARE YOU GETTING TIRED OF RETRIEVING RESOURCES DAY AFTER DAY?
NOT AT ALL!
FLYING WITH YOU IS PURE JOY, MR. TANIKAZE...
I COULD KEEP GOING 'TIL THE RINGS WERE COMPLETELY GONE.
ME TOO.
MR. TANIKAZE...

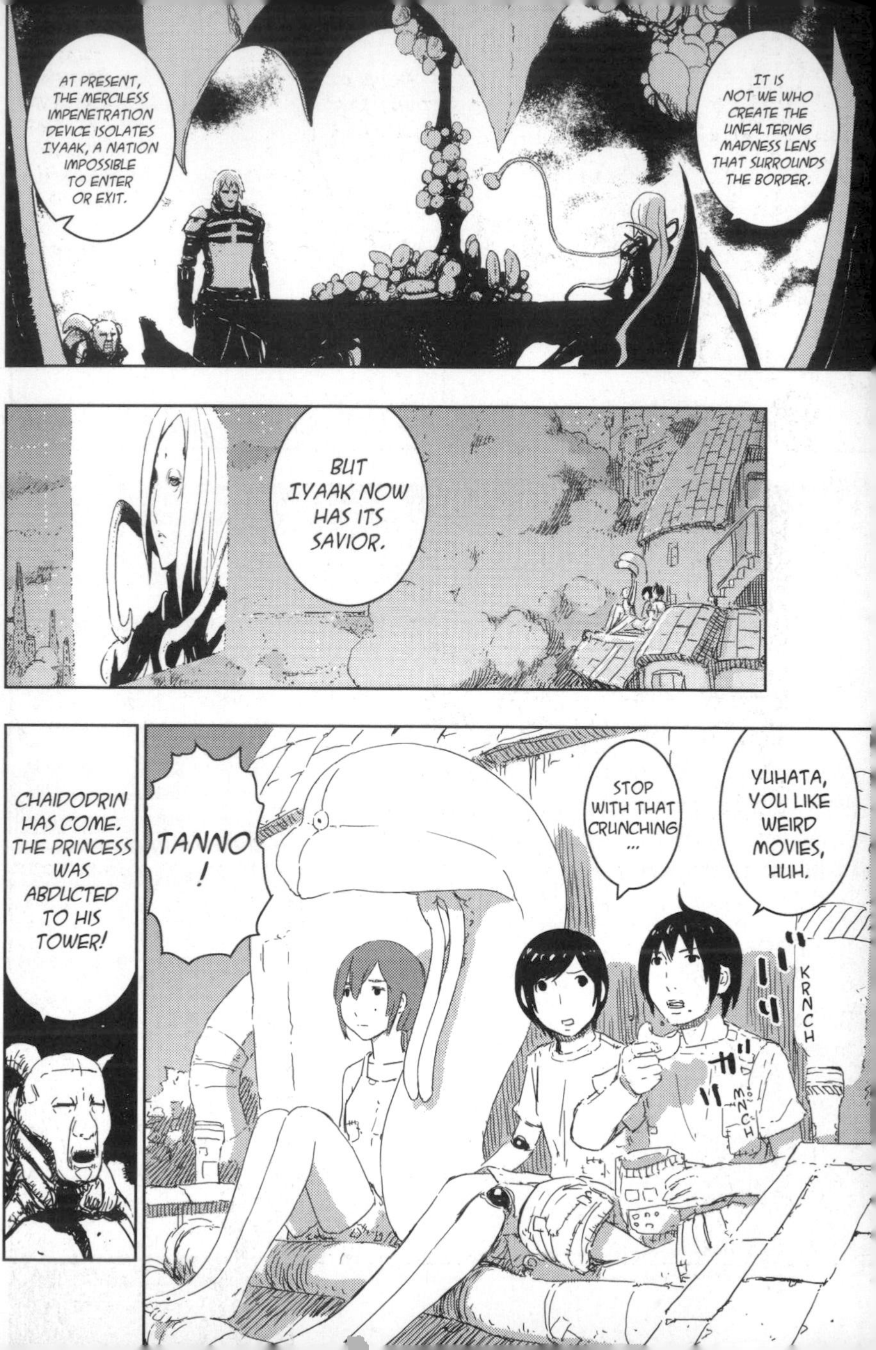

IT IS NOT WE WHO CREATE THE UNFALTERING MADNESS LENS THAT SURROUNDS THE BORDER.
AT PRESENT, THE MERCILESS IMPENETRATION DEVICE ISOLATES IYAAK, A NATION IMPOSSIBLE TO ENTER OR EXIT.
BUT IYAAK NOW HAS ITS SAVIOR.
YUHATA, YOU LIKE WEIRD MOVIES, HUH.
KRNCH
STOP WITH THAT CRUNCHING...
MONCH
TANNO!
CHAIDODRIN HAS COME. THE PRINCESS WAS ABDUCTED TO HIS TOWER!

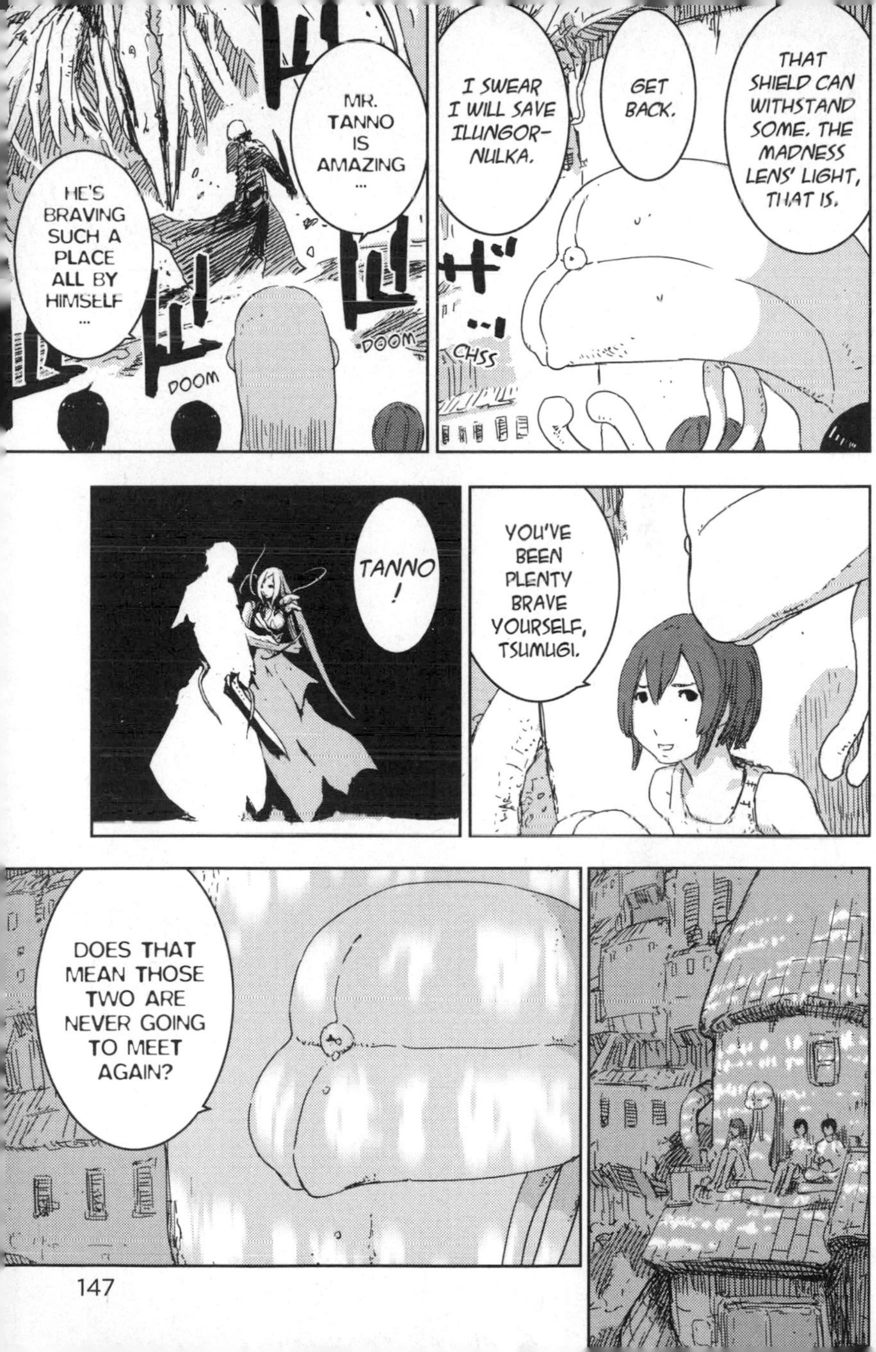
THAT SHIELD CAN WITHSTAND SOME. THE MADNESS LENS' LIGHT, THAT IS.
GET BACK.
I SWEAR I WILL SAVE ILUNGOR-NULKA.
CHSS
MR. TANNO IS AMAZING...
HE'S BRAVING SUCH A PLACE ALL BY HIMSELF...
DOOM
DOOM
YOU'VE BEEN PLENTY BRAVE YOURSELF, TSUMUGI.
TANNO!
DOES THAT MEAN THOSE TWO ARE NEVER GOING TO MEET AGAIN?

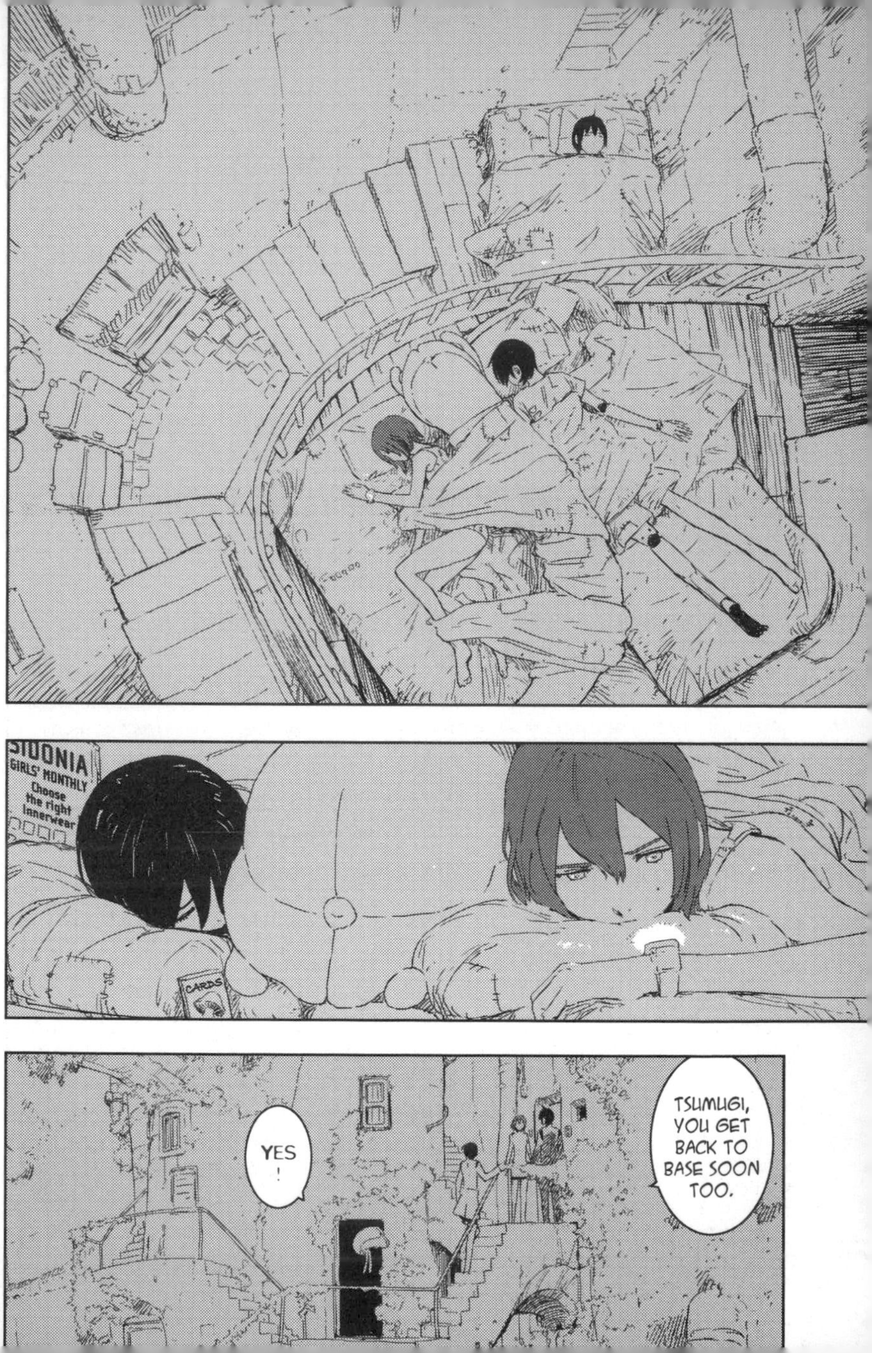
SIDONIA
GIRLS' MONTHLY
Choose the right Innerwear
CARDS
TSUMUGI, YOU GET BACK TO BASE SOON TOO.
YES!

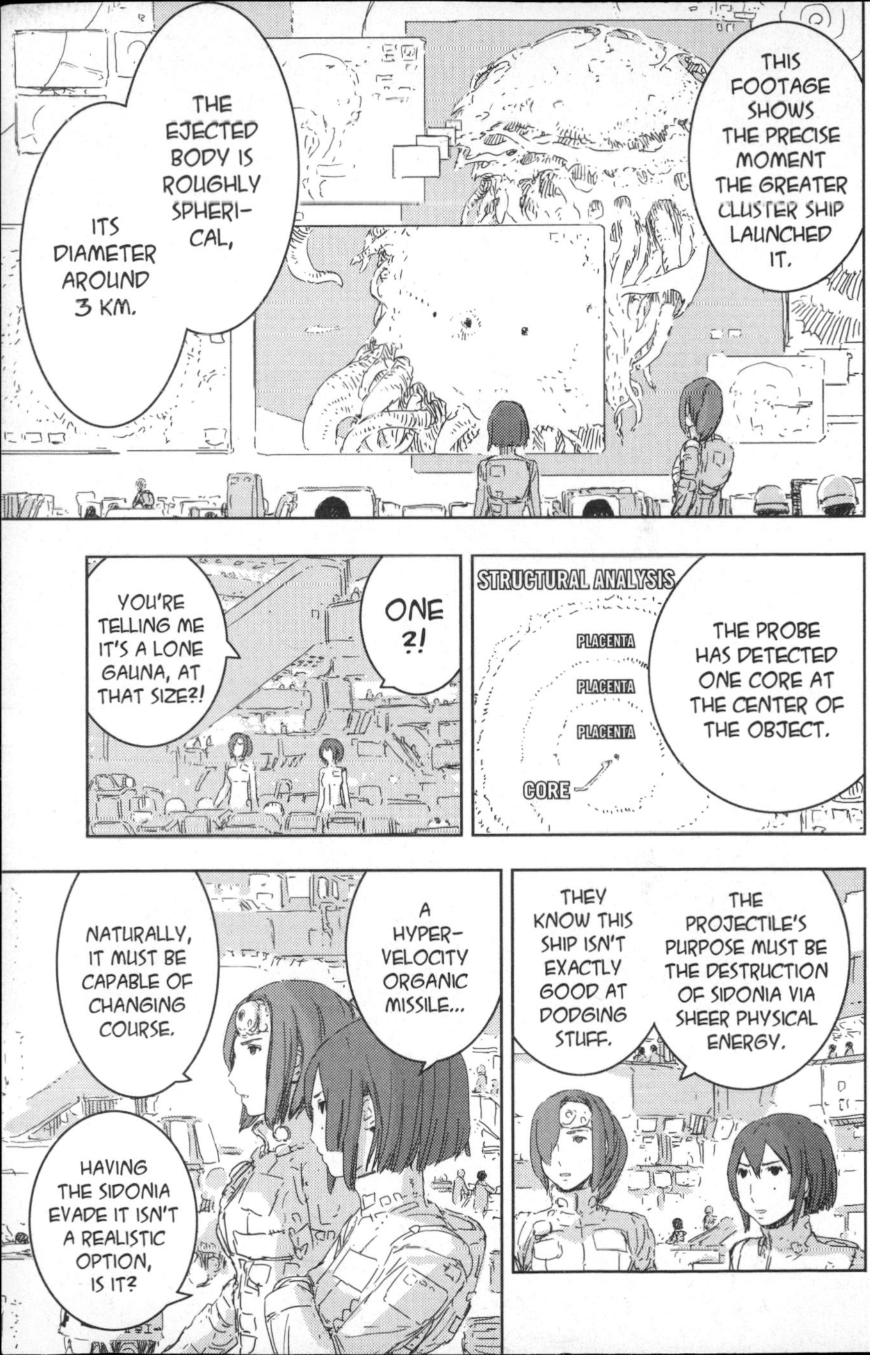
THIS FOOTAGE SHOWS THE PRECISE MOMENT THE GREATER CLUSTER SHIP LAUNCHED IT.
THE EJECTED BODY IS ROUGHLY SPHERI-CAL,
ITS DIAMETER AROUND 3 KM.
STRUCTURAL ANALYSIS
PLACENTA
PLACENTA
PLACENTA
CORE
THE PROBE HAS DETECTED ONE CORE AT THE CENTER OF THE OBJECT.
ONE ?!
YOU'RE TELLING ME IT'S A LONE GAUNA, AT THAT SIZE?!
THE PROJECTILE'S PURPOSE MUST BE THE DESTRUCTION OF SIDONIA VIA SHEER PHYSICAL ENERGY.
THEY KNOW THIS SHIP ISN'T EXACTLY GOOD AT DODGING STUFF.
A HYPER-VELOCITY ORGANIC MISSILE...
NATURALLY, IT MUST BE CAPABLE OF CHANGING COURSE.
HAVING THE SIDONIA EVADE IT ISN'T A REALISTIC OPTION, IS IT?

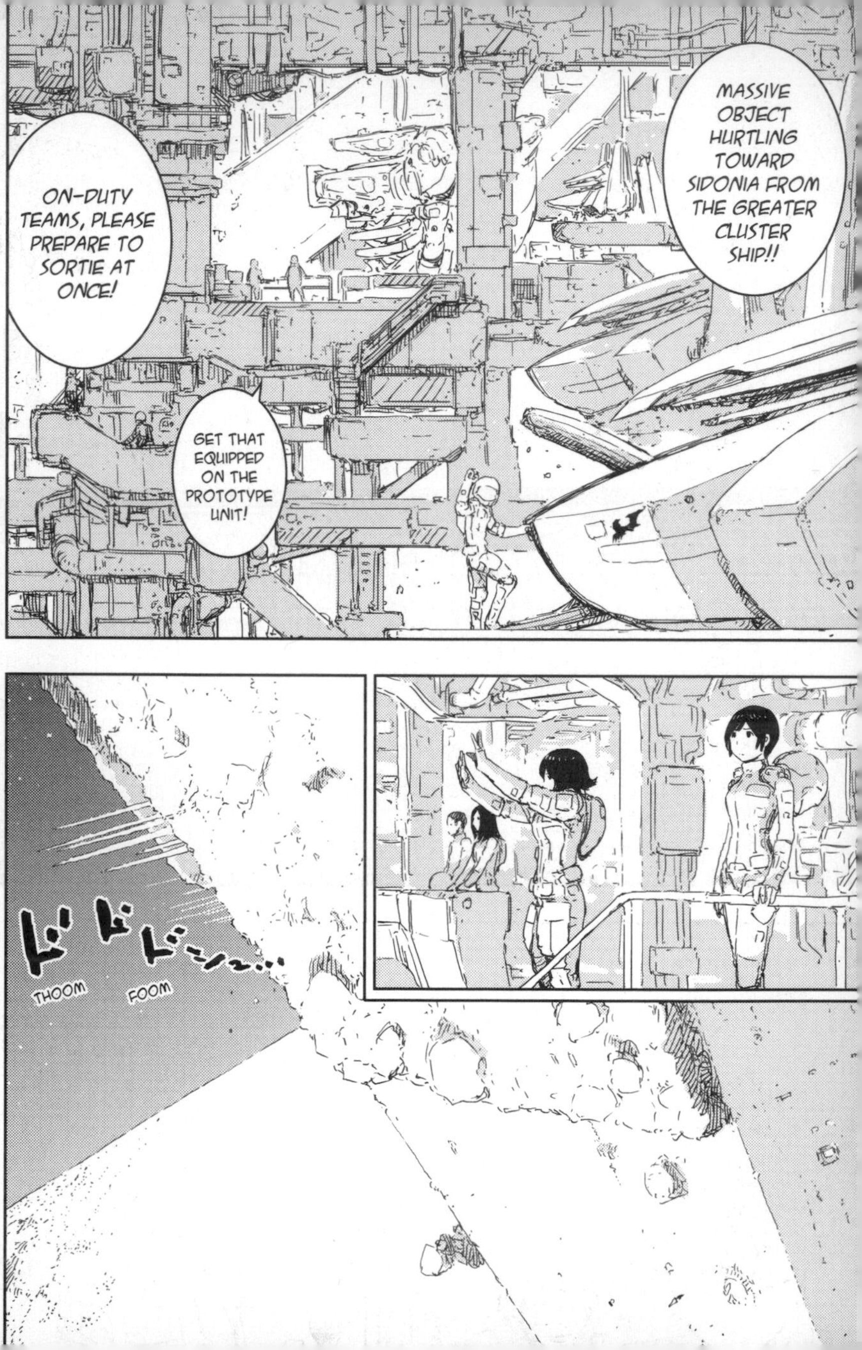
MASSIVE OBJECT HURTLING TOWARD SIDONIA FROM THE GREATER CLUSTER SHIP!!
ON-DUTY TEAMS, PLEASE PREPARE TO SORTIE AT ONCE!
GET THAT EQUIPPED ON THE PROTOTYPE UNIT!
THOOM
FOOM

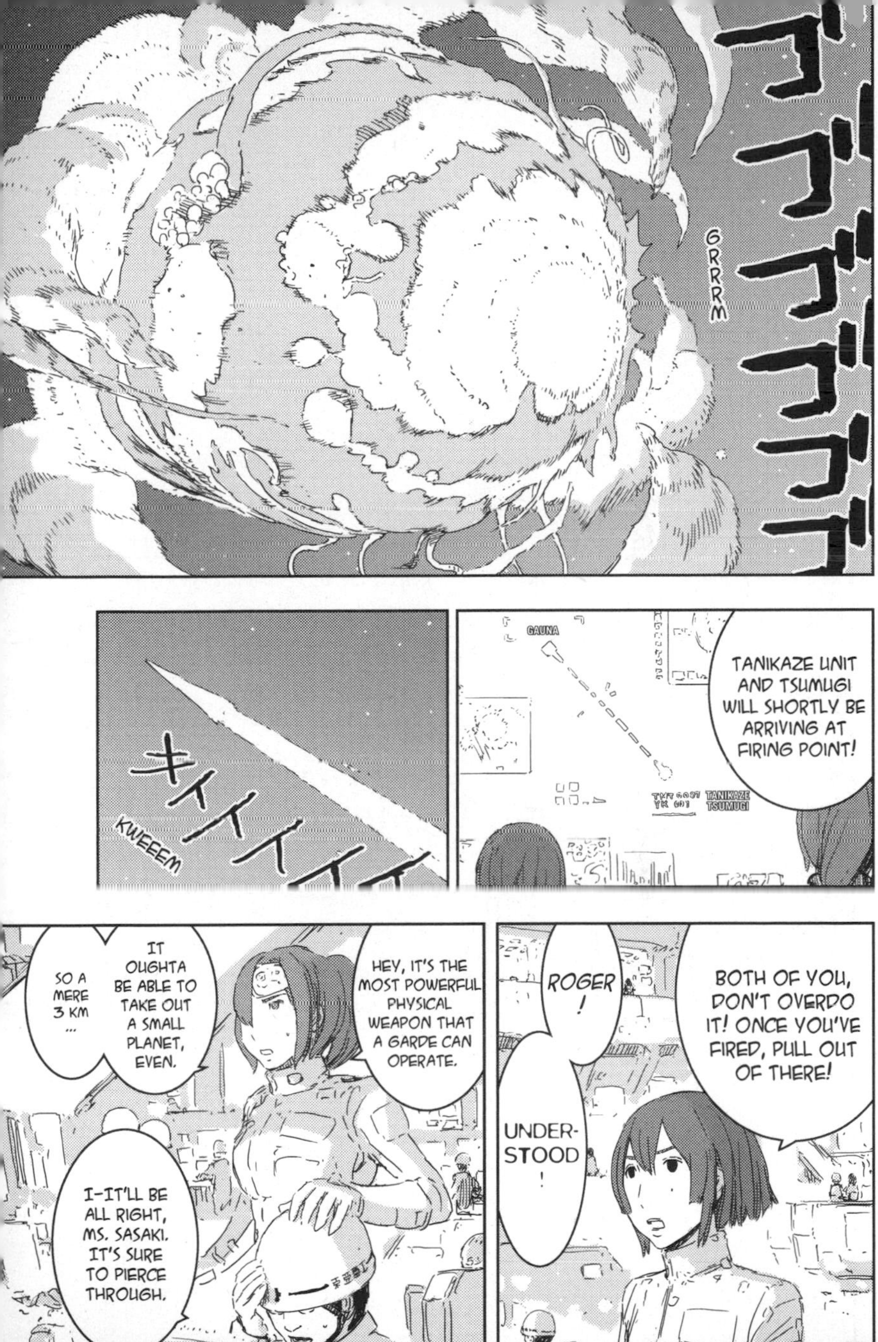
ゴゴゴゴ
GRRRM
GAUNA
TANIKAZE UNIT AND TSUMUGI WILL SHORTLY BE ARRIVING AT FIRING POINT!
TANIKAZE
TSUMUGI
キイイイ
KWEEEM
BOTH OF YOU, DON'T OVERDO IT! ONCE YOU'VE FIRED, PULL OUT OF THERE!
ROGER!
UNDERSTOOD!
HEY, IT'S THE MOST POWERFUL PHYSICAL WEAPON THAT A GARDE CAN OPERATE.
IT OUGHTA BE ABLE TO TAKE OUT A SMALL PLANET, EVEN.
SO A MERE 3 KM ...
I-IT'LL BE ALL RIGHT, MS. SASAKI. IT'S SURE TO PIERCE THROUGH.

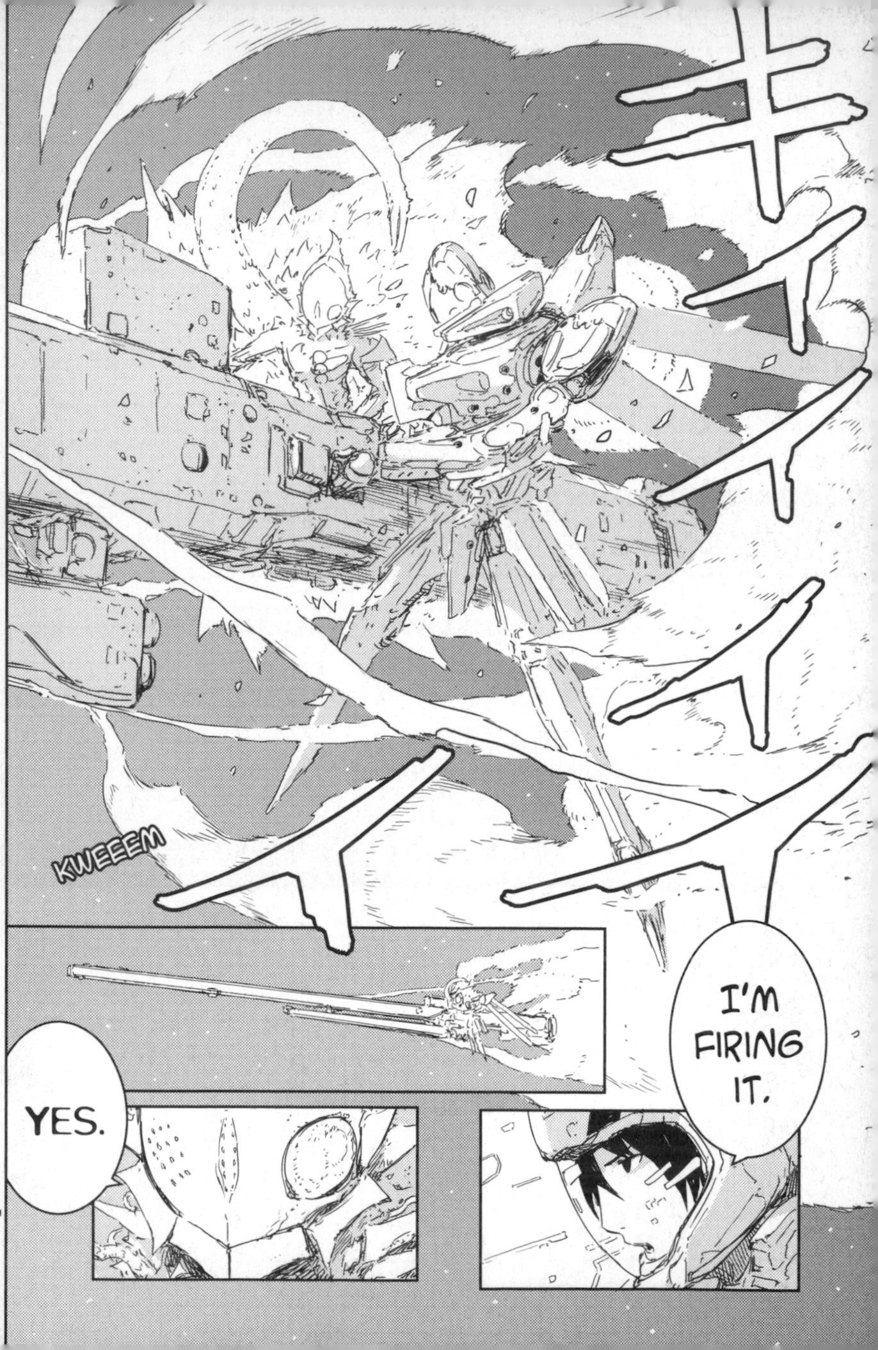
KWEEEM
I'M FIRING IT.
YES.

Chapter 43: END

シドニアの騎士
KNIGHTS OF SIDONIA

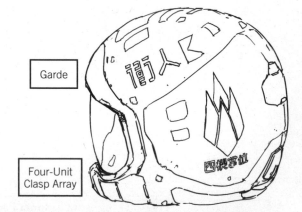

Garde

Four-Unit
Clasp Array

Chapter 44: Yuhata Midorikawa's Decision

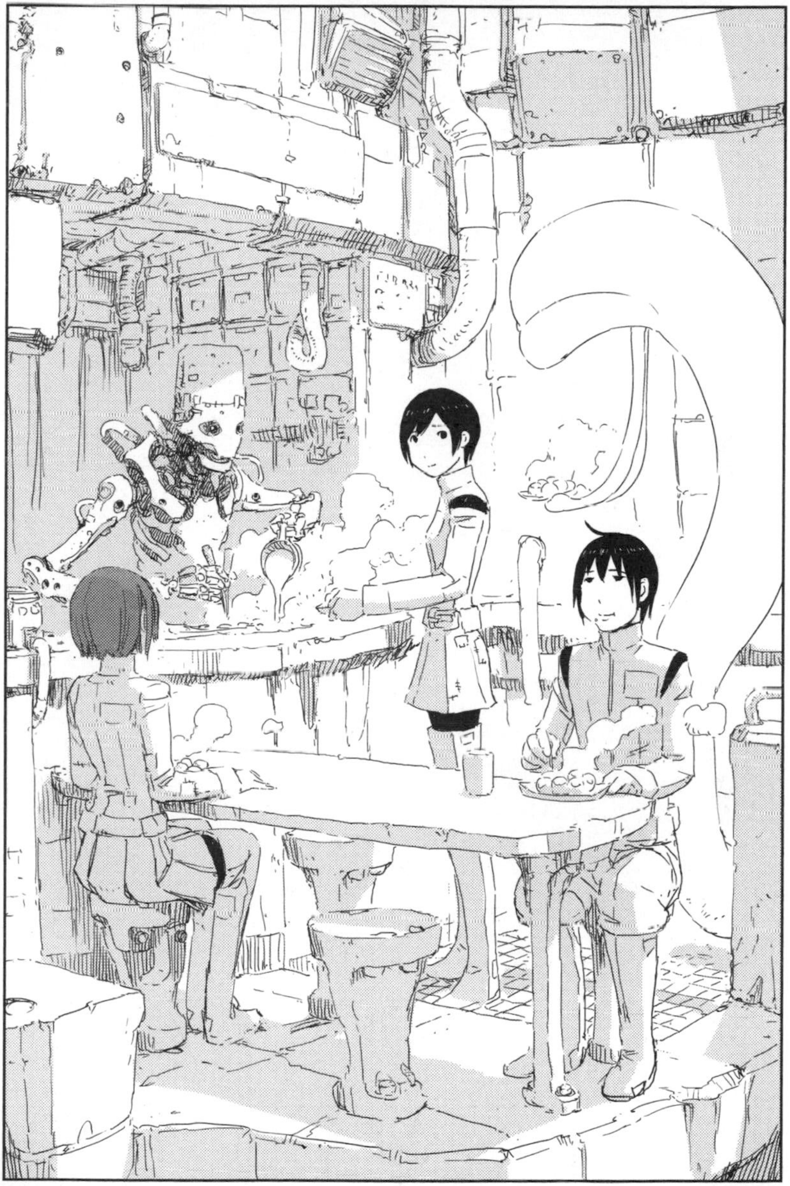

One Hundred Sights of Sidonia Part Thirty-Three:
Automated Stalls Floor

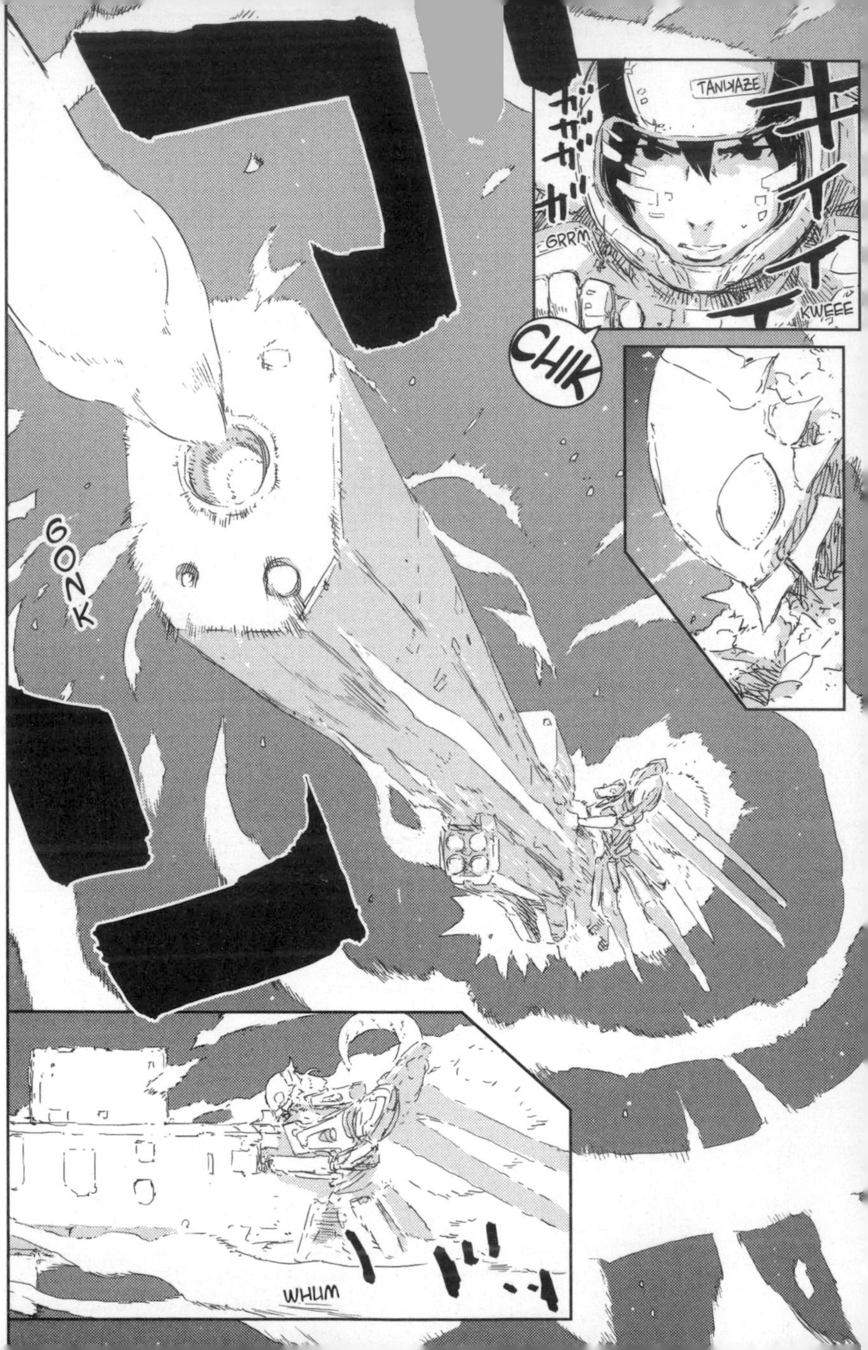
TANKAZE
GRRM
KWEEE
CHIK
GONK
WHUM

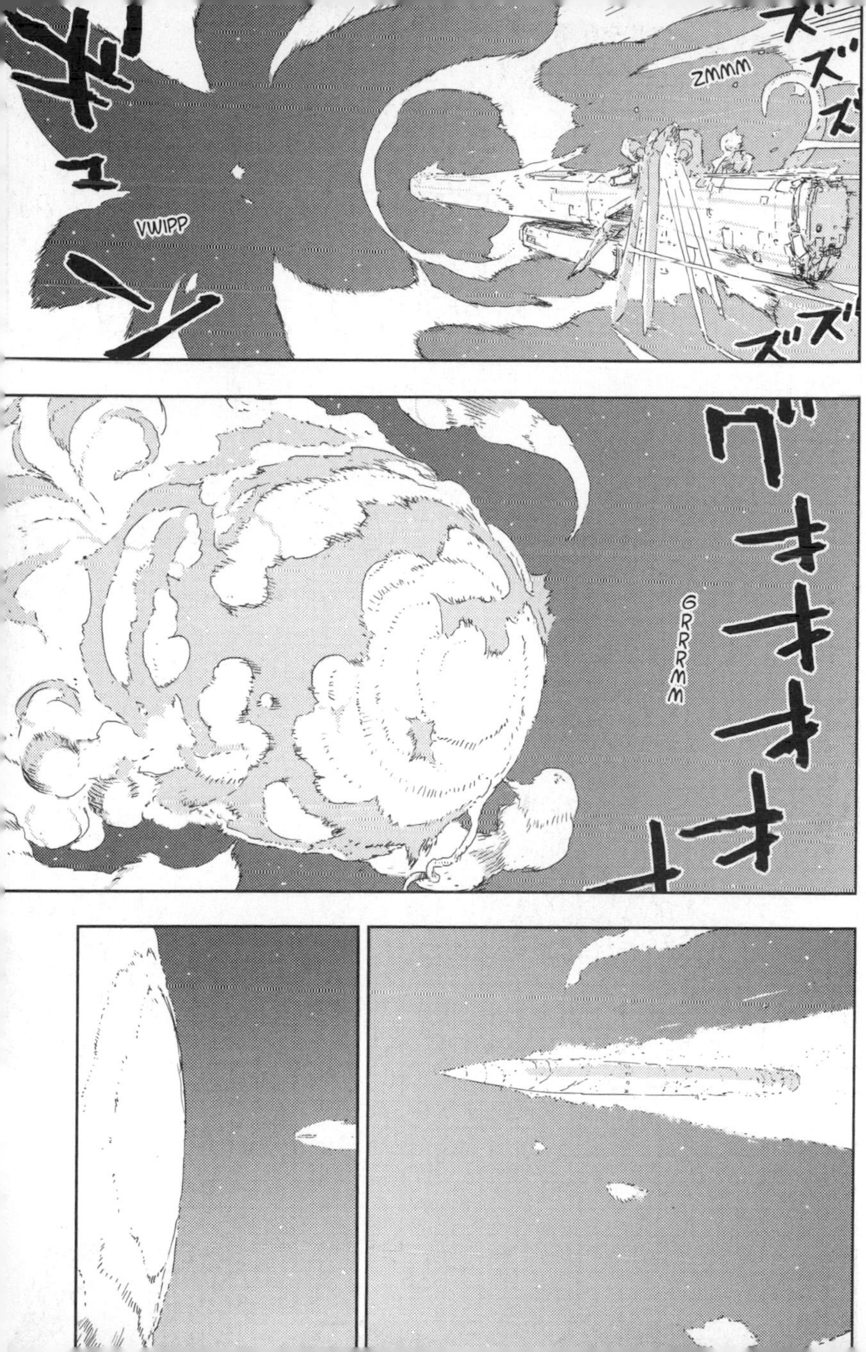
ズズズ
ZMMM
ズズズ
ギュン
VWIPP
グオオオオ
GRRRMM

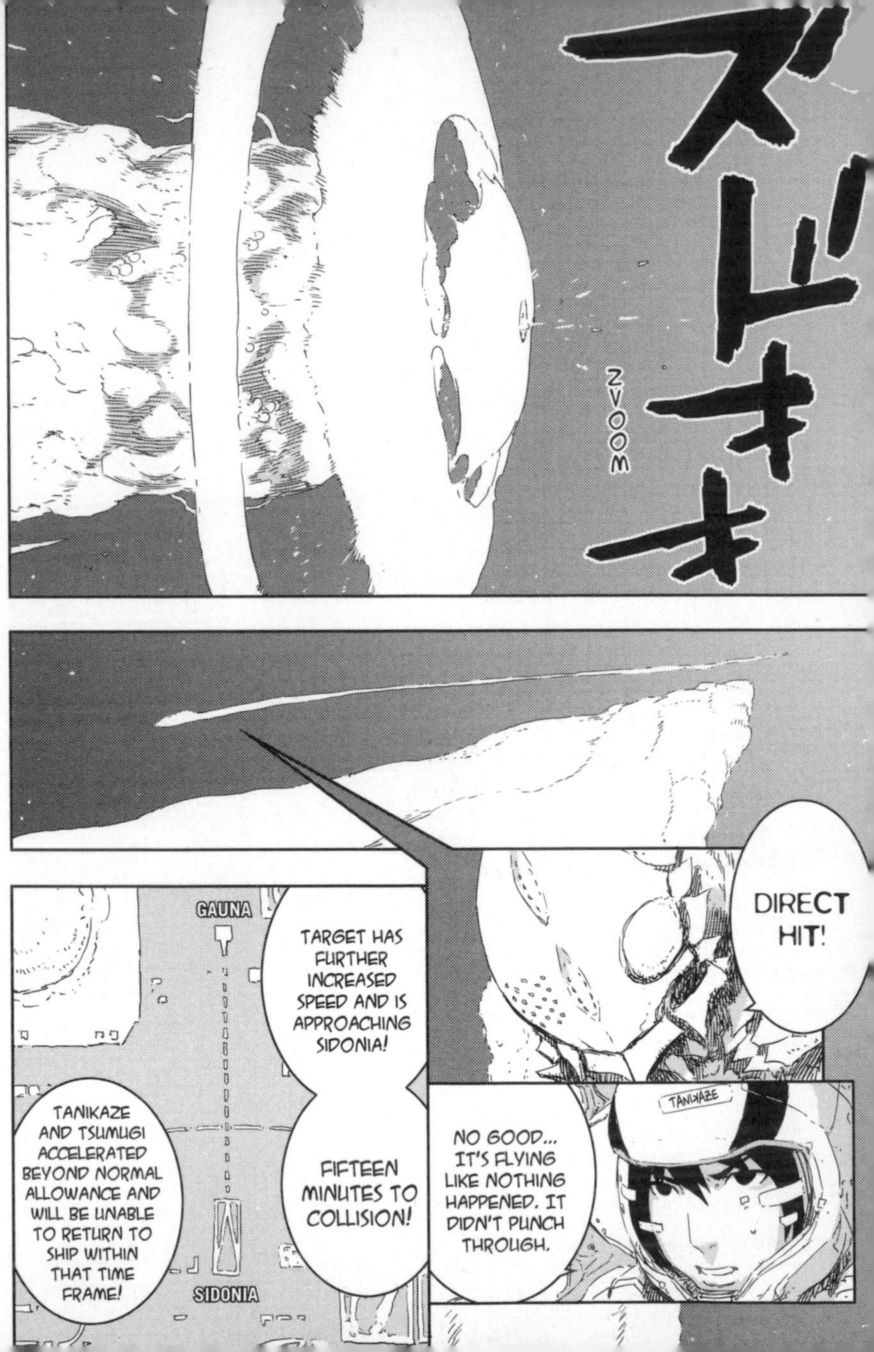
ズドォォ
ZVOOM
DIRECT HIT!
TARGET HAS FURTHER INCREASED SPEED AND IS APPROACHING SIDONIA!
GAUNA
SIDONIA
TANIKAZE
NO GOOD... IT'S FLYING LIKE NOTHING HAPPENED. IT DIDN'T PUNCH THROUGH.
FIFTEEN MINUTES TO COLLISION!
TANIKAZE AND TSUMUGI ACCELERATED BEYOND NORMAL ALLOWANCE AND WILL BE UNABLE TO RETURN TO SHIP WITHIN THAT TIME FRAME!

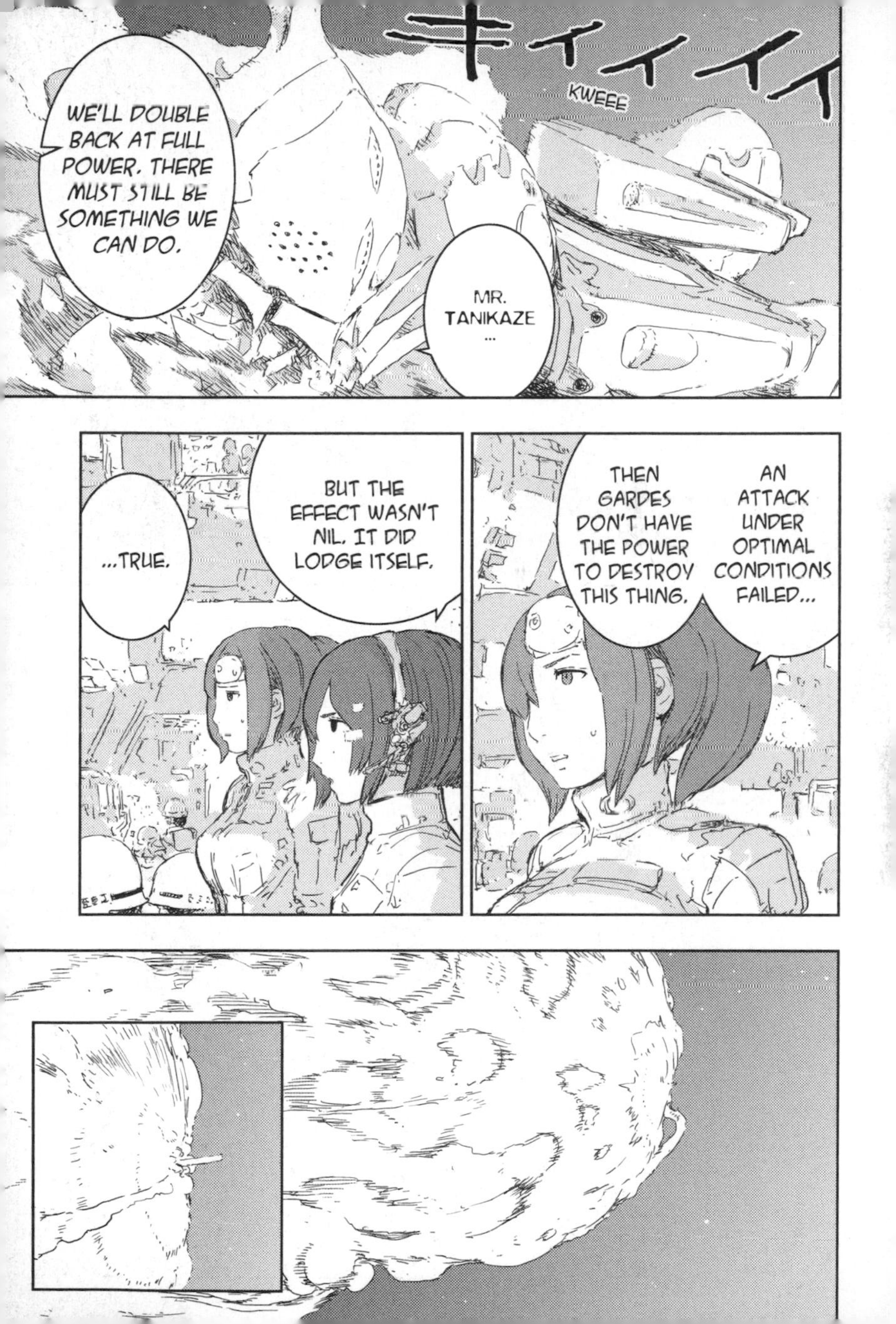
キィイイ
KWEEE
MR. TANIKAZE ...
WE'LL DOUBLE BACK AT FULL POWER. THERE MUST STILL BE SOMETHING WE CAN DO.
AN ATTACK UNDER OPTIMAL CONDITIONS FAILED...
THEN GARDES DON'T HAVE THE POWER TO DESTROY THIS THING.
BUT THE EFFECT WASN'T NIL. IT DID LODGE ITSELF.
...TRUE.

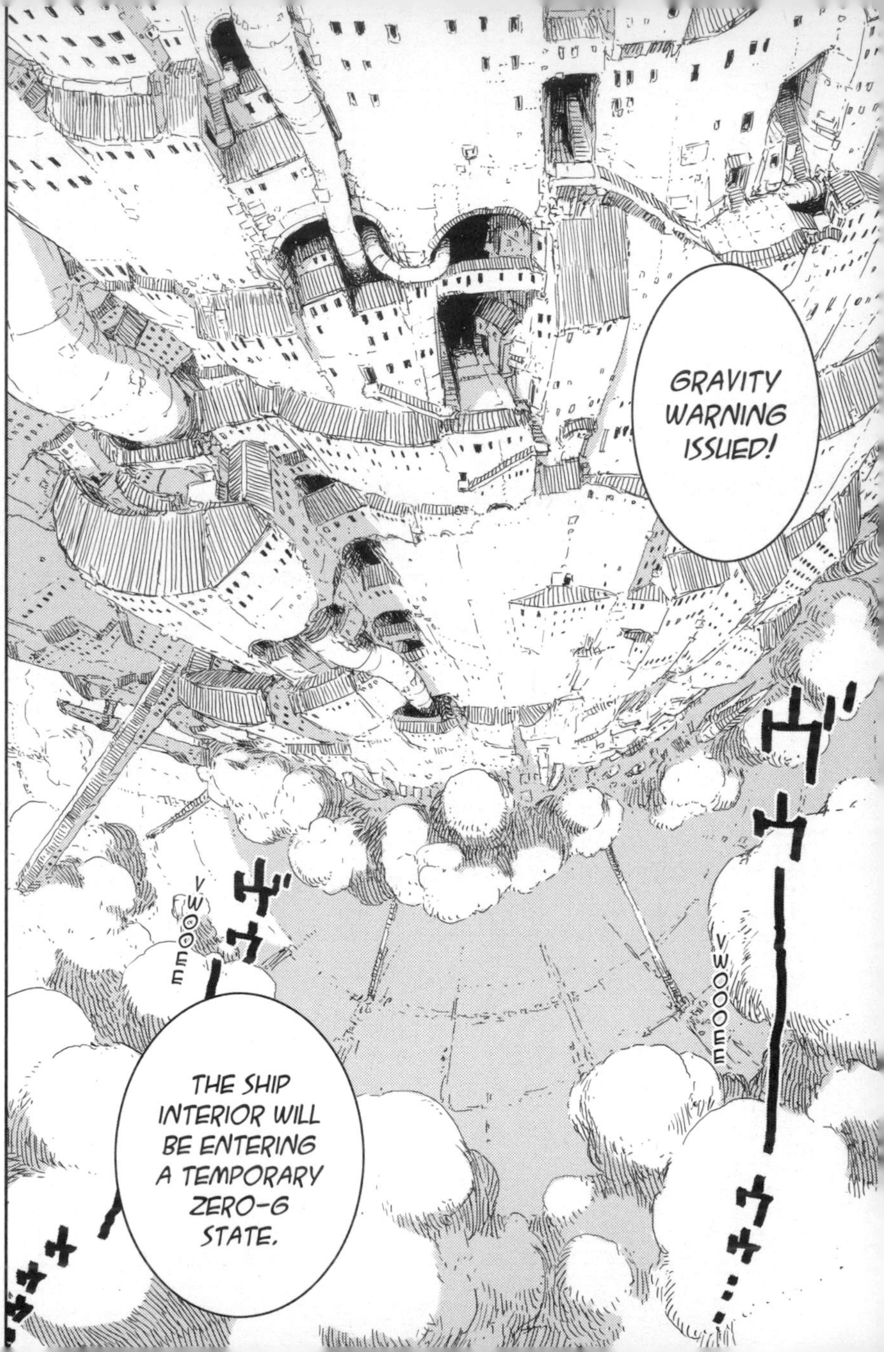
GRAVITY WARNING ISSUED!
VWOOOEE
VWOOOEE
THE SHIP INTERIOR WILL BE ENTERING A TEMPORARY ZERO-G STATE.

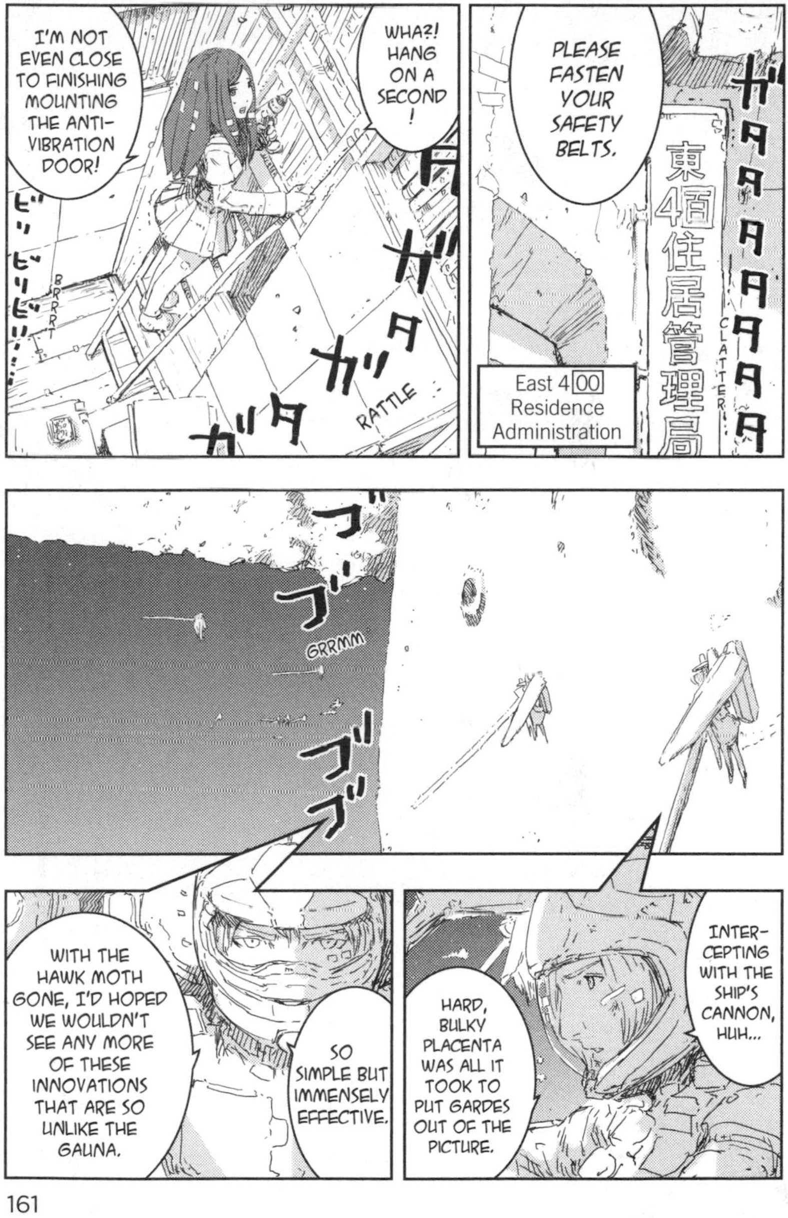
PLEASE FASTEN YOUR SAFETY BELTS.
East 4 00 Residence Administration
CLATTER
WHA?! HANG ON A SECOND!
I'M NOT EVEN CLOSE TO FINISHING MOUNTING THE ANTI-VIBRATION DOOR!
RATTLE
BRRRT
GRRMM
INTER-CEPTING WITH THE SHIP'S CANNON, HUH...
HARD, BULKY PLACENTA WAS ALL IT TOOK TO PUT GARDES OUT OF THE PICTURE.
SO SIMPLE BUT IMMENSELY EFFECTIVE.
WITH THE HAWK MOTH GONE, I'D HOPED WE WOULDN'T SEE ANY MORE OF THESE INNOVATIONS THAT ARE SO UNLIKE THE GAUNA.

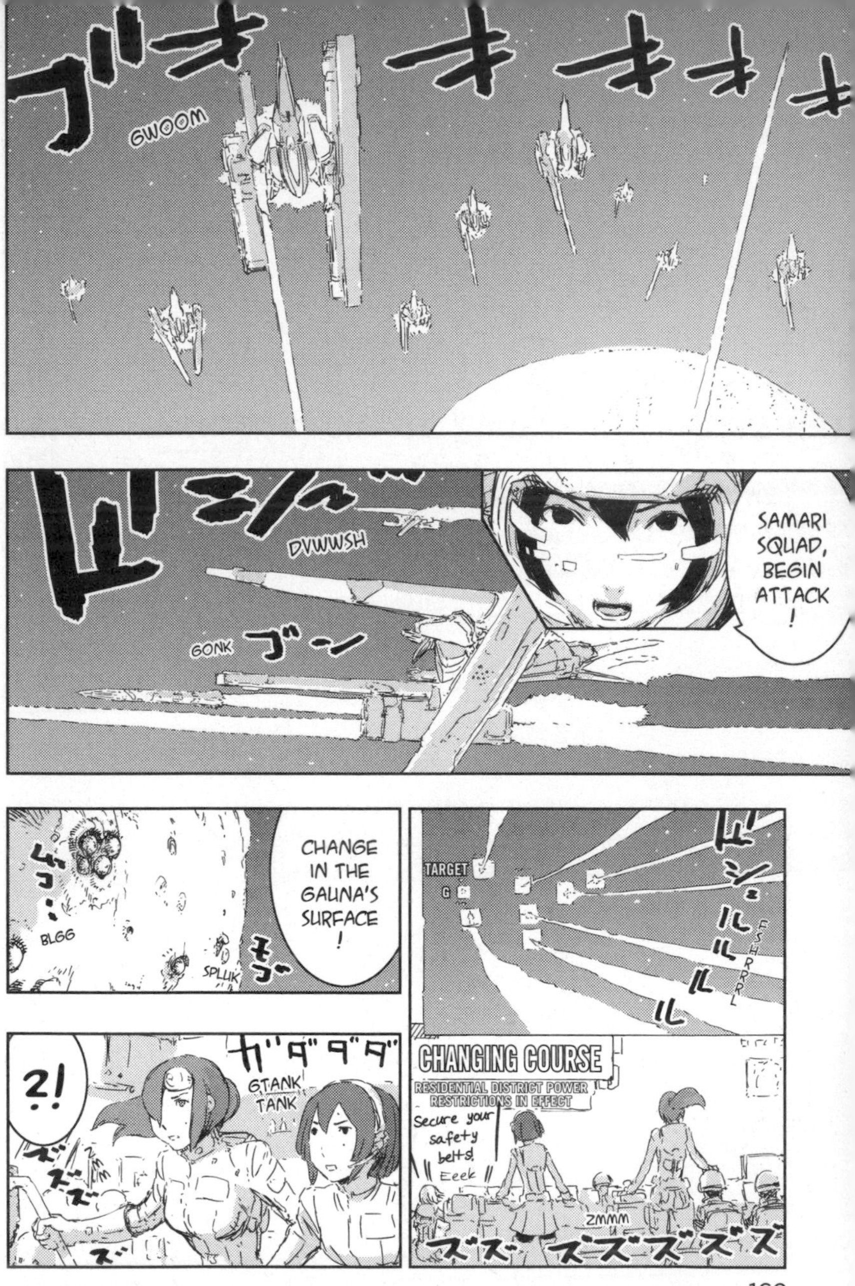
GWOOM
SAMARI SQUAD, BEGIN ATTACK!
DVWWSH
GONK
ゴーン
TARGET
G
FSHRRRL
CHANGE IN THE GAUNA'S SURFACE!
BLGG
SPLUK
CHANGING COURSE
RESIDENTIAL DISTRICT POWER RESTRICTIONS IN EFFECT
Secure your safety belts!
Eeek
ZMMM
?!
ガダダダ
GTANK TANK
ZMM

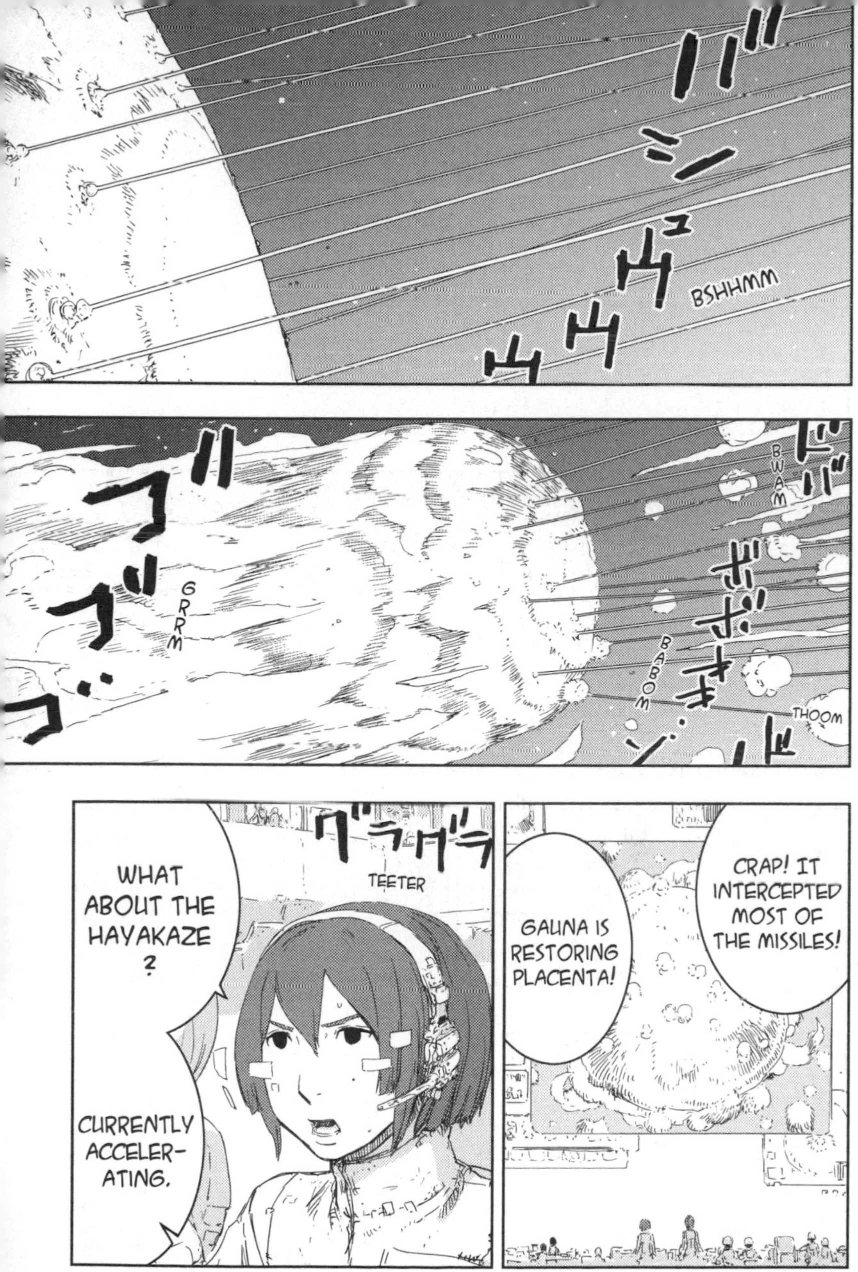
BSHHMM
BWAM
BABOOM
THOOM
GRRM
CRAP! IT INTERCEPTED MOST OF THE MISSILES!
GAUNA IS RESTORING PLACENTA!
WHAT ABOUT THE HAYAKAZE?
グラグラ
TEETER
CURRENTLY ACCELER-ATING.

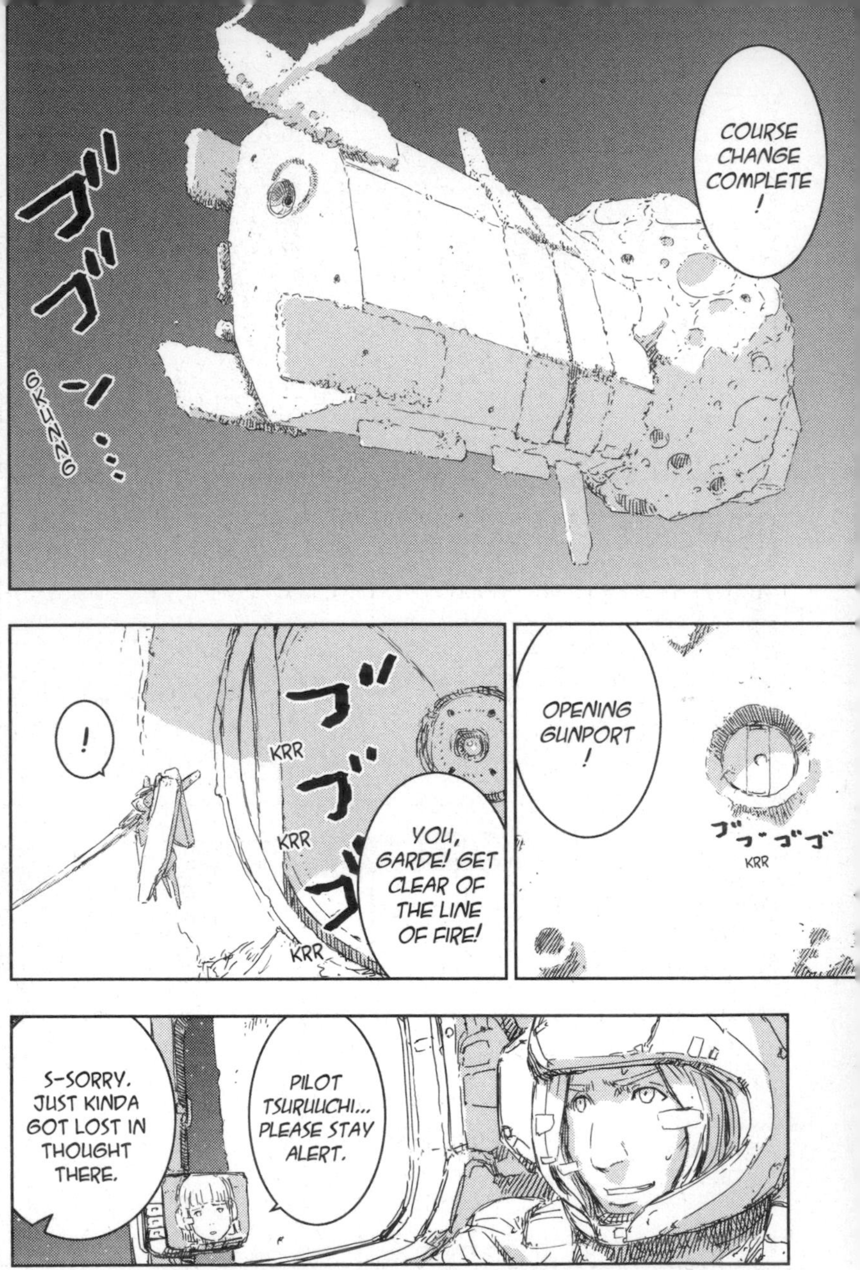
COURSE CHANGE COMPLETE!
ゴゴゴン…
GKUNNG
OPENING GUNPORT!
ゴゴゴゴ
KRR
YOU, GARDE! GET CLEAR OF THE LINE OF FIRE!
KRR
KRR
KRR
!
PILOT TSURUUCHI... PLEASE STAY ALERT.
S-SORRY. JUST KINDA GOT LOST IN THOUGHT THERE.

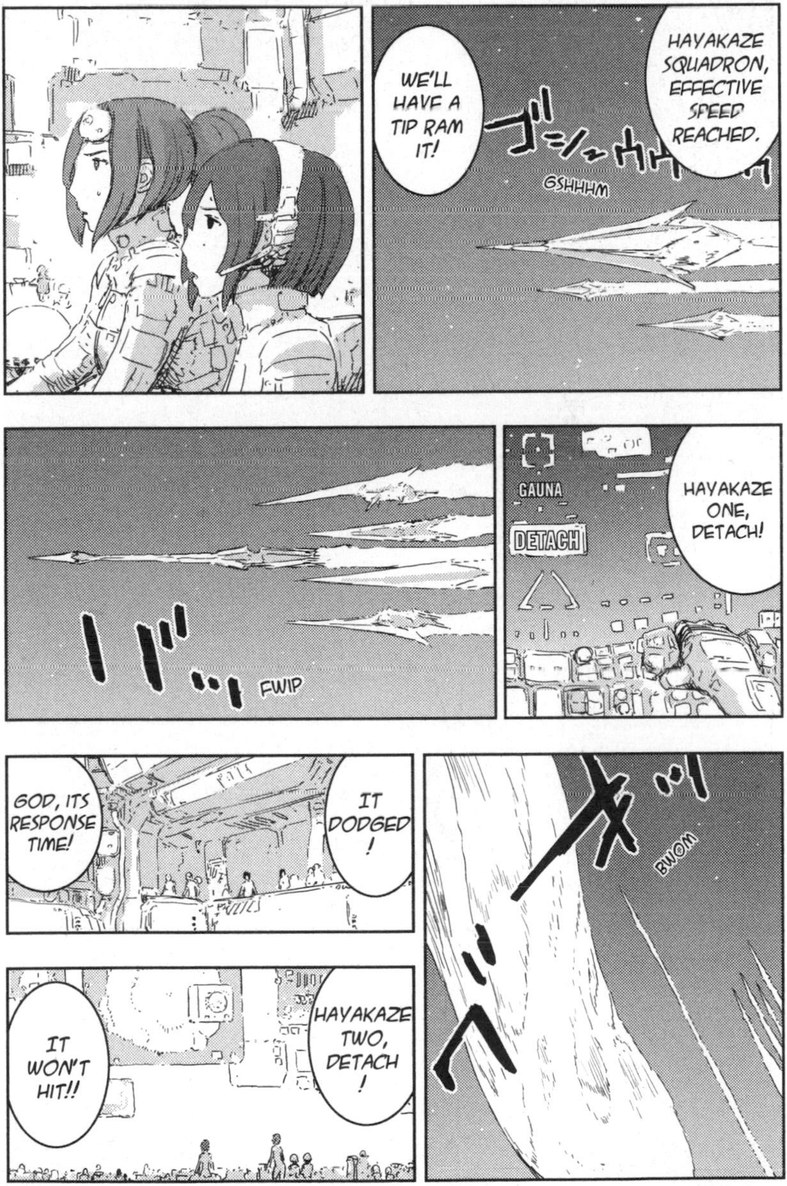

HAYAKAZE SQUADRON, EFFECTIVE SPEED REACHED.
WE'LL HAVE A TIP RAM IT!
GSHHHM
GAUNA
DETACH
HAYAKAZE ONE, DETACH!
FWIP
BWOM
IT DODGED!
GOD, ITS RESPONSE TIME!
HAYAKAZE TWO, DETACH!
IT WON'T HIT!!

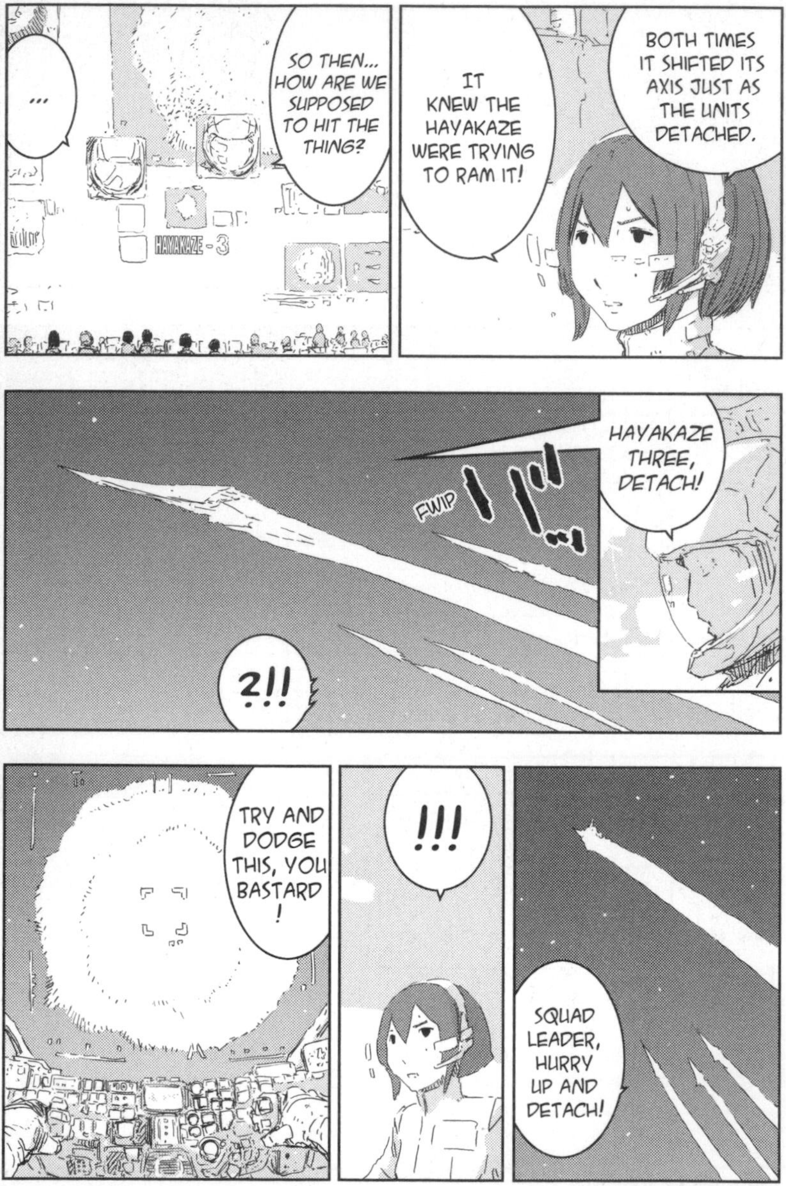
BOTH TIMES IT SHIFTED ITS AXIS JUST AS THE UNITS DETACHED.
IT KNEW THE HAYAKAZE WERE TRYING TO RAM IT!
SO THEN... HOW ARE WE SUPPOSED TO HIT THE THING?
...
HAYAKAZE-3
HAYAKAZE THREE, DETACH!
FWIP
?!!
SQUAD LEADER, HURRY UP AND DETACH!
!!!
TRY AND DODGE THIS, YOU BASTARD!

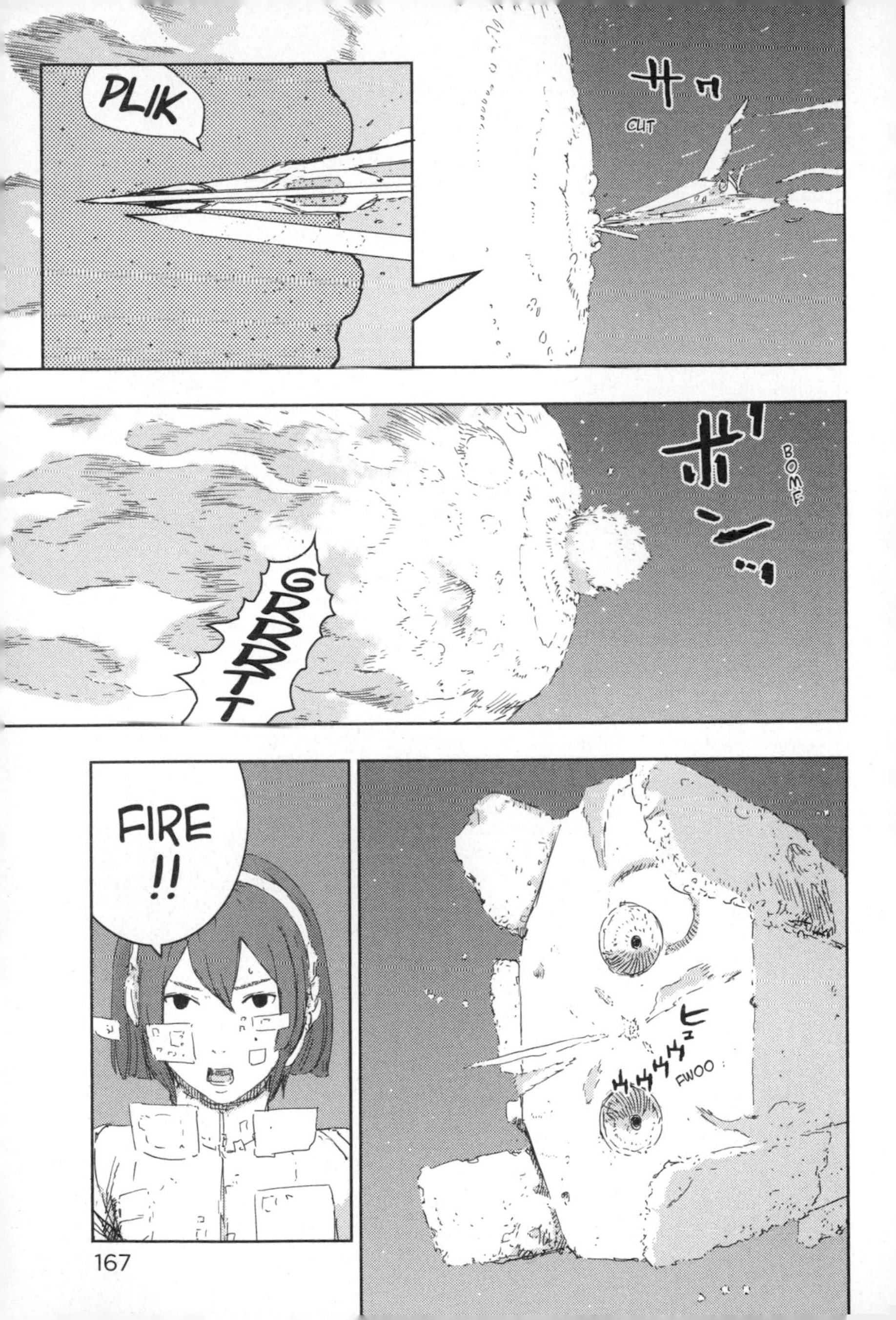
サッ
CUT
PLIK
ボンッ
BOMF
GRRRTT
FWOO
FIRE !!

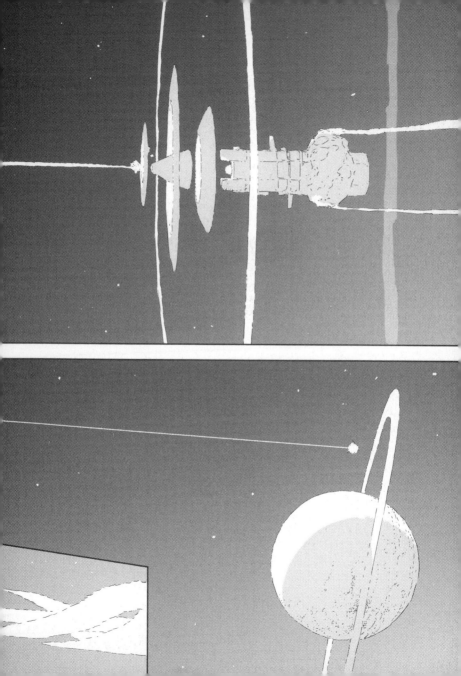

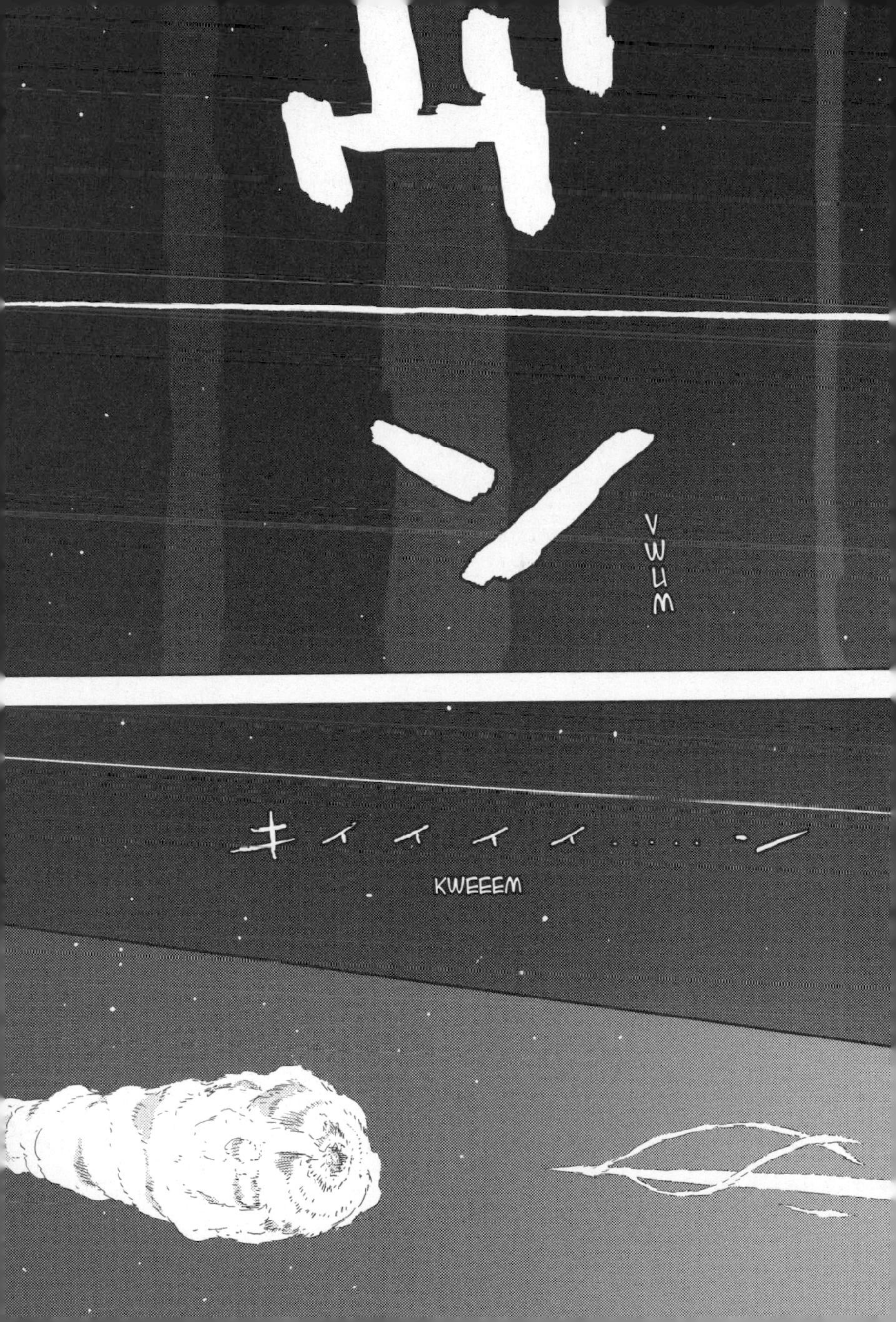
ン
VWUM
キイイイイ……ン
KWEEEM

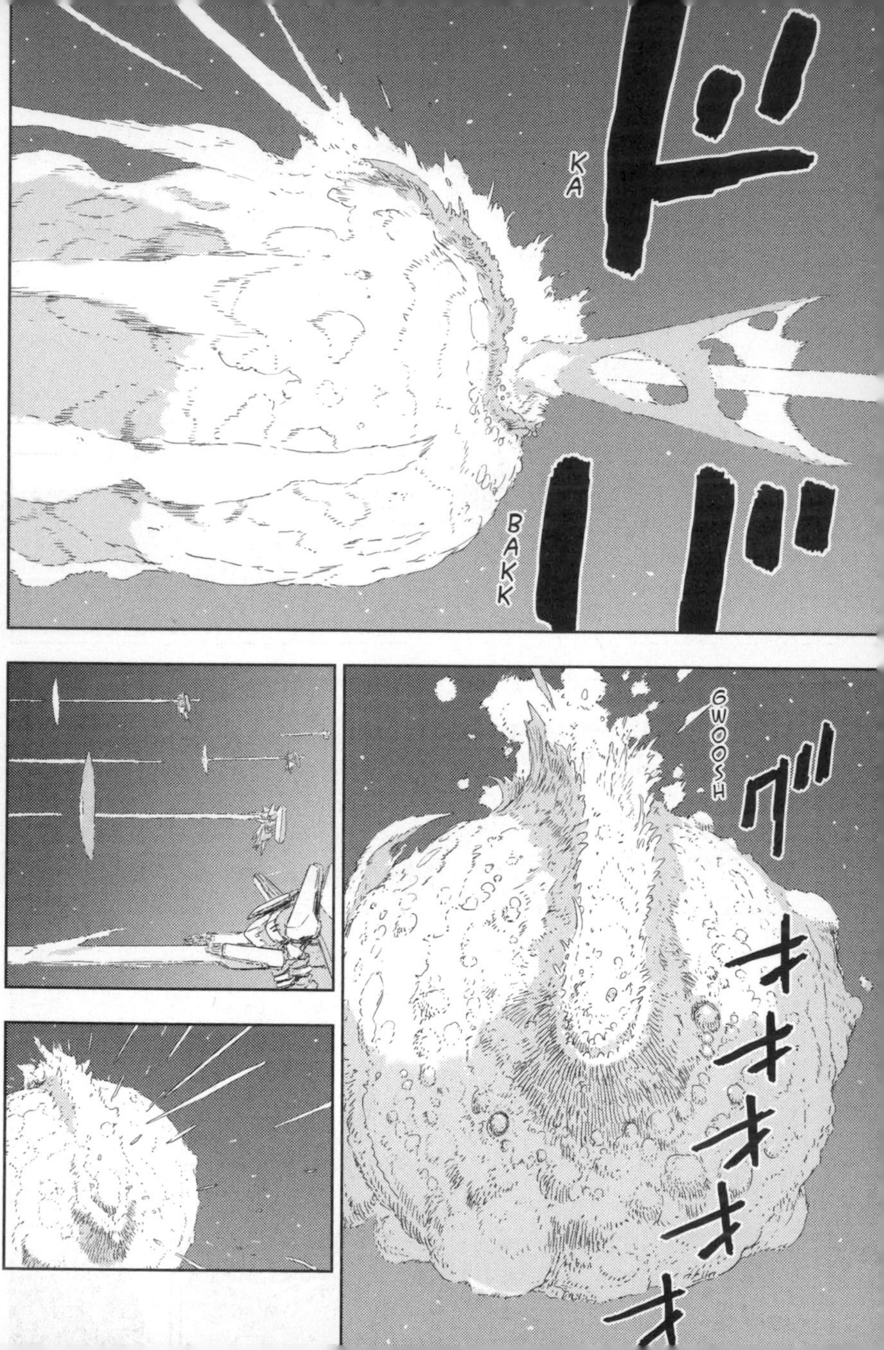
KA
BAKK
GWOOSH

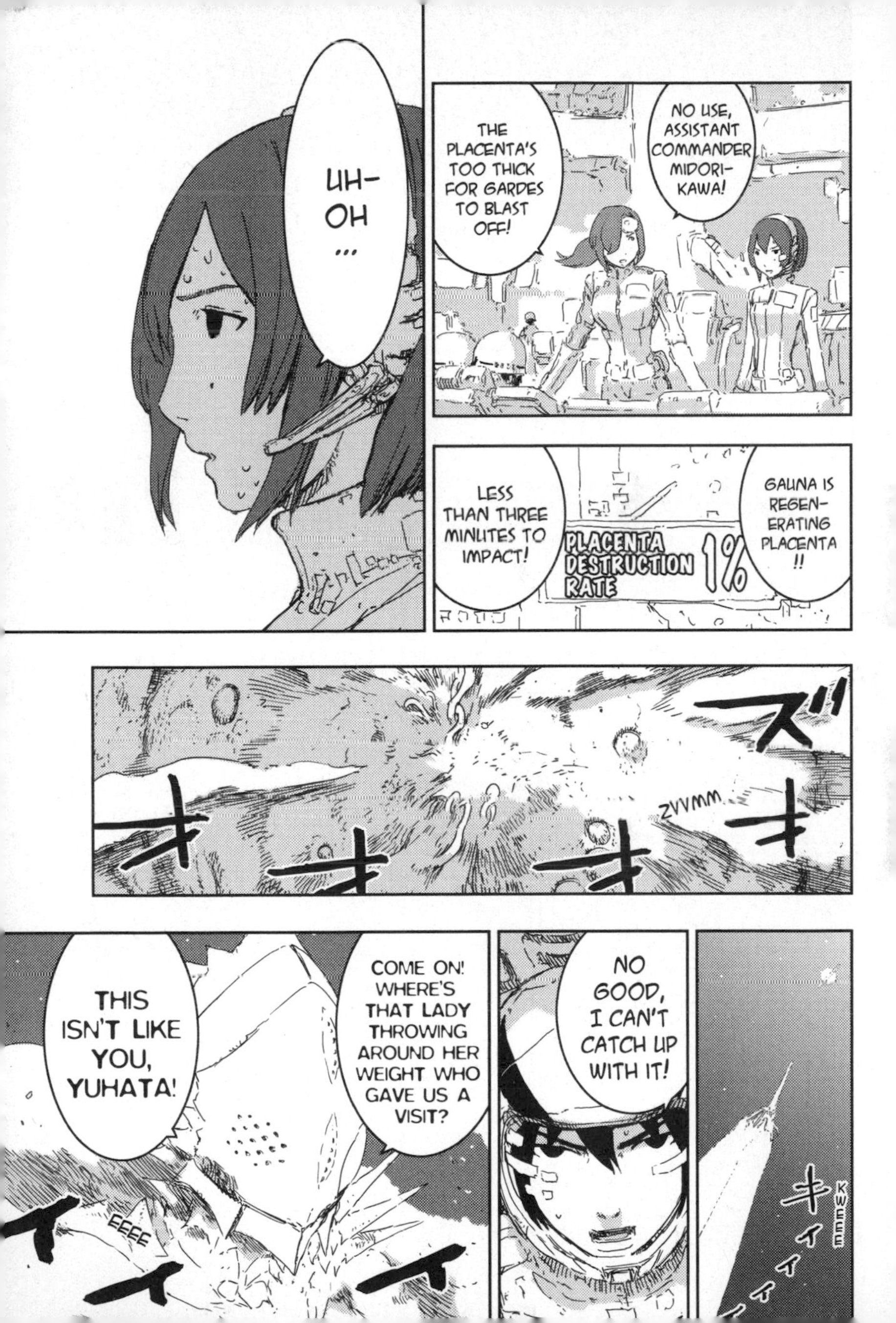
NO USE, ASSISTANT COMMANDER MIDORI-KAWA!
THE PLACENTA'S TOO THICK FOR GARDES TO BLAST OFF!
GAUNA IS REGEN-ERATING PLACENTA !!
PLACENTA DESTRUCTION RATE 1%
LESS THAN THREE MINUTES TO IMPACT!
UH-OH ...
ズオオオオ
ZVVMM
キイイイ
KWEEE
NO GOOD, I CAN'T CATCH UP WITH IT!
COME ON! WHERE'S THAT LADY THROWING AROUND HER WEIGHT WHO GAVE US A VISIT?
THIS ISN'T LIKE YOU, YUHATA!
EEEE
イイイ

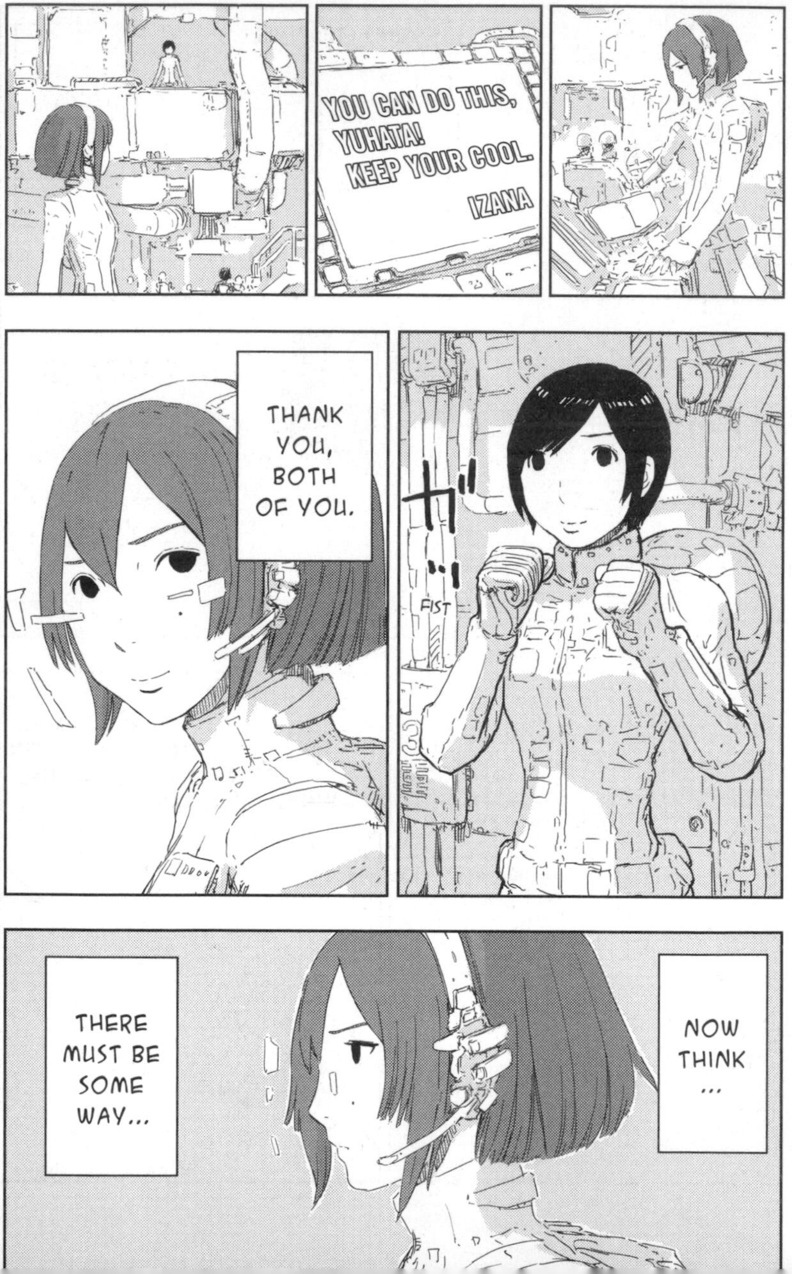
YOU CAN DO THIS, YUHATA! KEEP YOUR COOL.
IZANA
ガッ
FIST
THANK YOU, BOTH OF YOU.
NOW THINK ...
THERE MUST BE SOME WAY...

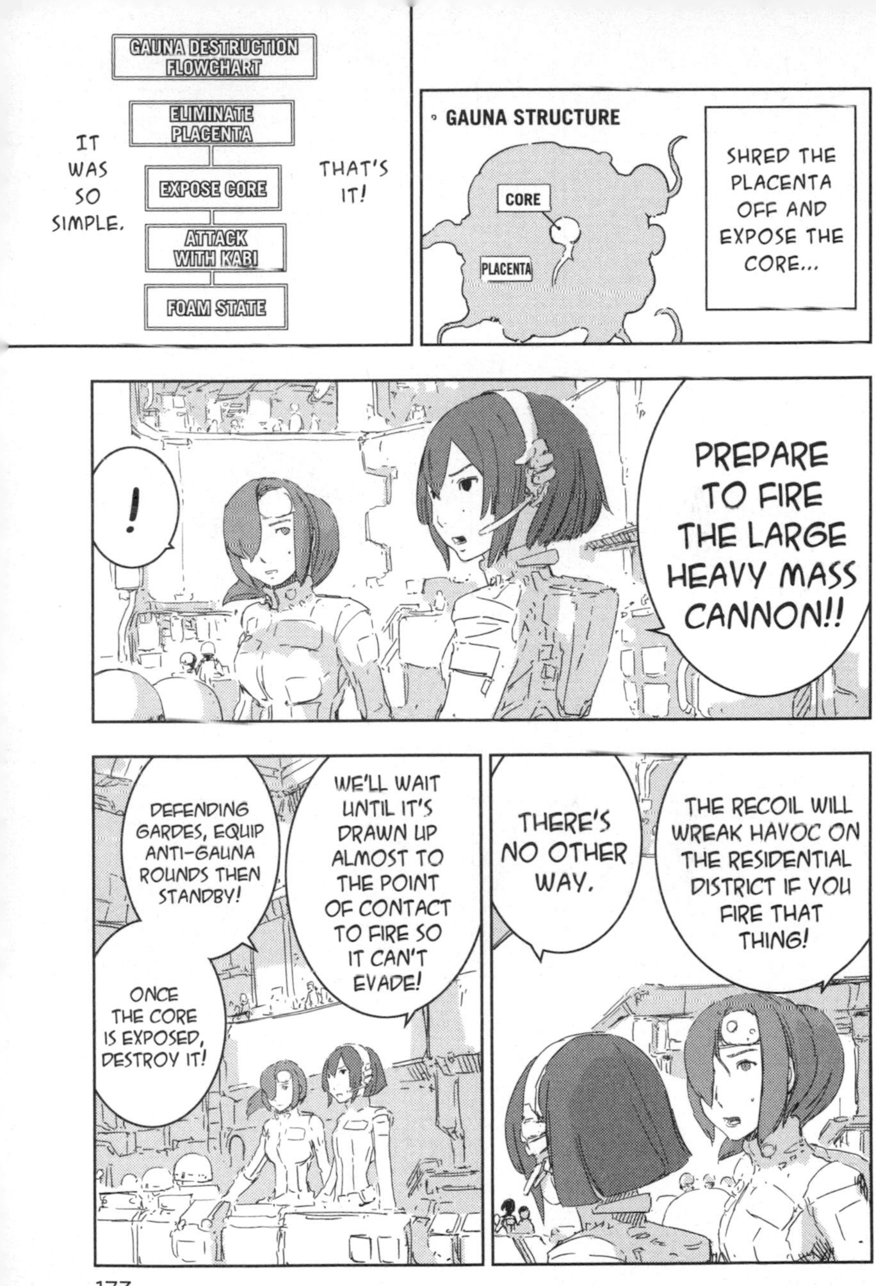
GAUNA STRUCTURE
CORE
PLACENTA
SHRED THE PLACENTA OFF AND EXPOSE THE CORE...
GAUNA DESTRUCTION FLOWCHART
ELIMINATE PLACENTA
EXPOSE CORE
ATTACK WITH KABI
FOAM STATE
THAT'S IT!
IT WAS SO SIMPLE.
PREPARE TO FIRE THE LARGE HEAVY MASS CANNON!!
!
THE RECOIL WILL WREAK HAVOC ON THE RESIDENTIAL DISTRICT IF YOU FIRE THAT THING!
THERE'S NO OTHER WAY.
WE'LL WAIT UNTIL IT'S DRAWN UP ALMOST TO THE POINT OF CONTACT TO FIRE SO IT CAN'T EVADE!
DEFENDING GARDES, EQUIP ANTI-GAUNA ROUNDS THEN STANDBY!
ONCE THE CORE IS EXPOSED, DESTROY IT!

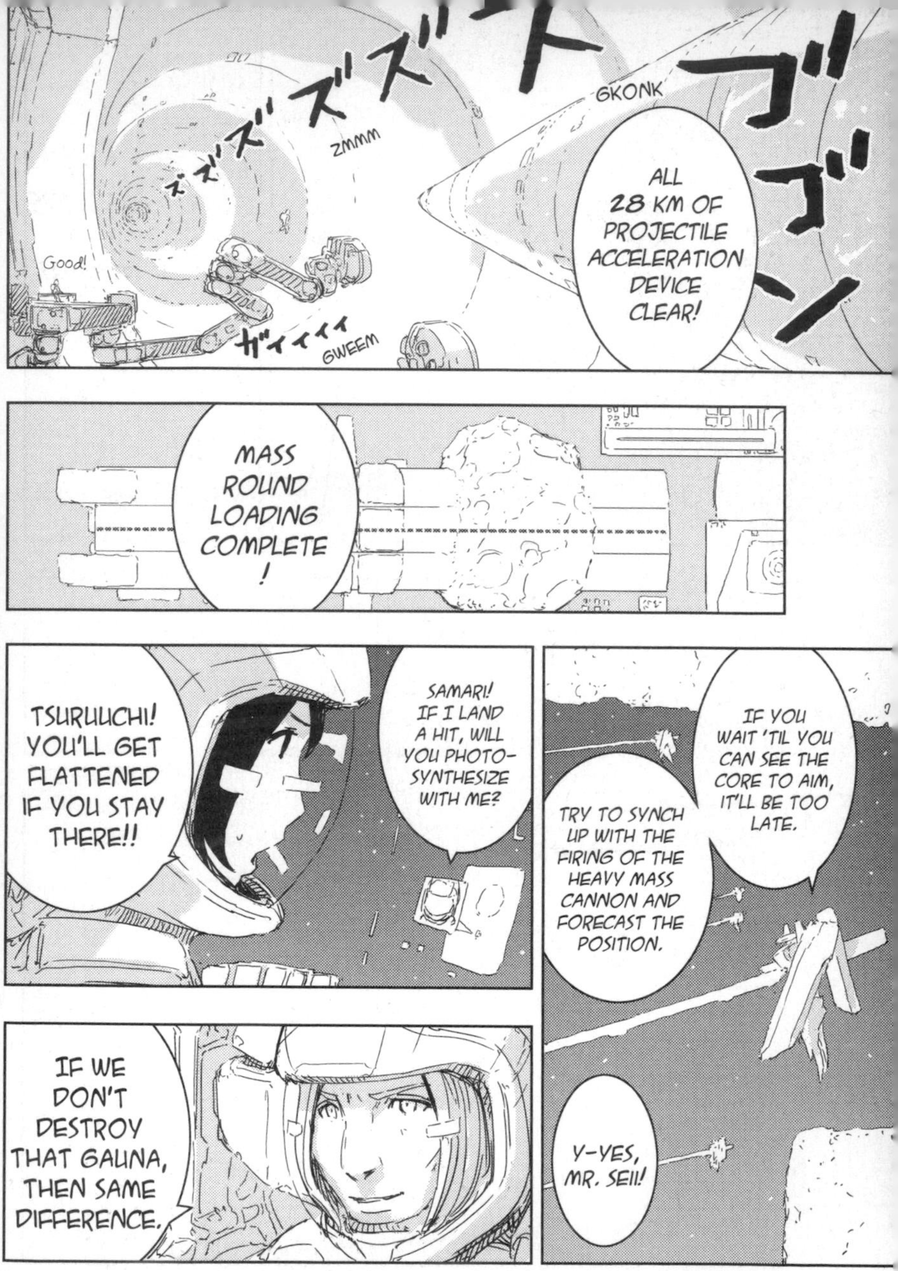
ゴゴン
GKONK
ALL 28 KM OF PROJECTILE ACCELERATION DEVICE CLEAR!
ズズズズズン
ZMMM
Good!
ガイイイイ
GWEEM
MASS ROUND LOADING COMPLETE!
IF YOU WAIT 'TIL YOU CAN SEE THE CORE TO AIM, IT'LL BE TOO LATE.
TRY TO SYNCH UP WITH THE FIRING OF THE HEAVY MASS CANNON AND FORECAST THE POSITION.
Y-YES, MR. SEII!
SAMARI! IF I LAND A HIT, WILL YOU PHOTO-SYNTHESIZE WITH ME?
TSURUUCHI! YOU'LL GET FLATTENED IF YOU STAY THERE!!
IF WE DON'T DESTROY THAT GAUNA, THEN SAME DIFFERENCE.

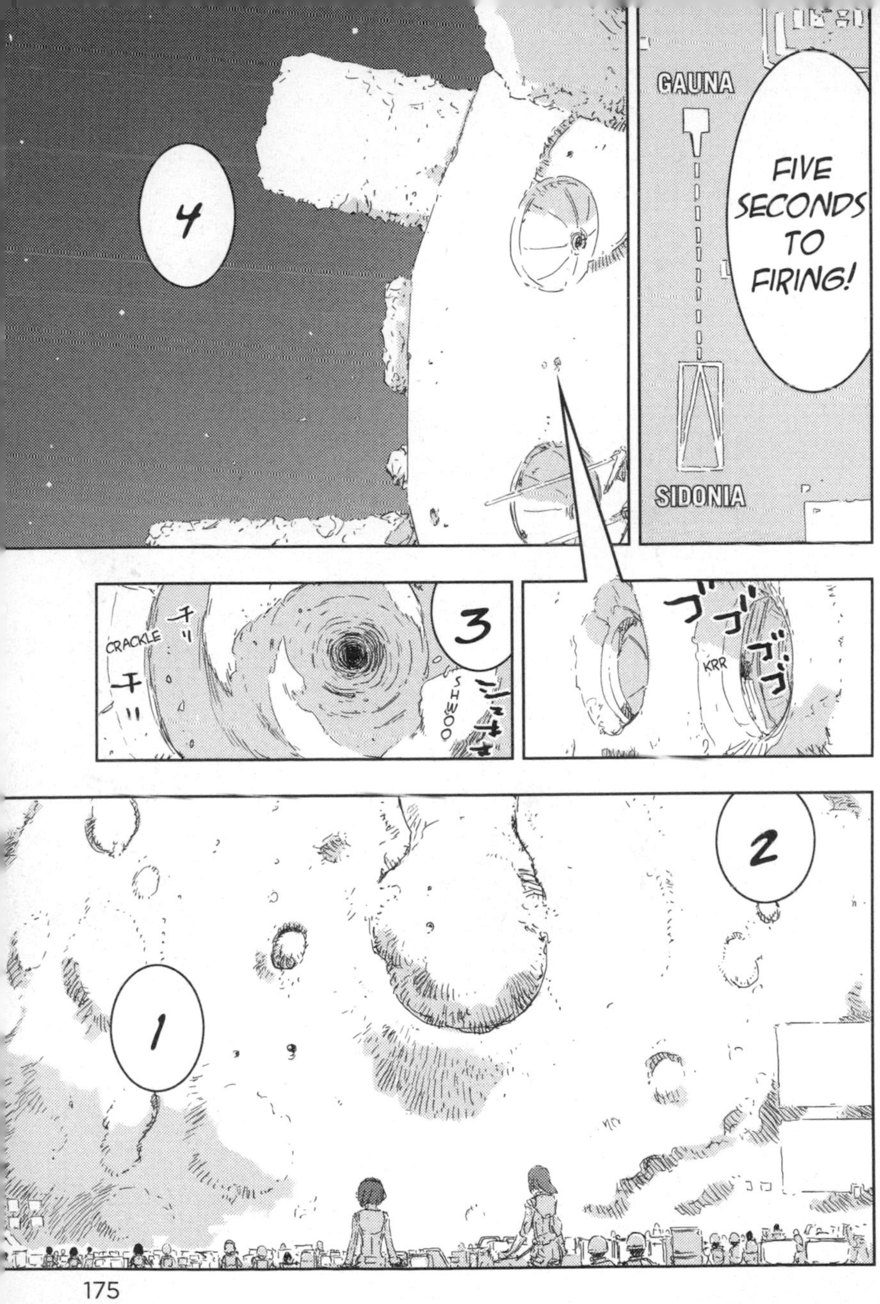
GAUNA
SIDONIA
FIVE SECONDS TO FIRING!
4
KRR
3
CRACKLE
SHWOO
2
1

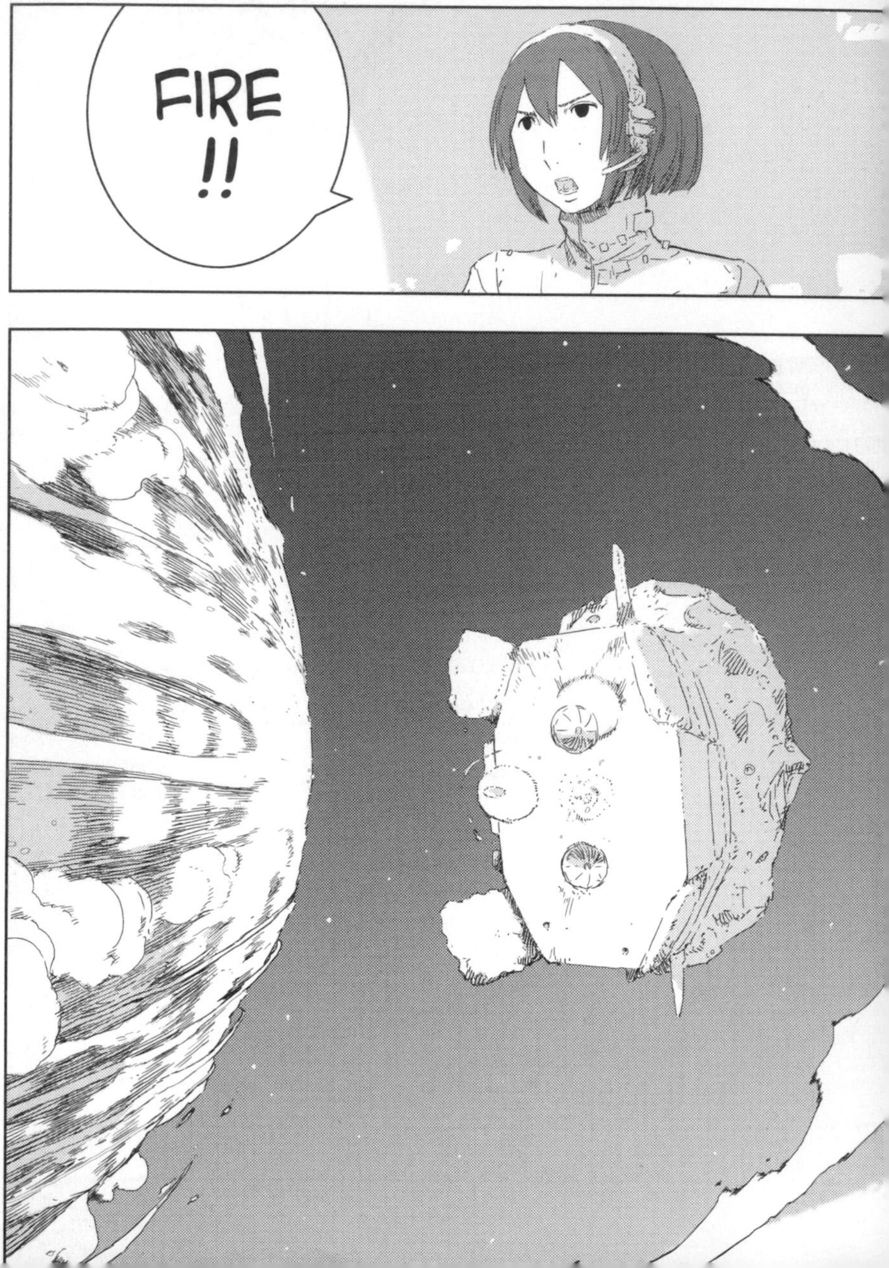
FIRE !!

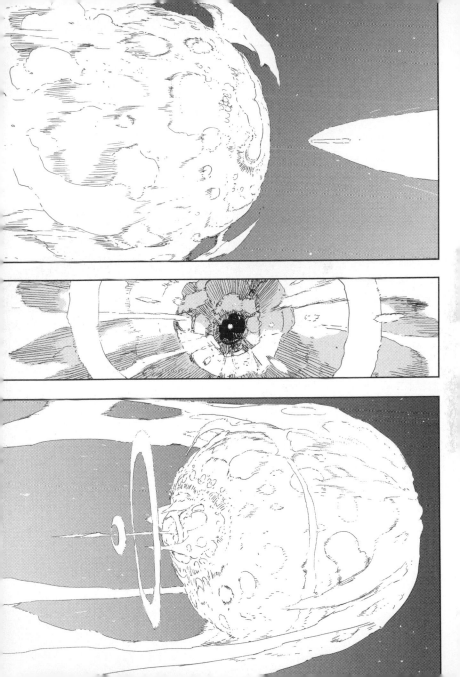

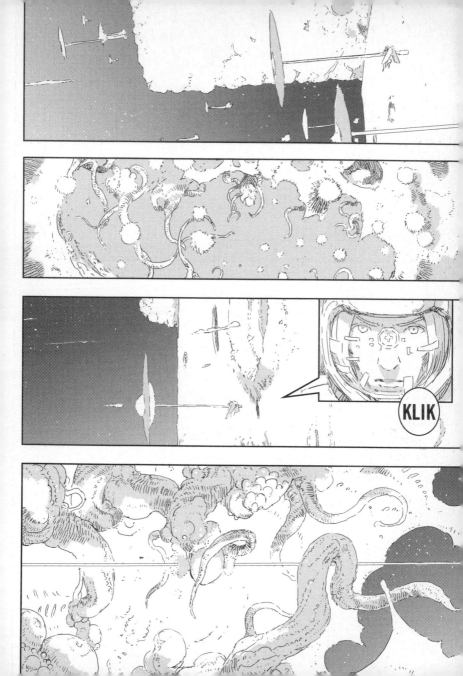

KLIK

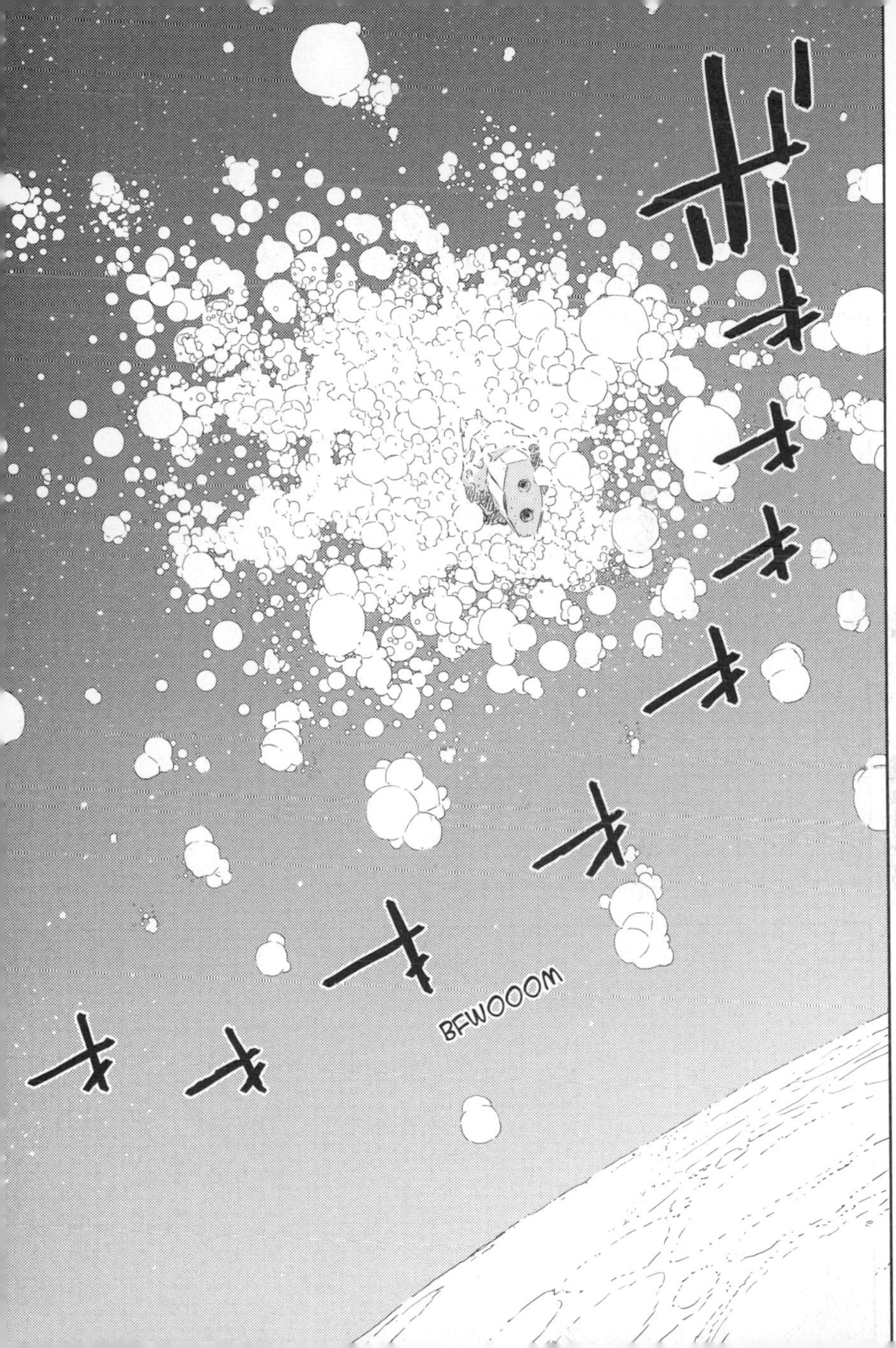
ボオオオオオオオ
BFWOOOM

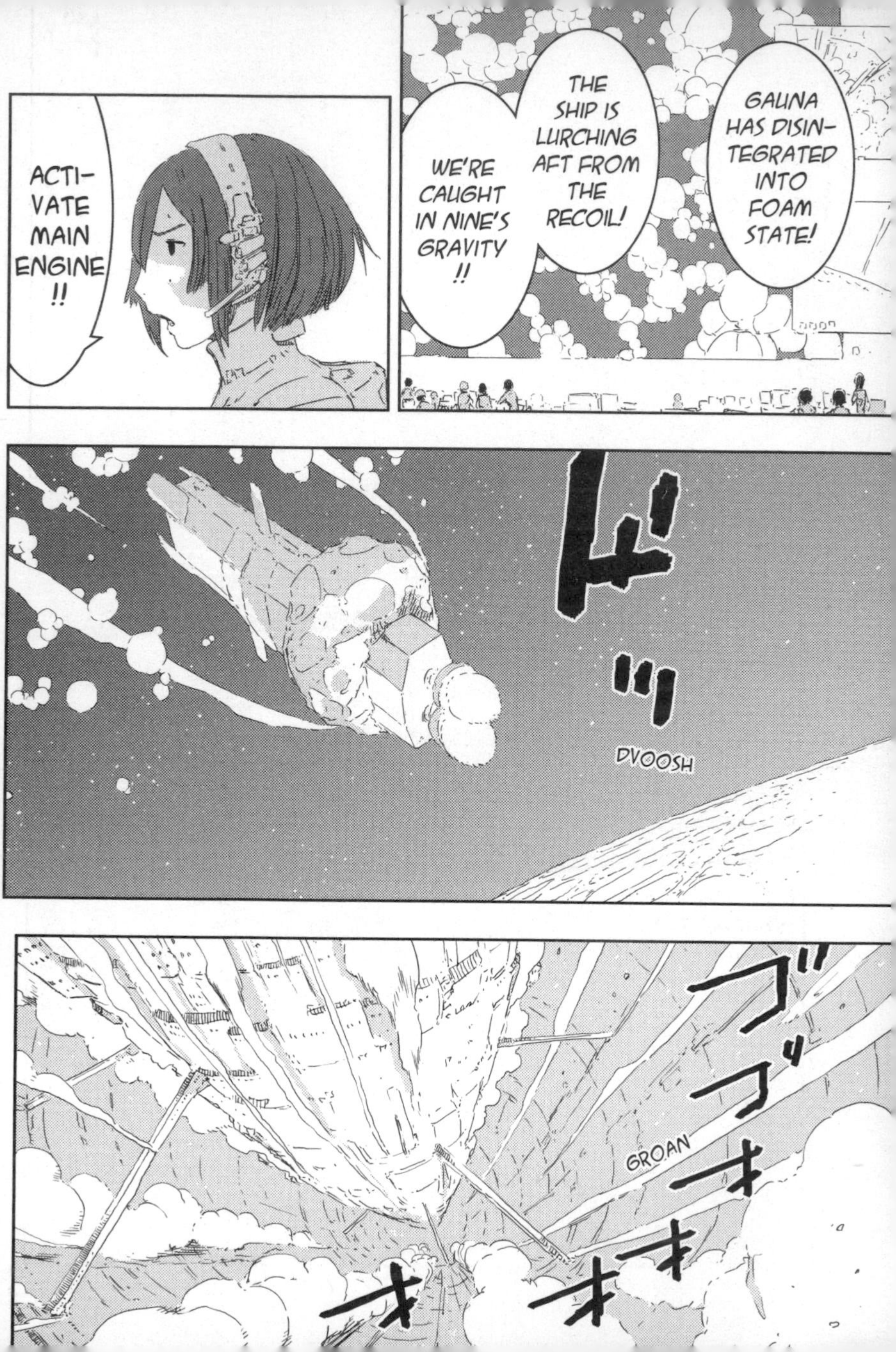
GAUNA HAS DISIN-TEGRATED INTO FOAM STATE!
THE SHIP IS LURCHING AFT FROM THE RECOIL!
WE'RE CAUGHT IN NINE'S GRAVITY !!
ACTI-VATE MAIN ENGINE !!
DVOOSH
GROAN

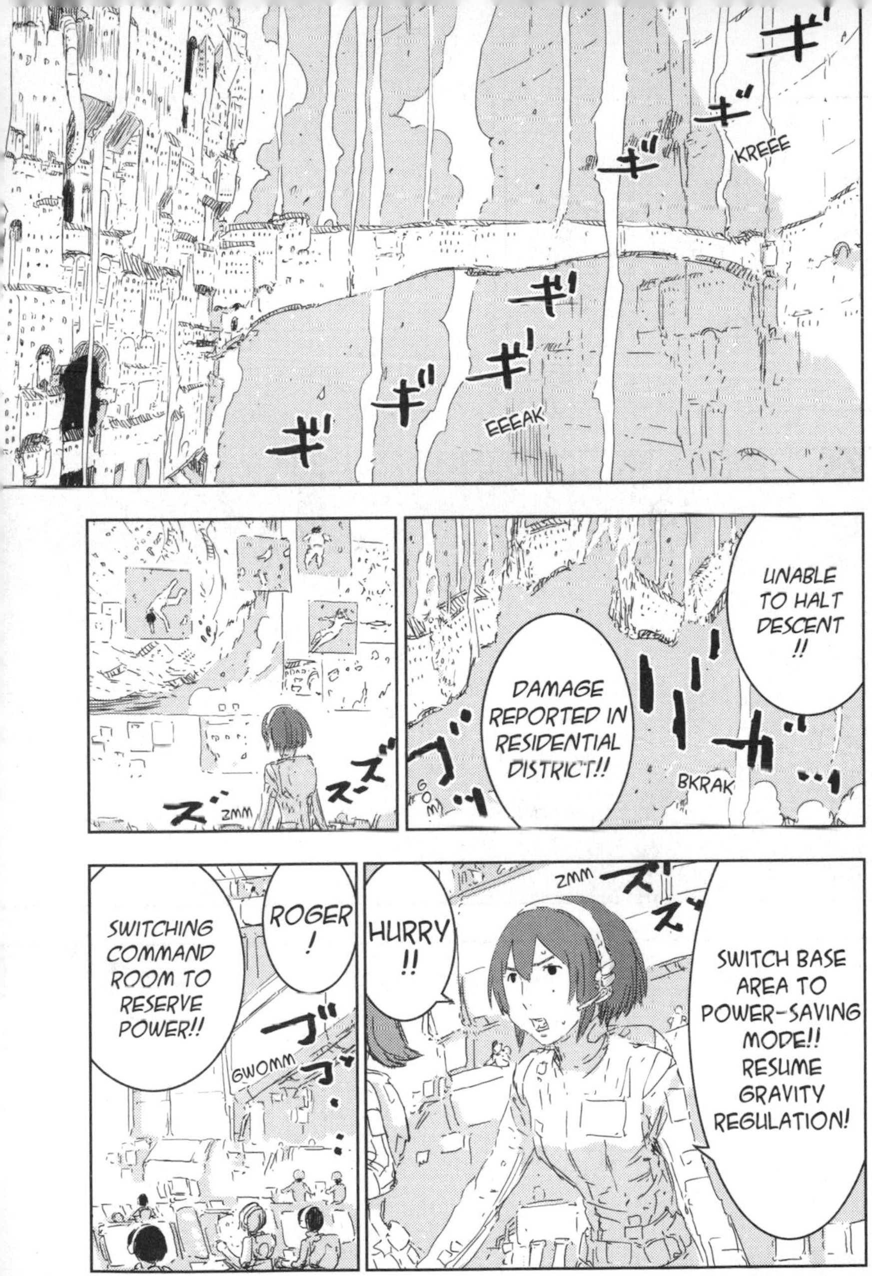
KREEE
EEEAK
UNABLE TO HALT DESCENT!!
DAMAGE REPORTED IN RESIDENTIAL DISTRICT!!
BKRAK
GOM
ZMM
SWITCH BASE AREA TO POWER-SAVING MODE!! RESUME GRAVITY REGULATION!
ZMM
HURRY!!
ROGER!
SWITCHING COMMAND ROOM TO RESERVE POWER!!
GWOMM

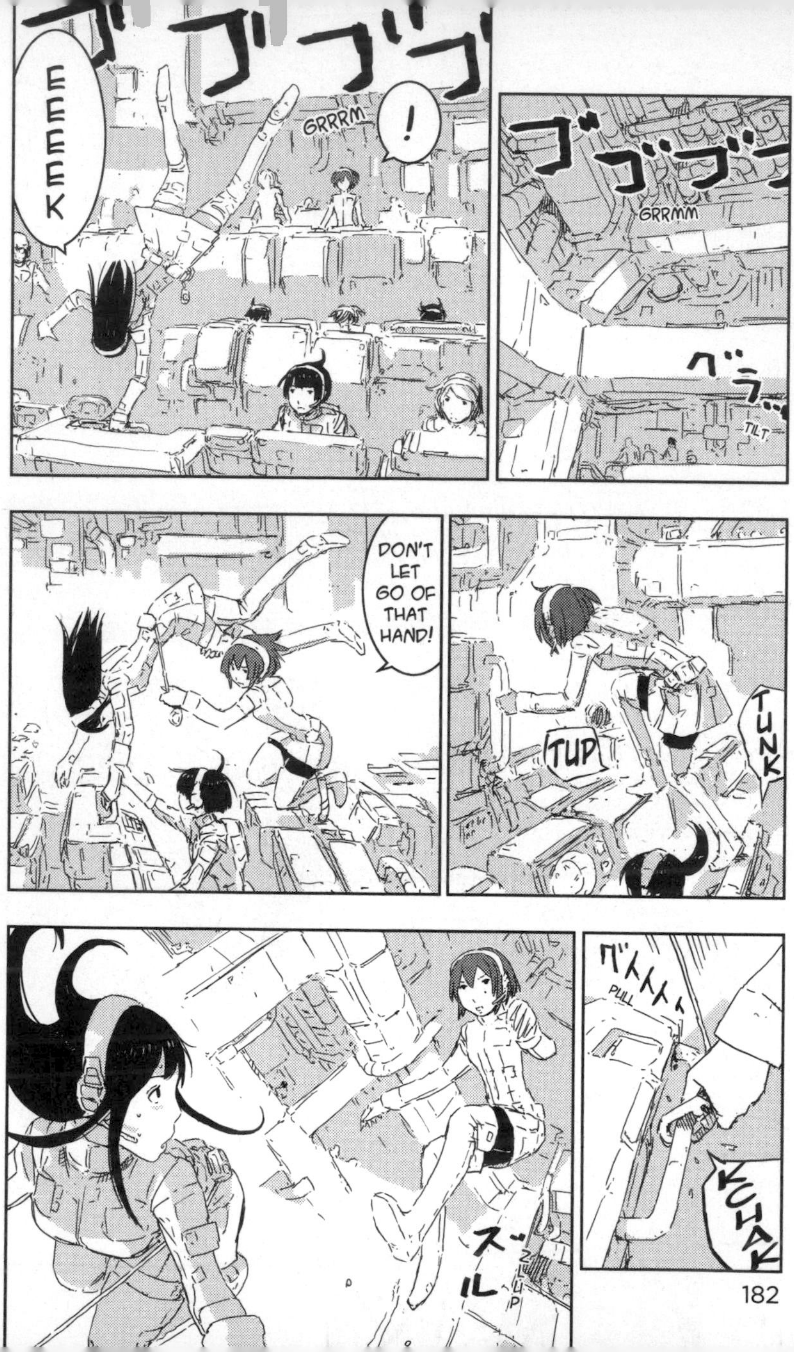
GRRMM
TILT
EEEEK
GRRRM
!
TUP
TUNK
DON'T LET GO OF THAT HAND!
PULL
KCHAK
ZLUP

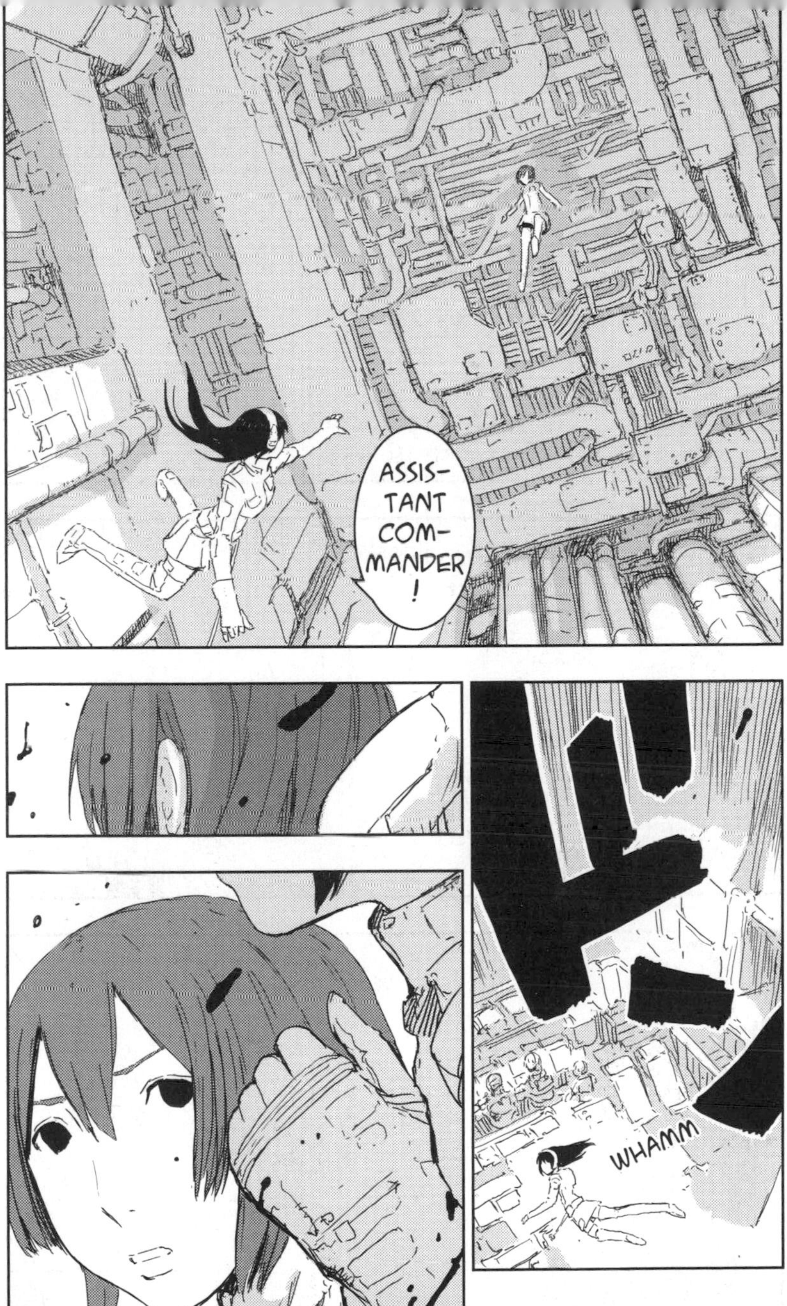
ASSIS-TANT COM-MANDER!
WHAMM

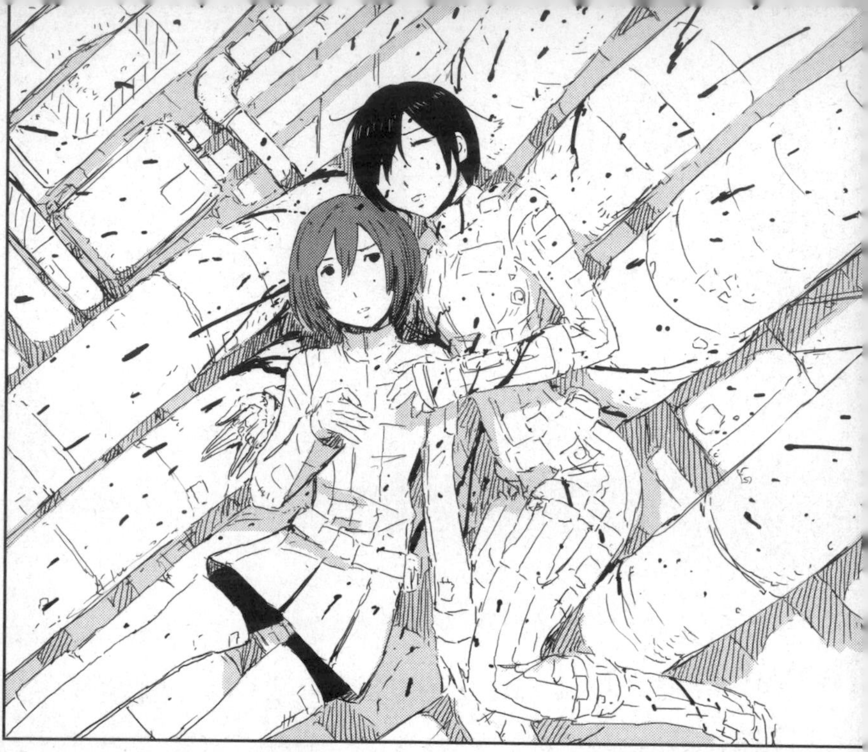

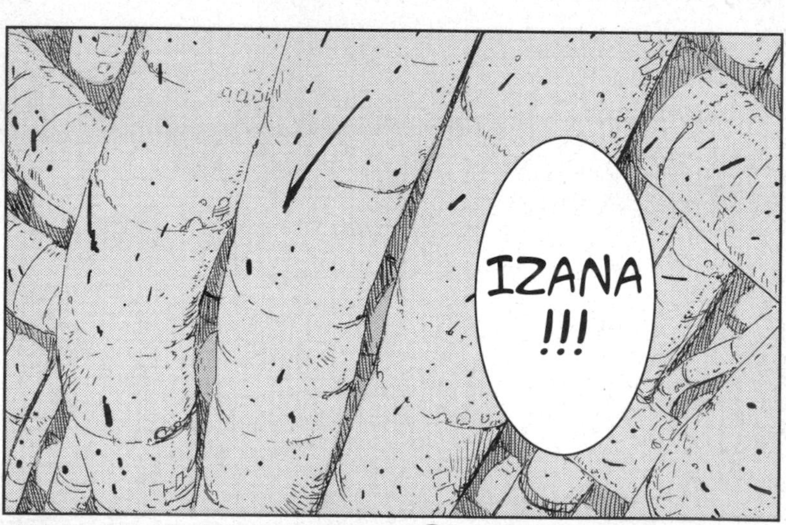
IZANA
!!!

シドニアの騎士
KNIGHTS OF SIDONIA

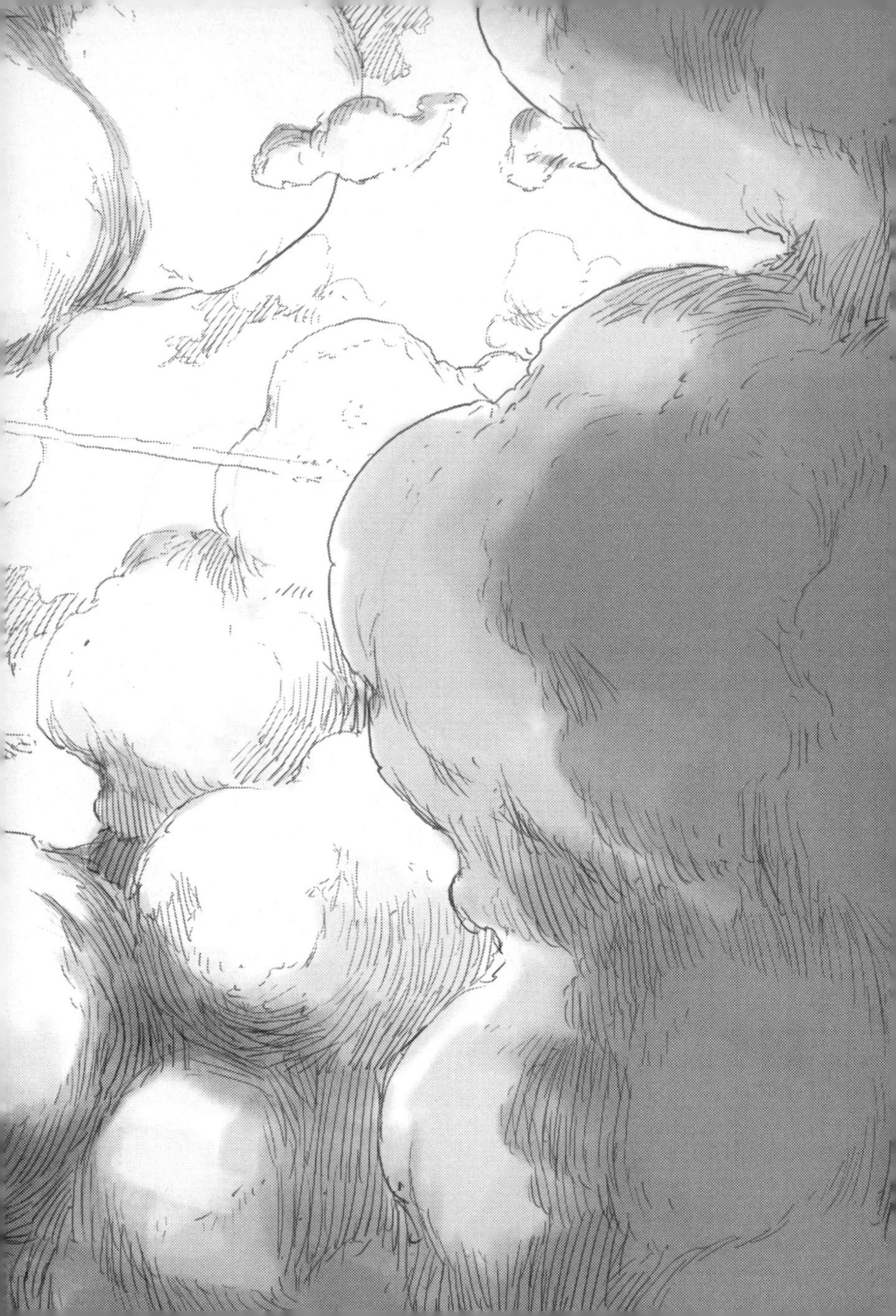

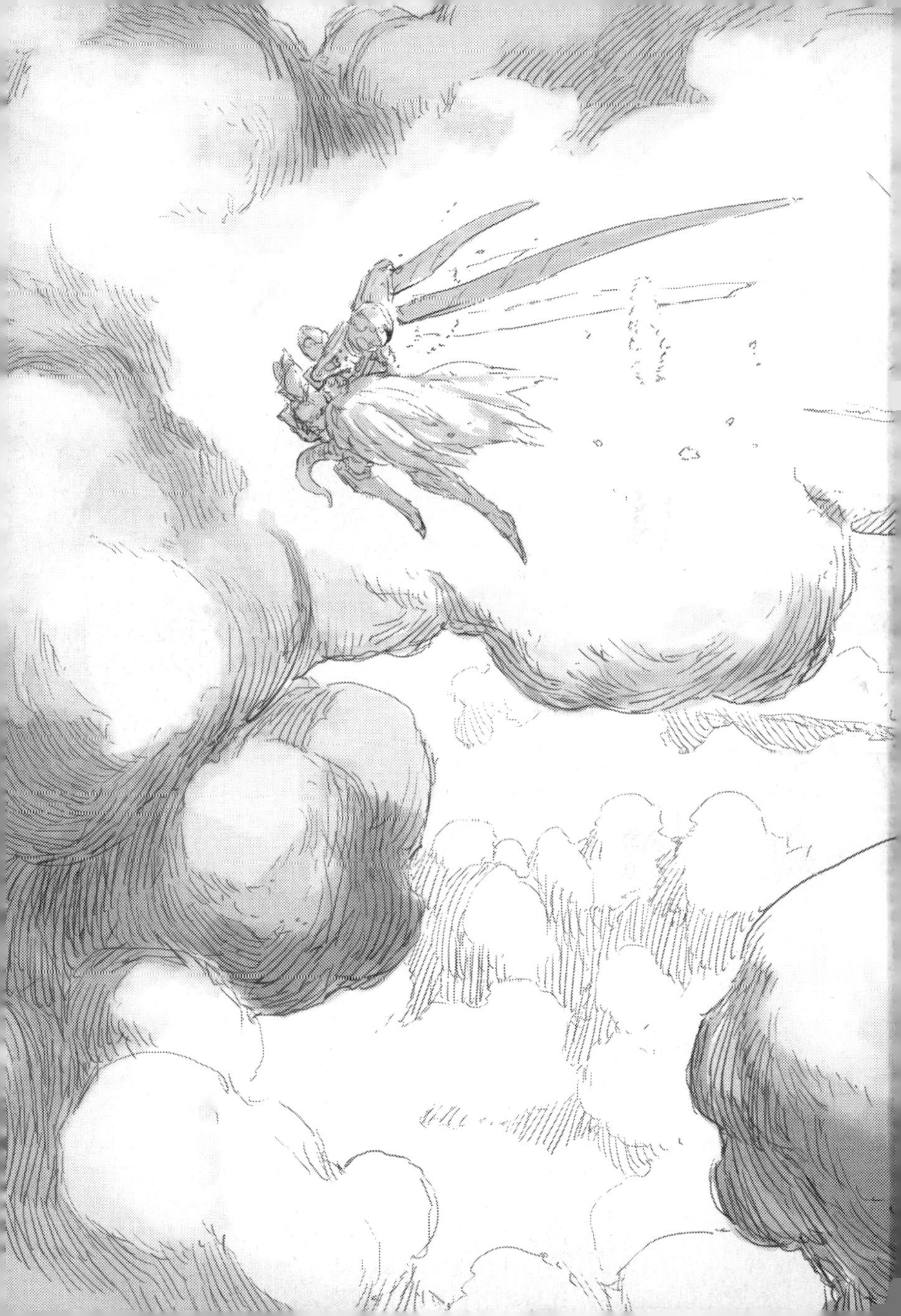

Knights of Sidonia, volume 9

Translation: Kumar Sivasubramanian
Production: Grace Lu
Daniela Yamada
Anthony Quintessenza

First published in Japan in 2012 by Kodansha, Ltd., Tokyo
Publication for this English edition arranged through Kodansha, Ltd., Tokyo
English language version produced by Vertical, Inc.

Translation provided by Vertical, Inc., 2014
Published by Vertical, Inc., New York

Originally published in Japanese as *Shidonia no Kishi 9* by Kodansha, Ltd.
Shidonia no Kishi first serialized in *Afternoon*, Kodansha, Ltd., 2009-2015

ISBN: 978-1-939130-22-8

Manufactured in Canada

First Edition

Second Printing

Vertical, Inc.
451 Park Avenue South
7th Floor
New York, NY 10016
www.vertical-inc.com